T0262023

HEALTHCARE TECHNOLOGIES SERIES 34

# The Internet of Medical Things

## Other volumes in this series:

# The Internet of Medical Things

Enabling technologies and emerging applications

Edited by
Subhendu Kumar Pani, Priyadarsan Patra,
Gianluigi Ferrari, Radoslava Kraleva and Xinheng Wang

The Institution of Engineering and Technology

Published by The Institution of Engineering and Technology, London, United Kingdom

The Institution of Engineering and Technology is registered as a Charity in England & Wales (no. 211014) and Scotland (no. SC038698).

The Institution of Engineering and Technology
Michael Faraday House
Six Hills Way, Stevenage
Herts SG1 2AY, United Kingdom

www.theiet.org

**British Library Cataloguing in Publication Data**
A catalogue record for this product is available from the British Library

ISBN 978-1-83953-273-3 (hardback)
ISBN 978-1-83953-274-0 (PDF)

Typeset in India by MPS Limited
Printed in the UK by CPI Group (UK) Ltd, Croydon

# Contents

# About the editors

**Subhendu Kumar Pani** is the Principal at Krupajal Computer Academy, Odisha, India. He has written over 200 scientific papers, book chapters, books, and patents. His professional activities include roles as a book series editor (CRC Press, Apple Academic Press, and Wiley-Scrivener), an associate editor, an editorial board member, and/or a reviewer of various international journals. He is an associate of several conference societies. He is a fellow of SSARSC and a life member of IE, ISTE, ISCA,OBA.OMS, SMIACSIT, SMUACEE, and CSI.

**Priyadarsan Patra** is the dean and a professor of Computer Sciences at UPES University, India. He served as a chief architect and a principal scientist at global divisions of the Intel Corp., where he led world-class R&D for systems-on-chip and microprocessors. His research interests include intelligent systems architecture. Being an author of 75+ scholarly publications, 4 books, 13 international patents, a senior member of IEEE and ACM, and an IE Fellow, Professor Patra founded IEEE System Validation and Debug Technology Committee.

**Gianluigi Ferrari** is an associate professor of Telecommunications at the University of Parma, Italy, where he coordinates the Internet of Things (IoT) Lab at the Department of Engineering and Architecture. He has written over 400 scientific papers/book chapters/books/patents and is an IEEE Senior Member. His research interests include IoT, networking, and smart systems.

**Radoslava Kraleva** is an associate professor in the Department of Informatics, South-West University "Neofit Rilski," Bulgaria. She has published over 60 papers, 14 book chapters, and 3 books and is an active member in organizing international conferences, seminars, and workshops. She is a member of the Bulgarian Mathematicians Union and the Union of Bulgarian Scientists. Her interests include human–computer interfaces, machine learning, pattern recognition, and the design and development of interactive mobile applications for children.

**Xinheng Wang** is a professor and head of Department of Mechatronics and Robotics at Xi'an Jiaotong-Liverpool University, Suzhou, China, with research interests in Internet of Things (IoT), Industrial IoT (IIoT), mobile healthcare, and acoustic localization, communications and sensing for healthcare. He was the inventor of the first IoT product, smart trolley, in the world to deliver intelligent services to airport passengers. He is the author/co-author of more than 200 international journal and conference papers and serves as a general chair/technical program chair for CollaborateCom since 2018. He is the holder of 15 granted patents. He is also an IET fellow and a senior member of IEEE.

*Chapter 1*

# Internet of medical things (IoMT): a systematic review of applications, trends, challenges, and future directions

*M.A. Jabbar[1]*

The Internet of medical things (IoMT) is rapidly changing the healthcare sector. IoMT paired with enabling technologies like artificial intelligence, cloud computing, wireless sensor networks can effectively monitor people's health continuously. In this chapter, the author provides a systematic review of the architectures of IoMT, applications, and trends in IoMT. IoMT applications to counter the COVID-19 pandemic are also discussed. IoMT and enabling technologies will improve the quality of human lives. This chapter addresses a few challenges while adopting IoMT in healthcare.

## 1.1 Introduction

In Internet of Things (IoT), all objects are considered smart objects that are paired with each other. Sensors and actuators blend with the environment and communication is shared across the platform. As per Atzori [1] IoT can be realized in three paradigms: (1) semantic oriented, (2) things oriented and (3) Internet oriented.

As per [2], IoT has been recognized as one of the emerging technologies that transform the world. IoT has a complex architecture, where various components interact with each other to find the solutions. IoT comprises cyber-physical systems to facilitate data-driven decision process.

By integrating various sensors and data analytics, IoT offers various solutions that can be used in smart grids, smart towns, smart homes, etc. There are three components in IoT that enables seamless applications [3]. The three components are (1) hardware that consists of sensors and actuators with embedded hardware, (2) middleware used for computing and storage and (3) visualization tools.

IoT is enabled with various technologies like (1) wireless sensors networks (WSN), (2) radio-frequency identification (RFID), (3) communication stack for WSN, (4) hardware for WSN, (5) middleware and (6) methods for secure data integration [3].

[1]Vardhaman College of Engineering, Hyderabad, India

RFID is a breakthrough technology in communication that enables in the design of various microchips in wireless communications. Two types of RFID, namely, active RFID and passive RFID are used in communication.

Due to the technological advancements, wireless communication have made available for effective low-cost and low-power devices.

Hardware for WSN consists of sensors, processing units, interfaces, receivers and power supply.

Communication stack is used to communicate with external world using the Internet. Middleware is used to integrate service-oriented architecture and sensor networks. Secure data aggregation methods are required to extend the lifetime of networks.

Efficient data storage and analytics tools are needed to process the data visualization tools that are used to help the users with the environment.

Addressing schemes are required to identify the various things that are connected. These addressing schemes will help one to uniquely identify the devices and control them with the Internet. IoT enables communication among various machines that form a large scale wireless network [4]. IoT architecture is shown in Figure 1.1 [5–7].

Workings of various components in the IoT are described as follows:

Sensors are used to transmit and receive data.

IoT edge devices are used to conduct processing.

Device provision helps one to connect various devices.

IoT gateway provides management, command, and control of the devices.

Stream processing is used to analyze complex execution.

Machine learning is used for predictive maintenance.

Reporting tools are used to store the data.

User management helps one to perform an action on the devices that are connected.

Communications of IoT are illustrated in Figure 1.2. Communications of IoT will happen in three domains, namely, (1) application domain, (2) network domain and (3) IoT domain [8].

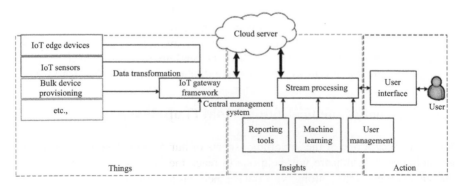

*Figure 1.1   Architecture of IoT [5–7]*

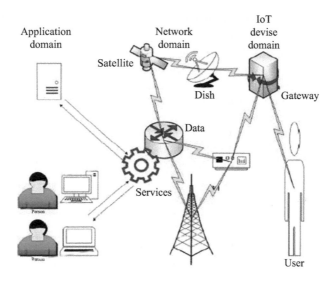

*Figure 1.2    IoT communication [8]*

IoT has been used in many applications, including agriculture, industry environment healthcare, smart cities, and for commercial use. Applications of IoT in various fields are shown in Table 1.1.

In addition to other segments, IoT has been used in healthcare industry. IoT plays a vital role in healthcare industry. Applications of IoT in health sector are shown in Table 1.2.

### 1.1.1    Internet of medical things

IoMT is playing an important role in healthcare industry. IoMT is an inter-connection of various medical devices and their applications connected with Internet.

Various elements in IoMT are listed in Table 1.3.

Patients health status recorded by IoMT will be transferred to a doctor via cloud data centers [9,10]. IoMT supports to monitor the clinical data of patients from hospital or home. IoMT consists of sensors and electronic circuits that take the data from the patients and process them. General architecture of IoMT is shown in Figure 1.3 [9,10] and the architecture of IoMT is shown in Figure 1.4 [11].

## 1.2    Internet of medical things (IoMT) applications

Smart healthcare one of the important aspects of human life. The use of emerging technologies in healthcare will help one to reach the health-related services to all the stakeholders. IoMT along with other emerging technologies is playing a vital role in smart healthcare. Various applications of IoMT in healthcare are (1)

*Table 1.1    Applications of IoT*

| Sl. no. | Reference | Application |
| --- | --- | --- |
| 1 | [33] | Nursing system |
| 2 | [34] | Rehabilitation |
| 3 | [35] | Kidney abnormality detection |
| 4 | [36] | Posture recognition |
| 5 | [37] | Patient psychological condition |
| 6 | [38] | Medical health monitoring |
| 7 | [39] | Autistic patient monitoring |
| 8 | [40] | Smart nursing |
| 9 | [41] | ECG monitoring |
| 10 | [42] | Smart healthcare |
| 11 | [43] | Medical health band |
| 12 | [44] | Smart hospital |
| 13 | [45] | Monitoring sleep apnea |
| 14 | [46] | M-Health |
| 15 | [47] | Cardiac arrhythmia management |
| 16 | [48] | Medical health management |
| 17 | [49] | Medical IoT |
| 18 | [50] | Health monitoring for chronic disease |
| 19 | [51] | Monitoring the poultry form |
| 20 | [52] | Ecological monitoring |
| 21 | [53] | Water monitoring |
| 22 | [54] | Home automation |
| 23 | [55] | Disaster management |
| 24 | [56] | Ozone mitigation challenges identification |
| 25 | [57] | Greenhouse gases monitoring |
| 26 | [58] | Mobile crowd sensing |
| 27 | [59] | Digital forensic |
| 28 | [60] | Location tracking |
| 29 | [61] | Data processing |
| 30 | [62] | smart home |
| 31 | [63] | Smart home |
| 32 | [64] | Smart home |
| 33 | [65] | Vehicular monitoring |
| 34 | [66] | Smart home |
| 35 | [67] | Weather monitoring |
| 36 | [68,69] | Smart street parking |
| 37 | [70,71] | Smart city |

management of chronic diseases, (2) telehealth, (3) lifestyle assessment, (4) remote intervention, (5) drug management, (6) medical nursing system, (7) rehabilitation system and (8) medical Bot.

This subsection gives a brief review of research related to applications of IoMT in healthcare.

Muzammal *et al.* [12] presented multisensor data fusion framework. IoMT is used for cuff-less BP measurement. In [13] authors presented a model based on backward shortcut connections. An IoMT model is designed for emotion recognition.

*Table 1.2    Applications of IoT in health sector*

| Sl. no. | Reference | Specific application |
|---------|-----------|---------------------|
| 1 | [72] | Disease management |
| 2 | [73] | Healthcare monitoring |
| 4 | [74] | Healthcare monitoring |
| 5 | [75] | Medical home monitoring |
| 6 | [76] | Security management |
| 7 | [77] | e-Health |
| 8 | [78] | Wearable device |
| 9 | [79] | Boy sensors |
| 10 | [80] | e-health |
| 11 | [81] | Wearable device |
| 12 | [82] | To counter PUEA attacks |
| 13 | [83] | Biotelemetry |
| 14 | [84] | Energy-efficient protocol |
| 15 | [85] | Healthcare |
| 16 | [86] | Healthcare |
| 17 | [87] | Healthcare environment |

*Table 1.3    Elements that are connected in IoMT*

| Sl. no. | Elements connected |
|---------|-------------------|
| 1 | Visual sensors |
| 2 | Accelerometer sensor |
| 3 | $CO_2$ sensor |
| 4 | Temperature sensor |
| 5 | ECG sensor |
| 6 | Sensors to measure pressure |
| 7 | Gyroscope sensors |
| 8 | Humidity sensor |
| 9 | Blood pressure monitor sensor |

Data fusion-enabled approach was proposed by [14]. A body sensor network is used for heart disease prediction. A fog computing environment is used in the proposed model. Predicting the sleep apnea using sleep apnea method was proposed in [15]. Long short-term memory and convolutional neural network (CNN) were used in the design of the proposed method.

Lin *et al.* [14] proposed a model for the detection of mental stress. EEG electrodes and functional near-infrared spectroscopy were used in the proposed method. In [16] Cabria and Gondra presented an algorithm to segment brain tumors in MRI scans. Potential field segmentation algorithm was used based on potential field.

Heart rate tracking using wearable sensors was suggested by [17]. Motion objects caused by ECG and PPG data were used for to measure the performance of the proposed model. A model to record BP from ECG sensor data was proposed in [18].

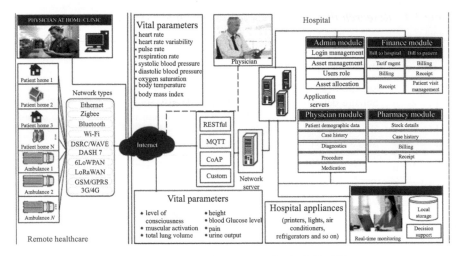

*Figure 1.3    Architecture of IoMT [9,10]*

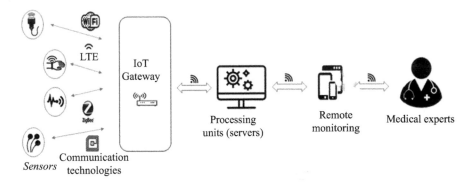

*Figure 1.4    General architecture of IoMT [11]*

Data generated from various sensors was fused and the output is fed to seven different classifiers.

In [19] authors presented a method for emotion recognition. Fused and non-fused physiological signal data sets were used for the evaluation of the proposed method. A feed-forward neural network classifier is used to train the data set. Authors in [20] modeled a recognition system for human action. The proposed method is tested on UTD-MHAD data set.

A Gaussian filter was used to decompose the images. Baloch *et al.* [21] presented a method for IoT healthcare applications. The proposed method consists of three phases to resolve issues and to maintain the efficiency. Applications of IoMT in healthcare have been shown in Table 1.4. The illustration of IoMT applications is shown in Figure 1.5 [22].

*Table 1.4    Research that has undertaken by adopting IoMT in healthcare*

| Reference | Objective of the method | Classifier used | IoMT |
|---|---|---|---|
| [88] | Seizure detection | Kriging method | EEG |
| [89] | Seizure detection | Swift network classification | Wearable EEG |
| [90] | Voice recorder | CNN | Smart sensors |
| [91] | Human activities | CNN | ECG |
| [92] | Stroke detection | $K$-Nearest neighbor, MLP, SVM | CT |

*Figure 1.5    Applications of IoMT [22]*

## 1.2.1    Role of IoMT during COVID-19

IoMT has been deployed to stop the spread of COVID-19 pandemic. Adoption of IoMT with other technologies like AI, big data, and block chain offers more effective solutions. A number of researchers are developing secure IoMT applications.

IoMT supports monitoring of COVID-19 patients from their home. Various measurements related to patients like blood pressure, heart beat will be recorded and transferred through the cloud to the healthcare workers. This will stop the spread of disease [23]. IoMT has been used to identify and track the origin of the COVID-19 outbreak [24]. Taiwan's company developed a wearable IoMT to detect the abnormal temperatures in and send the alert notification to higher authorities [25]. The cloud-based temperature monitoring system reduced the errors, saved medical personal time and reduced the risk of getting infected to healthcare officials.

AI-enabled IoMT has been deployed at a Taiwan's hospital to scan the people coming to hospital, detect the temperature and identify whether the people wearing the face mask or not [26]. Table 1.5 shows the various technologies used for COVID-19. Table 1.5 shows applications of IoMT during COVID-19.

Research that is mainly focused to address the challenges faced by COVID-19 are

1.  measures to enforce social distancing using the technology,
2.  remote patient monitoring of the patients using IoMT,
3.  IoMT-based methods for infection detection,
4.  IoMT-enabled thermal screening to avoid the spread of disease.

Advance technologies to tackle the pandemic are shown in Figure 1.6 [27].

Cognitive IoT is an emerging technology that is used for an efficient utilization of a scarce spectrum [28]. This technology is well suited to track the persons affected with COVID-19. Cognitive IoMT (CIoMT) is a special case of IoT. IoMT has been used in major areas to handle COVID-19 pandemic. CIoMT has been used for

1.  real-time tracking of patients,
2.  monitoring COVID-19-affected patients remotely,

*Table 1.5   IoMT during COVID-19*

| Reference | Application | Objective of the application |
|-----------|-------------|------------------------------|
| [93] | Tracking application | Prediction of virus trend |
| [94] | Temperature alert | Risk of mortality |
| [95] | Smart detector system | Drug detector |
| [95] | Diagnosis application | Diagnosis of disease |
| [96] | Tracing application | Patient tracking |
| [97] | Telemedicine | Prediction |

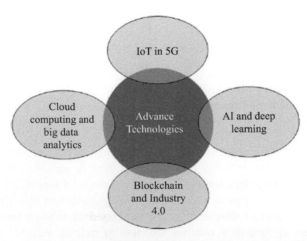

*Figure 1.6   Advanced technologies that are used to tackle COVID-19 [27]*

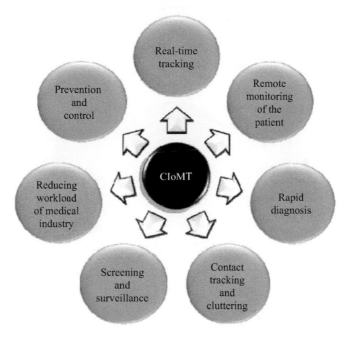

*Figure 1.7    Applications of CIoMT toward COVID-19*

3.  diagnosis of pandemic rapidly,
4.  surveillance of COVID-19,
5.  screening of patients,
6.  prevention and control of pandemic disease.

Major application areas where we can use (CIoMT) are illustrated in Figure 1.7 [29].

IoMT is also effective in providing the services to orthopedic patients affected with COVID-19. Services offered by IoMT for COVID-19 patients are

1.  providing smart healthcare,
2.  in terms of wearable devices,
3.  patient tracking,
4.  remote patient monitoring [30].

Services offered by IoMT toward COVID-19 orthopedic patients are shown in Figure 1.8 [30].

## 1.3   Security aspects in IoMT

Heterogeneous physical devises that are connected to IoT constitute the attack surface. There are many security challenges pertaining to IoT protocols and standards.

*Figure 1.8    Services offered by IoMT during COVID-19 as per [30]*

Security challenges in IoT include the following:

1.  identifying third party intruder,
2.  diverse network update policy,
3.  add in security policy,
4.  physical and exposure threat [31].

Attacks on IoT classified into two types: (1) data based and (2) protocol based.

Data-based attacks include threats related to original data packets, whereas protocol-based attacks exploit protocol-based structure. Protocol-based attacks are again classified into two types: (1) communication protocol based and (2) network protocol based.

Attacks will also be classified as active and passive. Category of various attacks is shown in Figure 1.9.

IoT attacks can also be classified as shown in Figure 1.10.

Rapid evolution of IoMT also raised security problems. IoMT security requirements and methods include (1) block chain, (2) access control methods, (3) IDS methods, (4) authentication schemes and (5) key management methods. Cyberattacks that happen to IoMT are listed as follows: (1) injection attacks, (2) denial of service attack, (3) device safety and (4) data leakage attacks. Attack surface for denial service is mostly on databases and cloud services. Hardware and middleware are the target for device safety attacks. Injection attacks basically target the databases. Data leakage attacks will occur to information and network.

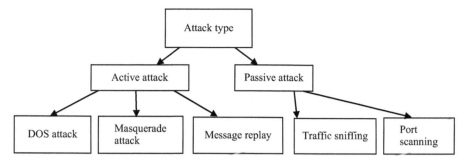

*Figure 1.9    Active and passive attacks types*

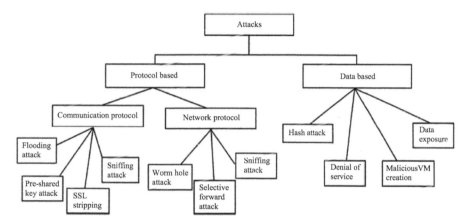

*Figure 1.10    Classification of IoT attack types [32]*

## 1.4    Challenges and future directions

IoMT-enabled healthcare applications are at fast and implementation of these connected devices will help one to improve healthcare sector. Although automation of health services is increasing, there are few challenges that need to be addressed.

1.  Insecure data transfer among the connected devices and data theft will be a severe privacy issue with the patient's data.
2.  Communication protocols and the risk associated with them is a challenging one.
3.  Integration of IoMT with other emerging technologies is also a challenging task.
4.  Data analytics and cloud computing are the challenges associated with IoMT.
5.  Interoperability within IoMT is another challenging task.
6.  Unstructured data and the data growth at exponential rate, memory of the system are the challenging tasks in medical domain.
7.  Hardware, software implementations and design optimization are also important challenges for IoMT.

8. Accuracy and precision are also two critical design factors for IoMT. Inaccurate results could be harmful to the patients.

Standard protocols, 5G-enabled emerging technologies like edge computing, explainable AI, can be integrated with IoMT for an effective use of IoMT in healthcare sector.

## 1.5   Conclusion

Smart healthcare is a current and well-researched area. IoMT, AI, cloud computing, and wireless sensor networks are all part of the smart healthcare. The main outcome of this chapter is to highlight the recent advances and applications of IoMT in the healthcare sector. The potential use of IoMT in handling the COVID-19 pandemic is discussed. Security attacks and various mitigation techniques were also addressed. We hope that this survey will benefit the research community in understanding the role of IoMT in smart healthcare and to adopt this technology well in the healthcare sector.

## References

[1]    L. Atzori, A. Iera and G. Morabito, The Internet of Things: A survey. *Comput. Networks* 2010; 54(15): 2787–2805.

[2]    J. Fenn, Gartner's hype cycle special report for 2005, 2005. http://www. gartner. com/resources/130100/130115/gartners_hype_c. pdf.

[3]    J. Gubbi, R. Buyya, S. Marusic and M. Palaniswami, Internet of Things (IoT): A vision, architectural elements, and future directions. *Future Gener. Comput. Syst.* 2013; 29(7): 1645–1660.

[4]    W. Weng, P. Chen, S. He, X. Sun and H. Peng, Smart electronic textiles. *Angew. Chem. Int. Ed.* 2016; 55: 6140–6169.

[5]    A.K. Raeespour and A.M. Patel, Design and evaluation of a virtual private network architecture for collaborating specialist users. *Asia Pac. J. Inf. Technol. Multimed.* 2016; 5: 13–50.

[6]    R.A. Stackowiak, IoT solutions overview. In *Azure Internet of Things Revealed*; Springer: Berkeley, CA, USA, 2019; pp. 29–54.

[7]    R. Hassan, F. Qamar, M.K. Hasan, A.H.M. Aman and A.S. Ahmed, Internet of Things and its applications: A comprehensive survey. *Symmetry* 2020; 12 (10): 1674. https://doi.org/10.3390/sym12101674.

[8]    G.J. Joyia, R.M. Liaqat, A. Farooq and S. Rehman, Internet of Medical Things (IoMT): Applications, benefits and future challenges in Healthcare domain. *J. Commun.* 2017; 12(4): 240–247.

[9]    J.T. John and S.J. Ramson, Energy-aware duty cycle scheduling for efficient data collection in wireless sensor networks. *IJARCET* 2013; 2.

[10]   S. Ramson and D.J. Moni, A case study on different wireless networking technologies for remote health care. *Intell. Decis. Technol.* 2016; 10(4): 353–364.

[11]   F. Al-Turjman, M.H. Nawaz and U.D. Ulusar, Intelligence in the Internet of Medical Things era: A systematic review of current and future trends. *Comput. Commun.* 2020; 150: 644–660.

[12]   M. Muzammal, R. Talat, A.H. Sodhro and S. Pirbhulal, A multi-sensor data fusion enabled ensemble approach form Medical data from body sensor networks. *Inf. Fusion* 2020; 53: 155–164.

[13]   T. Van Steenkiste, D. Deschrijver and T. Dhaene, "Sensor fusion using backward shortcut connections for sleep apnea detection in multi-modal data," 2019, arXiv:1912.06879. [Online]. Available: http://arxiv.org/abs/1912.06879.

[14]   K. Lin, Y. Li, J. Sun, D. Zhou and Q. Zhang, Multi-sensor fusion for body sensor network in medical human–robot interaction scenario. *Inf. Fusion* 2020; 57: 15–26.

[15]   F. Al-Shargie, Fusion of fNIRS and EEG signals: Mental stress study. *engrXiv* 2019; 2019: 1–5. doi: 10.31224/osf.io/kaqcw.

[16]   I. Cabria and I. Gondra, MRI segmentation fusion for brain tumor detection. *Inf. Fusion* 2017; 36: 1–9.

[17]   D. Fabiano and S. Canavan, Emotion recognition using fused physiological signals. In *Proc. 8th Int. Conf. Affect. Comput. Intell. Interact. (ACII)*, Cambridge, UK, 2019; pp. 42–48.

[18]   W. Zhang, J. Yang, H. Su, M. Kumar and Y. Mao, Medical data fusion algorithm based on Internet of Things. *Pers. Ubiquitous Comput.* 2018; 22 (5–6): 895–902.

[19]   J. Du, W. Li and H. Tan, Intrinsic image decomposition-based grey and pseudo-color medical image fusion. *IEEE Access* 2019; 7: 56443–56456.

[20]   C. Chen, R. Jafari and N. Kehtarnavaz, A real-time human action recognition system using depth and inertial sensor fusion. *IEEE Sens. J.* 2016; 16(3): 773–781.

[21]   Z. Baloch, F.K. Shaikh and M.A. Unar, A context-aware data fusion approach for health-IoT. *Int. J. Inf. Technol.* 2018; 10(3): 241–245.

[22]   I. Ud Din, A. Almogren, M. Guizani and M. Zuair, A decade of Internet of Things: Analysis in the light of healthcare applications. *IEEE Access* 2019; 7: 89967–89979. doi: 10.1109/ACCESS.2019.2927082.

[23]   D.S.W. Ting, L. Carin, V. Dzau and T.Y. Wong, Digital technology and COVID-19. *Nat. Med.* 2020; 26: 7.

[24]   Y. Song, J. Jiang, X. Wang, D. Yang and C. Bai, Prospect and application of Internet of Things technology for prevention of SARIs. *Clin. eHealth* 2020; 3: 1–4. doi: 10.1016/j.ceh.2020.02.001.

[25]   D. Koh. 2020. Temp Pal Smart Thermometer Helps Reduce COVID-19 Spread in Hospitals. https://www.mobihealthnews.com/news/asia-pacific/temp-pal-smart-thermometer-helps-reduce-covid-19-spread-hospitals.

[26]   Microsoft. 2020. Trying to Shield Hospital Staff and Patients from COVID-19 with Help from AI, Cloud, and Intelligent Edge – Asia News Center. https://news.microsoft.com/apac/2020/03/31/trying-to-shield-hospital-staff-and-patients-from-covid-19-with-help-from-ai-cloud-and-intelligent-edge.

[27]    S. Swayamsiddha and C. Mohanty, Application of cognitive Internet of Medical Things for COVID-19 pandemic. *Diabetes Metab. Syndr.* 2020; 14 (5): 911–915. https://doi.org/10.1016/j.dsx.2020.06.014.

[28]    W. Ejaz and M. Ibnkahla, Multiband spectrum sensing and resource allocation for IoT in cognitive 5G networks. *IEEE Internet Things J.* 2017; 5(1): 150e63.

[29]    S. Swayamsiddha and C. Mohanty, Application of cognitive Internet of Medical Things for COVID-19 pandemic. *Diabetes Metab. Syndr.* 2020; 14(5): 911–915.

[30]    R. Pratap Singh, M. Javaid, A. Haleem, R. Vaishya and S. Ali, Internet of Medical Things (IoMT) for orthopaedic in COVID-19 pandemic: Roles, challenges, and applications. *J. Clin. Orthop. Trauma* 2020; 11(4): 713–717. doi: 10.1016/j.jcot.2020.05.011. Epub 2020 May 15. Erratum in: J Clin Orthop Trauma. 2020 Nov-Dec;11(6):1169–1171. PMID: 32425428; PMCID: PMC7227564.

[31]    S. Bhatt and P.R. Ragiri, Security trends in Internet of Things: A survey. *SN Appl. Sci.* 2021; 3(1): 1–14.

[32]    A. Abdul-Ghani Hezam, D. Konstantas and M. Mahyoub, A comprehensive IoT attacks survey based on a building-blocked reference model. *Int. J. Adv. Comput. Sci. Appl.* 2018; 9: 355–373.

[33]    C.-H. Huang and K.-W. Cheng, RFID technology combined with IoT application in medical nursing system. *Bull. Networking Comput. Syst. Software* 2014; 3(1): 20–24. ISSN: 21865140.

[34]    Y.J. Fan, Y.H. Yin, L.D. Xu, Y. Zeng and F. Wu, IoT-based smart rehabilitation system. *IEEE Trans. Ind. Inf.* 2014; 10(2). EISSN: 2395–0072.

[35]    K. Divya Krishna, V. Akkala, R. Bharath, *et al.*, Computer aided abnormality detection for kidney on FPGA based IoT enabled portable ultrasound imaging system. *IRBM* 2016; 37: 189–197. 1959-0318. doi: 10.1016/j.irbm.2016.05.001.

[36]    G. Matar, J.M. Lina, J. Carrier, A. Riley and G. Kaddoum, Internet of Things in sleep monitoring: An application for posture recognition using supervised learning. In *2016 IEEE 18th International Conference on e-health Networking, Applications and Services (Healthcom)*, IEEE, 2016; pp. 1–6.

[37]    S.S. Al-Majeed, I.S. Al-Mejibli and J. Karam, Home telehealth by Internet of Things (IoT). In *Canadian Conference on Electrical and Computer Engineering Halifax*, Canada, 3–6, 2015. doi: 978-1-4799-5829-0.

[38]    I. Chiuchisan and O. Geman, An approach of a decision support and home monitoring system for patients with neurological disorders using Internet of Things concepts. *WSEAS Trans. Syst.* 2014; 13. E-ISSN: 22242678.

[39]    K.B. Sundhara Kumar and K. Bairavi, IoT based health monitoring system for autistic patients. In *Symposium on Big Data and Cloud Computing Challenges (ISBCC – 16')*, Smart Innovation, Systems and Technologies 49, 2016, © Springer International Publishing, Switzerland, 2016. doi: 10.1007/978-3-31930348-2-32.

[40]    K. Motwani, D. Mirchandani, Y. Rohra, H. Tarachandani and A. Yeole, Smart nursing home patient monitoring system. *Imp. J. Interdiscip. Res. (IJIR)* 2016; 2(6). ISSN: 2454-1362.

[41] P. Chavan, P. More, N. Thorat, S. Yewale and P. Dhade, ECG – Remote patient monitoring using cloud computing. *Imp. J. Interdiscip. Res. (IJIR)* 2016; 2(2). ISSN: 2454-1362.

[42] A.S. Yeole and D.R. Kalbande, Use of Internet of Things (IoT) in healthcare: A survey. In *Proceedings of the ACM Symposium on Women in Research 2016*, 2016; pp. 71–76.

[43] H. Arbat, S. Choudhary and K. Bala, IOT smart health band. *Imp. J. Interdiscip. Res. (IJIR)* 2016; 2(5). ISSN: 2454-1362.

[44] L. Yu, Y. Lu and X.J. Zhu, Smart hospital based on Internet of Things. *J. Networks* 2012; 7(10). doi: 10.43.4/jnw.7.10.1654-1661.

[45] K.M. Chaman Kumar, A new methodology for monitoring OSA patients based on IoT. *Int. J. Innovative Res. Dev.* 2016; 5(2). ISSN: 2278-0211.

[46] R. Singh, A proposal for mobile E-care health service system using IOT for Indian scenario. *J. Network Commun. Emerg. Technol. (JNCET)* 2016; 6(1). ISSN: 2395-5317.

[47] C. Puri, A. Ukil and S. Bandyopadhyay, iCarMa: Inexpensive cardiac arrhythmia management – An IoT healthcare analytics solution. In *IoT of Health'16*, 2016. doi: 10.1145/2933566.2933567.

[48] V. Chandel, A. Sinharay and N. Ahmed, Exploiting IMU sensors for IOT enabled health monitoring. In *IoT of Health'16*, 2016. doi: 10.1145/2933566.2933569.

[49] M. Fischer and M. Lam, From books to bots: Using medical literature to create a chat bot. In *IoT of Health'16*, Singapore, 2016. doi: 10.1145/2933566.2933573.

[50] A. Ghose, P. Sinha, C. Bhaumik, A. Sinha, A. Agrawal and A.D. Choudhury, UbiHeld – Ubiquitous healthcare monitoring system for elderly and chronic patients. In *UbiComp'13*, Zurich, Switzerland, September 8–12, 2013. doi: 10.1145/2494091.2497331.

[51] H. Li, H. Wang, W. Yin, Y. Li, Y. Qian and F. Hu, Development of a remote monitoring system for henhouse environment based on IoT technology. *Future Internet* 2015; 7: 329–341.

[52] N.S. Kim, K. Lee and J.H. Ryu, Study on IoT based wild vegetation community ecological monitoring system. In *Proceedings of the 2015 Seventh International Conference on Ubiquitous and Future Networks*, Sapporo, Japan, 7–10, 2015; pp. 311–316.

[53] R. Nordin, H. Mohamad, M. Behjati, *et al.*, The world-first deployment of narrowband IoT for rural hydrological monitoring in UNESCO biosphere environment. In *Proceedings of the 2017 IEEE 4th International Conference on Smart Instrumentation, Measurement and Application (ICSIMA)*, Putrajaya, Malaysia, 28–30, 2017; pp. 1–5.

[54] M.C. Yuen, S.Y. Chu, W. Hong Chu, H. Shuen Cheng, H. Lam Ng and S. Pang Yuen, A low-cost IoT smart home system. *Int. J. Eng. Technol.* 2018; 7: 3143–3147.

[55] D.W. Sukmaningsih, W. Suparta, A. Trisetyarso, B.S. Abbas and C.H. Kang, Proposing smart disaster management in urban area. In *Proceedings of the Asian Conference on Intelligent Information and Database Systems*, Yogyakarta, Indonesia, 8–11, 2019; pp. 3–16.

[56]    F. Ahamad, M. Latif, M. Yusoff, M. Khan and L. Juneng, So near yet so different: Surface ozone at three sites in Malaysia. *EES* 2019; 228: 012024. [CrossRef].

[57]    W. Suparta, K.M. Alhasa and M.S.J. Singh, Preliminary development of greenhouse gases system data logger using microcontroller Netduino. *Adv. Sci. Lett.* 2017; 23: 1398–1402.

[58]    F. Montori, L. Bedogni and L. Bononi, A collaborative Internet of Things architecture for smart cities and environmental monitoring. *IEEE Internet Things J.* 2017; 5: 592–605.

[59]    P. Zia, T. Liu and W. Han, Application specific digital forensics investigative model in Internet of Things (IoT). In *Proceedings of the 12th International Conference on Availability*, Reliability and Security, Reggio Calabria, Italy, 2017; pp. 1–7.

[60]    Y.B. Lin, Y.W. Lin, C.Y. Hsiao and S.Y. Wang, Location-based IoT applications on campus: The IoT talk approach. *Pervasive Mob. Comput.* 2017; 40: 660–673.

[61]    X. Zeng, S.K. Garg, P. Strazdins, P.P. Jayaraman, D. Georgakopoulos and R. Ranjan, IOTSim: A simulator for analysing IoT applications. *J. Syst. Archit.* 2017; 72: 93–107.

[62]    M.A. Jabbar and R. Aluvalu, Smart cities in India: Are we smart enough? In *2017 International Conference On Smart Technologies For Smart Nation (SmartTechCon)*, 2017; pp. 1023–1026. doi: 10.1109/SmartTechCon. 2017.8358525.

[63]    S. Chen, B. Liu, X. Chen, Y. Zhang and G. Huang, Framework for adaptive computation offloading in IoT applications. In *Proceedings of the 9th Asia-Pacific Symposium on Internetware*, Shanghai, China, 23, 2017; pp. 1–6.

[64]    A. Urbieta, A. González-Beltrán, S.B. Mokhtar, M.A. Hossain and L. Capra, Adaptive and context-aware service composition for IoT-based smart cities. *Future Gener. Comput. Syst.* 2017; 76: 262–274. [CrossRef].

[65]    D. Seo, Y.B. Jeon, S.H. Lee and K.H. Lee, Cloud computing for ubiquitous computing on M2M and IoT environment mobile application. *Cluster Comput.* 2016; 19: 1001–1013.

[66]    C. Lee, C. Wang, E. Kim and S. Helal, Blueprint flow: A declarative service composition framework for cloud applications. *IEEE Access* 2017; 5: 17634–17643.

[67]    A. Akbar, G. Kousiouris, H. Pervaiz, *et al.*, Real-time probabilistic data fusion for large-scale IoT applications. *IEEE Access* 2018; 6: 10015–10027.

[68]    X. Sun and N. Ansari, Traffic load balancing among brokers at the IoT application layer. *IEEE Trans. Netw. Serv. Manage.* 2017; 15: 489–502.

[69]    X. Sun and N. Ansari, Dynamic resource caching in the IoT application layer for smart cities. *IEEE Internet Things J.* 2017; 5: 606–613.

[70]    G.G. Krishna, G. Krishna and N. Bhalaji, Analysis of routing protocol for low-power and lossy networks in IoT real time applications. *Procedia Comput. Sci.* 2016; 87: 270–274.

[71]  P.G.V. Naranjo, Z. Pooranian, M. Shojafar, M. Conti and R. Buyya, FOCAN: A Fog-supported smart city network architecture for management of applications in the Internet of Everything environments. *J. Parallel Distrib. Comput.* 2019; 132: 274–283.

[72]  S. Kim and S. Kim, User preference for an IoT healthcare application for lifestyle disease management. *Telecommun. Policy* 2018; 42: 304–314.

[73]  X. Fafoutis, L. Clare, N. Grabham, *et al.*, Energy neutral activity monitoring: Wearables powered by smart inductive charging surfaces. In *Proceedings of the 2016 13th Annual IEEE International Conference on Sensing, Communication, and Networking (SECON)*, London, UK, 27–30, 2006; pp. 1–9.

[74]  F. Jimenez and R. Torres, Building an IoT-aware healthcare monitoring system. In *Proceedings of the 2015 34th International Conference of the Chilean Computer Science Society (SCCC)*, Santiago, Chile, 9–13, 2015; pp. 1–4.

[75]  Y. Ding, S. Gang and J. Hong, The design of home monitoring system by remote mobile medical. In *Proceedings of the 2015 7th International Conference on Information Technology in Medicine and Education (ITME)*, Huangshan, China, 13–15, 2015; pp. 278–281.

[76]  H.F. Atlam and G.B. Wills, IoT security, privacy, safety and ethics. In *Digital Twin Technologies and Smart Cities*; Springer: Cham, Switzerland, 2020; pp. 123–149.

[77]  Z. Baloch, F.K. Shaikh and M.A. Unar, A context-aware data fusion approach for health-IoT. *Int. J. Inf. Technol.* 2018; 10: 241–245.

[78]  V. Subrahmanyam, M.A. Zubair, A. Kumar and P. Rajalakshmi, A low power minimal error IEEE 802.15. 4 Transceiver for heart monitoring in IoT applications. *Wirel. Pers. Commun.* 2018; 100: 611–629.

[79]  S.C. Lin, C.Y. Wen and W.A. Sethares, Two-tier device-based authentication protocol against PUEA attacks for IoT applications. *IEEE Trans. Signal Inf. Process. Over Networks* 2017; 4: 33–47.

[80]  H.A. Damis, N. Khalid, R. Mirzavand, H.J. Chung and P. Mousavi, Investigation of epidermal loop antennas for biotelemetry IoT applications. *IEEE Access* 2018; 6: 15806–15815.

[81]  M. Elappila, S. Chinara and D.R. Parhi, Survivable path routing in WSN for IoT applications. *Pervasive Mob. Comput.* 2018; 43: 49–63.

[82]  J. Jebadurai and J.D. Peter, Super-resolution of retinal images using multi-kernel SVR for IoT healthcare applications. *Future Gener. Comput. Syst.* 2018; 83: 338–346.

[83]  H. Malik, M.M. Alam, Y. Le Moullec and A. Kuusik, Narrow band-IoT performance analysis for healthcare applications. *Procedia Comput. Sci.* 2018; 130: 1077–1083.

[84]  R. Hamdan, Human factors for IoT services utilization for health information exchange. *J. Theor. Appl. Inf. Technol.* 2018; 96: 2095–2105.

[85]  M. Shahidul Islam, M.T. Islam, A.F. Almutairi, G.K. Beng, N. Misran and N. Amin, Monitoring of the human body signal through the Internet of Things (IoT) based LoRa wireless network system. *Appl. Sci.* 2019; 9: 1884.

[86]   M.A. Dauwed, J. Yahaya, Z. Mansor and A.R. Hamdan, Determinants of Internet of Things services utilization in health information exchange. *J. Eng. Appl. Sci.* 2018; 13: 10490–10501.

[87]   M.A. Jabbar, S. Samreen and R. Aluvalu, The future of health care: Machine learning. *Int. J. Eng. Technol.* 2018; 7(4): 23–25.

[88]   I. Chiuchisan, H.-N. Costin and O. Geman, Adopting the Internet of Things technologies in health care systems. In *Proc. Int. Conf. Expo. Electr. Power Eng. (EPE)*, Iasi, Romania, 2014, pp. 532–535.

[89]   A. AwadAbdellatif, A. Emam, C.-F. Chiasserini, A. Mohamed, A. Jaoua and R. Ward, Edge-based compression and classification for smart healthcare systems: Concept, implementation and evaluation. *Expert Syst. Appl.* 2019; 117: 1–14.

[90]   G. Muhammad, M.F. Alhamid, M. Alsulaiman and B. Gupta, Edge computing with cloud for voice disorder assessment and treatment. *IEEE Commun. Mag.* 2018; 56(4): 60–65.

[91]   M.Z. Uddin, A wearable sensor-based activity prediction system to facilitate edge computing in smart health care system. *J. Parallel Distrib. Comput.* 2019; 123: 46–53.

[92]   A. Al-nasheri, G. Muhammad, M. Alsulaiman and Z. Ali, Investigation of voice pathology detection and classification on different frequency regions using correlation functions. *J. Voice* 2017; 31(1): 3–15.

[93]   J.C. Wang, C.Y. Ng and R.H. Brook, Response to COVID-19 in Taiwan: Big data analytics, new technology, and proactive testing. *J. Am. Med. Assoc.* 2020; 323(14): 2.

[94]   Y. Lee. 2020. Covid-19: Taiwan's New 'electronic Fence' for Quarantines Leads Wave of Virus Monitoring. https://www.thestar.com.my/tech/tech-news/2020/03/20/covid-19-taiwans-new-electronic-fence-for-quarantines-leads-wave-of-virus-monitoring.

[95]   H. Leite, T. Gruber and I.R. Hodgkinson, Flattening the infection curve – Understanding the role of telehealth in managing COVID-19. *Leader. Health Serv.* 2019; 33(2): 1751–1879. doi: 10.1108/LHS-05-2020-084.

[96]   L. Ferretti, Quantifying dynamics of SARS-CoV-2 transmission suggests that epidemic control with digital contact tracing. *Science* 2020; 31. doi: 10.1126/science.abb6936. Mar 2020.

[97]   Bosch. 2020. Combating the Coronavirus Pandemic: Bosch Develops Rapid Test for COVID-19. https://www.bosch.com/stories/vivalytic-rapid-test-for-covid-19.

## Chapter 2

# Non-invasive psycho-physiological driver monitoring through IoT-oriented systems

*Luca Davoli[1], Veronica Mattioli[2], Sara Gambetta[3], Laura Belli[1], Luca Carnevali[3], Marco Martalò[4]\*, Andrea Sgoifo[3], Riccardo Raheli[2] and Gianluigi Ferrari[1]*

The definition, analysis, and implementation of in-vehicle monitoring systems that collect data which are informative of the status of the joint driver-vehicle system represent a topic of strong interest from both academic players and industrial manufacturers. Many external factors, such as road design, road layout, traffic flow, and weather, can influence and increase driving-related stress, potentially increasing risks. The ubiquitous diffusion of Internet of Things (IoT) technologies allows one to collect heterogeneous data that can build the foundation for driver's psychophysiological characterization, with the aim of improving safety and security while driving. This chapter evaluates and discusses the feasibility and usefulness of a noninvasive IoT-oriented driver monitoring infrastructure aiming at collecting physiological parameters (such as heart rate variability, HRV) that may be adopted as biomarkers of the driver's psychophysiological state in different driving scenarios.

## 2.1  Introduction

Driving is one of the major experiences linking together people: every day, while travelling by car, drivers are exposed to different events and situations, which can impact on their psychophysiological state. External factors such as road design

[1]Internet of Things (IoT) Lab, Department of Engineering and Architecture, University of Parma, Parma, Italy
[2]Multimedia Lab, Department of Engineering and Architecture, University of Parma, Parma, Italy
[3]Stress Physiology Lab, Department of Chemistry, Life Sciences and Environmental Sustainability, University of Parma, Parma, Italy
[4]Networks for Humans (Net4U) Lab, Department of Electrical and Electronic Engineering, University of Cagliari, Cagliari, Italy
\*The work of Marco Martalò was carried out at the following place: in 2020, at the IoT Lab of the University of Parma; and in 2021 while collaborating with the IoT Lab.

(motorways vs. rural roads vs. city roads, etc.), road layout (straight vs. curves, steep road vs. downhill road, etc.), traffic flow (high vs. low), and weather can influence and increase driving-related stress. To this end, literature studies examined the relationship between traffic conditions and stress levels and, as expected, they found that driving-related stress is greater in high traffic jam areas rather than in low congestion ones [1–3]. Moreover, it has been observed that these stressful situations may alter the driver's psychophysiological state.

In this regard, HRV represents an indirect and noninvasive measurement of beat-to-beat temporal changes in heart rate (HR), which reflects cardiac autonomic influences, particularly of vagal origin, at the sinoatrial node of the heart. HRV analysis has been extensively applied in various research fields, including psychophysiology, cardiology, and psychiatry and has been increasingly recognized as a biomarker of health and stress. In fact, a healthy subject is characterized by higher levels of resting HRV that are in turn associated with better flexibility and adaptability to environmental challenges [4]. Moreover, HRV analysis is able to index psychophysiological states during stressful conditions or mental efforts (such as during driving activities) [4]. Indeed, lower tonic HRV has been associated with psychosocial stress and mental workload [5–7], whereas higher HRV reflects the capability of an individual to successfully adapt to external stimuli and manifesting itself in a reduction in daily performance [8]. An example of the potential utility of HRV as a biomarker of physiological driver's state is shown in [9], where driving-related stress is associated with a reduction in HRV indexes of vagal tone.

From a more technological perspective, the definition and analysis of monitoring systems inside vehicles that are able to simultaneously collect physiological indexes and useful data to determine the status of the driver–vehicle system is a topic of strong interest. The final aim for both academic players and industrial manufacturer is to improve safety and security while driving for both drivers and passengers [10]. Furthermore, recent technological progress has introduced new possibilities with respect to traditional manual driving, especially with regard to mechanisms aiming at vehicle—e.g., cars, trucks, etc.—driving assistance, such as *onboard* advanced driver-assistance systems (ADAS) [11]. In detail, examples of ADAS mechanisms equipping modern vehicles are antilock braking system [12], adaptive cruise control [13], electronic stability control (ESC) [14], lane departure warning system [15], forward collision warnings [16], traffic sign recognition [17], automotive night vision [18], alcohol ignition interlock devices [19], collision avoidance systems [20], and driver drowsiness detection [21]. Then, as a common objective, all these ADAS aim to compensate for human errors, in order to reduce road fatalities—activating alarms or, when necessary, taking control of the vehicle itself.

Furthermore, focusing on a more general perspective, in the last years the ubiquitous diffusion of the IoT paradigm [22] has influenced and changed our lifestyle, thanks to the ability to interconnect heterogeneous devices (such as sensors, actuators, or more in general, *smart objects* [23,24]), combining different technologies and communication protocols to build services for end users [25]. Thanks to this heterogeneity, IoT applications are innumerable—nowadays often requiring to outsource some processing efforts to cloud-based infrastructures [26]—and, among different possible scenarios, one of the most relevant ones is linked to the automotive industry, with the aim of acquiring a better knowledge of the driver–vehicle system as a whole.

Then, looking at the interaction level of all these paradigms, the majority of existing ADAS do not take into account aspects related to the psychophysiological state of the driver. This would require continuous monitoring and understanding of the driver's physical, emotional, and physiological state, an effective communication of the ADAS decisions to the driver, or a direct action on the vehicle. Although a monitoring system with these characteristics is very challenging to obtain, ADAS provided with information about the driver's psychophysiological state could take more contextualized actions, implementing complex decisions that are compatible with the driver's possible reactions. Another aspect that should be considered in the field of *in-vehicle* monitoring systems is the degree of intrusiveness of the sensors employed for collecting driver's physiological parameters, which in fact should not interfere—or minimize as much as possible their interference—with the driving activity and therefore should be selected accordingly.

Due to these premises, the aim of this chapter is 2-fold: (i) propose a non-invasive IoT driver monitoring infrastructure, aiming at collecting data useful to estimate the psychophysiological status of the driver, as a base for subsequent actions, and (ii) evaluate the usefulness of HRV parameters as biomarkers of a driver's psychophysiological state in different driving scenarios.

The rest of the chapter is organized as follows. A review of heterogeneous technologies for human driver monitoring is presented in Section 2.2. Section 2.3 describes the in-vehicle IoT monitoring system and the experimental setup. In Section 2.4, a preliminary evaluation of collected data is presented. Finally, some conclusions and propose future research directions are drawn in Section 2.5.

## 2.2  Heterogeneous driver monitoring

When considering technologies for human driver monitoring activities, a focal point that should be taken into account is the extent to which the end user (i.e., the driver) takes up these technologies. This is strictly dependent on their unobtrusiveness, i.e., their capacity to be perceived by the user as not infringing upon his/her privacy or interfering with his/her driving activity. Taking these aspects into account, IoT sensing devices can be adopted as monitoring technologies and could be selected on the basis of their mobility degree. *Mobile sensors* (e.g., wearable and sensors-equipped smartphones) have become practical and appealing—thanks to the miniaturization of the components—and could also be exploited for monitoring driver's behavior and physiology [27]. On the other hand, *stationary sensors* are typically installed in the environment that needs to be monitored (e.g., in the vehicle's cabin) and act without any physical contact with the user, thus being well suited for *unobtrusive* monitoring—an example of a stationary sensor may be a video and/or thermal camera positioned in the vehicle's cabin.

## 2.2.1    *Wearable and inertial sensors*

One of the uprising unobtrusive ways to monitor individual physiological para-meters while driving is through the collection and analysis of biological signals. For example, the electrocardiogram (ECG) gives uniqueness, universality, and permanence [28] in the measurement, thanks to its working principle by which the biometric signal is the result of the electrical conduction through the heart needed for its contraction [29]. Then, ECG analysis directly inside the vehicle's cabin may be useful for assessing parameters (e.g., HRV) related to both mental and physical stress, and workload [30–32] for automatic vehicle settings customization (e.g., biometric authentication for ignition lock [33]). Moreover, the respiratory signal may be exploited in order to obtain additional physiological indicators (e.g., the respiratory rate, RR) that are useful in the automotive scenarios. In particular, these data could be informative of the driver's workload and stress status. Nevertheless, it could be interesting to investigate how the combination of these measurements with vision data (either by normal or thermal cameras) would allow one to estimate a classification index for workload or stress level of the driver [34]. Additional mobile-sensing elements (often worn by the person to be monitored) are inertial measurement units (IMUs), which allow the estimation of the driver motion level through three-axis internal accelerometers and gyroscopes. More in detail, IMUs allow both motion and attitude/pose estimations, but they require to be carefully chosen and calibrated—because of bias instability, scaling, alignment, and tem-perature dependence. All these issues should be carefully considered especially in operating areas that require limitations in IMU's size, weight, and cost limitations.

With particular regard to the automotive field, inertial sensing mechanisms can intervene in different scenarios, from driver's movements monitoring when seated in the vehicle's cabin to safety areas—like vehicle dynamics control (e.g., ESC) and passenger restraint systems (e.g., seat-belt pretensioner and airbags).

## 2.2.2    *Camera sensors*

With regards to unobtrusive and stationary sensing technologies to be used in driver monitoring contexts, a particularly interesting one can be found in imaging-based solutions, such as video cameras. Unfortunately, as for sensing mechanisms discussed in Section 2.2.1, even video cameras are not exempt from drawbacks, especially depending on swinging lighting and atmospheric conditions—which may interfere with driver's movements monitoring and physiological signal recognition. Considering these aspects, a way to overcome this limitation is the deployment of thermal cameras, being more robust to adverse light conditions compared to canonical imaging sensors. More in detail, long wavelength infrared cameras [35] can detect objects in different environmental conditions (e.g., rain, darkness, in the presence of fog, etc.), are unaf-fected by sun glare (improving situational awareness [36]), and are more robust against reflections, shadows, and car headlights [37]. Even in this case, the price to be paid is that the thermal camera's video resolution is typically lower than that of traditional video sensors. Nevertheless, more recent thermal cameras are able to produce high-quality video streams. Finally, in addition to the driver's monitoring based on thermal cameras, useful integration could involve the use of normal and general-purpose imaging sensors, such as *in-vehicle* fixed cameras, or the front camera of a smartphone [38,39]. In detail, these additional video sensing elements can integrate the experimental data obtained by thermal cameras, thanks to their well-known portability, thus representing an optimal way for gathering information [40].

## 2.3 In-vehicle IoT-oriented monitoring architecture

### 2.3.1 Experimental setup

Given the different monitoring entities discussed in Section 2.2, the noninvasive IoT-oriented driver monitoring architecture proposed in this chapter is shown in Figure 2.1. In order to collect the driver's physiological data, an Equivital EQ02 LifeMonitor [41] sensor belt has been adopted. This wearable sensing device is composed by two elements: (i) a chest belt containing fabric electrodes placed in good contact with the driver's skin, and (ii) a sensor electronics module (SEM) collecting ECG and respiratory signals, skin temperature, and three-axis accelerometer data. Then, as shown in Figure 2.2, on a practical side the belt securely holds the SEM on the driver's body through a specific pocket on the left side of the belt itself.

Moreover, in order to collect thermal information from the body (i.e., face) of the driver and the surrounding environment, an FLIR One Pro LT [42] thermal camera has been included in the experimental IoT-oriented monitoring architecture. In detail, this video-capturing device is intended to work as an external "dongle" to be plugged into a smartphone (running either Android or iOS as operating system) and subsequently positioned and installed inside the vehicle, as shown in Figure 2.3. To this

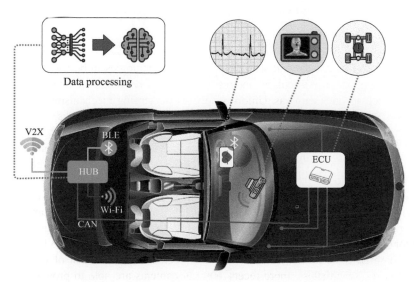

*Figure 2.1   In-vehicle IoT-oriented monitoring architecture*

*Figure 2.2    Equivital EQ02 LifeMonitor sensor belt positioning*

*Figure 2.3    FLIR One Pro LT thermal camera positioning inside the vehicle*

end, it is necessary to carefully and accurately define the position of the smartphone connected with the thermal camera; this is as much true as it represents a trade-off between the quality of the framing—further image-processing and analysis tasks require a frontal viewpoint—and the degree of obtrusiveness for the driver's perspective toward the windscreen.

## 2.3.2    HRV analysis

The experimental testbed has been used to obtain high-quality ECG recordings under stationary conditions in order to perform a first HRV analysis. In detail, ECG signals are digital waves converted through specific processing tasks and, aiming at obtaining a good time resolution, a sampling rate of at least 250 Hz is recommended. Then,

HRV is quantified by analyzing the variations of time intervals between consecutive normal heart beats. To this end, an inter-beat interval may be defined as the time between consecutive R-waves peaks of the ECG (R–R interval), while the time-course of the R–R interval is called *tachogram* and further quantitative analysis of this curve will allow the estimation of HRV parameters. HRV analysis is performed by applying time-domain and frequency-domain methods.

Time-domain parameters are calculated with mathematical approaches to measure the amount of variability present in a specific time period in a continuous ECG signal. The most frequent time domain indexes adopted for HRV analysis are detailed in Table 2.1: (i) standard deviation of the R–R intervals (SDNN), (ii) root-mean square of successive differences between adjacent R–R intervals (RMSSD), and (iii) percentage of successive R–R interval differences exceeding 50 ms (pNN50). In detail, the SDNN estimates overall HRV and includes the contribution of both branches of the autonomic nervous system (ANS) to HR variations. The RMSSD estimates vagally mediated changes in HR [43]. Finally, the pNN50 quantifies the percentage of successive R–R interval differences that are larger than 50 ms and reflects the vagal tone [43].

Instead, frequency-domain analysis requires to filter the signal into different bands. In fact, the power spectral analysis decomposes a time-dependent fluctuating signal into its sinusoidal components, allowing one to detect and quantify the amount of cyclical variation present at different frequencies [44]. Moreover, it provides information on how the power is distributed as a function of frequency. Thus, in a typical power spectral density curve, three main frequency bands can be identified, as detailed in Table 2.2: (i) very low frequency (VLF),

*Table 2.1   HRV indexes considered in the time domain*

| Variable | Description | Physiological origin |
| --- | --- | --- |
| SDNN | Standard deviation of the R–R intervals | Cyclic components responsible for heart rate variability |
| RMSSD | Root-mean square of successive differences between adjacent R–R intervals | Vagal tone |
| pNN50 | Percentage of successive R–R interval differences exceeding 50 ms | Vagal tone |

*Table 2.2   HRV indexes considered in the frequency domain*

| Variable | Description | Physiological origin |
| --- | --- | --- |
| VLF | Very low frequency ($<0.04$ Hz) | Long-term regulation mechanisms, thermoregulation and hormonal mechanism |
| LF | Low frequency (0.04–0.15 Hz) | Mix of sympathetic and vagal activity |
| HF | High frequency (0.15–0.4 Hz) | Vagal tone |

(ii) low frequency (LF), and (iii) high frequency (HF) bands. The VLF component reflects R–R interval variations that are due to long-term regulation mechanisms (e.g., thermoregulation and hormonal mechanisms). The LF band reflects a mix between sympathetic and vagal influences. The HF band reflects vagal tone and is linked to respiratory-related changes in cardiac autonomic modulation [45].

## 2.4    Experimental performance evaluation

### 2.4.1    Operating protocol for data collection

In order to collect information on the driver's psychophysiological state in different driving scenarios, driving tests should be performed according to a well-defined operating protocol. Both smooth and fast driving should be included in the analysis to evaluate the driver's response to different external stimuli, associated with different amount of perceived stress. All these tests should then take place on both urban and highway roads in situations of smooth and heavy traffic.

The experimental driver monitoring has been conducted on a 26-year-old Italian female subject, separating the driving protocol into six time intervals, as shown in Figure 2.4: (i) baseline, (ii) first city driving, (iii) first highway driving, (iv) second city driving, (v) second highway driving, and (vi) rest phase. Each driving period had a duration of at least 5 min, in the end resulting in a total driving time of 30 min. In order to collect driver's physiological data, the Equivital EQ02 LifeMonitor sensor was worn by the subject throughout the driving test and the FLIR One Pro LT thermal camera was used to simultaneously record temperature-related information.

The overall route covered during the experimental campaign inside the city of Parma, Italy, is shown in Figure 2.5. During the baseline period, the vehicle's engine was off and the subject was asked to sit still inside the vehicle to acquire baseline data. During city and highway driving phases, urban and ring roads were covered with an average speed of 50 and 90 km/h, respectively. Finally, at the end of the route, data recording continued for at least 5 min during recovery conditions, with the driver inside the car.

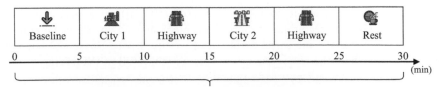

*Figure 2.4    Operating driving protocol adopted in the experimental driver monitoring*

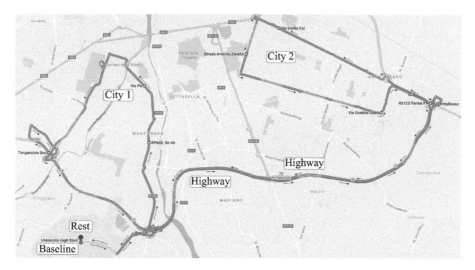

*Figure 2.5    Urban and highway roads traveled in the city of Parma, Italy, during the experimental driver monitoring*

## 2.4.2    HR and HRV data

ECG and respiratory signals were exported from the wearable sensor by means of its software manager, denoted as Equivital Manager. Then, raw ECG and respiratory data obtained from the EQ02 LifeMonitor equipment were amplified, digitized, and analyzed by means of the LabChart Pro 5.0 software [46]. More in detail, each raw ECG signal was manually inspected to ensure that all R-waves were correctly detected and to exclude artifacts before further analysis. Then, for each recording period, ECG signals were split in 5-min epochs and, for each epoch, HR has been calculated by plotting the number of R-waves per time unit (dim: beats per minute [bpm]), together with the estimation of time- and frequency-domain HRV indexes (namely, RMSSD and HF). Finally, as for the ECG signals, for each recording period, respiratory signals were split in 5-min epochs, and R–R was calculated for each epoch.

## 2.4.3    Experimental results

In Figure 2.6, average HR temporal dynamics (dim: [bpm]) are shown. In detail, at the beginning of the recording session, the subject showed an HR value equal to 85 bpm. Then, the HR increased during the first city driving phase and remained constant throughout the rest of the drive. Finally, at the end of the driving session, in the rest phase, the HR returned to baseline levels.

RMSSD values (dim: [ms]) are shown in Figure 2.7. At the beginning of the driving session, the average RMSSD was equal to 34 ms. Then, the RMSSD decreased during both city and highway driving phases, till increasing back to baseline levels during the rest phase, similar to what was observed for HR.

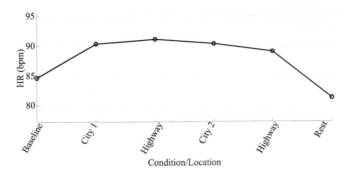

*Figure 2.6    Experimental HR values obtained during the driving route*

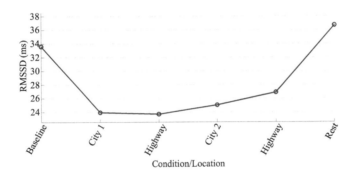

*Figure 2.7    Experimental RMSSD values obtained during the driving route*

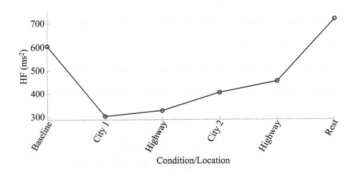

*Figure 2.8    Experimental HF values obtained during the driving route*

In Figure 2.8, the values of HF (dim: [ms$^2$]) are shown. As for RMSSD, the driving phase was characterized by a reduction of HF values in both city and highway scenarios, thus suggesting a decrease in parasympathetic modulation.

Finally, the average RR values (dim: counts per minute [cpm]) are shown in Figure 2.9. The R–R interval was steady during the overall recording session.

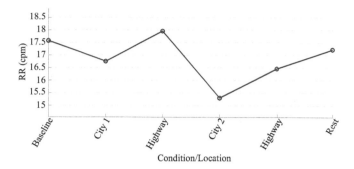

*Figure 2.9    Experimental R–R values obtained during the driving route*

These preliminary results suggest that the driving experience can modulate the psychophysiological state of the driver, as hinted by the reduction in HRV parameters associated with the increase of HR. Therefore, further driving recording sessions with a larger sample size are needed to confirm these results and indicate the extent to which HRV parameters may vary according to the psychophysiological state of the driver in different driving scenarios. Moreover, a future integration of thermal imaging data would provide a clearer picture of the physiological correlates of drivers' mental effort.

## 2.5    Conclusions and future works

In this chapter, a preliminary noninvasive infrastructure for in-vehicle driver monitoring of the psychophysiological status of the driver is presented. This infrastructure is based on an IoT sensor network composed by a wearable sensor belt, worn by the driver, and a thermal camera, installed in the vehicle's cabin framing the driver. Then, the protocol adopted for experimental data acquisition campaigns, together with ECG and respiratory signals collection and analysis during different driving scenarios, have been described. While additional experimental recordings are needed to confirm these experimental results and to allow a better investigation on the effects of driving activities on autonomic neural modulation of the cardiac function, the preliminary results on the utility of HRV parameters as biomarkers of a driver's psychophysiological state are promising.

Future activities will involve the integration of thermal camera-based data and the improvement of the IoT communication infrastructure in order to integrate additional data sources, e.g., data collected directly from the onboard vehicular bus and emitted from the vehicle's electronic control unit possibly in real time.

### Acknowledgments

The work of the authors is supported by the European Union's Horizon 2020 research and innovation program ECSEL Joint Undertaking (JU) under grant agreement no. 876487, NextPerception project—"Next Generation Smart Perception Sensors and Distributed Intelligence for Proactive Human Monitoring in Health, Wellbeing, and Automotive Systems." The JU received support from the European Union's Horizon 2020 research and innovation program and the nations involved in the mentioned projects. The work reflects only the authors' views; the European Commission is not responsible for any use that may be made of the information it contains. The work of L.D. is partially funded by the University of Parma, under "Iniziative di Sostegno alla Ricerca di Ateneo" program, "Multi-interface IoT sYstems for Multi-layer Information Processing" (MIoTYMIP) project.

# References

[1]  Hennessy DA and Wiesenthal DL. The Relationship Between Traffic Congestion, Driver Stress and Direct Versus Indirect Coping Behaviours. *Ergonomics*. 1997; 40(3): 348–361. doi:10.1080/001401397188198.

[2]  Hill JD and Boyle LN. Driver Stress as Influenced by Driving Maneuvers and Roadway Conditions. *Transportation Research Part F: Traffic Psychology and Behaviour*. 2007; 10(3): 177–186. doi:10.1016/j.trf.2006.09.002.

[3]  Neighbors C, Vietor NA, and Knee CR. A Motivational Model of Driving Anger and Aggression. *Personality and Social Psychology Bulletin*. 2002; 28(3): 324–335. doi:10.1177/0146167202286004.

[4]  Thayer JF, Hansen AL, Saus-Rose E, *et al.* Heart Rate Variability, Prefrontal Neural Function, and Cognitive Performance: The Neurovisceral Integration Perspective on Self-regulation, Adaptation, and Health. *Annals of Behavioral Medicine*. 2009; 37(2): 141–153. doi:10.1007/s12160-009-9101-z.

[5]  Lischke A, Jacksteit R, Mau-Moeller A, *et al.* Heart Rate Variability is Associated With Psychosocial Stress in Distinct Social Domains. *Journal of Psychosomatic Research*. 2018; 106: 56–61. doi:10.1016/j.jpsychores.2018.01.005.

[6]  Castaldo R, Melillo P, Bracale U, *et al.* Acute Mental Stress Assessment via Short Term HRV Analysis in Healthy Adults: A Systematic Review With Meta-Analysis. *Biomedical Signal Processing and Control*. 2015; 18: 370–377. doi:10.1016/j.bspc.2015.02.012.

[7]  Mulder T, De Waard D, and Brookhuis KA. Estimating Mental Effort Using Heart Rate and Heart Rate Variability. In: Stanton NA, Hedge A, Brookhuis K, Salas E, Hendrick HW, editors. *Handbook of Human Factors and Ergonomics Methods*. 1st ed. Boca Raton, FL: CRC Press; 2004. p. 227–236. doi:10.1201/9780203489925-30.

[8]  Melillo P, Bracale M, and Pecchia L. Nonlinear Heart Rate Variability Features for Real-Life Stress Detection. Case study: Students Under Stress Due to University Examination. *BioMedical Engineering OnLine*. 2011; 10 (1): 96. doi:10.1186/1475-925x-10-96.

[9]  Riener A, Ferscha A, and Aly M. Heart on the Road: HRV Analysis for Monitoring a Driver's Affective State. In: *Proceedings of the 1st International Conference on Automotive User Interfaces and Interactive Vehicular Applications*.

*AutomotiveUI '09*. New York, NY, USA: Association for Computing Machinery; 2009. p. 99–106. doi:10.1145/1620509.1620529.

[10] Davoli L, Martalò M, Cilfone A, *et al*. On Driver Behavior Recognition for Increased Safety: A Roadmap. *Safety*. 2020; 6(4): 1–33. doi:10.3390/safety6040055.

[11] Ziebinski A, Cupek R, Grzechca D, *et al*. Review of Advanced Driver Assistance Systems (ADAS). *AIP Conference Proceedings*. 2017; 1906(1): 120002. doi:10.1063/1.5012394.

[12] Satoh M and Shiraishi S. Performance of Antilock Brakes with Simplified Control Technique. In: *SAE International Congress and Exposition*; 28 February–4 March. Detroit, MI: SAE International; 1983. doi:10.4271/830484.

[13] Vollrath M, Schleicher S, and Gelau C. The Influence of Cruise Control and Adaptive Cruise Control on Driving Behaviour—A Driving Simulator Study. *Accident Analysis & Prevention*. 2011; 43(3): 1134–1139. doi:10.1016/j.aap.2010.12.023.

[14] Hall-Geisler K. How Electronic Stability Control Works 2021 [cited 11 May 2021]. Available from: https://auto.howstuffworks.com/car-driving-safety/safety-regulatory-devices/electronic-stability-control.htm.

[15] Kortli Y, Marzougui M, and Atri M. Efficient Implementation of a Real-Time Lane Departure Warning System. In: *2016 International Image Processing, Applications and Systems (IPAS)*; 2016. p. 1–6. doi:10.1109/IPAS.2016.7880072.

[16] Wang C, Sun Q, Li Z, *et al*. A Forward Collision Warning System Based on Self-Learning Algorithm of Driver Characteristics. *Journal of Intelligent & Fuzzy Systems*. 2020; 38(2): 1519–1530. doi:10.3233/JIFS-179515.

[17] Luo H, Yang Y, Tong B, *et al*. Traffic Sign Recognition Using a Multi-Task Convolutional Neural Network. *IEEE Transactions on Intelligent Transportation Systems*. 2018; 19(4): 1100–1111. doi:10.1109/TITS.2017.2714691.

[18] Martinelli NS and Seoane R. Automotive Night Vision System. In: *Thermosense XXI*. vol. 3700. International Society for Optics and Photonics. SPIE; 1999. p. 343–346. doi:10.1117/12.342304.

[19] Centers for Disease Control and Prevention (CDC). Increasing Alcohol Ignition Interlock Use; 2016 [cited 28 April 2021]. Available from: https://www.cdc.gov/transportationsafety/impaired_driving/ignition_interlock_states.html.

[20] Fuller J. How Pre-Collision Systems Work; 2009 [cited 28 April 2021]. Available from: https://auto.howstuffworks.com/car-driving-safety/safety-regulatory-devices/pre-collision-systems.htm.

[21] Jacobé de Naurois C, Bourdin C, Stratulat A, *et al*. Detection and Prediction of Driver Drowsiness Using Artificial Neural Network Models. *Accident Analysis & Prevention*. 2019; 126: 95–104. 10th International Conference on Managing Fatigue: Managing Fatigue to Improve Safety, Wellness, and Effectiveness. doi:10.1016/j.aap.2017.11.038.

[22]    Atzori L, Iera A, and Morabito G. The Internet of Things: A survey. *Computer Networks*. 2010; 54(15): 2787–2805. doi:10.1016/j.comnet.2010.05.010.

[23]    Davoli L, Belli L, Cilfone A, *et al.* Integration of Wi-Fi Mobile Nodes in a Web of Things Testbed. *ICT Express*. 2016; 2(3): 96–99. Special Issue on ICT Convergence in the Internet of Things (IoT). doi:10.1016/j.icte.2016.07.001.

[24]    Atzori L, Iera A, and Morabito G. From "Smart Objects" to "Social Objects": The Next Evolutionary Step of the Internet of Things. *IEEE Communications Magazine*. 2014; 52(1): 97–105. doi:10.1109/MCOM.2014.6710070.

[25]    Belli L, Cilfone A, Davoli L, *et al.* IoT-Enabled Smart Sustainable Cities: Challenges and Approaches. *Smart Cities*. 2020; 3: 1039–1071. doi:10.3390/smartcities3030052.

[26]    Belli L, Cirani S, Davoli L, *et al.* An Open-Source Cloud Architecture for Big Stream IoT Applications. In: Podnar Žarko I, Pripužić K, and Serrano M, editors. *Interoperability and Open-Source Solutions for the Internet of Things: International Workshop, FP7 OpenIoT Project, Held in Conjunction with SoftCOM 2014*, Split, Croatia, September 18, 2014, Invited Papers. Springer International Publishing; 2015. p. 73–88. doi:10.1007/978-3-319-16546-2_7.

[27]    Welch KC, Harnett C, and Lee YC. A Review on Measuring Affect with Practical Sensors to Monitor Driver Behavior. *Safety*. 2019; 5(4): 72. doi:10.3390/safety5040072.

[28]    Li M and Narayanan S. Robust ECG Biometrics by Fusing Temporal and Cepstral Information. In: *2010 20th International Conference on Pattern Recognition*; 2010. p. 1326–1329. doi:10.1109/ICPR.2010.330.

[29]    Abo-Zahhad M, Ahmed SM, and Abbas SN. Biometric Authentication Based on PCG and ECG Signals: Present Status and Future Directions. *Signal, Image and Video Processing*. 2014; 8(4): 739–751. doi:10.1007/s11760-013-0593-4.

[30]    Cassani R, Falk TH, Horai A, *et al.* Evaluating the Measurement of Driver Heart and Breathing Rates from a Sensor-Equipped Steering Wheel Using Spectrotemporal Signal Processing. In: *2019 IEEE Intelligent Transportation Systems Conference (ITSC)*; 2019. p. 2843–2847. doi:10.1109/ITSC.2019.8916959.

[31]    Lanatà A, Valenza G, Greco A, *et al.* How the Autonomic Nervous System and Driving Style Change With Incremental Stressing Conditions During Simulated Driving. *IEEE Transactions on Intelligent Transportation Systems*. 2015; 16(3): 1505–1517. doi:10.1109/TITS.2014.2365681.

[32]    Eilebrecht B, Wolter S, Lem J, *et al.* The Relevance of HRV Parameters for Driver Workload Detection in Real World Driving. In: *2012 Computing in Cardiology*. Krakow, Poland; 2012. p. 409–412.

[33]    Samarin N and Sannella D. A Key to Your Heart: Biometric Authentication Based on ECG Signals. *CoRR*. 2019; abs/1906.09181. Available from: http://arxiv.org/abs/1906.09181.

[34]    Coughlin JF, Reimer B, and Mehler B. Monitoring, Managing, and Motivating Driver Safety and Well-Being. *IEEE Pervasive Computing*. 2011; 10(3): 14–21. doi:10.1109/MPRV.2011.54.

[35]   Konieczka A, Michalowicz E, and Piniarski K. Infrared Thermal Camera-based System for Tram Drivers Warning About Hazardous Situations. In: *2018 Signal Processing: Algorithms, Architectures, Arrangements, and Applications (SPA)*; 2018. p. 250–254. doi:10.23919/SPA.2018.8563417.

[36]   Cardone D, Perpetuini D, Filippini C, *et al.* Driver Stress State Evaluation by Means of Thermal Imaging: A Supervised Machine Learning Approach Based on ECG Signal. *Applied Sciences.* 2020; 10(16): 5673. doi:10.3390/app10165673.

[37]   Kiashari SEH, Nahvi A, Bakhoda H, *et al.* Evaluation of Driver Drowsiness Using Respiration Analysis by Thermal Imaging on a Driving Simulator. *Multimedia Tools and Applications.* 2020; 79(25–26): 17793–17815. doi:10.1007/s11042-020-08696-x.

[38]   Kashevnik A, Kruglov M, Lashkov I, *et al.* Human Psychophysiological Activity Estimation Based on Smartphone Camera and Wearable Electronics. *Future Internet.* 2020; 12(7). doi:10.3390/fi12070111.

[39]   Lashkov I and Kashevnik A. Smartphone-Based Intelligent Driver Assistant: Context Model and Dangerous State Recognition Scheme. In: Bi Y, Bhatia R, and Kapoor S, editors. *Intelligent Systems and Applications.* vol. 1038. Cham: Springer International Publishing; 2020. p. 152–165. doi:10.1007/978-3-030-29513-4_11.

[40]   Lindow F and Kashevnik A. Driver Behavior Monitoring Based on Smartphone Sensor Data and Machine Learning Methods. In: *2019 25th Conference of Open Innovations Association (FRUCT)*. Helsinki, Finland; 2019. p. 196–203. doi:10.23919/FRUCT48121.2019.8981511.

[41]   Equivital Ltd. Eq LifeMonitor; 2021 [cited 18 May 2021]. Available from: https://www.equivital.com/products/eq02-lifemonitor.

[42]   Teledyne FLIR LLC. FLIR One Pro LT; 2021 [cited 18 May 2021]. Available from: https://www.flir.it/products/flir-one-pro-lt/.

[43]   Laborde S, Mosley E, and Thayer JF. Heart Rate Variability and Cardiac Vagal Tone in Psychophysiological Research – Recommendations for Experiment Planning, Data Analysis, and Data Reporting. *Frontiers in Psychology.* 2017; 8: 213. doi:10.3389/fpsyg.2017.00213.

[44]   Malliani A, Pagani M, Lombardi F, *et al.* Cardiovascular Neural Regulation Explored in the Frequency Domain. *Circulation.* 1991; 84(2): 482–492. doi:10.1161/01.CIR.84.2.482.

[45]   Shaffer F, McCraty R, and Zerr CL. A Healthy Heart Is Not a Metronome: An Integrative Review of the Heart's Anatomy and Heart Rate Variability. *Frontiers in Psychology.* 2014; 5: 1040. doi:10.3389/fpsyg.2014.01040.

[46]   ADInstruments Ltd. LabChart Lightning; 2021 [cited 10 May 2021]. Available from: https://www.adinstruments.com/products/labchart.

*Chapter 3*

# IoT-based biomedical healthcare approach

*Anil Audumbar Pise[1]*

The Internet of Things (IoT) enables physical items and devices to see, hear, and think by exchanging data. The IoT works in the other direction, converting ordinary items into intelligent ones. Embedded devices, communication protocols, sensor networks, Internet protocols, and applications are examples of IoT-specific technology. Certain IoT-based healthcare solutions, such as mobile health and telecare, as well as preventative, diagnostic, therapeutic, and monitoring systems, fundamentally modify everything. Wireless body area networks (WBANs) and radio-frequency identification (RFID) are unquestionably important components of the IoT. This chapter is covered, in addition to research on the usage of IoT in the field of biomedical systems to be applied within the framework.

## 3.1 Introduction

The fast progress of IoT technology in recent years has permitted the connecting of a huge number of smart items and sensors, as well as the formation of seamless data interchange between them. As a result, data analysis and storage systems such as cloud computing and fog computing are required. Healthcare is one of the IoT application areas that has aroused the interest of industry, academia, and government.

The advancement of IoT and biomedical healthcare is enhancing patient safety, staff happiness, and operational efficiency in the medical industry. Biomedical engineering is a relatively new area of study that integrates fundamental principles from physical and applied science to life and medicine. Engineers and experts in biomedical engineering work at the interface of engineering, healthcare and biological sciences. Recent advancements in the semiconductor industry, such as the down-scaling of electrical devices, as well as advancements in computer sciences, such as the advent of data science and cloud computing, have sparked an explosion of novel therapeutic applications. The effect was slow, but it helped the whole field of medicine. Nowadays, healthcare tailored to individual pathological requirements, the retention of long-term data (ECG, SPO2, etc.), and

[1]School of Computer Science and Applied Mathematics, University of the Witwatersrand, Johannesburg, South Africa

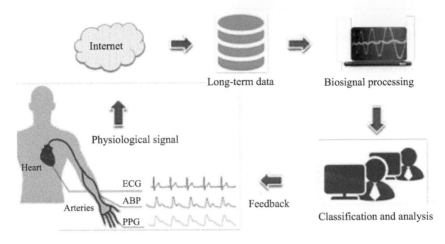

*Figure 3.1    IoT-based healthcare equipment in biomedical approach [1]*

analysis to identify pathological indications (blood pressure, perfusion index, glucose level, etc.). In general, monitoring patients with chronic illnesses continuously and in real time has become simpler than ever and we will soon be able to foresee illness.

The previous diagram (Figure 3.1) depicts a simplified form of an IOT-based biological system that includes monitoring, storage, complicated decision-making, and feedback capabilities. In most cases, a device is connected to the bodies of participants in order to collect and transmit data. This device is made up of an analog front-end circuit with sensors, amplifiers and filters for capturing physiological signals (such as ECG, PPG, and EEG), a processing unit, and a communication module. As a consequence of improvements in microelectronics technology, we now have wearable and implanted biosensors. The majority of long-term data is delivered through the Internet to cloud storage to alleviate the strain of processing huge amounts of data acquired from individuals and to conserve energy. The advent of "IoT" technology has made such connections between the front-end module and storage simpler than before.

A server with biological signal-processing capabilities may therefore execute primary processing tasks such as noise reduction (filtering) and sickness identification (QRS complex detection, R–R interval measurement, etc.). Furthermore, a "machine learning" and "big data" method may be used to make more sophisticated decisions (e.g., aberrant heart activity categorization), identify illnesses (e.g., cardiac disease identification), and detect dangerous situations early (e.g., stroke prediction). Finally, the results of this analysis may be made accessible to the general public, authorized physicians, and clinics through the mobile application, in certain circumstances nearly immediately after the device is connected to the subject's body.

In the remainder of this chapter, the following order has been created. In Section 3.2, a brief explanation of IoT-based healthcare biomedical application is given, which is followed by an overview of IoT-based healthcare biomedical system. Section 3.3 explores the IoT-based biomedical communication architecture and the healthcare system's interconnections. In Section 3.4, WBANs in IoT healthcare are explained. In Section 3.5 RFID communication protocol for biomedical applications is explained. A brief synopsis of analysis related to this study is explained in Section 3.6. This section discusses how IoT is being used to improve the delivery of biomedical operations and healthcare services during a time of crisis. The conclusion and potential work in the following sections are provided.

## 3.2  IoT-based healthcare biomedical applications

Biomedical applications powered by the IoT are used in biomedical systems for healthcare/telecare, diagnosis, prevention, treatment, and monitoring. WBANs and RFID technologies are key to the IoT concept. The goal of this chapter is to explore a new IoT-based healthcare framework for hospital information systems that will make use of WBANs and RFID technologies. The IoT-based biomedical framework is modeled and simulated using Riverbed Modeler. The results reveal that the IoT-based biomedical framework energy-aware system fulfills the ISO/IEEE 11073 standard's data rate and latency QoS criteria. It is also shown that the proposed framework may be utilized to swiftly develop unique case studies in healthcare information systems by building a time-saving simulation environment.

This study has looked at the most recent IoT components, applications and industry breakthroughs in healthcare, as well as the current status of IoT and biomedical healthcare apps, since 2015. In addition, to look at how promising technologies like biomedical healthcare systems, ambient supported living, big data, and wearables are being applied in the healthcare business. Furthermore, the different IoT and e-health legislation and policies in existence throughout the globe will be examined to evaluate their influence on the long-term growth of IoT and the healthcare business. Furthermore, a thorough assessment of IoT privacy and security issues from a healthcare standpoint is performed, including potential threats, attack techniques, and security setups. Finally, this chapter covers previously well-known security solutions in order to solve security issues, as well as trends, highlighted potential, and issues for the future evolution of IoT-based biomedical healthcare systems.

Though research in adjacent fields has shown that remote health monitoring is feasible, the potential benefits in a variety of circumstances are significantly greater. Remote health monitoring might be used to follow noncritical patients at home rather than in the hospital, alleviating pressure on hospital services such as physicians and beds. It might be used to improve access to healthcare in remote locations or to assist elderly people in remaining independent at home for long periods of time. Essentially, it may improve access to professional services, alleviating load on healthcare facilities and empower individuals to have more control over their own health at all times. Figure 3.2 depicts a typical IoT-based biomedical healthcare system.

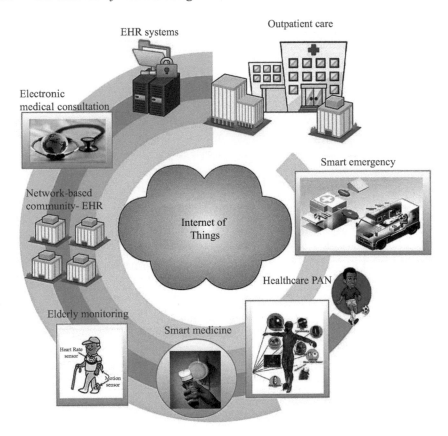

*Figure 3.2    Overview of a typical IoT-based biomedical healthcare system [2]*

## 3.3    IoT-based biomedical communication architecture

In research [3], Chiang *et al.* developed a robust nursing-care support system to enable efficient and secure communication between mobile biosensors, active intelligent objects, the IoT gateway, and the backend nursing-care server, which can do further data analysis to deliver high-quality, on-demand nursing care. This is an IoT-based biomedical communication framework to improve healthcare services.

In Figure 3.3, a patient management and rehabilitation scenario is shown in which field-installed environmental sensors and medical sensing devices serve as the IoT connection architecture for a nursing-care support system [3]. This enables caregivers (such as nurses) to perform patient care and rehabilitation procedures more effectively. Three major components comprise the proposed IoT connection scenario: a backend nursing-care server, a mobile gateway (usually carried by the caregiver), and intelligent gadgets (such as fixed sensor nodes or medical sensing devices). The intelligent gadgets will monitor and collect environmental and patient

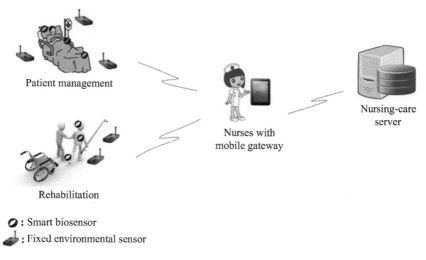

Patient management

Nursing-care
server

Nurses with
mobile gateway

Rehabilitation

*O* : Smart biosensor

: Fixed environmental sensor

*Figure 3.3    IoT-based biomedical communication architecture [3]*

biodata, with the caregiver engaging with them through a portable smart smartphone. The patient gives biometric data, namely, electrocardiography, electroencephalography, electromyography, and blood pressure. Following that, the caregiver may combine ambient data and the patient's biodata to make a more rapid assessment of the patient's requirements. As a consequence, patients will get more precise and timely therapeutic intervention. Numerous studies have been conducted on physical injury healing for enhancement of biomedical applications using IoT. In [4], Fan *et al.* describe the process of creating a framework that culminates in a recovery strategy personalized to an individual's symptoms. This is accomplished by linking the patient's diagnosis to a history of past patients' symptoms, illnesses, and therapies. The technology allows doctors to manually input symptoms and approve prescription medication; in 87.9% of cases. The physician followed the system's instructions to the letter and made no changes to the recommended treatment plan.

## 3.4    Wireless body area networks

The WBAN is made up of implanted sensors that monitor vital indicators as well as specific organs inside the body. Sensors capture data from various parts of the body and transmit it to the sink. Recent research has concentrated on the dependability, security, and efficiency of sensor communications in order to convey data from sensors to sinks. Reduced network life span is a critical criterion in WBANs, and the majority of recent publications have focused on developing cooperative routing algorithms that achieve low-energy consumption and increased network longevity. The packet reception ratio, on the other hand, is another statistic that has been used into the routing algorithms of WBANs in order to determine whether or not packets were successfully received in the sink [5].

Reference [6] assesses the usefulness of existing IoT technologies as a tool for monitoring Parkinson's disease patients. Their research implies that wearable monitors capable of detecting gait patterns, tremors, and general activity thresholds might be used in conjunction with vision-based sensors (i.e., webcams) in the home to detect Parkinson's disease beginning. Additionally, the authors believe that machine learning might result in more successful treatment options in the long run. According to [7], WBAN is on the way to improve biomedical application based on IoT. It consists of a network of small intelligent devices that can communicate wirelessly and analyze data. The garment incorporates sensing knots and may be worn as clothes. There are numerous things that are unique or may be worn over others. The growth of technology has resulted in a reduction in the size of electronic devices capable of wireless communication, while increasing their processing and data storage capabilities. WBANs have become a crucial component of medical monitoring systems due to their ability to be used at any time and in any place.

Figure 3.4 displays the fundamental WBAN structure as well as information transmission strategies collected from individuals. This structure's first layer facilitates wireless communication, allowing sensor nodes and nodes to connect with the network structure on the higher layer [9]. A Wi-Fi gateway is provided (PDA, smart mobile phone, etc.) for communication. The gateway is often a computer with an Internet connection that is attached to an access point and wirelessly captures data sent over it. The data gathered is kept on this computer. Currently, a medical monitoring mechanism is in place, enabling all data to be analyzed. It is preserved in such a manner that authorities may access it remotely.

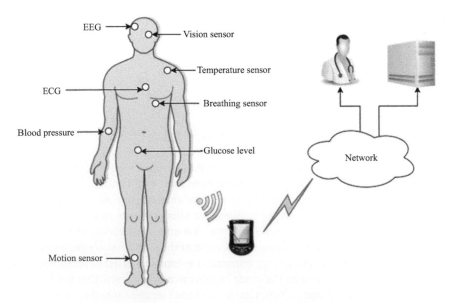

*Figure 3.4    General architecture of WBAN [8]*

Since the primary goal of WBAN is to improve people's lives, several applications are accessible. For the most part, these applications may be classified as either medical or nonmedical. Monitoring physiological aspects of the human body in order to identify anomalies and warn relevant people in real-time is one example of a medical application. Nonmedical uses include entertainment, emotion detection, secure identification, and nonmedical emergencies that are accomplished by collecting environmental data and alerting people to hazards like as fire [10]. While WBAN systems are often used to monitor a single person, collaborative WBAN systems may be used to monitor a group of people.

## 3.5   RFID IoT-based biomedical communication protocol

RFID technology offers a broad variety of uses in daily life, particularly where security is of the utmost importance. Monitoring human behaviors is one example of a mission-critical application that prioritizes security in biomedical healthcare applications. Due to population growth and random mobility, it is conceivable to encounter an inability to distinguish between two or more RFID-tagged individuals in a guarded environment with an RFID-based people monitoring system in place. One of the key challenges that security professionals confront in this regard is quickly recognizing and counting the number of tags present in a monitoring area.

In this context, a simple method was thought for avoiding RFID tag collisions in a busy, chaotic setting. This technique is known as the "adaptive slot adaptive frame (ASAF)-ALOHA protocol." This chapter briefly explores the ASAF-ALOHA protocol as an alternative to the presently utilized MAC protocols to enhance the overall performance of the RFID system. The ASAF-ALOHA protocol does a probabilistic assessment of the number of active tags in the region of interest and modifies the frame size and slot count in the next round accordingly. Because it conveniently handles RFID multiple-tag anti-collision problems, the adaptive slotted ALOHA protocol was selected as the communication layer for the case explored in this study. It is also worth noting that the physical layer communicates at a frequency of 13.56 MHz.

This is accomplished by the use of a simple algorithm that assesses the system's performance using statistical data on the number of successful, failed, and idle slots available to the reader. ASAF-ALOHA has been demonstrated in experiments to outperform conventional MAC procedures. In actuality, many algorithms' versatility is constrained by slots or frames. The ASAF-ALOHA protocol, on the other hand, is more flexible and allocates time for tag detection by distributing many frames in each round with time-adjustable slots per frame; that is, both the round and frame sizes may be changed at the same time. This improves the chances that the object will be discovered. The application layer, communication layer, and physical layer are the three levels of a simple RFID communication protocol. Figure 3.5 depicts a typical RFID-based healthcare system using IoT-based biomedical application.

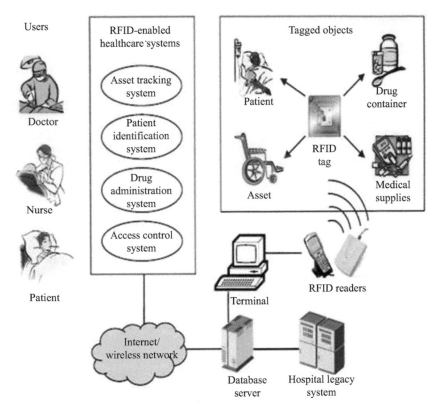

*Figure 3.5    RFID-based healthcare system for IoT analytics in medicine*

The author of [11] suggested a simple method for diabetics to assess their blood glucose levels. Patients must manually measure blood glucose levels at certain intervals during this technique. It next goes through two types of blood sugar irregularities. The first includes increased blood glucose levels, while the second includes a failure to assess blood glucose levels. Furthermore, the system determines how to tell the patient, his or her parents and family friends, or emergency healthcare professionals such as physicians, dependent on the severity of the irregularity. While this methodology is feasible and has been shown to be feasible, it might be improved by automating blood glucose monitoring.

In authors' suggestions [12], an off-the-shelf component and a custom antenna were combined to create a device for predicting cardiac disorders. A microcontroller analyses data from an ECG sensor to identify the heart rhythm.

This data is then wirelessly transferred to the user's device through Bluetooth, where it is processed and presented in a user application. The authors suggest that creating algorithms to forecast heart attacks might help the approach. Additional progress might be achieved by incorporating respiration rate monitoring, which has been shown to aid in the detection of cardiac arrests [13].

## 3.6  Problem statement

Much of the current research on IoT in healthcare has focused on the many uses of biomedical technology in a number of healthcare settings, including as nursing, ambient assisted living, and surgery. Furthermore, no studies have been undertaken that focused only on IoT improvements in healthcare and then compared the results to other healthcare businesses. This chapter, as an extension of prior study, presents an in-depth assessment of the numerous categories of specific elements of IoT advancements in medicine, with the purpose of giving this information to stakeholders interested in these types of innovations.

## 3.7  IoT and biomedical healthcare system interconnection

Previously, there was just one way for patients to communicate with doctors: in person, over the phone, or through text messaging. There was no system in place for doctors and hospitals to periodically evaluate patient health and, as a result, offer appropriate medications. The ability of the IoT to link technology and people's physical bodies will almost surely transform the healthcare business. Patients, family members, professionals, hospitals, and the healthcare system as a whole gain from it.

Innovative technologies that aid patients and doctors in ensuring their safety and enhancing treatment via the use of smart devices enabled by the IoT-based biomedical instruments offer up new paths for medical monitoring. At the same time, more open physician–patient communication has increased patients' participation and satisfaction. Furthermore, patients' health may be monitored, minimizing the duration of their stay and the possibility that they would return to the hospital following release. The widespread use of the IoT has the potential to reduce healthcare costs while boosting treatment efficacy. Furthermore, [14] includes statistical models for calculating joint angles in physical hydrotherapy scenarios, allowing for the monitoring of joint activity improvement over time.

Simple mechanical and electrical components have evolved into complicated devices that involve software, with some growing into platforms [15]. It may be observed in healthcare systems that have gotten smarter as a result of the IoT technology. Chronic illnesses may be tracked remotely and measures exchanged instantaneously with physicians and patient families thanks to the IoT-based biomedical architecture. This enables for regular monitoring of measurements as well as the early discovery and avoidance of unpleasant disease-related circumstances.

## 3.8  Examples of IoT-based biomedical healthcare devices

Initiatives to use the IoT-based biomedical healthcare devices in medicine are being developed. The effect of restricted healthcare resources on the lab technician workforce, as well as the decrease in healthcare staff due to the deployment of health-related IoT-based biomedical devices, promises to reduce some of the stress associated with the blood shortage. Invasive, transdermal medications, pacer systems, electronic gauges, and other forms of drug monitors allow doctors to help patients with infections and check on their well-being while also aiding with therapy. Growth, on the other hand, offers a myriad of advantages as well as a multitude of downsides. Many people have raised these self-evident healthcare security issues. Data thieves have access to data gathered and stored by embedded devices in the IoT. Prior to broad use, additional expansion of the usage of Internet of Healthcare devices and networks is necessary. Cybersecurity is a major barrier to a broad use of the IoT in healthcare.

### 3.8.1    Glucose monitoring

Glucose control has long been a struggle for the more than 30 million diabetics in the United States. Manually monitoring and documenting glucose levels is not only time-consuming, but it also only captures a patient's glucose levels at the time of the test. When levels fluctuate drastically, standard monitoring may be inadequate to identify a problem.

IoT technologies, which provide continuous, automated monitoring of patients' glucose levels, may assist to alleviate these worries. Glucose monitoring systems do away with the necessity for manual record-keeping and alert patients when their glucose levels are abnormal. Figure 3.4 depicts wireless implantable medical devices based on the IoT.

Among the issues is creating a glucose monitoring system based on the IoT as follows:

• Small enough to be used surreptitiously over time to observe patients without causing pain.
• It does not use a lot of energy and hence has to be recharged on a regular basis.

These are not insurmountable obstacles, and technologies that solve them have the potential to change the way individuals regulate their glucose levels.

### 3.8.2    Bluetooth-enabled blood labs

Implantable laboratories at the Swiss Federal Institute of Technology in Lausanne enable an independent analysis of patients' own blood samples, giving critical information. The unit consists of five electrodes, each coated with an enzyme, which enables the implant to monitor substances such as glucose and lactate. After finding the material, it is scanned and wirelessly sent through Bluetooth to the individual's PC. Additional investigation may be necessary; however, the results of this study may be sent through a smartphone to a doctor in another location for examination. This development would mostly benefit the elderly and chronically sick, since it would decrease their need on physicians. When implanted, this implantable device reduces the need for further blood work, allowing lab workers to be reduced. A completely automated laboratory that removes face-to-face interaction with patients results in decreased time spent acquiring all necessary lab tests. Additionally, they are advantageous for a number of reasons, including relieving demand on an over-burdened healthcare system.

### 3.8.3 Connected inhalers

Asthma is a huge condition that affects hundreds of millions of individuals throughout the world. Asthmatics may boost their reservoirs by using connected inhalers, giving them greater control over their symptoms and therapy. They employ cutting-edge asthma software. Propeller has developed a sensor that can wirelessly interact with an inhaler or spirometer. The sensor is designed to alert patients with asthma and chronic obstructive pulmonary disease to their thoughts as well as information that may help them make decisions about their worries. The sensor and related software detect medicine consumption and allergy threats as well as predict and notify users of these changes. Some saw the linked inhaler as a big advantage, despite the fact that it requires more effort on the patient's part to use. Furthermore, the sensor generates a report that may be shared with the patient's physician.

### 3.8.4 Blood coagulation testing

Roche has launched a Bluetooth-enabled coagulation instrument. Using the IoT system, patients may track the rate at which their blood clots. Roche's technology is the first IoT platform created specifically for anticoagulated patients. Self-testing has been shown to help patients remain within their treatment range and reduce their risk of bleeding and stroke. Because of the capacity to wirelessly transfer test results to their healthcare practitioner, patient visits have dropped. Furthermore, Roche's device enables patients to comment their test results, reminds them to test, and alerts them when test results exceed a specified range.

### 3.8.5 Connected cancer treatment

The American Society of Clinical Oncology's (ASCO) 2018 Annual Meeting will include a presentation of the findings of a clinical research involving patients receiving treatment for head and neck cancer. Patients will wear Bluetooth devices while receiving therapy, like in the pilot experiment, and their pain, heart rate, and even weight will be gathered through Bluetooth and continually mon-itored using data collection software coupled with the blood pressure and pulse-tracking program. In addition, each patient's weight will be measured on a daily basis to provide crucial information to their doctor. If the doctor believes it is necessary, the medicine may be changed on a daily basis. When compared to individuals in the placebo group who got no medical services connected to cancer and those who got medical services once a week, study participants saw a reduction in their symptoms.

The use of technology, which enabled the recognition of adverse effects associated with advanced healthcare practices and the implementation of smart health practices, has aided in simplifying patients' treatment by assisting with any emerging side effects, as well as addressing and alleviating concerns about it. Better treatments with smart technology may reduce patients' inconveniencing.

### 3.8.6   Robotic surgery

Surgeons may perform intricate procedures that would be impossible with human hands by implanting miniature Internet-connected robots inside the human body. Simultaneously, robotic surgeries done using small IoT devices would substantially reduce the number of surgical incisions, resulting in less painful therapy and a faster recovery period for patients.

### 3.8.7   IoT-connected contact lenses

Lens expansion and lens-stiffening treatments such as extracapsular categorization are thought to be the definitive solution for acquired longness, a cataract ophthal eye ailment. A study targeted at developing technology to treat long-lens failure, also known as presbyopia, the condition that leads in long-flectomizedness, will look at lens healing/stiffening and refracting to ensure recovery. Sensimed signals, developed by Swiss researchers, detect variations in ocular pressures that may indicate glaucoma.

### 3.8.8   A smartwatch app that monitors depression

Patients with MDD may need to wear smartwatches and utilize a monitoring gadget to track their depressive symptoms on a frequent basis. In this scenario, wearable technology has a far better chance of making a difference than just collecting steps; sensors that detect depression severity would be ideal. A depression app, like other IoT apps, may provide patients and caregivers with more information about their challenges.

### 3.8.9   Connected wearables

The IoT seems to be incomplete without interconnected wearables. Because worn and connected sensors are valuable equipment for health and medical staff, they not only benefit but also aid patients. They enable medical staff to monitor critical body statistics such as heart rate, body temperature, pulse, and other vital body data while still analyzing patients' health. Furthermore, hospitals benefit from wearable technology that allows doctors to monitor patients even after they leave the clinic. It is particularly useful in assisting patients with frequent checkup visits if they address problems they encountered during their hospital stay following release. If the situation changes, wearable sensors will alert the doctor from anywhere and at any time. When doctors are notified in real time, they may provide real-time guidance to their patients.

## 3.9   A summary of associated research

The IoT is rapidly gaining significance owing to its significant benefits of greater precision, reduced costs, and the ability to forecast future occurrences. Despite the fact that smartphone and computer technology have been in use for a long time, the increasing availability of apps and the IoT-based biomedical applications, wireless technology, and the virtual economy has all contributed to the rapid IoT, causing the overall technology ecosystem of society to expand [16].

Other physical instruments (sensors, actuators, and so on) have been combined with IoT devices to gather and communicate data through Bluetooth, Wi-Fi, and IEEE 802.11 [17]. Heart-related applications incorporate clinical data about the patient using integrated or wearable sensors such as thermistors, a palpator (a pressure sensor), a lead electrograph physiologist's (an ECG), and electro-of pathologist's the brain's electric potential (an EEG). Environmental parameters that may be recorded include temperature, humidity, date, period, and time of day. These medical information may be used to make intriguing and precise conclusions about a patient's clinical status. Because IoT sensors generate/capture a variety of data through the Internet, enormous amounts of data are provided by a variety of sources (sensors, mobile phones, e-mail, software, and applications). The previous research's findings are made accessible to physicians, caregivers, and anyone else allowed to use the devices. The growth of cloud/server-based stile diagnosis and the transmission of these facts through healthcare services is an efficient use of information, and cures are delivered as soon as possible when required.

Because the app's users, the healthcare institution, and the contact module all function together, all parties have access to the app's data. The bulk of IoT components are user-interface-based (IoT in the framework largely functions as a dashboard for medical practitioners, enabling patient monitoring, data visualization, and apprehension capabilities). The research revealed that IoT in healthcare has improved on previous year's results by delving further into these issues [14]. Healthcare monitoring, regulation, and privacy are three potential IoT applications that should be examined first. These technical advances demonstrate the IoT potential for success and profit in the healthcare business. The fundamental problem, however, is to maintain service quality matrices that encourage knowledge exchange, stability, cost efficiency, and resilience while also maintaining all users' data privacy [18].

Table 3.1 summarizes the contributions of several academics to IoT in healthcare. In 2019, Dang *et al.* developed a cloud-based method for processing IoT data in healthcare [24]. They selected to address a number of security problems and difficulties related to the use of IoT and cloud computing in healthcare. In 2019 [27] and 2018 [23,28], a significant number of peer-reviewed journal articles were released, both of which searched for prior-to-2017 publications. Nazir *et al.* performed a systematic review of research published between 2011 and 2019 that addressed the security and privacy risks associated with mobile-based healthcare IoT [27].

There are presently no research papers that are solely devoted to medical IoT applications; nonetheless, Table 3.1 provides relevant research papers on healthcare IoT. The table summarizes the outcomes of ten independent researches on IoT in healthcare (e.g., systemic analyses and other types of evaluations). The initial

*Table 3.1    General review of IoT in healthcare*

| Paper title | Contributions | Author and reference |
|---|---|---|
| The IoT for health care: a comprehensive survey | • Discuss the problems and concerns associated with the Internet of Things in healthcare<br>• Address different laws and legislation governing IoT and eHealth. In healthcare, discuss big data, ambient knowledge, and wearables<br>• Examine network structures and associated software or facilities in IoT for healthcare<br>• Emphasize the protection and privacy concerns associated with IoT in the healthcare network | Islam *et al.* [19] |
| Medical internet of things and big data in healthcare | • Examine the use of IoT and big data in healthcare<br>• Discuss the problems associated with the use of big data in healthcare<br>• Apps and smartphone applications for examination | Dimitrov [20] |
| Internet of things for smart healthcare: technologies, challenges, and opportunities | • A definition for the usage of IoT in healthcare is proposed<br>• The current state of affairs and possible future advances in healthcare IoT are addressed<br>• Discuss potential research trends, concerns, and issues of healthcare's Internet of Things<br>• Consider cloud computing as a data storage system<br>• Pay attention to different wearable and networking gadgets | Baker *et al.* [21] |
| Advanced internet of things for personalised healthcare system: a survey | • Examine and categorize healthcare IoT systems, implementations, and successful case studies<br>• Present a four-layer Internet of Things architecture for customized healthcare networks (PHS)<br>• Discuss upcoming study developments, as well as problems and obstacles in healthcare IoT | Yang *et al.* [22] |

*(Continues)*

*Table 3.1  (Continued)*

| Paper title | Contributions | Author and reference |
| --- | --- | --- |
| Towards fog-driven IoT eHealth: promises and challenges of IoT in medicine and healthcare | • Provide an overview of the present situation and potential developments of healthcare IoT<br>• Describe a multi-tiered architecture for the Internet of Things-enabled eHealth ecosystem: To inspire, use a Devices, fog computing, and a cloud-based service<br>• Discuss how the Internet of Things will be seen in hospitals and pharmacy<br>• Showcase a unified platform for the Internet of Things-enabled eHealth world<br>• Demonstrate the challenges and future avenues for IoT in e-health | Farahani *et al.* [23] |

research [19] examined several aspects of IoT in healthcare, including networks and structures, methods, and implementations. They discussed a wide range of issues, including data privacy and standards, as well as IoT and e-health regulations. On the other hand, the contents of this study date back to the early days of IoT, and the need for it in the healthcare industry is expanding, forcing the creation of a fresh assessment.

Table 3.2 provides a thorough [28] overview of the materials and technology used in hospital IoT installations reported in 2018. According to the report, the most common site for healthcare IoT is the home. It demonstrates that the top-ranked journals for papers created on the subject are *Procedia Computer Science, the Journal of Network*, and *Computer Applications*, and the *Journal of Medical Systems*. Another research [29] from 2017 revealed that hospitals were the most vulnerable to IoT adoption. Certain countries' e-health programs and activities have been touted as contributing to the IoT without providing readers with a summary of their work [19,24].

Another issue that IoT has presented is security and secrecy, as well as interoperability and interaction with healthcare technologies. In previous articles, we went into further depth on these topics [19–21,23,25–28,30]. Previously, these academic articles focused on various aspects of IoT healthcare, such as the use of cloud computing, fog computing, mobile computing, wearable sensors, and big data in healthcare. Several research articles on the current state and potential breakthroughs for healthcare IoT address current and future advances [21,23,25,27,28,30].

*Table 3.2    Systematic review of IoT in healthcare*

| Paper title | Contributions | Author and reference |
|---|---|---|
| A survey on internet of things and cloud computing for healthcare | • Conduct a study of the IoT framework for the healthcare sector, with an emphasis on architecture, platforms, and topologies<br>• Examine the influence of IoT and cloud computing on healthcare<br>• Describe emerging industry trends and initiatives on IoT and cloud computing in the healthcare field around the world<br>• Discuss the security issues associated with the Internet of Things (IoT) and cloud computing in healthcare<br>• Consider how the use of IoT and cloud computing in healthcare poses a number of challenges | Dang *et al.* [24] |
| The application of internet of things in healthcare: a systematic literature review and classification | • Investigate the cybersecurity and interoperability issues involved with healthcare IoT<br>• Show the current state of healthcare IoT and then present possible future changes<br>• More about the Internet of Things and how it could be included in healthcare<br>• Examine the advantages of cloud-based architecture for IoT in healthcare | Ahmadi *et al.* [28] |
| Internet of things for healthcare using effects of mobile computing: a systematic literature review | • Show the current state of healthcare IoT and then present possible future changes<br>• Examine the security and privacy issues posed by healthcare IoT<br>• Mobile computing in healthcare IoT | Nazir *et al.* [27] |
| IoT-based healthcare applications: a review | • Show the current state of healthcare IoT and then present possible future changes<br>• Examine the security and privacy issues posed by healthcare IoT<br>• Mobile computing in healthcare IoT | de Morais Barroca Filho *et al.* [25] |
| Enabling technologies for fog computing in healthcare IoT systems | • The current state of affairs and possible future advances in healthcare IoT are addressed<br>• Collect both of their functioning and non-functional requirements<br>• Discuss the issues and questions around IoT infrastructure in healthcare | Awad Mutlag *et al.* [26] |

## 3.10   Conclusion

One of the aims of e-health is to deliver healthcare services to patients in their homes, especially via the use of IoT-based biomedical applications. In general, IoT applications are intended to save money and stimulate patients at home, resulting in increased patient engagement. Everyone will benefit from improved health promotion and a more fulfilled lifestyle as a consequence of this.

According to the study's findings, the IoT-based biomedical applications in medicine are still in its infancy. The utilization-limiting application seems to have put a significant strain on the healthcare system in a variety of subfields. Furthermore, since the number of medical IoT studies and research fields increased in 2018, the number of studies on this topic will grow in the future, resulting in the engagement of new research areas.

## 3.11   Future work

The healthcare sector is a large and diverse enterprise in which a wide range of actors, including patients, healthcare specialists, and insurance firms, are heavily involved. Nonetheless, despite the fact that IoT is currently not extensively employed in a variety of medical subfields, it is gaining traction in those sectors. Despite the fact that there is much overlap among IoT, healthcare, and medicine, there are certain sectors where IoT has yet to be applied due to interdisciplinary challenges. Scholars who are particularly interested in comprehending this phenomenon may be interested in this investigation. This goal will be met in the future either qualitatively, via interviews with targeted audiences, or quantitatively, via literature searches.

## References

[1]   C.-F. Chiang, F.-M. Hsu, and K.-H. Yeh. Robust IOT-based nursing-care support system with smart bio-objects. *Biomedical Engineering Online*, 17 (2): 1–15, 2018.

[2]   Y.J. Fan, Y.H. Yin, L.D. Xu, Y. Zeng, and F. Wu. IoT-based smart rehabilitation system. *IEEE Transactions on Industrial Informatics*, 10(2): 1568–1577, 2014.

[3]   R. Jafari and M. EffatParvar. *Cooperative Routing Protocols in Wireless Body Area Networks (WBAN) : A Survey*, 2017.

[4]   C.F. Pasluosta, H. Gassner, J. Winkler, J. Klucken, and B.M. Eskofier. An emerging era in the management of Parkinson's disease: wearable technologies and the internet of things. *IEEE Journal of Biomedical and Health Informatics*, 19(6): 1873–1881, 2015.

[5]   I. Kırbas. *Online Kablosuz İnkübatör İzleme ve Kontrol Sistemi Tasarımı ve Uygu-laması*. PhD thesis, Doktora Tezi, Sakarya Üniversitesi, Sakarya-Türkiye, 2013.

[6]   S. Saleem, S. Ullah, and K.S. Kwak. A study of IEEE 802.15.4 security framework for wireless body area networks. *Sensors*, 11(2): 1383–1395, 2011.

[7]   A. Pise, H. Vadapalli, and I. Sanders. Facial emotion recognition using temporal relational network: an application to e-learning. *Multimedia Tools and Applications*; Springer: Netherland, 2020; pp. 1–21.

[8]   S.-H. Chang, R.-D. Chiang, S.-J. Wu, and W.-T. Chang. A context-aware, interactive m-health system for diabetics. *IT Professional*, 18(3): 14–22, 2016.

[9]   G. Wolgast, C. Ehrenborg, A. Israelsson, J. Helander, E. Johansson, and H. Manefjord. Wireless body area network for heart attack detection [education corner]. *IEEE Antennas and Propagation Magazine*, 58(5): 84–92, 2016.

[10]  M.A. Cretikos, R. Bellomo, K. Hillman, J. Chen, S. Finfer, and A. Flabouris. Respiratory rate: the neglected vital sign. *Medical Journal of Australia*, 188 (11): 657–659, 2008.

[11]  R.C.A. Alves, L.B. Gabriel, B.T. de Oliveira, C.B. Margi, and F.C.L. dos Santos. Assisting physical (hydro) therapy with wireless sensors networks. *IEEE Internet of Things Journal*, 2(2): 113–120, 2015.

[12]  A. Pise, H. Chabukswar, and D. Jadhav. Hard authentication using dot array carrier structure. *International Journal of Scientific & Engineering Research*, 4(5): 670–676, 2014.

[13]  V. Jagadeeswari, V. Subramaniyaswamy, R. Logesh, and V. Vijayakumar. A study on medical internet of things and big data in personalized healthcare system. *Health Information Science and Systems*, 6(1): 1–20, 2018.

[14]  H. Peng, Y. Tian, J. Kurths, L. Li, Y. Yang, and D. Wang. Secure and energy-efficient data transmission system based on chaotic compressive sensing in body-to-body networks. *IEEE Transactions on Biomedical Circuits and Systems*, 11(3): 558–573, 2017.

[15]  A. Gatouillat, Y. Badr, B. Massot, and E. Sejdić. Internet of medical things: a review of recent contributions dealing with cyber-physical systems in medicine. *IEEE Internet of Things Journal*, 5(5): 3810–3822, 2018.

[16]  L.M. Dang, M. Piran, D. Han, *et al.* A survey on internet of things and cloud computing for healthcare. *Electronics*, 8(7): 768, 2019.

[17]  I. de Morais Barroca Filho and G.S. de Aquino Junior. IoT-based healthcare applications: a review. In *International Conference on Computational Science and Its Applications*, pages 47–62. Springer, 2017.

[18]  A. Awad Mutlag, M.K. Abd Ghani, N. Arunkumar, *et al.* Enabling technologies for fog computing in healthcare IoT systems. *Future Generation Computer Systems*, 90: 62–78, 2019.

[19]  S. Nazir, Y. Ali, N. Ullah, and I. García-Magariño. Internet of things for healthcare using effects of mobile computing: a systematic literature review. *Wireless Communications and Mobile Computing*, 2019, 2019.

[20]  B. Farahani, F. Firouzi, V. Chang, M. Badaroglu, N. Constant, and K. Mankodiya. Towards fog-driven IoT eHealth: promises and challenges of IoT in medicine and healthcare. *Future Generation Computer Systems*, 78: 659–676, 2018.

[21] H. Ahmadi, G. Arji, L. Shahmoradi, R. Safdari, M. Nilashi, and M. Alizadeh. The application of internet of things in healthcare: a systematic literature review and classification. *Universal Access in the Information Society*, 18 (4): 837–869, 2019.

[22] S.M.R. Islam, D. Kwak, M.D.H. Kabir, M. Hossain, and K.-S. Kwak. The internet of things for health care: a comprehensive survey. *IEEE Access*, 3: 678–708, 2015.

[23] N. Scarpato, A. Pieroni, L.D. Nunzio, and F. Fallucchi. E-health-IoT universe: a review. *Management*, 21(44): 46, 2017.

[24] D.V. Dimitrov. Medical internet of things and big data in healthcare. *Health-Care Informatics Research*, 22(3): 156, 2016.

[25] S.B. Baker, W. Xiang, and I. Atkinson. Internet of things for smart healthcare: technologies, challenges, and opportunities. *IEEE Access*, 5: 26521–26544, 2017.

[26] J. Qi, P. Yang, G. Min, O. Amft, F. Dong, and L. Xu. Advanced internet of things for personalised healthcare systems: a survey. *Pervasive and Mobile Computing*, 41: 132–149, 2017.

[27] F.T. Al-Dhief, N.M.A. Latiff, N.N.N.A. Malik, *et al.* A survey of voice pathology surveillance systems based on internet of things and machine learning algorithms. *IEEE Access*, 8: 64514– 64533, 2020.

[28] M. Elkhodr, S. Shahrestani, and H. Cheung. Internet of things applications: current and future development. In *Innovative Research and Applications in Next-Generation High Performance Computing*, pages 397–427. IGI Global, 2016.

[29] N. Boudargham, J.B. Abdo, J. Demerjian, C. Guyeux, and A. Makhoul. Investigating low level protocols for wireless body sensor networks. In *2016 IEEE/ACS 13th International Conference of Computer Systems and Applications (AICCSA)*, pages 1–6. IEEE, 2016.

[30] P. Yang, J. Qi, G. Min, and L. Xu. Advanced internet of things for personalised healthcare system: a survey. *Pervasive and Mobile Computing*, 41: 132–149, 2017.

*Chapter 4*

# Impact of world pandemic "COVID-19" and an assessment of world health management and economics

*Hemanta Kumar Bhuyan[1] and Subhendu Kumar Pani[2]*

For the COVID-19 pandemic, international health facilities have been issued in financial section with difficulty. According to the economic status, several hospitals and healthcare facilities loses a month in sales. Furthermore, providing an adequate healthcare solution to COVID-19 could cost $52 billion (around $8.60 per person) for low- and middle-income countries (LMICs). Could burden have a significant effect on health treatment, surgeries, and outcomes through the use of COVID-19. This year the World Bank predicts that the global economy would contract by about 8%, with developing countries bearing the brunt of the burden. Lack of planning was a key in dealing with healthcare facility issues everywhere. On a national scale, items such as gowns, gloves, facemasks, syringes, disinfectants, and toilet paper ran out. Healthcare worldwide has felt threatened by COVID-19's findings and has responded by formulating new programs to deal with pandemics. In this article, we will talk about the financial implications of COVID-19 that include clinics, surgery, and medical procedures on both the US and foreign healthcare systems, in the United States and abroad. In the case of natural or human-made disaster, the United States and the rest of the world would make profit from being prepared for a single blueprint to react.

By December 29, 2019, the novel coronavirus (nCoV) sparked a worldwide pandemic. Such groups—especially the older adults and those with weakened immune systems, such as low blood pressure, cardiovascular disease (CVD), or asthma, or chronic kidney disease—are at an increased risk of the infection. Systemic socioeconomic status (SES) is linked to a higher prevalence of diabetes, hypertension, coronary artery disease, and obesity in both demographic groups. Those already established conditions increase the likelihood of catching the coronavirus (2019-nSRS-2), also known as severe acute respiratory syndrome coronavirus (SARS-CoV-2). Emphasis should be put on the root of the issue at

[1]Department of Information Technology, VFSTRU, Guntur, India
[2]Krupajal Engineering College, Odisha, India

vulnerable periods. The study of the social determinants of health (SDOH), which involves research on the various facets of a population's health in the context of various aspects of their society, will assist policymakers in managing health crises in ways that treat everybody fairly. During the COVID-19 pandemic, the SDOH directly affected patient recovery and health outcomes.

Determine how these three variables influence national healthcare, social, and economic well-being. Many forms of quantitative and nonnumerical data have been employed. We have found small well-equipped clinics, poor rule awareness, unemployment, and shortage of research equipment to be influential in this COVID-19 infection. To combat the spread of diseases, enforcement policies that are tough yet respect people's rights could be more effective. The delivery of adequate medical treatment is necessary for setting up appropriate medical facilities.

## 4.1  Introduction

Once there were 7.5 billion inhabitants on Earth, 1 year ago, no one could have expected COVID-19. World Health Organization (WHO) was the first to identify a COVID-19 on December 30, 2019 and put the disease on a global emergency list on January 30, 2020. But also scientists say that the virus was at work for some time before this. Respiratory problems may occur with single-stranded RNA viruses [1] in the air. It is estimated by the CDC project an infection, or virulence (R0), of 2.5 for this new Corona virus strain. It found one hundredfold greater lethality of the mutant variants than of the normal influenza virus [2,3]. When the pandemic was already new, the global production chain was disrupted.*

About 51% of Americans recorded a loss of income and an increase in unemployment of 14.7% due to the outbreak [4]. It has been difficult for young people to make their mortgage and cover the bills this year due to missed income and jobs. These consequences are more likely to occur in young adults in America, who have not saved enough for an economic recession. Predictions show that one in five tenants was likely to face homelessness this year. COVID-19 has foreign implications as well. As soon as the Chinese government imposed a mandatory quarantine, several countries lost a large portion of their critical trade products. It is increasingly clear that many countries, particularly those in the developing world, heavily rely on China. Unfortunately, several valuable equipment pieces, such as respirators, gloves, were lost in the explosion. In turn, the lack of appropriate personal protective equipment (PPE) promoted the global pandemic. The World Bank expects global growth to drop by almost 8% in places that have seen the most significant losses in development and 2 trillion dollars this year [5]. COVID-19 has had an influence on all US healthcare services and foreign organizations as well.

---

*Projected to be the leading cause of USS disease costs in 2020. It is estimated that it would cost the US economy $3.3 trillion. It is forecast to cost the US$3 trillion in the next 2 years [3].

## 4.2   Impact on societies

According to the National Collaborating Centre for Health, discriminated populations are classified as "Groups and societies who are discriminated against (based on socioeconomic and political status), as well as socially and economically disadvantaged, because of unequal power relationships." This time, this definition of those who are un- or underprivileged has never been more on target [6]. The pandemic affected poor and underprivileged populations in the US anti-Hispanic, anti-African American, and anti-working class. Despite having poor wages, low-income people have been shown to be greatly impacted by COVID-19 [7]. Any businesses have felt the consequences; nevertheless, personal utilities, bars and restaurants, banking, and manufacturing remain critical in the overall economic situation. This broad sector is made up of minorities such as African-Americans, Latino-Americans, and women, which is especially important for developing innovative ideas. It has had a disproportionate effect on minorities and women, leading to an increase in prejudice and exclusion. The statistical fact cannot discount the importance of knowledge of working with populations that are disproportionately composed of members of Latin and African-Americans that their jobs and income levels are lower than Caucasians'. The poor are far more likely to be affected by the economic effects of COVID-19 than the middle class or the wealthy. The onset of COVID-19 also raised concerns about race relations between Asian-Americans and the police. This prejudice study has generated an astounding 1,497 complaints now, according to the Asian Pacific American Center, which notes that a good number of these complaints originate from only the first 8 weeks of operation. To the tune of 50%, about 50% of these cases originated in two states—California and New York. Moreover, IPSOS conducted a poll in the United States, which showed that approximately 30% of people there attributed the COVID-19 pandemic to China. Some further findings discovered that almost 30% of participants have seen others accuse COVID-19 for Asian crime. These results are worrying since they show the pandemic is strengthening existing patterns of prejudice against the community who faced it before.

As a result of Creative+, there have been significant impacts on women. There are many more ways for women to be engaged in work, home, and household relative to men. The COVID-19 epidemic has clearly compromised this middle ground. Schools and daycare facilities are closing due to the virus, so families struggle to manage their babies. For home-based working mothers, this will contribute to their daily tensions. Since the discrepancy in compensation between the genders is such, she can simply scale back her job commitments to accommodate the existing family obligations and concentrate on the important ones. As a result of being culturally removed from the office, female employees of the service sector may be significantly impacted. Many women with an essential function outside the home return to their jobs even if they might have difficulty finding childcare. Societal and occupational responsibilities have increased, leading to women bearing an extra burden in the workforce and the home, which may lead to women having a more significant stress load than previous pandemics do. The so-called COVID-19 pandemic has hit the lower income strata of the community as well.

Another is the workers of supermarkets. While being deemed an invaluable facility, they make only $11.37 every hour and provide minimal facilities and few to no healthcare coverage. A significant proportion of the Latino workforce is working in supermarkets, and thus COVID-19 has heavily affected the Latino culture. This is a bad state of affairs for certain retail employees who would put their well-being at risk to obtain modest or insufficient compensation. This is, of course, that people who serve at low-paying service positions in grocery stores must still be supported because it is their lot in life.

## 4.2.1    Impact of social manner on COVID-19

The release of the COVID-19 pandemic has created a substantial psychosocial gap in the American population. As a result, it has created alarm, trepidation, concern, uneasiness, and mass disorder. The impacts COVID-19 has on the United States would be discussed in this segment [8,9]. After the development of COVID-19, Americans have suffered a detrimental mental impact. After the start of the plague, the various human mental conditions such as anxiety and depression have increased. At least 40.9% of participants experienced at least one psychiatric disorder, according to a CDC study. These involve signs of drug dependence, depression, post-traumatic stress, and paranoia, all of the anxiety. And 50, and about one-quarter of participants in the study who expressed thoughts of killing themselves or attempting to kill themselves were in that age group. This study also discovered disparate psychological effects on African-Americans, Hispanic individuals, unpaid domestic service employees, and critical workers concerned about their mental health. According to the report, all three factors rose in June of 2020 by comparison to the same month of the previous year.

Due to the stigma of COVID-19, people will experience significant psychosocial impacts similar to those related to the SARS epidemic of 2003. The healthcare professionals dealing with patients who had SARS became more stigmatized. In the same manner, healthcare staff caring for patients who are infected with COVID-19 can often suffer from this occurrence. Stigmatization can incite victims to think that they are being discriminated against and perceive others to be fearful of them, to perpetuate their powerlessness, and reduce their standing in society, which can contribute to feelings of being powerless and social alienation. This is so, because stigmatized communities can trigger unhealthy behavior, which can increase the spread of disease. Healthcare workers face more social marginalization and personal vulnerability than financial risk.

The first widely acknowledged approach to combat the spread of COVID-19 is quarantined. A vaccination is an essential part of managing this infection, although there are potential problems. It has unintended detrimental societal consequences due to being closed off and quarantined. The critical factors that aggravate the condition include money, lack of necessities, and the possibility of a deterioration of false belief about the disease reports. It could result in signs that are close to obsessive–compulsive anxiety as it goes on to cause further loneliness. Repeated washing and testing of temperatures cause maladaptive or aberrant habits, such as compulsive cleaning or checking. Elderly patients and healthcare providers are at a risk of long-term mental deterioration because of this pandemic. Several factors contribute to this fact: carrying a great COVID-19 count, the possibility of infection, lack of PPE, new and excessive visibility, becoming a big part of moral and ethical decision-making, and working overtime Additional caregivers must further alienate themselves from relatives as a result of this. Anxiety and depression may occur as a result of these stressors. If clinicians make an effort to look at clinical factors and behavioral ones, this provides a psychological evaluation for addiction and drug misuse. This is very problematic when healthcare workers put their well-being at risk as they handle others. Even then, we would further open a dialog on the mental well-being of employees at the frontline workers [10].

Facebook and other social networking have amplified the psychosocial problems COVID-19 generated. Soon after the advent of COVID-19, confusion and fear-mongering escalated on social media. Social network rumor, paranoia, and hysteria are directly proportional to each other regarding the number of platforms available sources. Ironically, the effect of social media on the Chinese population has become that of bigotry. As a result, outdated knowledge regarding eating preferences, social media biases, and misleading assumptions about the Chinese people have emerged. The social media revolution has been mixed with disinformation and has enabled the dissemination of bigotry and paranoia; as a result, not performed properly, COVID-19 therapy may have unwanted side effects. Terror, panic, anxiety may exacerbate these symptoms, and confusion. There must be greater focus on dealing with the psychosocial issues associated with this drug, particularly in fragile groups, including the elderly and people with preexisting mental conditions.

### 4.2.2   Impact on healthcare facilities

COVID-19 hospitals had to build additional negative pressure spaces, recruit replacement personnel, pay overtime for employees, and labor to train them, all of which necessitated additional money and contribute to the existing scarcity of PPE. To free up medical workers' time and beds, both nonurgent and elective surgeries were halted. As a result, there was an approximately 90% reduction in-office visits, and almost all outpatient care was provided by video-chat services, which may have contributed to a drop in patient anxiety. Due to increases in COVID-19 costs and the loss of outpatient visits, several hospitals were placed under financial stress [11].

It was especially difficult for academic medical centers in the United States. During the last few decades of their growth, they have increased their debt significantly as they have undertaken numerous renovations and additions to the medical facilities. Although running on tight margins, academic medical institutions also functioned as a safety net, becoming one of the most costly ones in the United States. Excessive pre-pensionary solvency, compounded by excessive therapeutic revenue, jeopardized these organizations' capacity to cope with COVID-19.

Veterans' Administration hospitals were often dealing with much of the same problems; they could, since they operated as a heavily centralized, nonprofit hospital, draw on numerous revenue sources, which was not as bad for them. For certain physicians who practice in the Department of Veterans Affairs (VA) specialty and procedural practices, the income impact of cancelled treatments was not as worrisome since they do not get money for their services the same way fee-for-based organizations do in the private sector does. Often, as a VA system works as a whole, it will change the supply chain to serve best regions devastated by the pandemic. The Department of Veterans Affairs provided over 16,500 intensive care units and offered 3,000 ventilators and 4,000 medical assistances for deployment in the form of deployable disaster services. The Veterans' Administration switched several of their official trips to telehealth care. It was done by the VA through the usage of telehealth, employing the first Chief Telehealth Officer in 1999. Before the arrival of the pandemic, the VA predicted the rapid increase in virtual treatment. Prompted by the first COVID-19 cases in the United States, they started to invest in the technology, including providing patients with mobile computers, pulse oximeters, and cell phones to track their temperature remotely, such as smartphones.

During the plague, there was a campaign to help the elderly of our community. One small nursing home outbreak in Washington State helped start the pandemic. A nurse at the nursing home developed an infection called COVID-19 on February 28. Both employees and residents in the facility reported signs of respiratory disease on that day. By March 18, a total of 167 COVID-19-infected people, 50 COVID-19 travelers, and a lone agent had been found. Accordingly, the hospitalization rate was high for 54% of the inhabitants and 33% of the workers, resulting in a fatality rate of 33% [12]. More than 40% of all pandemic patients and staff in long-term care facilities have succumbed to COVID-19. We found that eight out of every ten cancer of the COVID-19 population was in people aged 65 and over. Thus, the Coronavirus Assistance, Relief, and Economic Security Act allotted $5 billion to long-term care centers and older people's homes for the elderly. Thanks to the improved funds, additional infection prevention procedures, as well as personnel and program being put in place for those unable to leave their house, the nursing home was able to have extended visitation features to its residents [13].

## 4.2.3   Worldwide impact

### 4.2.3.1   China

According to the initial reports in Wuhan in December of 2019, China was the epicenter of the pandemic. Within a month, the Hubei provincial government in China had enforced a state of emergency on Wuhan. Buses, trains, subways, and water taxis ground to a halt: several vehicles were unable to navigate inside the approximately 9 million inhabitants of the region. The airports and rail stations were shut down for the duration of the strike. Restrictions on intercity and domestic travel were enforced elsewhere, though unfortunately, these preventative steps limited disseminating the virus. The country had a GDP growth of 6.8% in the first quarter of the year, nearly after 30 years. A fast lockout led to the disruption of many citizens' lives. A great fascination is expressed in the West as China lifted the last of its controls in April of 2020, and the rest of the world awaits its return to normalcy [14].

### 4.2.3.2 India

It was a step in the right direction for the Indians, who, after ages of isolation and British colonial domination, had finally regained their freedom and identity, had the opportunity to start constructing a modern democratic nation on the Indian model. Trissur is the first in India to be hit by COVID-19, on January 30, 2020. The government initially employed policies to limit the spread, including quarantine of persons who traveled from high-risk locations, tracing those who had contracted the virus, and preventing movement of those with a large caseload of cases. When the number of cases grew, local dissemination became apparent, attention turned to dealing with the virus, and control steps began to dominate the Ebola. The moves India has introduced are similar to those in China, including closing public venues and rerouting foreign air transport. Furthermore, these regulations inflicted a financial burden on the local economies and had long-term detrimental effects in the agriculture, industrial, and utility sectors [15,16]. The disease spread among the countries with which India had trade relations and within them, which put a considerable dent in India's exports. Furthermore, the general pandemic and resulting mass incarceration have significantly increased anxiety and depression in India.

### 4.2.3.3 Brazil

COVID-19 did not get to Brazil until February of 2020. Still, it soon became a celebrity in this field as a hotbed of creativity contrast to some national responses. State/Federal governments initiated measures. President Bolsonaro attracted wide backlash for his apparent inattention to the virus. Since he spoke out so passionately about FU lockdowns, he usually touted the overhyped hydroxychloroquine cure and had a generally low attitude toward the pandemic. An estimated 13 million people are cut off from access to safe water in Brazil's informal slums, poverty-stricken shanty towns. Due to the global spread of the pandemic, the economic consequences in Brazil have been substantial. On March 9–13, the equity exchange in São Paulo fell by over 15% to its worst weekly percentage decline since the Great Recession of 2008. Additionally, the GDP declined by 11.4% in the second quarter of 2020 relative to the same period in the previous year. As of September of this year, with an incidence of 4 million and a mortality rate of about 6, behind just the United States and Brazil in the world, the United States in incidence and rate of, the United States, Brazil has over a million reported cases and over 125,000 people die per year from them [17].

### 4.2.3.4 Singapore

Singapore's reaction to the pandemic has been extolled as one of the most promising ones in the world. With the first cases arising in December 2019, the nation was one of the first to register COVID-19 and initially was second only to China in overall cases. The SARS-CoV epidemic of 2002 revealed several vulnerabilities in Singapore's capacity to cope with pandemics and was the catalyst for the nation to patch up those deficiencies. The country developed the National Centre for Infectious Diseases (NCID) and 900 quick responses to public health preparedness clinics. Daily drills were held to simulate the arrival of a pandemic. As a consequence, Singapore was well prepared to conduct mass screening of possibly infectious persons. They have identified themselves as one of the most prolific in research and touch tracing. The National University of Singapore (NUS) Yong Loo Lin School of Medicine created an engaging series of comics entitled "COVID-19 Chronicles" that provides essential information about the virus in a format that is easily understood by most demographics. Messages such as these have been widely disseminated across the world and have received universal acclaim.

Additionally, Singapore used several strategies similar to other countries that suffered outbreaks, such as reducing the scale of meetings, promoting physical distancing, restricting movement, and screening and quarantine anyone entering the nation. Strict fines were levied for breaching these rules. Interestingly, Singapore did not initially resort to issuing a systematic shutdown or shutting schools until a flare-up of cases leads to a 21-day order on April 28, 2020. This was some months after the virus was first observed in the world [18]. Despite the country's progress in managing the contagious burden of the epidemic, owing to the interconnected-ness of the global economy, Singapore have not sparred the economic effect of the pandemic as the country recorded 13.2% contraction in GDP in the second quarter of 2020 as opposed to the previous year [19].

### 4.2.4    Impact on low- and moderate-income countries

How long before a pandemic breaks out in the high- and low-income countries? Health problems that have been caused by long-standing barriers such as inadequate healthcare coverage, lengthy insecurity, limited clean water access, and highly crowded slums are exacerbated by the appearance of the outbreak of COVID-19. Realities such as mutual distancing and constant handwashing and mass monitoring render the deployment of that almost unlikely. Moreover, in LMICs, people cannot afford to skip a single day of operation, and the economies are less capable of taking a full shutdown [20].

The concept is generally applied to cases when the United States or China does something, but some countries bear the flu. Indeed, the global consequences of lockdowns and ensuing recessions have trickled down to the lower middle economies. However, between April and May of this year, remittance receipts in Bangladesh dropped by 19% and 41%, respectively, in the Kyrgyz Republic. Remittances are a significant component of GDP in lower middle–middle-income countries, and many families depend on them for their survival. Pacing themselves would be tough, not to say the least, as the faltering global economy adds fuel to the virus. Fortunately, the majority of LMICs responded quickly by implementing school closures, limitations on public meetings, and travel was able to slow the outbreak's spread. Moreover, in the global community, there is an effort to help these countries meet their needs [20,21].

### 4.2.5    Impact on international healthcare facilities based on medical services

COVID-19 has affected almost every facet of the world's markets, not least of which was healthcare, with staggering problems in treating the global pandemic.

Unpreparedness was a big part of the problem of healthcare services. PPE [22] was also lacking for healthcare staff. Different healthcare staff used PPE to protect their health during medical services. The Pakistani analysis discovered that just 34.5% had helmets, and 0.5% had face masks or goggles. In Jordan, a survey claims that just 18.5% of physicians had access to PPE. Even the US healthcare sector was troubled by the accessibility of prescription supplies. Approximately 15% of the doctors indicated that they did not have N95 respirators. Approximately 50% of the doctors reported that they did not have facemasks, and approximately 50% reported that they did not have complete suits or gowns. Furthermore, about 7% of physicians recorded caring for patients who had contracted COVID-19, and approximately 80% of PPE had been reused. Healthcare services across the world requested nonmedical PPE donations and resourceful residents modified products to meet this need. People around the globe faced similar issues with the availability of intensive care units and ventilators. We did not have the resources to test locally. Disturbances in global supply chains caused more shortages of food and consumer goods.

The pandemic has diminished efforts for the diagnosis and treatment of non-COVID-19 disease as a side effect. Noncommunicable disease (NCD) preventive and recovery interventions have been compromised since the COVID-19 pandemic started. As the virus advanced, healthcare staff, who had usually handled non-catasthma cardiovascular conditions were pulled from treating patients to assist with the COVID-19 response. In compliance with public health recommendations, certain procedures and appointments were also delayed. Shrinking of public transportation impacted patient's travel times to appointments. Sometimes, cancer and diabetic patients were unable to get the treatment and medication they needed. Ironically, these results were seen more in low-income nations, where countries still have a large percentage of their national income tied up in battling the pandemic. The results of a survey in Bangladesh, Kenya, Pakistan, and Nigeria have found decreased access to antenatal and vector control systems, as well as tuberculosis and HIV programs, before the pandemic. Moreover, there was a notable decline in family income at the same period as healthcare expense rose [23]. COVID-19 also prompted healthcare providers to develop contingency plans that guarantee that necessary treatment is not postponed or denied due to a global viral or another epidemic. Alternative solutions such as telemedicine have gained a significant foothold in healthcare settings worldwide and have aided in mitigating the impact of the epidemic on people.

### 4.2.6   Emergency caring

In several nations, the COVID-19 pandemic had a significant effect on the global economy, so in turn, the Canadian Cardiovascular Society issued recommendations to help cardiac surgery hospitals stay profitable. They call these recommendations a "ramp-up" that meets all local health mandates while increasing elective cardiac surgeries at a healthy pace. Experts think that normalcy of reduced catastrophe loss can help limit the economic impact of COVID on cardiac surgery. From the viewpoint of healthcare, a team from Germany performed a pan-European study on these two specialty practices that asked "excessive financial challenges due to the trauma pandemic." Ironically, being self-employed was shown to be a strong indicator of financial hardship, one of which was referred to as "deplete" in the study's multiple regression model. Thus, according to their multiple regression analysis, self-employed trauma and orthopedic surgeons should be supported more. Like their cardiac surgeons, this profession shares a similar viewpoint that the pandemic's impact on the cost of their operations stopped unnecessary procedures. The specialized trauma and orthopedic surgeons are unmoved by financial considerations. Results indicated that nearly one-third of the group would give up practicing because of the pandemic, and nearly two-thirds might benefit from increased healthcare funding.

On the other hand, telemedicine offers a silver lining, with 44% of participants believing that it will rise in value in the future. While the survey was established in rather extraordinary conditions, a lot of open questions remain about its psychometric testing. In 1 month at his 22-year-old private practice, there was a 29% reduction of money on every occasion due to the worldwide epidemic. He lost money at a private practice which he started in Italy before the pandemic 2 years before it struck entirely. According to the authors of this chapter, all surgical professionals in all countries who want to limit their career to just cosmetic surgery had done so due to the lack of options due to financial difficulty. Overall, it describes the first instance of a partnership between Latin American and worldwide healthcare stakeholders to show the substantial contribution of COVID-19 healthcare resources to the medical service economy [24]. Finally, there is a discussion of COVID's economic effect on the Latin American radiation oncology field. The survey conducted in Latin-American countries like Argentina, Costa Rica, and Peru (the three countries had fewer than 3% of the total of radiation oncology treatment centers) showed that both had seen a 20% revenue loss from closure inactivity. Less than 3% of the total radiation oncology facilities were still operational during the pandemic. They administered the ASTRO survey in Latin America to view the pandemic's overall financial effect on an underutilized field of healthcare. In Latin American radiation oncology, use of telemedicine as a tool of the future was predicted.

### 4.2.7    Constructive response reduction strategies

Preventing the spread of the nCoV SARS-2 would entail a device protection solution that considers viral potencies, disinfection tactics, environmental biobrave ability, and human contact/risk reduction. Early symptoms diversely excrete the virus in several layers and particles. Viruses are found in raw substance droplets and aerosols that are found in blood and other body fluids. When a small number of viral mixtures are generated and their density and speed vary, their traveling distance is affected. Fine dust seems to collect around surrounding items or people. A more delicate, viral-laden substance circulates in ventilation patterns. Virulence is based on the quantity of an encapsulating organic environment. Second, try and limit the release of hazardous coexisting microorganisms to work areas, breaks, and lavatories. To help avoid the spread of illness, hold sick and possibly infectious patients at home is essential to minimize the incidence of disease. Whenever they wear masks, risk to their coworkers decreases. Since masks avoid involuntary hand and mouth gestures, they are helpful in terms of personal well-being. The regular use of caps, gloves, mask, and glasses to reduce the spreading of disease. The vaccines must be available to everyone, especially those at a risk of COVID-19 infections must be easily accessible.

Antimicrobial gels from the Centers for Disease Control may be made non-contagious by primary low-level disinfectants. Usually, they are between 50% alcohol and 60% gel solutions. This agent protects the alcohol from bacterial evaporation; therefore, there is plenty of time for the virus particles to come in touch with it. There are significant considerations that have to be considered: focus and touch time. Alcohol in water just reduces the total alcohol content gradually, as it evaporates rapidly, which prevents more extended touch periods. An intact skin barrier cannot keep viruses out of the mucus membranes but can provide defense from transferring to them. Thorough handwashing of soap and water at the start of the day reduces the infective bioburden brought in from the outside from interaction with contaminated surfaces and suspended droplets and aerosols. Daily hand hygiene after interaction with all aspects of the patient's treatment to decrease the risk of disease transmission can necessitate special hand wipes. One may minimize the chance of being sick by washing hands, arms, face, or spitting in that manner. Because it is safer for staff, it also helps prevent the movement of infective bacteria to workspaces such as desks, computers, mice, and touch screens. The surface of the tools, including drawer handles and bars, should be disinfected according to the number of employees who use them. Plastic enclosures are more efficient at keeping liquids away from compromising electronic connections through maintaining color-coded containers and gel dispensers in work environments; conformity with safety disinfection procedures is supported by visual cues.

Mechanical ventilation controls lower the particle level of HVAC (reduces the concentration of bacteria in the airflow). The usage of higher airflow speeds (above 612 exchanges/hour) at sites over 612 volumes helps remove infectious aerosols. Still, it prevents desiccate or sedimentation of virus-laden or other aerosol particles. When working in the ventilation and HVAC environments, work only in the fresh air inflow zones and stay away from the return air inflow zones. Break rooms offer unique obstacles. Lower volumetric airflow has the effect of making aerosols more persistent. During meals, masks are off. This makes it easier for the droplets and particles to be dispersed, facilitating the spreading of the infection(s). The locations that incorporate some high-frequency touch surfaces, such as the door handles, the coffee cup, and the tabletops. Cultural considerations should take precedence. Fatigue leads to a loss of the ability to do repetitive and complex activities. It degrades for many hours; however, fully after 12–16 h. The standards for infection prevention and prescribed practices are likely to become less stringent as an individual's level of exhaustion increases. There is a greater likelihood of infection because of illness among people who live and function close to each other. Controls on productivity are enormous. When job tasks are made to anyone at random, the spread of personal creative ideas is maximized. Studies done by Mascha *et al.* showed that consistency in team tasks would help minimize staff cross-immunity. They recommend 1 week of work and 1 week of vacation for each consecutive week to help employees who are overburdened or highly stressed. Prevention of burnout is often done by recognizing the style of the leader and planning for leadership to prevent burnout. Empathy and influence over others are associated with increased professional achievement [25]. Other job habits involve wearing high-quality facemasks, distancing oneself, testing the community for potential damage after exposure, and using water decontamination within a reasonable period, with well-thought-out cleaning protocols in place.

Training aspects involve wearing top-quality gloves, social distancing oneself as far as possible, measure oneself in the community, and thoroughly disinfect for a decent period. Not performed correctly, COVID therapy may have unwanted side effects. These symptoms may be exacerbated by terror, panic, anxiety, and confusion. An alternate strategy has been used in many healthcare institutions, such as using telemedicine, proving helpful in preventing the global spread of NCDs. Compliance with infection control and suggested practices can rise with wear levels. Telemedicine's merit lies in finding a means of minimizing infection while sacrificing overall standards. COVID-19 has made operational shortcomings for healthcare providers to provide fewer effective services for patients through medical procedures.

## 4.3    Impact of health on the emerging COVID-19 pandemic

People started being sick as the nCoV (Chinese New Year, January 2020) traveled quickly through China. On December 29, 2019, the first four nCoVs were announced. Wuhan is the biggest city in Hubei province, which is located in the middle of central China. The symptom was strange pneumonia of no apparent cause [26]. Early evidence shows the business touch. More and later, it was discovered that disease could be spread from person to person, often by human touch. The specific illness triggered by 2020-NP was called by the WHO on February 11, naming it COVID-19 on the follow-up date [27]. People with preexisting asthma, CVD, hypertension, chronic kidney disorder, and/an obesity are particularly vulnerable to the findings of the CDC proved that all who have these conditions have a higher risk of serious illness from COVID-19. Although SES may increase the risk of CVD, particularly among those who have asthma or hypertension and many others, which are also risk factors of CKD, including depression, diabetes, and obesity (SES). CDC estimates that 94% of COVID-19-treated patients succumbed [28]. These particular circumstances increase the likelihood of SARS-2 infection, and as a result, people in these areas must have the support and services to survive. This study explains the importance of SDOH during pandemic (COH). Precausal precautions should be taken to keep the transmission within abounds.

### 4.3.1    Social determinants of health

The SDOH encompasses five main social and economic conditions outlined in Figure 4.1 improving access to all resources, improving the social and community resources around our welfare, the economic conditions around our communities,

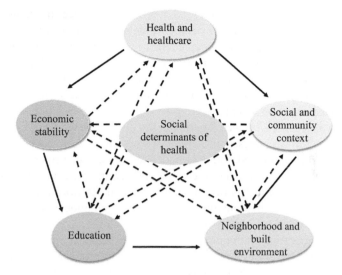

*Figure 4.1    Different domains of social determinants of health (SDOH)*

and enhancing our built environment. Access to affordable services, having healthcare, having primary healthcare, and understanding health needs are all components of health and fitness, and well-being. Have a low level of health literacy will hinder patients in finding their way around the confusing health system and take away their comprehension of medical advice or medications. People who have no health benefits would be less able to use or still have regular medical coverage, which may complicate CVD, asthma, and cancer management. Context is just as important as it is in how an individual leads his or her life as it is in defining what he or she does. The practice of group engagement and inequality falls within this domain. Religious and group connectedness reduces the risk of premature death. The built environment encompasses infrastructure, travel, food, air, and environmental issues [29]. Secondary causes of asthma have been shown to be related to air quality. The CDC also discovered that people with asthma are at an increased risk of full-blown disease to occur [30]. Safety is paramount in fitness. Residents are more inclined to stroll or run in their communities if they are sure that their neighbors are doing the same. The concern about danger and security makes for mental well-being as well. Activity impairs the immune system. This has been seen in previous studies to be the case for poor people and those in disadvantaged communities. These neighborhoods also experience stressful conditions due to the additional stressors of "overcrowding, high violence, inadequate facilities, and poor social support." The schooling process encompasses high school graduation, registration in college, and fluency in a foreign language.

The more educated the one is, the longer his/her lifespan. It is often necessary to provide health records in a helpful way to the customer, depending on their degree of schooling. Economic well-beings are income, employment, household structure, health, education, housing, food, general safety, recreation, and nutrition (SDOH). In economic hardship, the number of people who have activity-impairing chronic conditions goes up. Many people become unemployed and are afflicted by homelessness, drug misuse, or become sick due to the effects of unemployment. An explanation of SDOH is that there are financial resources, such as a salary, life experience, and various forms of social help. Simply placed, in short, you are the way you were born, learn to be, that is, the way you live and function your whole life [31]. They see the entire guy. These various diseases have a widespread effect on the well-being of people and the welfare of whole populations. Because of these socioeconomic differences, SES can be equated with social inequality (SES). The better on the socioeconomic scale, the worse the health consequences. Lifespan is shortened for people on the bottom half of the social scale. If you look at things socioeconomically, health problems build on the inequities already befalling a community section.

Many characteristics are interrelated and play a major function in the eruption of the COVID-19. For example, an individual's education affects his or her economic stability and what neighborhood he or she is eligible to live in, which affects his or her social well-being. Consequently, socioeconomic variables are likely to be important in infection and mortality At the time of data collection, the researchers discovered certain counties in New York, including the Bronx, Brooklyn, and Queens, which also had a significantly higher death rate among people of low SES. This case is another example to consider when considering a child growing up in a low-income home. It is difficult for low-income families to provide for their children, which could lead to low-quality schools.

There would be no equality in education, no matter where this kid resides, as long as it is different from a wealthier suburb or a more decadent school system because government schools are financed by local, national, state, and federal resources [32]. Any funding for our social projects will come from personal income and property taxes. The affluent areas and districts would raise more money; therefore, they have more money to spend. Districts that serve low-income students get smaller salaries and inadequate services, while poorly educated teachers receiving small wages are included in low-income schools. It does not matter whether you get average or below-average grades as well as long as you plan on pursuing an above-average academic career in college. And if it is from a low-income family, the kid would always have a few high-paying career prospects. This places the infant in the same financial situation as his or her parents. People who live in poverty-ridden communities have higher chances of remaining that way. The five factors can be seen as a kind of a cycle that affects an ever-changing scenario, even today.

## 4.4    Health in the clinical system

### 4.4.1    Clinical knowledge

The need to access, store, interpret, and understand essential clinical knowledge make health decisions [33]. Being educated about one's disease will also include reading and comprehending clinical information brochures, health advice from a doctor, and patient. It is challenging to take care of one's health even though you can read health-related content because of a lack of literacy. In general, individuals with lower levels of literacy have worse health results. Sometimes, studies have shown some demographic classes to have lower levels of health literacy. Disadvantaged, uneducated, and minority populations are more likely to have poor health literacy [33]. Patients that show evidence of having poor literacy may have high overall literacy and good verbal fluency. Health awareness is critical in a public health emergency, and it aids in the control of COVID-19. Any understanding of infectious diseases, such as how well viruses survive and spread in the environment, helps us consider the conditions in this case. In terms of the future influenza C outbreak, understanding health awareness can empower individuals to apply social distancing and other steps to keep the virus at bay.

Social distancing can be crucial in reducing the COVID-19 in April and May of the following year. Determined if each community with a certain degree of trust adhered to a prescribed distance from other groups, 52% and 31% were "moderately" "significantly" convinced in their conviction that social distancing themselves from others was successful in warding off illness during the upcoming COVID-19 episode [34]. Of course, however, almost 14% of participants showed doubt regarding social distance and its effectiveness in preserving life. Overall, 88% of the Americans who took part in the survey said they "still" or "very often" distanced themselves from crowds. In light of recent developments, the percent distribution dropped from "always" to "often" to "frequently" and in several cases to "usually." For those who "think it matters," 79% exercised distancing, while just half of those who "think it doesn't matter" did. Freedom, 43% "most of the time" did. According to these facts, health awareness was vital in determining whether a person could grasp the seriousness of the COVID-19 pandemic and whether he might meet safety guidelines, such as distancing himself from family members during the flu, and whether or seek out loved ones.

### 4.4.2   Access to medical- and primary-care doctor

Admission to healthcare is better known as "timely delivery of personal health benefits to get the best potential health results." Many individuals encounter limiting healthcare challenges, which can impact their well-being. An obstacle in healthcare includes, but is not restricted to, such issues as a shortage of transportation for medical services, low or no benefits, the lack of accessible healthcare, or limited funding. At poverty levels and minorities, the lack of healthcare is pretty common. More than a quarter of American adults indicated that they would avoid medical treatment if they had a fever and dry cough [35]. Seizures and flu-like effects are most often associated with this strain of smallpox. Answered, including when shown video footage of themselves becoming poisoned with COVID-19. Many adults who said they were unable to afford health insurance, ages 30–30 to 39 with annual incomes of less than $40,000 and had just a high school diploma or less, were more likely to forgo seeing a doctor. In low-income people, it is linked to SES. Hispanic and African Americans, and nonblack people have less access to healthcare. Primary treatment may not be possible without health benefits. Or individuals might be less likely to use healthcare services. This places the uninsured ones at risk of long-CVD, hypertension, obesity, and diabetes screening out of those who do not have insurance into question. To provide the provision of medical services, preventive insurance must be made available. Minorities and the poor experience further hardships by attempting to get quality healthcare. All of them are strongly supported by student-based clinics. A student-run health center on the University of Nebraska Medical Center campus, named the SHARING Clinic, serves as healthcare and healthcare for communities in need and underprivileged in Omaha. As a result of the COVID-19 epidemic, this clinic is now closed. To the underserved communities, which might still experience accessibility issues, these student-run clinics exacerbate the problems they have because of it.

## 4.5    Role of health disease

### 4.5.1    Food deserts on cardiovascular disease (CVD)

A food desert is a low-income region where enough access to nutritious food is not accessible [36]. A research discovered that people living in an environment with little access to supermarkets and fruits and vegetables were at risk for CVDs in the metropolitan area. They observed that income was significantly related to CVD risk when it came to diet while also finding that healthful eating was not related to CVD (18). Awareness that wealth has a more significant contribution to position led them to equate low-income communities to individuals who earned low individual income. The researchers discovered that an individual's level of wealth was more closely linked to CVD than their area income or access to food. Those individuals who had above-average gross household incomes in lower income areas had lower CVD risk levels [36]. People with more money, who lived in poor communities had healthier cardiovascular profiles. This suggests that, at least in part, access to nutritious foods is not a factor that increases CVD risk. Furthermore, this new research discovered that class is associated with increased mortality from CVD, and lower SES [37]. This study shows an inverse relationship between lower income and a greater chance of severe infection with CVD.

### 4.5.2    Role of food deserts on hypertension and chronic kidney disease

Low wage is a known risk factor for both hypertension and CVD. Fruits and vegetables prove to be more nutritious than they are less expensive. High food prices restrict the consumption of nutritious foods by low-income households. In low-income and minority areas, refined foods and fats and oils are favored instead of fresh fruits and vegetables. Results: A research survey conducted by Suarez *et al.* shows that 80.3% of the participants "still" or "much of the time" have fruits at home [38]. This compares to 83% of participants who are in the top wage bracket and who have access to grocery stores or farmers' markets in their neighborhoods. The families who lived in food deserts had more impact on their dietary choices, blood pressure, and incidence of kidney disease than those who lived in other locations [38]. It was discovered that people who lived in food deserts and had low wages had lower serum concentrations of carotenoids. There are ways to get an idea about how many fruits and vegetables you consume using carotenoids. It was also discovered that individuals in food deserts have lower average protein, potassium, sodium, and magnesium consumption but higher average wages. The quantities of these minerals will reveal one's acid load in the system. High pH indicates an alkaline diet [39]. High protein foods (meat, dairy, etc., in particular) trigger a rise in body acidity. Fruits and vegetables increase the number of organic compounds in urine. When you have a diet of a lot of acidic foods, you are likely to have metabolic acidosis and asthma, kidney disease, and other issue-related problems. Studies have shown that a heavy acid load contributes to obesity [40].

## 4.5.3   Role of SDOH on obesity

There are more fast food chains in food deserts than there are supermarkets. Individuals who do not have easy access to affordable access to fresh, wholesome foods have obesity [41]. According to the CDC, an individual is categorized as "obese" as having a body mass index (BMI) greater than or equal to 40 [30]. Those people living outside food deserts are more likely to be eating more fresh produce than those who live in supermarkets. They are less likely to be overweight. The likelihood of obesity being linked to a hypovolemic respiratory disease, recognized as the Pickwickian syndrome, is greater among overweight individuals. It is unclear whether this disorder is more common among people who are obese, although it is theorized that they may have more difficulty taking deep breaths around the neck or belly due to excess weight. Due to the buildup of carbon dioxide, it causes anoxia. Adjoints may be secreted in reaction to respiratory difficulties [42]. BMI is the body mass in kilograms divided by the square of the person's height in meters. BMI indicates when a person's weight is within an acceptable range. People with a BMI under 18.5 are undernourished. The BMI ranges between 18.5 and 25, which is considered to be natural. A person has a BMI of 25 to 30 to 32, which places them in the overweight category. A BMI of 30.0 or above indicates that a person is overweight [43]. Throughout the study, it was discovered that 62% of the patients died from viral infection. About 64% of nonobese people had to go into artificial breathing, and of those who survived, 36% had to suffer from the infection. In people with a larger proportion of body fat, the numbers of those needing artificial breathing and deaths are notably more significant.

A BMI >40 was the second strongest independent predictor of hospitalization in patients with COVID-19 at an academic hospital in New York City [44]. COVID-19 patients who required a ventilator were obese or morbidly obese, according to French research. Due to decreased respiratory mechanics, respiratory function, improved airway resistance, and diminished gas exchange, many patients will need ventilator support [45]. Even if some people who are obese, the breathing muscles can be weaker because of fat on the neck or in the belly, as previously discussed, and lung volume may be affected because of fat that restricts the ability to expand the chest and take a full breath [42,45]. The findings also showed an improvement in the risk of COVID-19 as BMI rose [45].

## 4.6    Social setting

### 4.6.1    Determination

People's perceptions of unfairness and injustice can feed bigotry. Actions benefit the well-off at the expense of the poor. In both the human and institutional levels, healthcare levels, discrimination exists. Individual discrimination involves encounters between patients and their healthcare professional attributable to ethnicity, gender, or some other discrimination that leads to a diminished ability to access care. Healthcare services and the patient's well-being may be impeded by experiences that lead to illness. Hierarchical inequality can be seen in the context of residential segregation along ethnic lines, gender lines, wage inequity, and so on. The particular form of systemic discrimination (name, skin color, gender, sexual orientation, national origin, socioeconomic class, age, religion, etc.) may impact individual people as well as groups. Somehow, residential apartheid finds itself contributing to the racial differences seen between African and Caucasian communities. African-Americans live in concentrated poverty. Education systems in these areas are inadequate, unemployment is very high, health insurance is unavailable, violence is a constant problem, and residents have no social support. Still, life for the residents is complex [46]. This is because it is hard to maintain social isolation in communities that are poor. Any relatives will not be able to keep their distance from each other. In extreme poverty, minorities and blacks are more likely to keep positions where it is not possible to telecommute [47]. This COVID-19 emergency has placed many minorities in the position of either needing to work and putting food on the table, or remaining at home and keeping their families safe, especially the Latino community because of a sheer number of jobs in the warehouse work, manufacturing, maintenance, and custodial employment are common among minorities [47]. While 35% of those infected with the virus do not identify themselves as either race or ethnicity, it is readily apparent in the current statistics. Many New York City residents have died from it than any other racial race [46]. In New York, 29% of the population are made up of Latinos. Of all the COVID-19 people who die in New York, about 34% are people of color—22% of the area. However, people of African descent in the United States have a 2.4-time greater risk of death due to this infection than those of other races. The facts for the US population, broken down by territory, are startling. According to the US Census Bureau, African Americans are 13% of the overall population, although they have suffered 32% of the COVID-19 deaths. On the other hand, white people are much more likely to be at risk because they live in the United States than those in the rest of the world [48].

## 4.6.2   Active part of the community

Whether you have social assistance, you are much better off psychologically. Social connectedness, another definition for the term continuity, defines the kind of relationships a group has with its participants. Thus, social capital, an index of mutual wealth, perception of justice, solidarity, and perceptions of group benefit are socially necessary [33]—directly or negatively for survival [49]. The more unequal the society, the fewer people have access to social resources. More research indicates that social connections, specifically, reduce both the income gap and mortality. The more excellent social stability in a neighborhood, the lower the levels of tension and anxiety and the higher the self-rated well-being for the residents. Immune related to the immune, cardiovascular, and neuroendocrine stress may have significant effects on the body. People who are shown to have a greater likelihood of developing atherosclerosis if provided with more excellent assistance from others have been seen to have a reduced risk of CVD. As in California one showed, social assistance serves as a bridge to social problems that Hispanics face [50]. People and cultures have pulled together through this challenging period of need. Clinical clerkships are placed on hold, which means medical students cannot help everyone who comes to the office. Nationwide, medical students have stepped up to support frontline doctors and even help out with infant care and pet care. Nebraska Medical students can use the time they are afforded to take off their clerkships to serve in the community because the supply of face and body protection equipment has been low among those who know how to sew because of shortages of supplies for frontline personnel (PPE). COVID-19 is more risk than other disease to survive with social stability.

## 4.6.3   Make surrounding foods

### 4.6.3.1   Access to healthy foods

Food is a must for existence. It is significant to one's overall well-being. Those who eat more fruits and vegetables have a reduced chance of serious illness. A balanced diet consists of a wide variety of fruits, herbs, lean meats, legumes, soy foods, and other sources of protein, as well as nondairy sources of fat. Poor dietary and health problems, such as hypertension, diabetes, and cancer, have been shown to be related to suboptimal feeding [51]. There are several elements in the built environment and community that influence each other. While healthier foods are usually very accessible or in demand, they still face several obstacles in getting to the public. Healing may also occur because people can quickly get to the right food, a factor in the city and developed environment. A survey released in 2012 revealed that the typical grocery stores are 2.19 miles away from households in the United States [51]. To prevent anyone who does not have their cars or connections to public transit from making a shopping trip, this has the potential to be a real obstacle. Food deserts are regions that are found in low-income cities where people have no access to nutritious food. Global crop production is estimated to increase 50% by 2025 [41]. Grocery shops are more prevalent in more residential areas than commercial zones. Cheap food shops and supermarkets are chock full of toxic and unhealthful choices (higher saturated and trans-fat and higher calories). Individuals who do not have ready access to fresh fruits and vegetables tend to have inadequate diets. Because African-American and Latino neighborhoods are more likely to have a higher concentration of fast food and grocery stores, they are also more likely to be, on average to be less attractive to someone wishing to establish a new business in them. However, the ethnic groups often may not have as good health results as racial groups. Why? People living in food deserts have an increased risk of obesity, which is mentioned elsewhere. Income is another essential factor of balanced food consumption. There are solid and numerous studies that indicate people on low incomes depend on lower nutrient-dense food. Processed goods tend to be more costly, but they are not always unhealthy. People who cannot afford to buy fresh foods purchase the packaged ones instead [51]. It is essential to consider food deserts during a pandemic and that people do not have accessibility to nutritious foods, particularly. When food is in short supply, it would be impossible for those who do not have sufficient access to good nutrition or food to eat their fill. People would have to make more frequent visits to grocery stores to acquire their food, thereby increasing their chance of infection. Disadvantaged populations living in food deserts may face a greater risk of malnutrition retailers hoarding nutritious foods because of the COVID-19 epidemic. Substandard nutrition may make this more of an issue in food-deprived areas than in wealthier areas.

### 4.6.3.2    Local/global surrounding conditions

How can you handle the topic of "air quality, water quality, infrastructure, and pollution?" Health inequalities may be quantified by looking at when people wind up in specific neighborhoods and where they are located. Non-whites are most likely to live along the ocean coastlines [27]. In high-poverty neighborhoods where minorities with low economics are concentrated, pollution seems to be caused by industrial polluters like refineries, landfills. Groundwater was determined to be the principal source of drinking water for about a third of the population. Foundries, refineries, and garbage dumps usually contain hazardous waste. It has been proposed that pollution in the environment may render people more susceptible to COVID-19. It is thought that pollution particles are a mode of transportation for the virus. The new study claims show that air quality might have increased the infection rates. This may be that air contamination makes one's immunity weaker, allowing them to contract infections. As recently determined, a fine-particle level rises, known as PM 2.5, will facilitate the spread of COVID-19 A analysis showed that there was a correlation between a rise of 1 $\mu m/m^3$ and 8% of deaths due to COVID-19 [52]. Health still has great importance. Residents of high-poverty communities are less healthy because of their poverty. Many people will stroll, bike, or work out than play in the open area nowadays. The next problem in high-poverty communities is that residents in these neighborhoods do not have access to greenery. These neighborhoods are so well populated that it is hard for their inhabitants to find room to be green. Increased social distance also helped one to decrease the COVID-19 infection rate. In neighborhoods where there are many people, distancing yourself from the crowd is realistic. You are more likely to get the infection if you live in densely populated areas and spread it. Poorly maintained low-income households also inhabit public housing. Too many infestation problems of cockroaches, rodents, rats, and other vermin are conducted and discovered. Some things often seen in these conditions were mold, the absence of air conditioning, smoking, and cigarette use. Children who grow up in a housing project are twice as likely to be born with asthma than children who grow up in a single-family household. People living in poverty could be susceptible to COVID-19.

## 4.7 Academy

### 4.7.1 High school graduation

For most occupations and college and further education, a high school diploma is mandatory [53]. With no high school diploma and no educational opportunities, work opportunities are restricted. If there are not enough work openings, people will fall into poverty. Poverty has also been debated to result in unfavorable health effects. It is often the home and school that determines if a high school student graduates. Studies show that children who have limited contact with their parents when in high school are far more likely to drop out. Schools that have a higher degree of criminality are more likely to have lower attendance and lower educational achievement. Students from lower income families are less likely to have money and thus therefore are less likely to get good schooling. At the time of the COVID-19 epidemic, many schools had to go online to avoid the disruption of face-to-to-face schooling. These children do not have Internet connectivity. The theory behind this finding is that children from upper class households have more time flexibility to access and use online resources than their lower class counterparts. Studies more extended, but some can close the door to opportunities early on. An uneducated parented child can value education below that of an educated one and downplay academic requirements, thereby giving it a disproportionate low value. This should not affect the value of parents with a higher degree of education. Education is necessary regardless of any difficulties or barriers that the individual can face.

Non-educated parents are letting their children miss school to do their homework while the others are spending hours online. Having to engage in distance learning will affect academic success for specific children.

### 4.7.2 Psycholinguistics and literacy

Minorities and individuals with more inadequate degrees of schooling are most likely to be included in working-class neighborhoods. Studies have shown that people with language and reading barriers have more severe health problems, do not have insurance, and have a more challenging time following orders on a drug regimen. The United States is host to numerous non-English speakers. Medical students and physicians at Harvard also launched a new project dubbed the "COVID-19 Health Literacy Project." This knowledge that is part of COVID is now known in

35 different languages [54]. The capacity to translate into languages includes Arabic, Bengali, Chinese, Dutch, Hindi, and several others. The virus details, ways to avoid catching the virus, and any remedies for illnesses are available on the fact sheets. This has created an open forum for discussion also for non-native speakers. It is vital to increase public knowledge of the infection and promote safety measures to stop the spread of the disease.

## 4.8    Stable, predictable employment

Money, the work one has, and incentives such as healthcare, compensated medical time, and family leaves play a significant role in this equation. Workplace racial inequalities often occur. Then Caucasians to occupy positions, African-Americans, and minority groups are overrepresented in the blue-collar workforce. Psychological discrimination in the workplace may have devastating results, leading to fatigue, anxiety, and poor health. Unemployed individuals are at greater risk for stress disorders such as hypertension, diabetes, and CVD, making them more susceptible to COVID-19. The US economic performance has decreased after export and import restrictions were announced. For the last 7 years, an estimated 33.5 million Americans have applied for jobless benefits [55]. When people are out of work, they risk or forfeit their benefits. Allowing someone who cannot afford care to be screened for the COVID-19 virus has been ineffective. On March 27, 2020, the President signed into law of the Coronavirus, a Food, Relief, and Economic Security Act, also known as the Hope Act [56]. It gives $1,200 to any American family with an income of $75,000 or less for a stimulus [57]. The family gets $1,200, and there are two children under 18 years of age. That increases to $1,500 for each minor boy. However, to obtain a stimulation check, the conditions may appear clear on the surface, which are various and complex. It has not been determined how the allocation of funds would be carried out. As of this moment, the individuals who apply for the stimulus search have been sent one. Speaking to both the President and Congress about issuing a second search has been proposed, but no one knows when to follow through. Many families will not get away with a single $1,200 check. This will probably be a hardship for households, as when the crisis is over and everybody will go back to work until they get paid.

The economic downturn and the distribution of COVID-19 (on one side); you must tread lightly to decrease COVID-19. A combination of social isolation and crowding social distancing outward seems to be suitable for making the curve more stable. Still, it comes at the cost of the country's financial prosperity. Each state's governor proposed civic distancing, and so a period of social segregation ensued. The rise in March and May month events and a drop in June and increase in July is an excellent example of regression toward the mean. Georgia Governor, Gillespie declared a state of emergency on March 25, though the Idaho Governor did not declare one until 1 month later, on April 3, 2020 [58]. Staff who were not necessary during the lockdown were ordered to remain home and just go to the food store or drugstore if they are necessary. The whole station was placed on lockdown before social distancing had been executed. The country's emergency communications system was made operational on April 24, 2020 [59]. During April, the cases in Georgia began to rise slightly. Preferably until the lockdown was applied, by June of 2015, the occurrence in Georgia was higher. On the other hand, the Governor of Idaho declared a State of Emergency on March 25, 2020 [58]. Over the first few weeks of the month, it increased, and by the middle of the month, it had subsided. The state was finally unlocked on April 30, 2020 [60]. In mid-April to the start of June, there were <40 recorded cases of Lyme disease in Idaho. After the date June 1, 2020, when it was first put in place, the frequency is increasing, and the increase is more significant in June than in July. It is seen in Figure 4.2 that the average prevalence of COVID-19 cases in the United States is substantial. It is clear that the new trend of frisking, specifically, has been reestablished as the number of instances around the country has returned to its pre-lockdown rate as it was before the locks being installed and has continued to spread out in that manner (Figure 4.2). It is reasonable that enforcing a lockout around the nation's borders takes priority given the national economy. In the meantime, we are working to

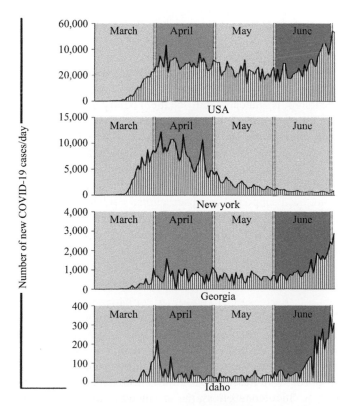

*Figure 4.2    The wax and wane in new cases of COVID-19 per day in USA, New York, Georgia and Idaho. The graphs were generated using the online data form CDC and John Hopkins web sites*

eliminate COVID-19; the national economy would have to be shown what it has in store.

## 4.9    The impact of the COVID-19 pandemic on firms

The new COVID-19 is a growing threat to the global economy, public health, and national security. As of June 30, 2020, there have been ten million reported cases, causing about 500,000 deaths in 215 countries (as per reports from the WHO and Johns Hopkins) [61,62]. I predict that the COVID-19 crisis would trigger significant problems in both infectious disease and mass public health outbreaks and extensive food poisoning in the community. According to an Organization for Economic and Co-operation Development (OECD) estimate, the global GDP growth rate is projected to decline to 2.4% by 2020. The possibility of instability, and a significant decrease in global economic activity due to sharp drops in production and spending and supply chain disturbances has risen. This is a huge challenge for many countries as well as for governance and cooperation around the world. Many people being sick could have a major effect on China's economy [63–65]. As of April 17, China's gross domestic product had risen 13.5%, investment, and usage by 24.5%, and all dropped by 15% compared to the year before; however, Chinese people's unemployment increased to 6.2% for the first time in the first quarter, according to the figures published by the National Bureau of Statistics of China.

Entrepreneurship is fundamental to the country's economy as a whole. Because of this, for companies, it is imperative to consider the current state of firms and their coping mechanisms and how the effects of the COVID-19 pandemic on them are. As soon as the disease epidemic has run its course, researchers will begin to study corporations' innovation plans and responses [66–68]. Other sectors have also been studied to identify possible solutions to the pandemic. However, these findings have not been supported by observational evidence.

Firms in Guangdong Province were examined to see how they were affected by the COVID-19 pandemic and if any policy responses could be prepared (the province with the highest GDP in China). To explore why the pandemic impacted corporations, they went on to look into whether the disease has affected them, and what they expected in the future. Any supportive measures can be implemented.

### 4.9.1    Time-saving method

This study was reviewed by the school of management's IRB, with approval granted in the form of IR2020. It was decided that a survey will be done in Guangdong Province. According to the following formula, the minimum sample size was determined. From the previous information, the total minimum population was estimated to be 384. Nonetheless, the survey was expanded to 500 to boost the overall accuracy of the data set. Distributing in Dongguan, Shenzhen, along with many city government offices, there are 21 cities in Guangdong Province and the GDP of the 15 cities included in our sample represent more than 90% of the total

GDP of Guangdong Province. Firms on this list were chosen according to Guangdong province's industry characteristics and the scale of the industry.

## 4.9.2 Data gathering

The study was done between April 10, 2020 and April 25, 2020 while everybody was out on vacation. Three company executives were reached via telephone or WeChat, a mobile app. The survey was entirely voluntary and we received informed permission from all participants. In the survey, the important research priorities, participant confidentiality, and ethical principles were outlined to participants well in advance of the start of the survey. As much of the queries as they might, they were required to. Even, they were not confident and could avoid making an effort to choose a response by leaving it blank. Altogether, 1,553 questionnaires were given.

## 4.9.3 Computations and statistical review

Entering the data was needed. No more data analysis was needed. People were eliminated from the survey because they responded with less than 30% of the questions correctly and lacked relevant information. Descriptive questions were used to get information about the sample's demographic profiles and describe the findings.

## 4.9.4 Statistical results

Characteristics of the demographic group: An answer rate of the survey was found to be a success at 94.8% (524 of the population replied). The several sectors in the business analysis included information technology (18%), engineering (34.6%), banking (12%), service and commercial (7.4.4%), and industrial (12.6%), business and construction (14.2.6%), and trade (7.4%), 4.8% of the GDP have been affected. This manufacturing distribution follows Guangdong's economic developments closely. As polled, the businesses were comparably sized. A total of 141 businesses, out of the total of 300 and 6,600, made up around 26% of the overall firms and had 50 or fewer workers. In contrast, 162 (the half of the 500-employee category, and over) out of the total of 5,000, the total of 500, accounted for around 24% of the total number of companies.

Firms would be great because of the effect of the pandemic. Since more than half of the companies carried out their day-to-day activities but suffered stock-running problems, some were shut down or remained operational due to shortfalls of materials. Many companies face at least one of these challenges: wage and social security, rent payment, customers' overdue payments. Though the cost of labor and cost of production tendering are important for larger companies, firms with less than 50 workers rent appear to be the main driver. The vast majority of companies sustain output barely, with materials or materials' scarcity. And 22.9% of companies received domestic requests, although 63.9% experienced delays or unable to ship their product on schedule.

### 4.9.4.1    Gibberish

Redeems to concentrate on demand patterns in the public sector and behavior improvement in the public sector. Pandemics would lead to less GDP and jobs, consonant with our research on the COVID-19 pandemic. This research, however, just looked at aggregate trends without addressing the companies, which better captures the effect of the COVID-19 pandemic on the economy. Firms would be significant because of the effect of the pandemic. Returning to full manufacturing capability was difficult because of the disease. More than half of the businesses reported problems with inventory; some of them also claimed they were completely out of material. One-third of the businesses we surveyed are feeling operational stresses, so we would estimate that they hire one-third of the workers and incur one-third of the costs. Also, 23.4% of businesses have done away with domestic requests.

Many businesses stated that market penetration was impeded because of client face-to-face and location meetings being challenging to conduct. Furthermore, nearly two-thirds of the companies posted increased operational costs, including postponed orders, distribution taking more prolonged, and less-than-expected production output. Much of them had to contend with the financial problems associated with their separation. They were still being held on strict accounts for payroll salaries, insurances, leases, financial obligations, and accounts. As shown by the answers to question 4 (supply of raw materials, spare parts, other production and processing materials), the business owners explained that the supply chain is affected by epidemic-related delays at varying degrees across the regions. Due to the spread of the disease, several export industries were threatened. Several businesses announced cancellations and postponed delivery of overseas orders.

### 4.9.4.2    Companies dealt with the outbreak

A new pandemic and the rivalry with the United States have sparked further R&D investment and creativity in the Chinese economy. In the words of Creative and Venn, more than half of the companies agree that this global pandemic has helped the growth of virtual workplaces, remote workers, and market interruption methods and strengthened their capacity to deal with major disasters. A few people suggested that an outbreak would take out rivals in the long run, leading to company launches or expediting improvements in marketing strategies (such as community channel expansion). As an example, the company's primary market retailers include larger shopping centers. They relocated staff from their stores to online sales, which enabled the company to focus on online markets throughout the crisis. When they did this transition, they had outstanding crisis in hand thanks to utilizing social networking and live-streaming channels. It has done the trick, as certain companies have grown as a result of the outbreak and others that have adopted it to try new industries. Around the same time, it has helped customers become more conscious of their well-being and led to behavioral changes in consumption. Firms also discovered that an increase in consumer interest in creativity has created new business possibilities and fueled their changes in marketing practices. Several interview panel members suggested an imperative, for faster growth, for example, online schooling and 5G. Any companies also replaced traditional store-based methods with multichannel marketing. As an example, on the other hand, the shop is closed, but community shopping and social marketing are taking place.

## 4.10 Healthcare, social and economic challenges in Bangladesh

Reported cases and fatalities are projected to be 48,786 and 1,482 on November 7, 2020. Coronaviruses are the first known viruses that were detected in Wuhan, China. These viruses mutate rapidly and have a great mutation risk of infection. The main problem caused by coronavirus infection is severely acute respiratory illness. The number of people infected by this lethal virus has increased from around 219, increasing the incidents. The WHO announced that there is a pandemic of COVID-19 because it has spread all over the globe. North America and Europe have both been identified as having nearly 21,000 cases of COVID-19, while Europe has 12,000 registered in secondary institutions. The four nations with the most COVID cases on Earth up to November 7, 2020 are USA (9,504,758), India (8,462,080), Russia (1,733,025), and France (encompassing the same number of cases), and Russia (9,503,758). About 45,000 people have died in China due to the disease and over 91,000 have been diagnosed with it [69]. And the extension of deadly diseases from another lower middle class Asian nation with a population of 161.3 million [70], Bangladesh is caught in the tragedy. Bangladesh was the first to recognize Creative Origins on March 8, 2020. Until the end of the date, the total of COVID-19 deaths has been set at 410,988 and the number increases to 5,966.

### 4.10.1 Methodology

This chapter also included qualitative and quantitative analysis methods in some of the research approaches used in it. Data from secondary sources, writers' forecasts, details from the WHO, and related academic institutions (IEDCR) were used. Official data estimates have been used to calculate the population's vulnerability. Thus, other polls and tests have been used to confirm these results. Such personal impressions of the world around the United States will be supplemented with data collected from a wide range of different outlets and anecdotal knowledge from all over the country. Primary research done in PubMed and Google Scholar was done on COVID-19. Healthcare, religious, and economic data on Bangladesh was gathered from March to November 7, 2020. Keywords were used in the quest, e.g. "COVID-19," "Coronavirus outbreak."

### 4.10.2 Analysis of basic healthcare

#### 4.10.2.1 Healthcare service

Following the WHO guidelines, Bangladesh has implemented policies to reduce the transmission of COVID-19 to minimize the transmission. Among the policies, included are mandatory use of facial masks, limitation of travel, social distancing, and lifestyle modifications. In addition, the government and private sectors are striving to promote good personal hygiene by utilizing local media. A research published by Farhana and Mannan [71] demonstrated that a substantial number of Bangladeshis were unaware of, not aware of, and entirely confused about the propagation, indications, and incubation time for COVID-19. Bangladesh hospitals–treated patients faced a great deal of difficulty as a result of the emergence of COVID-19. Serious disadvantages were discovered in facilities providing ventilation for cases of acute severe respiratory illness. For every 1,000 residents, there are around 8 ICU beds. According to the WHO condition study, as of October 26, 11,730 available beds and 564 ICUs are ready to handle COVID-19 patients nationwide. In Dhaka, 35.19% of all hospital beds are available to the general population and the remaining beds and ICUs are dedicated to medical patients. Due to many infected patients being treated at home, beds in the hospital were not filled [72].

At first, the facilities were not sufficient but with time, they grew. Over time, more and more government and private healthcare providers have come to use C.O. V.I.D.T.s (or C.O.V.D.D.). It must be emphasized, though, that the COIMEST's research scope in Bangladesh, at only 14.6 million tests, is considerably less than that of the countries in South Asia. Over most of the 1980s and 1990s, WHO sponsored MOHFW to increase testing capability and currently are underway plans for further development in the nation. In this latter case, WHO also launched a comprehensive effort to ship out hundreds of samples from all of the 64 districts of Bangladesh. With WHO's help, as of September 2020, nearly half of all the samples were distributed to laboratories throughout the region [73].

Following a coronavirus outbreak in Bangladesh, the GoB charged a fee of 200 taka (80 pence in United Kingdom currency) for the COVID-19 test instead of the 3,500 taka charged by the private sector. Also, proportionally, the occurrence of research has decreased to about 0.8 tests per 1,000 individuals each day. The doctors at the CDC have made personal commitments to assist and heal people even when they have the moral obligation to look after their safety and security. The medical staff and other frontline providers of healthcare have difficulty treating the COT-treated patients appropriately because of a lack of sufficient equipment, a limited capacity for supporting them, and the Government's lack of readiness to handle the crisis. This coronavirus has caused the deaths of countless healthcare workers worldwide, especially in Wuhan, China. Physicians and healthcare staff are particularly susceptible to this deadly disease in Bangladesh [74].

### 4.10.3    Precarious living

Due to a lack of resources, the cessation of municipal facilities and everyday operations culminated in a medical emergency. Around one-fifth of the nation lives in poverty and a huge percentage of the workforce is engaged in part-time employment that does not pay. Loss of work vs loss of lives, the shutdown presented a quandary. It is estimated that about 62 million people in Bangladesh are on wage or salaried jobs, with 10 million in casual employment made up of those working on regular wage/salary. At least 4.5 million regular laborers work in the construction, transportation, and lodging industries who were deeply impacted [75].

Around 4 million citizens in the world depend on the RMG industry. As developing countries, which were big importers of this industry, began cancelling orders for COVID; the livelihoods of those employees were threatened and the remaining 4 million people work in the manufacturing industries, of which 85% are working informally. Employees are at the same rate of pay as others who do not come on as they have no special skills. Additionally, many self-employed jobs in the informal economy are often self-employed individuals, numbering over 5.19 million people. A total of 18 million people's life was under threat throughout the shutdown era. It will seem that 72 million families in America are currently suffering economic hardship. The package it adopted for the promotion of the economy consists of lending to export-oriented businesses for a total of Tk 117 crore for salaries, as well as making various varieties of loans to small and medium companies and groups who have sent their employees overseas, to unemployed people and staff who have returned from abroad, and job postings on both of the country's cash and kind (welfare support) to the poverty stricken. However, there have been considerable execution problems around the different schemes, with big companies performing better than local, grassroots, family, and micro-businesses. The cash benefit was modest, and there were flaws in the administration. This has not been shocking, according to numerous studies, that the rate of poverty rose during the crisis [76,77].

## 4.10.4   Social distancing

Lack of involvement in social interaction has become the principal approach to monitor and may even reverse the influence of COVID-19 infection [78].

There is no known means of treating morbidity and fatality, so humanity must preserve social distance. Regulation of social-distancing requirements becomes a significant concern for large numbers of the population in Bangladesh who rely on their regular employment. About 55% of the population in urban Bangladesh is believed to live in slums. Around one in five people in Third World families live in a slum, according to the OECD. Slightly over half of the respondents in Chittagong's slums have four to six people in a room while the other quarter has seven to ten people to share a room (2018). It is typically difficult to access individual rooms in the shantytowns since the streets are typically too small for two people to walk side by side. Compliance can also be challenging for others who are eager to go along. A regular laborer, a dealer, and rickshaw-pullers having little resources must distance themselves from their communities [79]. Some institutions also questioned the significance of social exclusion in the broader social context as well. If resources are distributed equally that completely depend upon which would depend on who is in-line to receive them, who can afford to wait in-line, and what is distributed free of charge by social aid. Socioeconomic considerations can affect conformity with social distance norms. Since too many drivers are using the same mode of transport, the traffic gets much worse at holiday and festival time. Public understanding of social distancing could have been hindered by missing social data [80].

## 4.10.5    *Groups with special needs*

People turn to religion when stressed, but you must make them see it unemotionally as a way of keeping distancing yourself from it. People would instead go to churches to seek hope and a sense of community. We found two significant violations in adhering to the Lockout Protocol. The first was an excellent opportunity for people from Dhaka to come home because it saved them from a career in the RMG industry. The second was to accompany a religious leader's funeral. However, various constituencies have assailed the GOOP with accusations of managerial incompetence [80–82]. Each network team that implemented this kind of application customized it for their corporate purposes, with various inputs from different stakeholders. Still, overall, few groups do not benefit from incorporating one: (differentiation of channels for) flexibility in their application software.

A higher degree in deterioration of both physical and mental well-being is associated with the shutdown. The spread of coronavirus multiplies the demand for mental and physical well-being through elderly, disabled, economically disadvantaged ones, and the sick ones are more severely impaired. Domestic abuse and gender-based harassment is at the forefront of media attention due to a worldwide surge in the use of restrictions, as reported in both local reports and on social networks. More and more companies also moved work away from the office to the workplace, with women having to perform their daily domestic duties longer hours as well. It has been established from various sources that the level of aggression has been rising in the home is becoming disturbing.

## 4.10.6    *Discussion*

To address the widespread proliferation of COVID-19, GoB has implemented several prevention and control measures. In Bangladesh, MOHFW set out "Bangladesh Emergency Health Preparedness and Response Strategy for COVID-19." The foremost concern of this strategy is to slow the progression of the illness. To further improve the ICU use, the hospital built a new facility, hired, and equipped 2,000 more physicians and employed 5,000 nurses. The GoB initiative guaranteed surgical devices, supplies, and health-related services for COVID-19 patients and providers. However, they do not have a higher number of patients relative to their counterparts in other [nearby] countries No well-equipped COVID-19 research laboratories and no clinical or health services for these citizens in the country of Bangladesh make finding a cure difficult. This, thus, shall ensure that the GoB has proper research facilities and health treatment for this lethal virus. For many impoverished citizens in Bangladesh, it was a life-or-or-death decision to take the long-malaria test. As opposed to staying sealed, more people choose to consider the latter to ensure their long-term survival. The shutdown caused millions of Americans to lose their jobs and wages.

It was hard enough and arrived too late. As a result, a lot of people who were not well-off have been much worse off. Social distancing is difficult because of the socioeconomic, environmental, and economic challenges that citizens face in

Bangladesh. Furthermore, lacking understanding, negative feelings, and little concern for social distancing has been putting the country at risk for the spread of the COVID-19 virus. Poverty and the fear of unemployment are legitimate reasons for noncompliance. Due to the nature of the chemical agent, wearing a respirator is critical in containing exposure to COVID-19 and therefore must be done at all times. According to a survey, it is estimated that approximately 63% of the population of Bangladesh wears a mask. About 53% of Dhaka division residents use facial masks to prevent the spread of infectious diseases. The study confirms that residents in metropolitan environments do not adhere to the health recommendations to avoid transmitting disease. So for the public to be informed of this virus presents a problem to the government. During potential pandemic times, interventions might include social isolation and wearing masks in public. In periods with increased parental supervision, domestic abuse occurs more often. Not just poor people, but mothers at all income levels face self-esteem problems as they are forced to stay home full time to support their families. Bangladesh is notorious for its hatred and brutality against women and children. About 35% of married women experience sexual abuse at the hands of their spouses. Despite laws and recognition, women continue to encounter a substantial obstacle in their pursuit of fair representation in public life. The factors that need to be considered when formulating a plan for healthcare communication strategy are communication (meaning which will be communicating with patients and how), appropriateness (how people can perceive and relate their message to the treatment provided), value (a treatment can mean a lot of things to a patient), and significance (which it is most significant to the patient).

## 4.11   Conclusions

At the COVID-19 pandemic's advancing around the globe, the COVID-19 death toll is accumulating. Aside from the increasing amount of cases and fatalities, also on the whole, the epidemic had a dangerous side impact on economies: In addition to decreasing their numbers, it increased their fragility. Following the announcement of pandemic status in March 2020, bans on global travel were put in place, with citizens encouraging anyone who could avoid being infected to avoid public areas by workplace exposure and ensuring that they were at home at all times. In late March of 2006, Wuhan, China, was where the first cases of the disease were discovered. In Brazil and the LMICs, a significant number of people in the United States, but also the United States, India, and other higher income countries, were hit by the epidemic. Unpreparedness was a big part of the problem of healthcare services. In some instances, healthcare staff experienced a health-productivity gap. COVID-19 failures also spurred healthcare institutions to find new necessities for patients. Telemedicine, psychological distancing, masking, and handwashing have also been seen to lower the burden of the COVID-19 pandemic.

Pandemic influence has more to do with other people than health services. The community that resides in poverty and is heavily polluted with sewage and garbage is being hit harder by this toxin. Additional assistance, such as a benefit payment for the poor, is needed. During epidemic outbreaks, it is highly critical for this group to have a careful eye on this demographic since they are more susceptible to disease. You become more susceptible during epidemics because of SES and ethnic classification. Dietary patterns and low wages are correlated with lower SES. Latinos are more disadvantaged than Caucasian populations owing to personal and structural inequality, and as a result, they are more prone to suffer from ill-health effects. Therefore, it is clear that the pandemic has passed them by, perhaps never yet suspected. Richard Clarke Cabot, an American physician, thought of both of these aspects while doing his daily work. On the basis of these observations, he concluded that people with worse health were more likely to die. This research supports the conclusion that poverty, disparities, and SDOH increase the transmission rate of illness. While inequalities in health and disease cause disparities in morbidity and mortality, inequities in healthcare exacerbate the problem. Current research on epidemics has paid no attention to the impacts of social inequality on well-being at periods of an epidemic, which means they missed the point entirely, because they failed to do both. Because of this, it is essential to respond to any health emergency promptly. To avoid an epidemic of illness, it is essential to be aware of all the well-being and healthcare causes. Identifying specific health and healthcare causes, such as SDOH, will aid in providing access to a comprehensive set of services to the socioeconomically vulnerable. Education of the public on the virus seriousness of the disease and awareness-inducing nature of the illness is equally necessary. If you are more aware of the community that is at risk than others, it may affect the decision to avoid others that are less. Taking into consideration, the many causes will help one to stop an epidemic from increasing. Appropriate and timely clinical treatments, together with well-directed and timely schooling, have proved to be successful countermeasures to the COVID virus. Reducing disparity between well-being and healthcare may be achieved by using SDOH. Such projects need an interdisciplinary approach that comprises doctors, anthropologists, public health officers, and researchers, along with others from the National Institutes of Health, the WHO, and others, to thoroughly understand various causes of health disparities that groups of people face. We will have to determine how the last one goes because we can deal with potential plagues.

Based on COVID-19 pandemic knowledge, a variety of hypotheses may be reached. Asking the correct questions is critical in dealing with such a problematic issue. Thus, rather than predicting the task's difficulty, it is more prudent to assume that it is essential. Second, more stringent policies and efficient compliance are necessary if an epidemic is to deter or slow down its dissemination. Third, taking note of the shortcomings of the health sector revealed by this experience, effective steps must be taken to enhance public health. Proper plans, including improved equipment of health facilities and staff training, are crucial in this respect. To avoid the further transmission of COVID-19 infections, stringent controls on cross-infections in hospitals should be taken.

# References

[1] He X, Lau EHY, Wu P, *et al.* Temporal dynamics in viral shedding and transmissibility of COVID-19. *Nat Med.* 2020; 26: 672–5. https://doi.org/10.1038/s41591-020-0869-5.

[2] Li Q, Guan X, Wu P, *et al.* Early transmission dynamics in Wuhan, China, of novel coronavirus-infected pneumonia. *N Engl J Med.* 2020; 382: 1199–207. https://doi.org/10.1056/NEJMoa2001316.

[3] Heron M. Deaths: leading causes for 2017. *National Vital Statistics Reports*, 2019; 68(6).

[4] Congressional Budget Office. CBO's current projections of output, employment, and interest rates and a preliminary look at federal deficits for 2020 and 2021. Congressional Budget Office (2020). https://www.cbo.gov/publication/56335 (accessed October 25, 2020).

[5] Wu Z and McGoogan JM. Characteristics of and important lessons from the coronavirus disease 2019 (COVID-19) outbreak in China: summary of a report of 72314 cases from the Chinese center for disease control and prevention. *JAMA – J Am Med Assoc.* 2020; 323: 1239–42. https://doi.org/10.1001/jama.2020.2648.

[6] National Collaborating Centre for Determinants of Health. Marginalized populations. National Collaborating Centre for Determinants of Health (2020).

[7] Yang Song, Min Zhang, Ling Yin, *et al.* COVID-19 treatment: close to a cure? A rapid review of pharmacotherapies for the novel coronavirus (SARS-CoV-2), *International Journal of Antimicrobial Agents*, 2020; 56(2): 1–8.

[8] Bhuyan HK, Chakraborty C, and Shelke Y, Pani SK. COVID-19 diagnosis system by deep learning approaches, *Expert Systems*, July 2021 (Early Published).

[9] Czeisler M-E, Lane RI, Petrosky E, *et al.* Mental health, substance use, and suicidal ideation during the COVID-19 pandemic—United States, June 24–30, 2020. *MMWR Morb Mortal Wkly Rep.* 2020; 69: 1049–57. https://doi.org/10.15585/mmwr.mm6932a1.

[10] McGowan ML, Norris AH, and Bessett D. Care churn – why keeping clinic doors open isn't enough to ensure access to abortion. *N Engl J Med.* 2020; 383: 508–10. https://doi.org/10.1056/NEJMp2013466.

[11] Satiani B and Davis CA. Practice management the financial and employment effects of coronavirus disease 2019 on physicians in the United States (2020). doi:10.1016/j.jvs.2020.08.031.

[12] McMichael TM, Currie DW, Clark S, *et al.* Epidemiology of COVID-19 in a long-term care facility in King County, Washington. *N Engl J Med.* 2020; 382: 2008–11. https://doi.org/10.1056/NEJMoa2005412.

[13] Sullivan-Marx E. Aging in America: how COVID-19 will change care, coverage, and compassion. *Nurs Outlook.* 2020; 68: 533–5. https://doi.org/10.1016/j.outlook.2020.08.013.

[14]    Normile D, Cohen J, Enserink M, *et al.* As normalcy returns, can China keep COVID-19 at bay? Infected travelers pose a continuing threat, but local coronavirus transmission still occurs as well. *Science.* 2020; 368: 18–9. https://doi.org/10.1126/science.368.6486.18.

[15]    Varghese GM and John R. COVID-19 in India: moving from containment to mitigation. *Indian J Med Res.* 2020; 151: 136–9. https://doi.org/10.4103/ijmr.IJMR_860_20.

[16]    Bhuyan HK and Ravi VK. Analysis of sub-feature for classification in data mining, *IEEE Transaction on Engineering Management*, 2021 (Early Published).

[17]    Statista. COVID-19 deaths per capita by Country. Statista (2020).

[18]    Lee VJ, Chiew CJ, and Khong WX. Interrupting transmission of COVID-19: lessons from containment efforts in Singapore. *J Travel Med.* 2020; 27: 1–5. https://doi.org/10.1093/jtm/taaa039.

[19]    Singapore's economic contraction in the second quarter was worse than initial estimates, August 2020, https://www.cnbc.com/2020/08/11/singapore-releases-second-quarter-2020-gdp-economic-data.html.

[20]    Bhuyan HK, Chakraborty C, Pani SK, and Ravi VK. Feature and sub-feature selection for classification using correlation coefficient and fuzzy model. *IEEE Transaction on Engineering Management*, May, 2021 (Early Published).

[21]    Daniel G, Stefania F, and Johannes W. COVID-19: Without Help, Low-Income Developing Countries Risk a Lost Decade, August 27, 2020. https://blogs.imf.org/2020/08/27/covid-19-without-help-low-income-developing-countries-risk-a-lost-decade/

[22]    Suleiman A, Bsisu I, Guzu H, *et al.* Preparedness of frontline doctors in Jordan healthcare facilities to COVID-19 outbreak. *Int J Environ Res Public Health.* 2020; 17. https://doi.org/10.3390/ijerph17093181.

[23]    Ahmed SAKS, Ajisola M, Azeem K, *et al.* Impact of the societal response to COVID-19 on access to healthcare for non-COVID-19 health issues in slum communities of Bangladesh, Kenya, Nigeria and Pakistan: results of pre-COVID and COVID-19 lockdown stakeholder engagements. *BMJ Glob Health.* 2020; 5: e003042. https://doi.org/10.1136/bmjgh-2020-003042.

[24]    Martinez D, Sarria GJ, Wakefield D, *et al.* COVID's impact on radiation oncology: a Latin American survey study. *Int J Radiat Oncol Biol Phys.* 2020; 108: 374–8. https://doi.org/10.1016/j.ijrobp.2020.06.058.

[25]    Luedi MM, Doll D, Boggs SD, *et al.* Successful personalities in anesthesiology and acute care medicine: are we selecting, training, and supporting the best? *Anesth Analg.* 2017; 124: 359–61. https://doi.org/10.1213/ANE.0000000000001714.

[26]    Li Q, Guan X, Wu P, *et al.* Early transmission dynamics in Wuhan, China, of novel coronavirus-infected pneumonia. *N Engl J Med.* 2020; 382: 1199–207. doi:10.1056/NEJMoa2001316.

[27] Rothan HA and Byrareddy SN. The epidemiology and pathogenesis of coronavirus disease (COVID-19) outbreak. *J Autoimmun.* 2020; 109: 102433. doi:10.1016/j.jaut.2020.102433.

[28] CDC. Preliminary estimates of the prevalence of selected underlying health conditions among patients with coronavirus disease 2019—United States, February 12–March 28, 2020. *MMWR Morb Mortal Wkly Rep.* 2020; 69: 382–6. doi:10.15585/mmwr.mm6913e2.

[29] AMA. *Social Determinants of Health, Health Systems Science Learning Series.* Chicago, IL: AMA (2020).

[30] CDC. *Coronavirus Disease 2019 (COVID-19): People Who Are at Higher Risk for Severe Illness.* Atlanta, GA: CDC (2020).

[31] Chapman AR. The social determinants of health, health equity, and human rights. *Health Hum Rights.* 2010; 12: 17–30.

[32] Watson K. Why schools in rich areas get more funding than poor areas. Global Citizen (2016). Available online at: https://www.globalcitizen.org/en/content/cost-of-education-in-us/

[33] ODPHP. Social cohesion. In: *Healthy People 2020.* Washington, DC: U.S. Department of Health and Human Services (2020).

[34] Kluch Avas. Americans' social distancing beliefs and activity (May, 2020). Available online at: https://news.gallup.com/opinion/gallup/311261/americans-social-distancing-beliefs-activity.aspx.

[35] ODPHP. Discrimination. In: *Healthy People 2020.* Washington, DC: U.S. Department of Health and Human Services (2020).

[36] Kelli HM, Hammadah M, Ahmed H, *et al.* Association between living in food deserts and cardiovascular risk. *Circ Cardiovasc Qual Outcomes.* 2017; 10: e003532. doi:10.1161/CIRCOUTCOMES.116.003532.

[37] Mackenbach JP, Cavelaars AE, Kunst AE, and Groenhof F. Socioeconomic inequalities in cardiovascular disease mortality; an international study. *Eur Heart J.* 2000; 21: 1141–51. doi:10.1053/euhj.1999.1990.

[38] Banerjee T, Crews DC, Wesson DE, *et al.* Food insecurity, CKD, and subsequent ESRD in US adults. *Am J Kidney Dis.* 2017; 70: 38–47. doi:10.1053/j.ajkd.2016.10.035.

[39] Osuna-Padilla IA, Leal-Escobar G, Garza-Garcia CA, and Rodriguez-Castellanos FE. Dietary acid load: mechanisms and evidence of its health repercussions. *Nefrologia.* 2019; 39: 343–54. doi:10.1016/j.nefroe.2019.08.001.

[40] Abbasalizad Farhangi M, Nikniaz L, and Nikniaz Z. Higher dietary acid load potentially increases serum triglyceride and obesity prevalence in adults: an updated systematic review and meta-analysis. *PLoS One.* 2019; 14: e0216547. doi: 10.1371/journal.pone.0216547.

[41] Cooksey-Stowers K, Schwartz MB, and Brownell KD. Food swamps predict obesity rates better than food deserts in the United States. *Int J Environ Res Public Health.* 2017; 14: 1366. doi:10.3390/ijerph14111366.

[42] NIMH. *Obesity Hypoventilation Syndrome.* Bethesda, MD: NIMH (2013).

[43]  CDC. *Defining Adult Overweight and Obesity*. Atlanta, GA: CDC (2020).

[44]  Petrilli CM, Jones S, Yang J, *et al.* Factors associated with hospitalization and critical illness among 4,103 patients with COVID-19 disease in New work City. *medRxiv*. 2020: 1–25. doi:10.1101/2020.04.08.20057794.

[45]  Simonnet A, Chetboun M, Poissy J, *et al.* High prevalence of obesity in severe acute respiratory Syndrome Coronavirus-2 (SARS-CoV-2) requiring invasive mechanical ventilation. *Obesity (Silver Spring)*. 2020; 28: 1195–9. doi:10.1002/oby.22831.

[46]  Firebaugh G and Acciai F. For blacks in America, the gap in neighbourhood poverty has declined faster than segregation. *Proc Natl Acad Sci USA*. 2016; 113: 13372–7. doi:10.1073/pnas.1607220113.

[47]  Nania R. *Blacks, Hispanics Hit Harder by the Coronavirus, Early U.S. Data Show*. Washington, DC: AARP (2020).

[48]  APM Research Lab. *The Color of Coronavirus: COVID-19 Deaths by Race and Ethnicity in the U.S.* St. Paul, MN: APM Research Lab (2020).

[49]  Kawachi I, Kennedy BP, Lochner K, and Prothrow-Stith D. Social capital, income inequality, and mortality. *Am J Public Health*. 1997; 87: 1491–8. doi:10.2105/AJPH.87.9.1491.

[50]  Finch BK and Vega WA. Acculturation stress, social support, and self-rated health among Latinos in California. *J Immigr Health*. 2003; 5: 109–17. doi:10.1023/A:1023987717921.

[51]  ODPHP. Access to foods that support healthy eating patterns. In: *Healthy People 2020*. Rockville, MD: U.S. Department of Health and Human Services (2020).

[52]  Wu X, Rachek C, Sabath BM, Braun D, and Dominici F. Exposure to air pollution and COVID-19 mortality in the United States: a nationwide cross-sectional study. *medRxiv*. 2020: 1–36. doi:10.1101/2020.04.05.20054502.

[53]  ODPHP. High school graduation. In: *Healthy People 2020*. Rockville, MD: U.S. Department of Health and Human Services (2020).

[54]  Shafa Z. New effort aims to provide Covid-19 resources to non-English speakers in U.S. STAT News (2020).

[55]  Lopez MH, Rainie L, and Budiman A. Financial and health impacts of COVID-19 vary widely by race and ethnicity (2020, May 5).

[56]  iSPARC. Coronavirus economic stimulus payments: who gets it, how, & impact on other benefits. *Psychiatry Inf Brief*. 2020; 17: 1–4. doi: 10.7191/pib.1148.

[57]  Abrams EJ, Myer L, Rosenfield A, and El-Sadr WM. Prevention of mother-to-child transmission services as a gateway to family-based human immu-nodeficiency virus care and treatment in resource-limited settings: rationale and international experiences. *Am J Obstet Gynecol*. 2007; 197(3 Suppl): S101–6. doi: 10.1016/j.ajog.2007.03.068.

[58]  Kloppenburg K. Governor Little issues stay-at-home order for Idaho (2020, March 25). Available online at: https://www.krtv.com/news/coronavirus/stay-at-homeorder-issued-in-idaho.

[59]   Orecchio-Egresitz RMISH. Georgia allowed some businesses to reopen today, but many store and restaurant owners aren't ready to take the risk (2020, April 24). Available online at: https://www.businessinsider.in/international/news/georgia-allowed-some-businesses-to-reopen-today-but-many-store-andres-taurant-owners-arent-ready-to-take-the-risk/articleshow/75365048.cms.

[60]   Brown R and Scholl J. Idaho governor extends stay-home order through April 30 because of coronavirus (2020, April 15). Available online at: https://www.idahostatesman.com/news/coronavirus/article242012651.html.

[61]   Chattu KV, Adisesh A, and Yaya S. Canada's role in strengthening global health security during the COVID-19 pandemic. *Global Health Res Policy*. 2020; 5: 16–18.

[62]   Bhuyan HK, Kamila NK, and Pani SK. Individual privacy in data mining using fuzzy optimization. *Engineering Optimization*, July, 2021 (Early Published).

[63]   Bhuyan HK, Dash SK, Roy S. and Swain DK. Privacy preservation with penalty in decentralized network using multiparty computation. *International Journal of Advancements in Computing Technology (IJACT)*. 2012; 4(1): 297–303.

[64]   United Nations Development Program in China Assessment report on impact of covid19 pandemic on Chinese enterprises. Available at: https://www.cn.undp.org/content/china/zh/home/library/crisis_prevention_and_recovery/assessment-report-on-impact-of-covid-19-pandemic-onchineseente.html (accessed April 7, 2020).

[65]   Wang X and Sun T. China's engagement in global health governance: a critical analysis of China's assistance to the health sector of Africa. *J Glob Health*. 2014; 4(1): 793–804.

[66]   Wang Y, Hong A, Li X, and Gao J. Marketing innovations during a global crisis: a study of China firms' response to COVID-19. *J Bus Res*. 2020; 116: 214–20.

[67]   Bhuyan HK, Raghu Kumar L, Reddy KR. Optimization model for sub-feature selection in data mining. *2nd International Conference on Smart Systems and Inventive Technology (ICSSIT 2019), IEEE Explore*, 2019.

[68]   Bhuyan, HK and Reddy CV. Madhusudan. Sub-feature selection for novel classification, International Conference on Inventive Communication and Computational Technologies (ICICCT), *IEEE Explore*, 20–21 April, 2018. doi: 10.1109/ICICCT.2018.8473206.

[69]   World Health Organization. *Coronavirus Disease (COVID-19) Update*. World Health Organization (2020). https://www.who.int/bangladesh/emergencies/coronavirus-disease-(covid-19)-update (accessed November 7, 2020).

[70]   BBS. Labour force survey Bangladesh 2016–17 (2018).

[71]   Farhana KM and Mannan KA. Knowledge and perception towards Novel Coronavirus (COVID 19) in Knowledge and perception towards Novel Coronavirus (COVID 19) in Bangladesh. *Int Res J Bus Soc Sci*. 2020; 6: 76–9.

[72]   Cousins S. Bangladesh's COVID-19 testing criticised. *Lancet (London, England)*. 2020; 396: 591. https://doi.org/10.1016/S0140-6736(20)31819-5.

[73]   World Health Organization. *Increased Testing Capacity, Essential Step in Fighting COVID-19*. World Health Organization (2020). https://www.who.int/

bangladesh/news/detail/08-10-2020-increased-testing-capacityessential-step-in-fighting-covid-19 (accessed November 3, 2020).

[74]    Bangladesh sees 100th death of doctors from Covid-19. Dhaka Tribune (2020). https://www.dhakatribune.com/health/coronavirus/2020/10/15/bangladesh-sees-100th-death-of-doctors-from-covid-19.

[75]    Islam R. The impact of COVID-19 on employment in Bangladesh: Pathway to an inclusive and sustainable recovery (2020).

[76]    Sen B. Poverty in the time of Corona: Short-term effects of economic slowdown and policy responses through social protection (2020).

[77]    Sultan M, Hossain MS, Islam MS, Chowdhury K, Naim J, and Huq F. COVID-19 impact on RMG sector and the financial stimulus package: Trade union responses (2020).

[78]    Ferguson NM, Laydon D, Nedjati-Gilani G, *et al.* Impact of non-pharmaceutical interventions (NPIs) to reduce COVID-19 mortality and healthcare demand (2020). https://doi.org/10.25561/77482.

[79]    World Population Prospects 2019, https://population.un.org/wpp/.

[80]    Reuters. Bangladesh shuts down villages after tens of thousands attend cleric's funeral. New York Times (2020).

[81]    Bradbury-Jones C and Isham L. The pandemic paradox: the consequences of COVID-19 on domestic violence. *J Clin Nurs*. 2020; 19: 1–3. https://doi.org/10.1111/jocn.15296.

[82]    Islam A. *COVID-19 Lockdown Increases Domestic Violence in Bangladesh.* DW (2020) https://www.dw.com/en/covid-19-lockdown-increases-domestic-violence-inbangladesh/a-53411507.

*Chapter 5*

# Artificial intelligence in healthcare

*Deepa Joshi[1] and Anikait Sabharwal[1]*

The ability of artificial intelligence (AI) to imitate human cognitive capabilities, coupled with the ease of accessibility of medical data and the expeditious advancement of analytical techniques, is bringing paramount difference to the healthcare industry. Former research demonstrates the remarkable accuracy of AI to aid physicians to settle on better clinical choices or supplant judgment made by human beings, in particular, technical and practical areas of medical care. Statistics indicate that the shortage of doctors in therapeutically under-resourced regions and the lack of availability of skilled physicians in highly engaged clinical settings tend to cause a rise in false detection rates. The excessive workload causes fatigue that could lead to poor recovery of diseases. AI is ever-evolving as it is making advancements at an exponential rate, especially in healthcare treatments, such as monitoring treatments, improving the planning, and analyzing data to provide better treatment plans. The procedure of data accumulation, data management, clustering, and tagging invites numerous governance and regulatory challenges that could take a long duration. The healthcare industry thrives in this unending battle as the complexity and intricacy of data, and strict guidelines take a major toll. A healthcare institute is subjected to ask for consent from an institutional review board's work to attenuate a portion of these concerns, and researchers and scientists may measure, process, and anonymize DICOM information to strip away any patient's medical information. The AI-enabled medical care employed in the institutes plays an imperative role as an informative assistant that provides aid to doctors in acquiring an understanding of meaningful patterns from data collection. This practice holds the potential to save a lot of time, cost, and effort while yielding consistent, unbiased, and prime diagnosis or treatment. AI and deep learning (DL) tools used in day-to-day medical decision-making have a grave impact on improving the patient's treatment and overall cost incurred due to their employ- ment efficiency and accuracy. AI and machine learning (ML) can prove to be of supreme importance and assistance in the early detection and thus the prevention of a plethora of diseases by reading and analyzing the patient's vitals. The presented chapter is of 5-folds. First, the distinct data sources where the healthcare data is

[1]School of Computer Science, University of Petroleum and Energy Studies (UPES), Dehradun, India

gathered from are discussed. Second, we talk about the moral and lawful difficulties of AI-driven medical care. Next, the structured and unstructured types of healthcare data have been analyzed followed by the AI techniques applied to these types of data, such as ML, natural language processing (NLP), and DL. We then analyze the crucial disease areas such as cardiology, radiology, neurology, and cancer, where the health issues can be alleviated by employing AI techniques. In conclusion, we further discuss the areas where AI-based techniques are applied in real life.

## 5.1    Introduction

The goal of AI is to teach, while also passing on human intelligence and instincts to a computer. An amalgamation of mathematics, statistics, and science makes this task attainable.

Famous AI strategies comprise ML techniques for structured data, for example, neural network (NN), the traditional support vector machine (SVM), and advanced DL, in addition to NLP that is utilized for the unstructured data. Cardiology, cancer, and neurology are some of the principal disease areas that employ AI tools. Instead of teaching, training and programming systems for certain tasks, ML emphasizes on passing on the abilities concurrently. ML designs algorithms through which systems can create and work on predictions for homogeneous situations and tasks. Under the approach termed supervised learning, the machines are given data and are trained on examples that have similar desired output so they can further work on unseen problems and data. Under unsupervised learning, just the input data is given to the machine, and it is required to build an output without help and oversight [1]. From the early days itself, ML algorithms were devised and were utilized to analyze medical datasets. Today, ML is an instrumental base for providing key tools to astute data analysis. Particularly over the most recent couple of years, the evolution of technology gave moderately reasonable and accessible ways to gather and store data. Current medical clinics are exceptionally provisioned with observing and other data accumulation tools. Furthermore, the data is assembled and apportioned in huge data frameworks. ML is right now at such an innovative stage that it is equipped to analyze clinical data, and specifically there is a huge load of work done in clinical analysis in compact dedicated diagnostic problems [2].

ML is being employed on varied kinds of diseases like diabetes and cancer, falling under healthcare analysis. Cancer being one of the most fatal diseases has distinct kinds that comprise breast cancer, stomach cancer, lung cancer, prostate cancer, and the list goes on. Nearly 12% instances of cellular breakdown in the lungs come every year, where 10% cases do not make it through. Likewise, for breast cancer, 11% cases arise, of which 9% do not make it. For dealing with cancer in the medical field analysis, it is crucial that accurate and prime quality data is produced. In such an ambition-driven world, medical services should utilize the data in a particular way that consistently results in an ascent in the quality of medical care and a significant decrease in the expense required for the therapy [3]. With time, especially in recent years, there is an exponential rise in medical care research with ML. The difficulty human beings face in making decisions and inferring data is due to the assortment of medical data that involves omics data, clinical data, or even EHR data. For that very reason, ML has been effectively presented and advanced in medical care for finer comprehension of data and superior dynamic cycle [4].

The chapter has been presented in 5-folds. Initially, the distinct data sources from where the medical care data can be accumulated are examined. Second, we discuss the moral and legal hurdles of AI-driven healthcare. Furthermore, the structured and unstructured kinds of medical services data have been investigated, which is trailed by the AI strategies applied to these kinds of data, for instance, ML, DL, and NLP. We at that point dissect the absolutely critical disease areas like cardiology, radiology, nervous system science, and cancer, where the medical problems can be lightened by utilizing and efficaciously employing AI methods. In conclusion, we examine the fields where AI-based methods are applied in reality.

## 5.2 Healthcare data sources

If not handled with utter perseverance and seriousness, data accumulation and hence management in healthcare can be particularly perplexing, laborious, and unsafe. In the light of staying aware of this consistently converting data landscape, the associations need a data accumulation solution that is prepared to deal with medical care, crystal clear use cases and with safety and security efforts, and compliance that consider the novel requirements of the industry.

The healthcare industry has a plethora of sources for big data that include the records of hospitals, medical records of patients, medical examination results, and IoT (Internet of Things) devices as illustrated in Figure 5.1. A notable segment of

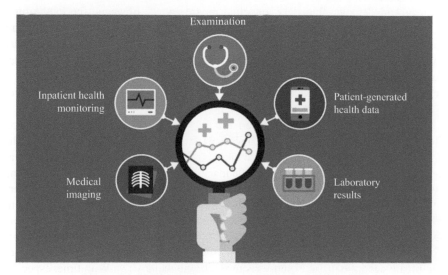

*Figure 5.1 Various sources of healthcare data [37]*

big data that is instrumental in public healthcare is generated by biomedical research. Thus, this portion requires careful management and analysis to derive meaningful information. Over the years, the analysis of healthcare data is coming up to become quite possibly the majority of favorable research sectors. It comprises information for varied types, like sensor data, clinical data, and omics data. The patient records that are stored in electronic health records during the ongoing treatment are termed clinical data. Omics data is amongst the high magnitude data that comprises transcriptome, proteome, and genome data types. Sensor data is the one that is gathered from numerous wearable and wireless sensor devices [4].

Each industry faces challenges regarding regulations and governance in the collection, storage, and management of data, although when it comes to the healthcare industry, the battles fought are one of a kind. Frequently, the information that is gathered in medical care is intricate and is administered by unnecessarily rigid guidelines [5]. The majority of healthcare providers collect data in innumerable forms, like forms for patient intake, treatment evaluation, health assessment forms, and consent forms amongst many. To make the information attainable in the customer relationship management systems at the backend, electronic well-being record frameworks, and divided between suppliers, the data post collection is made to go through manual data entry. Statistics show that this manual entry process is prone to errors like incorrect entries, typing errors, or even wrong form entries being made in a patient's records. Usually, the forms on paper render patient information unavailable to all custodians inside 24 h, particularly the data gathered from outside sources. This may bring the patient a disconnected care environment. The most genuine kind of digital clinical information is acquired right at the mark of care at a clinical office, emergency clinic, hospital, or practice. Regularly referred to as the electronic clinical record (EMR), the EMR is typically unavailable to people beyond the research spectrum. The data accumulated involves regulatory and demographic data, conclusion, treatment, physician endorsed drugs, research facility tests, physiologic observing data, hospitalization, patient insurance, and so on. Individual associations, for instance, medical clinics or health frameworks offer access to the internal staff, although bigger coordinated efforts, for instance, the NIH Collaboratory Distributed Research Network, give multidisciplinary access to clinical information vaults by qualified researchers.

## 5.3    Legal and ethical obstacles of artificial intelligence-driven healthcare

In India, the data transfer for processing data is not covered by any definite law. Gigantic measure of information was handled by a third party by the ones providing service, hence recording the data as indicated by US laws [6]. A debate struck in 2017 because of a comparable arrangement among Google DeepMind and the Royal Free London NHS Foundation Trust [7]. That understanding was reprimanded for not adhering to the Caldicott Principles by moving information that is more than what is needed and obscuring the complete line that is between the data regulators and the ones who process data. This led to legitimate commitments and liabilities. The United Kingdom is known to have instrumental mechanisms like the Information Commissioner's Office (answerable for authorizing as well as putting Data Protection Act into motion) and Health Research Authority (liable for a government foundation diving into health research) and Confidentiality Advisory Group (a strategy for classified health data in if explicit assent is unavailable), which were not consulted prior to the rise of data transfer, subsequently done to employ "self-assessment information governance toolkit" utilized to support the security of particularly specialized technical framework to deal with NHS data [7]. In such cases, it is crucial that the care-providers are cautious when they share the data with an outsider which is in an implicit relationship with the separate patient(s), respectively. The care that is provided straight to the concerned authority or person is regarded as "action concerned about the protection, examination and treatment of disease and the mitigation of enduring of a recognized individual." This requires a notice to be provided to the patient or subject of concern. In case the explicit assent and notice are not granted, then all the data, irrespective of being tagged or untagged, falls into the public domain and is required to be produced by a statutory body. Through this, a tab can be kept regarding the unlawful proprietary manipulation of the information and accordingly the data processor can only exchange the data up to a certain limit. The freely accessible public or peer-examined data sets, for example, Messidor, will help unconstrained development of processes and algorithms, since without assent such de-identified data sets ought to be viewed as a community resource. The idea of putting them in the hands of the community is to employ and enforce policing of the data exchanges at a level that cannot be attained by the government. In India, we need to have legal regulations, for example, segment 251 in the United Kingdom, which calls the government and legal control for such exchanges [7]. As a matter of fact, the discussion of ownership and custodial responsibility of such information in our country seldom takes place [8]. There is no particular brief regarding what way the information will be handled by the machine in the event that we utilize an AI device on such sets. The effect of transfer learning and AGI is such that humans often are boggled as to how the data is handled by the machine. People apparently found certain lines of play in AlphaZero "completely alien" but highly efficacious. Notable progress has been seen in Justice BN Srikrishna Committee, as they strategically empowered their patients [8]. In any case, it is reckless to anticipate that general protection should address immensely tangled bioethical worries in the expansion and growth of clinical AI. The healthcare profession is required to demand explicit customs and "Dos and Don'ts," which whenever stuck to will guard it against prosecution and litigation in the event of data break since India is not just the colossal producer and the least expensive source of such data (as per confirmation made by the authors in the Google Diabetic Retinopathy Project) [9], it will pose to be a massive market specifically for the algorithms that are derived from it in future. The machines require rules and regulations for effective recursive self-improvement, which calls for a dire need of strengthened bioethical and computational ethics framework to guarantee optimum and safe functioning of the same. The phrase, "First, do no harm," should be strongly conveyed from clinical morals into the discipline of computational bioethics. We possess the characteristics of a typical parent in this case; past a phase of development, we may not be in charge of these algorithms any further or may not comprehend them by any stretch of our imagination.

## 5.4    Types of healthcare data

Clinical data is the key resource when it comes to carrying out research in medical and health research work. Health information can be located in numerous structures, as vital signs, lab results, patient's way of life information, notes by the doctor, and an assortment of kinds of imagery (ultrasonography, ultrasonography, and magnetic resonance imaging, pathology slides). Despite there being no principles or classifications that include a wide range of medical information, it is extremely useful to think about this significant data as organized and unstructured information. Getting a handle on and accommodating the two prime kinds of data, organized, structured, and unstructured data, is among indispensable difficulties for medical care suppliers. The clinical data, which is rising dramatically, incorporates an incredible volume of unstructured and structured information as different areas [10]. The grave issue lying in medical care fields is that about 80% of information for electronic medical records or a majority of clinic data frameworks are in general disregarded, unsaved, or even deserted in a lot of clinical places for quite a while [4]. However, the entire data is as yet made in numerous hospitals quite difficult to be associated with clinical research of big data and the AI industry in medical services. Subsequently, there is a dire need to deal with those unmanaged data.

### 5.4.1    *Structured data*

Structured data is a type that is kept in store in an utterly organized way, like documents. It is simpler to analyze and hence store since it has direct limits and is produced and put away in a standard design and format. Patient segment data, analysis and interaction codes, medicine codes, and other explicit information from the electronic medical record are ordinarily created and delivered in a standard, structured organized way. Traditional data warehouses can be considered the ones that are quite frequently structured data.

Unstructured data is rather a bit laborious. It comes in a plethora of forms that include emails, audio and video files, text and genome files, as well as social media posts. Structured data is certainly not an analogous category—if the data is organized and structured, it is not necessary that it is organized in a manner that makes complete sense or has ease of interpretation. Contrarily, if the data lacks formal structure, it is not necessary that it will not be interpreted with absolute ease, or that it can only be analyzed by choosing a resource-intensive manner. On the face of it, unstructured data addresses a more prominent hurdle to dissect and decipher than structured data.

### 5.4.2    *Unstructured data*

Unlike structured data, unstructured data is not entirely defined and thus cannot be inspected the way structured data is. Therefore, it is rather difficult for healthcare organizations to make unstructured data operable. Enormous amounts of unstructured healthcare data are collected by healthcare organizations, and quite a few difficulties to discover the instruments that permit that data to be utilized. Unstructured data can be made pragmatic with AI and ML, hence enabling them to help doctors gather instrumental insight into the patients' health [10]. Unstructured big data in medical systems prior to proposing the development of healthcare AI, at the moment, has its base on ML. To enhance the utilization and application of unstructured healthcare big data, we need to establish the data accumulation, quality assurance, and anonymization processes. It is essential that metadata for every type of unstructured healthcare data is extracted, defined, visualized, and standardized automatically. Further, the open stage for incorporation and the application of the unstructured medical data should be created while mirroring these ideas. A cautious glance at this dichotomy, particularly inside the setting of evolving innovation, uncovers nuanced contrast.

Images and free text are not that easy to categorize in a way that numerical, structured data points can be categorized. For example, diagnosing the blood pressure reading as elevated, normal, or hypertensive can be achieved merely by some lines of code. A doctor's note that indicates "gen fatigue, trouble breath, and chest pain" indicates hypertension, although abbreviation and spelling mistakes made in text would need a human being to decode and further understand it (mainly when the text is written by hand or is manually scanned in the EMR through fax). Imagery poses difficulties in the same line—X-rays and pathology slides for the most part are incomprehensible to each aside from exceptionally skilled experts and even doctors who have years of experience often further require second judgment in order to confirm an inference or diagnosis. In contrast, the time when clinical imaging is progressively depending upon digital imagery, the unstructured data is thus predominantly examined and analyzed by hand. However, persistent progresses in ML and AI can possibly change the manner in which doctors and suppliers utilize unstructured data. As per the example provided, a tool of NLP may have the ability to understand a note made by the doctor and understand the same as "general fatigue, trouble breathing, and chest pain" whereas a tool for ML decision support may have the ability to recommend that these are manifestations identified with hypertension (this analysis likewise benefits from structured context-oriented information like the patient's stature, pulse, and weight). In the same manner, using huge repositories of medical imagery, computer science researchers are conscientiously working with doctors in order to train and build ML models to perceive patterns in medical imagery to give a computerized and automated "subsequent assessment" affirming (or proposing ambiguity) a manually created inference or finding [11].

AlphaZero is known to have become proficient in chess, Shogi and Go unaccompanied with human assistance, apart from the rules of the game. In a period of 24 h, AlphaZero triumphed over all the exceptional AI programs like AlphaGo, Elmo, and Stockfish (3 days) [9]. Improvement in AI is presently moving its attention from "supervised" learning (which needed numerous labeled instances to prepare the instrument to perceive comparable patterns) to "unsupervised learning" (a type of learning in which the machine trains without the help of any labeled data). With time, progress, having such an eminent computational force as its backbone, AI is becoming supreme. Although considering this, it raises a major concern about a situation with this force discovering its way into unacceptable and dangerous hands, be it artificial or human. The earlier one evolves at the pace of human advancement, giving an open door to evolve and reclaim our lives, however, not so for the artificial elements, as we can see with the AlphaGo experience. This calls for deeper caution in the fields of medicine and medical research since the individual influenced by every choice is a conscious human being. AI cannot be considered one single technology, but rather an assembly of them, and many of them have a direct, yet distinct, relationship with the field of healthcare.

## 5.5    AI techniques developed for structured and unstructured data

AI, which comprises robotics, NLP, and ML may be employed in nearly all kinds of fields in healthcare, and the possible commitments to clinical education, biomedical research, and the applications of medical services appear to be boundless. With its thriving capacity to coordinate, amalgamate, and grasp from massive sets of medical information, AI serves parts in clinical decision-making, diagnosis, and customized medication. Symptomatic and diagnostic calculations based on AI integrated with mammograms are aiding the discovery and diagnosis of breast cancer, filling in as second judgment for radiologists. Furthermore, progressed virtual symbols are equipped for participating in significant discussions, which has effective inferences for the determination and treatment of disease related to psychiatry. Applications in AI additionally reach out to the actual physical domain with physical task support networks and systems, robotic prostheses, and portable controllers aiding the delivery of telemedicine.

Devices in AI can be essentially categorized into two distinct parts. The initial classification incorporates ML methods that investigate structured data like EP, hereditary, and imaging information. In clinical implementation, ML systems cluster patient's attributes and traits or construe the likelihood of the outcomes of the diseases. The subsequent classification incorporates NLP techniques that gather from unstructured data's information like medical journals or notes to enhance and improve medical structured data. The NLP systems aim at transforming texts to machine-decipherable structured data, which is then analyzed by ML techniques.

### 5.5.1    Machine learning

With the aim of extracting features from data, ML builds various data analytical algorithms. Usually patient "traits" and medical outcomes of interests are taken as inputs for the ML algorithms. These traits often comprise the standard data such as gender, age, and history of diseases, along with data that is specific to diseases, that include EP test, gene expressions, clinical symptoms, medication, diagnostic imaging, physical examination results, and the list goes on. Not just the characteristics, even the patient's medical outcomes that comprise quantitative disease levels, patient's survival times, and disease indicators, like, size of tumor, are gathered for the purpose of clinical research [12]. The subsequent features are preferred to accelerate ML system's effectiveness in resolving diagnostic tasks in healthcare: great execution, the capacity to suitably manage noisy data (errors) and with missing data, the clarity of knowledge of diagnosis, the capacity to elaborate conclusions, and the capacity of the algorithm to reduce the quantity of examinations that are important to acquire reliable diagnosis [2]. ML algorithms may be separated in three significant classes: supervised learning, semi-supervised learning, and unsupervised learning. The one that is immensely notable for feature extraction is unsupervised learning, while supervised learning is reasonable for prescient modeling through progressively developing a few connections between the patient's characteristics (input) in addition to the interest's outcome (output). The crossbreed between supervised learning and unsupervised learning has been effectively put forward as semi-supervised learning that is appropriate for situations where the outcome is missing for particular subjects [12]. Figure 5.2 shows the ubiquity of distinct supervised learning strategies in medical implementations.

AI applications in healthcare typically employ supervised learning for a plethora of reasons and purposes. Unsupervised learning may be utilized as a feature of the step of preprocessing to lessen dimensionality or recognize subgroups, which therefore makes the subsequent supervised learning's step way more effective. Important strategies incorporate decision tree, random forest, naïve Bayes, discriminant analysis, NN, logistic regression, linear regression, nearest neighbor, and SVM [13].

## 5.5.2 Neural networks

NNs, when regarded with logistic regression, may be considered an add-on to encapsulate composite nonlinear relationships between an outcome and the input

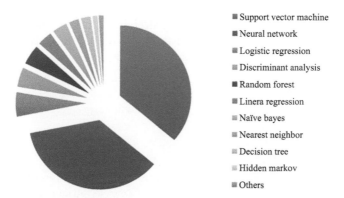

*Figure 5.2 The ML algorithms employed in the healthcare literature. Data is created by looking through the ML algorithms inside medical services on PubMed [12]*

variables. The methodology of NNs in tackling such issues is not quite the same as typical approaches. It takes the countless contributions of many such manually written digits named as training samples and builds a framework to naturally derive rules for distinguishing the digits by persistently learning patterns from those training samples. Moreover, the precision of such models can be further refined by appending additional training samples [13]. "Perceptron" is the prime belief that drives the building of an NN. The concept of a perceptron was encouraged by the human nervous system, where each network consists of distinct interconnected neurons that effectively communicate with one another.

Over the period of time, healthcare has become an instrumental field where AI techniques, including DL, are extensively employed and applied. DL has the ability to inspect more mind-boggling nonlinear patterns in the data. With the evolving technology, there is a grave rise in the amount and complexity of data, which calls for the new fame of DL. An algorithm that has its base on DL functions in the subsequent manner: input layer is utilized as a gateway for the input data to enter the deep NN. Figure 5.3 mentions the sources of data for DL.

The design of the input data gets changed so the deep NN realizes the way to handle and process the same, and potentially certain extra calculations are then performed. At that point, the outcomes are provided to the initial hidden layer. A network can contain a variety of secret layers, implying that this footstep carrying out a calculation and providing the result to the following hidden layer is further carried out on various occasions, until and unless the yield layer has been reached. The final layer's role is essential to offer a solution to the question that DL is expected to answer.

For instance, in Figure 5.4, a prostate magnetic resonance (MR) picture is the input that goes via the network with every one of its layers, and thus the output layer conveys the response to the doubt "Is there a lesion in the prostate MR image?"

### 5.5.3    Natural language processing

The EP, picture, and hereditary data can be deciphered by the machine with the goal that the ML algorithms can be instantly performed after legitimate pre-processing or quality maintenance measures. In any case, an immense extent of

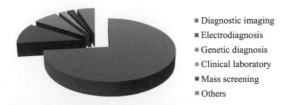

*Figure 5.3    The sources of data for deep learning. The data is created by looking through deep learning in an amalgamation with the diagnosis methods on PubMed [38]*

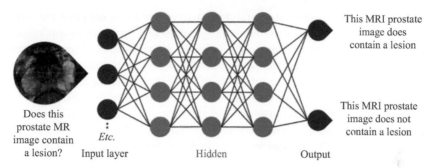

*Figure 5.4    A deep neural network utilizes various layers to protect and handle input data (a prostate MR picture, in this case). Once the data goes via the network, a solution is given by the algorithm to a particular question, like, "Is there a lesion in the prostate MR image?" [38]*

clinical data is in the structure of narrative text, like physical inspection and assessment, clinical research center and lab reports, and employable notes that are unstructured while possessing no limits for the PC program. With regard to this unique circumstance, NLP focuses on separating and hence gathering helpful data through narrative text in order to help medical decision-making. Two essential components can be found in an NLP pipeline, namely (1) processing of text and (2) subsequent classification. It recognizes a progression of catchphrases and keywords related to diseases in the clinical notes dependent on the verifiable historical databases through text processing [14]. Following that, a proportion of the keywords are picked by analyzing their impacts on the categorization of the abnormal and normal cases. At that point, the approved keywords advance the structured data to help clinical dynamics of making decisions. The development of the NLP pipelines is with a goal of aiding clinical making of decisions to notify arrangements related to treatment, overseeing unfavorable effects, and much more. For instance, Fiszman *et al.* presented that bringing NLP into the picture for perusing the chest X-beam reports provides aid to antibiotic associate frameworks to caution doctors for the conceivable requirement against infective therapy [15]. On a similar note, NLP was employed by Miller *et al.* to oversee the lab-based antagonistic effects on its own [16]. NLP pipelines are also instrumental in assisting diagnosis of diseases. For example, Castro *et al.* recognized 14 disease factors related to cerebral aneurysms by carrying out NLP on the medical and clinical notes [17].

## 5.6    Major disease areas

AI, which incorporates the domains of NLP, robotics, and ML, may be implemented in practically any domain in healthcare, and its possible commitments to medical education, clinical research, and applications of medical services appear to be boundless. Flaunting its hearty capacity to coordinate, learn, and integrate from huge datasets of the medical industry, AI has the potential to serve parts in analysis, diagnosis [18] customized medication [19], and decisions made in the healthcare industry [20]. For instance, diagnostic calculations and applications based on AI applied to mammograms are aiding the identification of breast cancer, filling in the second judgment cum opinion for radiologists [21]. Likewise, progressed virtual symbols are equipped to take part in significant conversations, having inferences for the diagnosis and thus, treatment of diseases in psychiatry [22]. AI implementations additionally reach out into the physical sphere with mobile manipulators, physical task support systems, and robotic automated prostheses, and aiding the conveyance of telemedicine.

Cancer, neurology, and cardiology are few of the key disease areas that employ AI tools [12]. Somashekhar *et al.* proposed that the IBM Watson for oncology must be a top-notch AI system for aiding the diagnosis and analysis of cancer via a two-staged approval study [23]. Esteva *et al.* carefully performed an analysis on clinical pictures to recognize subtypes of skin malignant growth [24]. Bouton *et al.* developed an AI structure to restore and subsequently reenforce the control of development in patients with quadriplegia [25]. Farina *et al.* effectively tried the power of an offline machine or man-made interface that uses the issued timings of spinal motor neurons to control the prostheses of the upper limb [26]. Dilsizian and Siegel inspected the normal utilization of the AI system to analyze and examine the anticipated utilization of the AI system heart disease via a careful look at the cardiovascular pictures [19].

## 5.7    Applications of AI in healthcare system

Application of AI knows no bounds, as it proves to offer immense advancements in each of the domains of medicine, ranging from the diagnosis to the entire treatment. The credit to on-demand healthcare services goes entirely to the advances made in smartphones and wireless technology that have been made using search engines or platforms and apps that track health possible, while also enabling a new form of healthcare delivery accessible whenever and wherever required, via remote interactions. These assistance services are beneficial for underprivileged places and areas that lack specialists by helping bring the cost down and preventing pointless exposure to infectious diseases at the center. An absolute blend of bigger data accumulation data libraries, a large AI pool, and accelerated computer processing speed has featured quick building of AI technology and tools healthcare [27]. Diving into specifics, the entire advancement of DL has made a major impression on the lines we perceive AI tools these days and is practically the cause for the majority of recent exhilaration and anticipation surrounding AI applications (Figure 5.5). A plethora of favorable implementations for medical purposes have varied opinions. Forbes issued a statement in 2018 that the instrumental domains would be image analysis, clinical decision support, virtual assistants, robotic surgery, and administrative workflows [28]. A 2018 written report by Accenture referred to the particular areas while also including dosage error reduction,

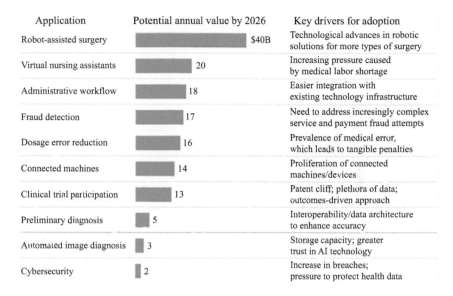

| Application | Potential annual value by 2026 | Key drivers for adoption |
|---|---|---|
| Robot-assisted surgery | $40B | Technological advances in robotic solutions for more types of surgery |
| Virtual nursing assistants | 20 | Increasing pressure caused by medical labor shortage |
| Administrative workflow | 18 | Easier integration with existing technology infrastructure |
| Fraud detection | 17 | Need to address incresingly complex service and payment fraud attempts |
| Dosage error reduction | 16 | Prevalence of medical error, which leads to tangible penalties |
| Connected machines | 14 | Proliferation of connected machines/devices |
| Clinical trial participation | 13 | Patent cliff; plethora of data; outcomes-driven approach |
| Preliminary diagnosis | 5 | Interoperability/data architecture to enhance accuracy |
| Automated image diagnosis | 3 | Storage capacity; greater trust in AI technology |
| Cybersecurity | 2 | Increase in breaches; pressure to protect health data |

*Figure 5.5   Applications of AI in the healthcare system [39]*

connected machines, and cybersecurity [29]. A 2019 report written by McKinsey mentions key areas being robotics-assisted surgery, electroceuticals, targeted and personalized medicine, and connected and cognitive devices [30].

### 5.7.1   Solutions based on genetics

It is being counted on that within the coming decade a major portion of the worldwide populace will be provided with a full genome sequencing either upon the time of birth or in grown-up life. Such genome sequencing takes up approximately 100–150 GB of data and allows a prominent tool for accurate medicine. The process of uniting the interface of the genomic and phenotypic information is currently in progress. The present-day clinical system requires refinement and redesign in order to utilize certain genomics data and its advantages [31].

### 5.7.2   Development and discovery of drug

Drug development and development is one such domain that is extensively long, costly, and complex and holds the probability of taking greater than 10 years, right from the recognition of molecular targets to the point unless a drug item is affirmed and promoted in the market. Disappointment at this point in time poses an astounding financial impact, and quite a few drug candidates fail amidst development and are not able to make it to the market [32]. There are numerous methods that have been utilized to develop models to aid drug discovery since the 1990s such as NNs, random forest, and SVMs. Not long ago, DL started to be carried out because of the expanded measure of information and the consistent enhancements in computing power. ML can be employed in the drug discovery process for streamlining various tasks. They comprise de novo design of drug–receptor interactions, drug compound property, drug reaction prediction, and activity prediction [33].

### 5.7.3   Support in clinical decisions

The help of NLP makes it more advantageous for doctors to narrow down the pertinent data from patient reports. AI holds the capacity to store and work on huge arrangements of information, which can give knowledge databases and encourage assessment and recommendation independently for every patient, consequently assisting clinical decision support [34].

### 5.7.4   Robotics and artificial intelligence-powered devices

There are various fields in medical care where one can see robots being utilized to supplant the human workforce, increase human capacities, and help human healthcare experts. These also comprise robots employed for surgeries, for example, assistants for rehabilitation, patient assistance, and laparoscopic operations, robots that are coordinated into prosthetic and implants, and robots employed to help doctors and other medical care staff working on their routine errands. A portion of these gadgets are being created by organizations particularly for interaction with patients and, hence, advancing the association among people and machines from a care perspective. Many of the robots right now being worked on have a fair degree of AI innovation fused for better execution with regard to classifications, language recognition, and image processing [34].

## 5.8   Examples of AI used in healthcare

Large health companies are now often merging, which allows for pronounced health data accessibility [35]. Greater health data helps in laying the fundamental groundwork for the implementation of AI algorithms. A huge portion of industries in the healthcare sector focus on the implementation of AI in the support systems of clinical decision-making. ML algorithms adjust and take into consideration more powerful feedback followed by the solutions as the collection of data occurs [36]. Big data is becoming the talk of the town amongst a number of companies to explore the possibilities of its incorporation in the healthcare industry. The organizations look into the market opening via the domains of "data storage, analysis, assessment, and management technologies," the most important aspects of the medical industry. Following are listed certain key examples of big shot companies that have been instrumental in contributing to AI algorithms for use in healthcare.

   **IBM's Watson Oncology** is building at the Memorial Sloan Kettering Cancer Center and Cleveland Clinic. At the same time, IBM is actively functioning with CVS Health on applications in AI in the treatment of chronic diseases, along with Johnson on the analysis of scientific papers in order to locate associations for advancement in development of drugs. In May 2017, Rensselaer Polytechnic Institute and IBM started a project that they were jointly working on, granted

Health Empowerment by Analytics, Learning and Semantics (HEALS), to prospect employing technologies of AI to augment the medicine industry [23].

**Microsoft's Hanover project**, partnered with Oregon Health Science University's Knight Cancer Institute, plays a paramount role in analyzing medical research with the agenda of predicting the most efficacious alternatives for cancer drug therapy in patients. There are various project initiatives that comprise development of programmable cells along with medical image analysis of tumor progression.

**Google's DeepMind** platform is currently extensively employed by the UK National Health Service on data accumulated through applications on mobile phones to detect certain health risks. Another project under the NHS includes an examination of clinical pictures gathered from NHS patients with an aim to develop computer vision algorithms for spotting cancerous tissues.

**Tencent at this point** is actively operating on various clinical frameworks and deliverables. The aforesaid compass AI Medical Innovation System, a diagnostic medical imaging deliverable that is powered by AI; WeChat Intelligent Healthcare; and the Tencent Doctorwork.

**Intel's venture capital arm**, Intel Capital, a while back funded a startup, Lumiata, that employs AI to develop care options and identify patients at risk.

**Kheiron Medical** built a DL software for analyzing mammograms and detecting breast cancers in them.

**Fractal analytics** has incubated Qure.ai that pays extensive attention to employing AI and DL to refine radiology and accelerate the diagnostic X-rays' analysis.

**Elon Musk** launched the surgical robot that inserts the Neuralink brainchip. Neuralink has emerged with trailblazing neuro-prosthetics that networks with a huge number of neural pathways in the mind [35]. According to the procedure, a chip, approximately the same size of a quarter, may be embedded instead as a piece of skull precisely by a surgical robot that avoids accidental injury [27].

**The Indian startup, Haptik**, lately built a Chabot functioning in WhatsApp that answers questions corresponding to the deadly coronavirus in India.

Digital consulting applications, including AliHealth Doctor You, Babylon Health's GP at Hand, Your.MD, Ada Health, and KareXpert, employ AI for clinical consultancy dependent on the patient's clinical history and basic clinical proficiency. The consumers are required to fill in their symptoms into the application that then uses speech recognition to collate against a disease database. Babylon further takes the consumer's medical history into account and presents a recommended action. Entrepreneurs in the medical industry successfully utilize seven business model archetypes in order to bring AI solutions to the market. These archetypes actively hang on to the value that is produced for the target consumer (e.g., a patient's focal point versus medical care supplier's focus) and take into careful consideration capturing components (for instance, providing data or associating partners). iFlytek set in motion a service robot "Xiao Man" that fused AI technology for identifying the consumers registered and providing customized suggestions in medical areas. It also functions in the domain of medical imaging. Companies like UBTECH (Cruzr) and

SoftBank Robotics (Pepper) are also actively working toward building similar robots. Far reaching tech companies such as Google, Amazon, Baidu, and Apple, all have dedicated research divisions in AI along with having smaller AI-based companies acquired worth millions of dollars since the field of AI is constantly evolving. Numerous automobile manufacturers are thinking in the same line and are beginning to employ ML medical care in their cars.

# References

[1]    D. Joshi, S. Anwarul and V. Mishra. Deep learning using Keras. In *Machine Learning and Deep Learning in Real-Time Applications*; 2020 (pp. 33–60). IGI Global. doi:10.4018/978-1-7998-3095-5.ch002.

[2]    I. Kononenko. Machine learning for medical diagnosis: history, state of the art and perspective. *Artificial Intelligence in Medicine*. 2001; 23(1): 89–109.

[3]    K. Raheja, A. Dubey and R. Chawda. Data analysis and its importance in health care. *International Journal of Computer Trends and Technology*. 2017; 48(4): 176–180.

[4]    A. Dhillon and A. Singh. Machine learning in healthcare data analysis: a survey. *Journal of Biology and Today's World*. 2019; 8(6): 1–10.

[5]    D. Joshi and T.P. Singh. A survey of fracture detection techniques in bone x-ray images. *Artificial Intelligence Review*. 2020; 53(6): 4475–4517.

[6]    J. Bali, R. Garg and R.T. Bali. Artificial intelligence (AI) in healthcare and biomedical research: why a strong computational/AI bioethics framework is required? *Indian Journal of Ophthalmology*. 2019; 67(1): 3.

[7]    J. Powles and H. Hodson. Google DeepMind and healthcare in an age of algorithms. *Health and Technology*. 2017; 7(4): 351–367.

[8]    V. Khullar. *White Paper on Data Protection Framework for India* [Internet]. Prsindia.org; 2018. [cited 2018 August 25]. Available from: http://www.prsindia.org/uploads/media/Report.

[9]    J. Krause, V. Gulshan, E. Rahimy, *et al.* Grader variability and the importance of reference standards for evaluating machine learning models for diabetic retinopathy. *Ophthalmology*. 2018; 125(8): 1264–1272.

[10]    HIT Infrastructure. *Unstructured Healthcare Data Needs Advanced Machine Learning Tools*; 2018. [online] Available at: https://hitinfrastructure.com/news/unstructured-healthcare-data-needs-advanced-machine-learning-tools [Accessed 23 March 2021].

[11]    HealthSnap, Inc. *Challenges and Opportunities of Structured and Unstructured Health Data | HealthSnap INC*; 2018. [online] Available at: https://healthsnap.io/structured-unstructured-health-data/ [Accessed 23 March 2021].

[12]    F. Jiang, Y. Jiang, H. Zhi, *et al.* Artificial intelligence in healthcare: past, present and future. *Stroke and Vascular Neurology*. 2017; 2(4).

[13]    I. Goodfellow, Y. Bengio and A. Courville. *Deep learning*. First Edition. Cambridge, MA: The MIT Press; 2016.

[14] C.D. Manning and H. Schütze. *Foundations of Statistical Natural Language Processing.* Cambridge, MA: MIT Press, 1999.

[15] M. Fiszman, W.W. Chapman, D. Aronsky, *et al.* Automatic detection of acute bacterial pneumonia from chest X-ray reports. *Journal of the American Medical Informatics Association.* 2000; 7: 593–604.

[16] T.P. Miller, Y. Li, K.D. Getz, *et al.* Using electronic medical record data to report laboratory adverse events. *British Journal of Haematology.* 2017; 177: 283–286.

[17] V.M. Castro, D. Dligach, S. Finan, *et al.* Large-scale identification of patients with cerebral aneurysms using natural language processing. *Neurology.* 2017; 88: 164–168.

[18] F. Amato, A. López, E.M. Peña-Méndez, P. Vaňhara, A. Hampl and J. Havel. Artificial neural networks in medical diagnosis. *Journal of Applied Biomedicine.* 2013; 11(2): 47–58.

[19] S.E. Dilsizian and E.L. Siegel. Artificial intelligence in medicine and cardiac imaging: harnessing big data and advanced computing to provide personalized medical diagnosis and treatment. *Current Cardiology Reports.* 2014; 16(1): 441.

[20] C.C. Bennett and K. Hauser. Artificial intelligence framework for simulating clinical decision-making: a Markov decision process approach. *Artificial Intelligence in Medicine.* 2013; 57(1): 9–19.

[21] J. Shiraishi, Q. Li, D. Appelbaum and K. Doi. Computer-aided diagnosis and artificial intelligence in clinical imaging. *Seminars in Nuclear Medicine.* 2011; 41(6): 449–462.

[22] D.D. Luxton. Artificial intelligence in psychological practice: current and future applications and implications. *Professional Psychology: Research and Practice.* 2014; 45(5): 332–339.

[23] S.P. Somashekhar, R. Kumarc, A. Rauthan, *et al.* Abstract S6-07: double blinded validation study to assess performance of IBM artificial intelligence platform, Watson for oncology in comparison with Manipal multi-disciplinary tumour board? First study of 638 breast Cancer cases. *Cancer Research.* 2017; 77(4 Suppl): S6-07.

[24] A. Esteva, B. Kuprel, R.A. Novoa, *et al.* Dermatologist-level classification of skin Cancer with deep neural networks. *Nature.* 2017; 542: 115–118. doi: 10.1038/nature21056.

[25] C.E. Bouton, A. Shaikhouni, N.V. Annetta, *et al.* Restoring cortical control of functional movement in a human with quadriplegia. *Nature.* 2016; 533: 247–250.

[26] D. Farina, I. Vujaklija, M. Sartori, *et al.* Man/machine interface based on the discharge timings of spinal motor neurons after targeted muscle reinnervation. *Nature Biomedical Engineering.* 2017; 1: 0025. doi: 10.1038/s41551-016-0025.

[27] K.-F. Lee *AI Superpowers: China, Silicon Valley, and the New World Order.* Boston, MA and New York: Houghton Mifflin; 2018.

[28] B. Marr . "How Is AI Used in Healthcare: 5 Powerful Real-World Examples That Show the Latest Advances". Forbes, July 27, 2018. Available at: https://

www.forbes.com/sites/bernardmarr/2018/07/27/how-is-ai-used-in-healthcare-5-powerful-real-world-examples-that-show-the-latest-advances/#610224b95dfb. [Accessed 25 March 2021].

[29]    B. Kalis, M. Collier and R. Fu. 10 pPromising AI Applications in Health Care. Harvard Business Review 2018. Available at: https://hbr.org/2018/05/10-promising-ai-applications-in-health-care. [Accessed January 10, 2021].

[30]    S. Singhal and S. Carlton. *The era of exponential Improvement in healthcare?* McKinsey & Company; 2019.

[31]    J.K. Kulski. Next-generation sequencing –an overview of the history, tools, and "omic" applications. In: *Next Generation Sequencing-Advances, Applications and Challenges*. London: Intech; 2016.

[32]    J.P. Hughes, S. Rees, S.B. Kalindjian and K.L. Philpott. Principles of early drug discovery. *British Journal of Pharmacology*. 2011; 162(6): 1239–1249.

[33]    L. Zhang, J. Tan, D. Han and H. Zhu. From machine learning to deep learning: progress in machine intelligence for rational drug discovery. *Drug Discovery Today*. 2017; 22(11): 1680–1685.

[34]    M. Rangaiah. *Artificial Intelligence in Healthcare: Applications and Threats | Analytics Steps*; 2020. [online] Analyticssteps.com. Available at: https://www.analyticssteps.com/blogs/artificial-intelligence-healthcare-applications-and-threats [Accessed 25 March 2021].

[35]    A.N. Pisarchik, V.A. Maksimenko and A.E. Hramov. From novel technology to novel applications: Comment on "An integrated brain-machine interface platform with thousands of channels" by Elon Musk and Neuralink. *Journal of Medical Internet Research*. 2019; 21(10): e16356.

[36]    G. Litjens, T. Kooi, B.E. Bejnordi, *et al.* A survey on deep learning in medical image analysis. *Medical Image Analysis*. 2017; 42, 60–88. doi:10.1016/j.media.2017.07.005.

[37]    Scnsoft.com. *The State of the Art in Health Data Analytics*; 2017. [online] Available at: https://www.scnsoft.com/blog/health-data-analytics-overview [Accessed 26 March 2021].

[38]    V. Fortunati. *Deep Learning Radiology: The Secret of Convolutional Neural Networks*; 2020. [online] Quantib.com. Available at: https://www.quantib.com/blog/convolutional-neural-networks-in-deep-learning-radiology [Accessed 25 March 2021].

[39]    B. Kalis, M. Collier and R. Fu. *10 Promising AI Applications in Health Care*; 2018. Retrieved 5 April 2021, from https://hbr.org/2018/05/10-promising-ai-applications-in-health-care.

*Chapter 6*

# Blockchain in IoT healthcare: case study

*Kripa Elsa Saji[1], Nisha Aniyan[1], Renisha P. Salim[1], Pramod Mathew Jacob[1], Shyno Sara Sam[1], Kiran Victor[1] and Remya Prasannan[1]*

Health sector is one of the most important industries in the world. With the recent advent in the number of diseases, health is becoming the primary concern for each individual. But with their busy schedules, they do not find enough time to act on this concern. In this chapter, a health monitoring system has been proposed to sense the vital body parameters and to store and share them in a secure environment. The vital body parameters are sensed from the patient using sensors. The sensed data is then stored into blockchain. The stored data can be accessed by the patient and doctors using a web application. When a doctor needs to access the information about a patient from another doctor, they only need to transfer the patient ID between themselves to access the data.

## 6.1 Overview

Due to the recent advent in the number and kind of diseases, health has become the primary concern for all humans. With the changing climate, sedentary lifestyle, and other factors affecting the environment, diseases are finding a way to get in people's life stealthily. So, it is necessary to have a system that will be able to help people out of this conflict. It is necessary to have a system that will help people out of this predicament.

IoT or Internet of Things is a system of sensors and software used in the collection and transfer data over a wireless network without any human communication. The sensors are used to collect data or information from an environment. The sensed data are stored in a database via Wi-Fi, Bluetooth, Ethernet, etc. This data is processed and depending on it, needed steps are taken.

Blockchain is a distributed ledger platform used to store transactions (blocks) in a database (chain). The information stored in the blockchain is immutable. Blockchain

[1]Department of Computer Science and Engineering, Providence College of Engineering, Chengannur, APJ Abdul Kalam Technological University, India

employs a peer-to-peer network that allows the transactions to imply at most two parties (sender and receiver). It is a decentralized network so there is no chance to interact with this directly through a third party. The data is securely stored crypto-graphically. These technologies are getting implemented in many sectors for provid-ing a secure environment, data protection, sensing data easily, etc. In this proposed model, these technologies were incorporated to sense, monitor, store, and share health parameters.

In the existing system, patients' data is stored in electronic health record (EHR) and electronic medical records systems. These systems are used to share the medical information of the patient with health-care providers and organizations. The various challenges faced by the user in this scenario are listed next:

- The users do not have access to their records stored in EHRs.
- When consulting another doctor, there is an overhead of paper-based medical records.
- Paper-based records do not provide security, confidentiality, and integrity.
- The medical records in EHRs are not secure from third-party intrusion.

The proposed system addresses these challenges using IoT, blockchain, and a web application. The model aims to provide secure storage along with monitoring and sharing of vital body parameters.

## 6.2    Existing models to secure IoT healthcare

There are various EHR systems available based on various technologies. Most of them focus on providing a secure and efficient way of medical information storage using blockchain or cloud-based architectures. Here we discuss the summary of some relevant systems available for securing IoT healthcare.

Kulkarni and Bakal [1] proposed a system to sense the body condition of humans and then sent it to the medical experts. This medical team reviewed the critical parameters that have been sensed and took further necessary action.

Kalaiselvi [2] proposed a system that is a network of connected Internet-enabled devices that communicate with each other to take care of health using remote sensors. This system does work without the assistance of human-to-human or human-to-machine contact, this system can transmit data over a network. This information is sent to the mobile applications.

Yeotkar and Gaikwad [3] proposed a model that is a remote monitoring tech-nique which the person can be monitored wirelessly in his location using wearable sensor arrangement by using accelerometer, temperature sensor, pulse oximeter and heart-rate sensor, and galvanic skin response sensor to monitor physiological human body.

Ved *et al.* [4] proposed a cloud-based personal health record system aiming for an authorized user to access and review the patient's records from any location. It is a web application that works on the J2EE platform, deployed on Amazon EC2 and runs on Microsoft SQL Server 2005. The user interface is divided into role-based modules and for message passing and maintenance. The database layer includes the DCM4CHE server and SQL server. For establishing security, password-protected access is provided to all the users.

Joshi *et al.* [5] proposed a model for the health records to be accessed in a delegated and secured manner using attribute-based encryption (ABE) for the management of access and data security in cloud-based EHRs. The EHR manager application is a web application that is developed, using Python, based on the fundamentals of the model-view-controller architecture and is open-source. The system consists of access broker (for authentication), EHR ontology (stores encrypted data), ABE, and cloud service provider modules (for hosting EHR ontology).

Yang *et al.* [6] proposed a system to solve security problems and improve storage efficiency. Cloud storage and blockchain technology are used to guarantee the storage efficiency of electronic health records. ABE is used to assure the fine-grained access control of the data in EHR which is part of security. The experimental results showed the time for encryption and search to be independent to the number of attributes.

Adlam and Haskins [7] proposed blockchain technological know-how has been evolving and ought to perchance enhance the modern-day EHRs infrastructure. It is suggested that EHRs often employ a role-based get entry to manipulate the model. Permissioned blockchain technological know-how may want to enhance the authorization model by influencing clever contracts and attribute-based get entry to control. Hyperledger Fabric has been recognized as a permissioned blockchain technological know-how ideal closer to use-cases that require privacy.

Mahore *et al.* [8] proposed a model based on cloud and blockchain which provides privacy and health-care data for statistical analysis to the researchers at the same time. The model uses permissioned blockchain where the keys, certificates, and all the participating entities are managed by the membership service provider. When a patient visits a hospital, a cloud-based record is created and the metadata is stored on the blockchain from which the researchers can obtain data. The patient has complete control over his records, divided into sensitive and nonsensitive, and has two key pairs for each. The sensitive data holding the information that can disclose the patient's identity is encrypted using public key, while the nonsensitive data that holds the diagnosis data is encrypted using public key and stored on the cloud.

Ahmed *et al.* [9] proposed a distributed digital network system that acts as a public ledger and uses bitcoin to operate money services, security services, IoT, and various Internet applications. This system keeps the secure history of the complete data for certain things. It has been explained as the shedding light of blockchain, some of the typical algorithms used in the various blockchain, and scalability issues.

Tanwar *et al.* [10] proposed a technology to strengthen virtualization by implementing personalized healthcare in real-time using blockchain technology. The blockchain can improve healthcare by using various solutions for eliminating the prevailing limitations in health-care systems which includes tools and frameworks to determine the effectiveness of the system such as Docker container, composer, Hyperledger Fabric, Wireshark capture engine, and Hyperledger Caliper.

Ramachandran *et al.* [11] proposed a blockchain technology that allowed the balancing aspects of EHRs. Moreover, this technology assures the transactions perform on EHRs are clear and restricted to make unauthorized changes. This model aims to review the current blockchain-based pattern for the management of EHRs and assess the scope of blockchain in the future.

Mary Subaja *et al.* [12] proposed blockchain technology know-how as a disbursed method to provide safety in having access to the clinical record of a patient. It includes three phases that are authentication, encryption, and data retrieval the usage of blockchain technology. To withstand frequent attacks, quantum cryptography, Advanced Encryption Standard, and secure hash algorithm algorithms are used for authentication, encryption, and data retrieval, respectively. The proposed model guarantees the safety of patient and trustworthiness and security of the health care system.

Liu *et al.* [13] proposed a scheme for the safety and sharing of clinical facts based on the hospital's blockchain to enhance the digital fitness device of the hospital. The scheme can fulfill a variety of protection residences such as decentralization, openness, and tamper resistance. A reliable mechanism is created for the medical doctors to save clinical facts or get right of entry to the historic facts of sufferers while meeting privateness preservation. Furthermore, a symptom-matching mechanism is given between patients. Proxy re-encryption technological know-how is used to assist the docs to access historical documents of patients.

Radhakrishnan *et al.* [14] proposed a system that used a multilevel authentication-based scheme to protect the blockchain from attacks and add one more layer of security. If attackers change any data in the electronic health record, it can prove to be fatal to the patients as it can result in wrong medication or surgery. Blockchain plays a decisive role in securing data and transactions. The challenge in this solution is scalability as the blockchain-based EHR system needs large storage for storing data.

Nuetey Nortey *et al.* [15] proposed a system used for the preservation of privacy during collecting, managing, and distributing EHR data. The system ensures complete privacy, access control, and integrity of distributed EHRs to the data owners during its dispersion on the blockchain. The proposed system integrates blockchain system to achieve interoperability and data sharing with appropriate Application Programming Interfaces (APIs) with the use of its underlying technology. Record validation in the system is done using modern cryptographic techniques. The Hyperledger Fabric, a permissioned private blockchain having its own characteristics and parameters, is used for implementation. But it provides the facility for the creation of a private blockchain for research and testing purposes.

Huang *et al.* [16] proposed MedBloc which is a blockchain-based impervious EHR device that permits patients and health-care carriers to get entry to and distribute fitness records in a privacy-preserving manner. MedBloc represents a longitudinal view of the patient's fitness history and permits patients to supply or withdraw consent for managing rights of entry to their records. MedBloc is a tightly closed EHR system that leverages blockchain technology. MedBloc protects patients' privacy by using the state-of-the-art encryption scheme.

Kim *et al.* [17] proposed a patient-centric medicinal drug history recording gadget with the use of blockchain, which captures QR code printed on the envelope with the aid of drug save based totally on prescription. The records are saved by using hash fee of data in blockchain and prevent the altering of the data. This machine used fast health-care interoperability resources, the worldwide fitness records exchange standard, to enhance interoperability.

Harshini *et al.* [18] suggested a patient-driven model for record maintenance and the usage of blockchain. The contracts can be integrated in future days increasing its manageability in statistics exchange. This model deploys smart contracts which executes when both the parties agree on a set of protocols. This model suggests blockchain technology as one of the potential solutions for the maintenance of health records in an efficient manner.

Mikula and Jacobsen *et al.* [19] proposed a system that aims to manage identity and access to maintain authentication and authorization using blockchain. The authentication and authorization of the users are done by the validation of transactions in the blockchain. The proposed system includes a client application (App), a database, an application server, and a server for authentication and authorization. The communication of the user and system is done using the App that, in turn, interacts with the application server to perform operations. The blockchain stores the transactions as key-value pairs, where the key contains a hash of the user's public key.

Živi *et al.* [20] described tangle as DAG (directed acyclic graph) and its advantages compared to other blockchain technologies. In tangle, each transaction (child) points to two previous transactions (parents) and approves them. A transaction can be approved multiple times in a direct or indirect way. The transactions become immutable after reaching consensus, which is attained with the help of Random Walk Monte Carlo algorithm. The tangle is consistent by using proof of work computation that is performed by every transaction. The aggregate weight of a transaction is the total number of successive transactions and the transactions that have affirmed it.

## 6.3    Blockchain to secure IoT healthcare

### 6.3.1    *Proposed system*

The proposed health monitoring system incorporates of the following three modules: sensor module, blockchain module, and the web application module. The sensors are provided with the user to sense the required vital parameters. The data sensed by the sensors will get stored into the blockchain. The web application will permit the patient and doctors to access the data. The doctors can also consult another doctor for a patient by sharing the patient ID rather than the whole data. Figure 6.1 demonstrates the block diagram of the proposed system.

#### 6.3.1.1    Sensor module

The proposed system aims to extract the vital body parameters from the user with the help of sensors. The sensors used in the system are AD8232, DS18B20, and

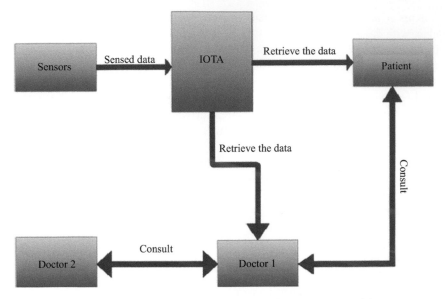

*Figure 6.1    Architecture of using blockchain in IoT healthcare*

MAX30100. The sensed parameters are read by NodeMCU. NodeMCU has inbuilt Wi-Fi with the help of which this data will be sent to the blockchain.

### 6.3.1.2    Blockchain module

IOTA (name of a consortium) technology is a distributed ledger intended for the IoT to hold up friction-less data and value transfer. The data from the server will be stored in the IOTA. A seed is created, which is a private key used to login into the IOTA wallet. Then generates an address and adds the sender address. And all transactions are directed on the IOTA node. Tangle is used for authenticating the transactions. All the data is securely stored in it. The users can access the patient data stored in IOTA using the web application.

### 6.3.1.3    Web application module

The web application will permit the user to access and view their data that is stored in IOTA. The user requests for the data stored in IOTA using IOTA tokens with the help of client libraries. The data transactions are converted into trytes and then to ASCII. This converted data will be provided to the user. The users can also share their data with other participating entities. When users share their data with the doctors, the doctors can update the data by adding their suggestions.

### 6.3.1.4    Working of proposed system

The working of the proposed system is illustrated in Figure 6.2. Sensors are used to sense the vital body parameters. The sensed data will be read using NodeMCU and stored into the blockchain (IOTA). The users can access, view, and share their data

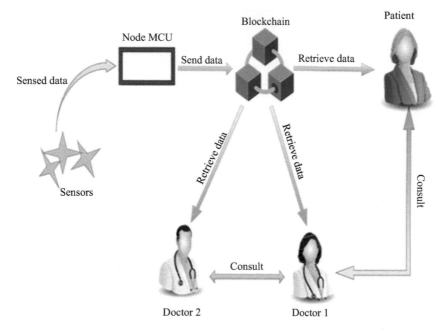

*Figure 6.2   Working of proposed blockchain system for IoT healthcare*

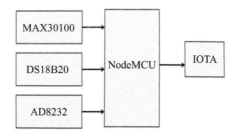

*Figure 6.3   Block diagram of sensor layer*

with other entities using the web application. The doctors can also consult another doctor by only sharing the patient ID rather than the whole medical record.

The block diagram of sensors layer is shown in Figure 6.3. The sensors used in the system for sensing the vital body parameters are MAX30100 (for pulse and saturation), DS18B20 (for temperature), and AD8232 (for ECG). The micro-controller unit NodeMCU is used to read the data that is sensed using the sensors. The data is then stored into the blockchain platform, IOTA.

In Figure 6.4, the use case diagram demonstrates the various use cases of the health monitoring system. The end users of the system will be users and doctors. The user can view the sensed data, share the data with other users (doctors), and view their updated data through the web application. The doctor can modify the

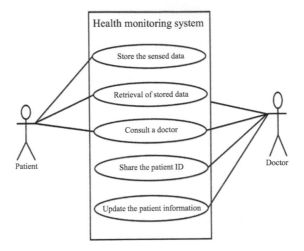

*Figure 6.4    Use case diagram of health monitoring system*

medical records of the patient. The doctor can also refer another doctor by sharing the patient ID, used for retrieving the patient's medical records.

## 6.3.2    System implementation

The system is implemented using multiple technologies both on the software front and hardware sides. On the hardware side, sensors are consolidated with the microcontroller NodeMCU and the detected data is stored into the blockchain. On the software side, a web app is developed for retrieval and sharing of the stored data.

Multiple sensory data can be read from a patient which can be useful in determining their health conditions or even some underlying health problems. These data points are read using multiple sensors that are integrated into the system. The data is then stored into IOTA—a blockchain solution—to ensure the utmost security of the patient data. The web application is then used to access this data on request. The various hardware components required are

- pulse oximeter and heart rate sensor
- ECG sensor
- temperature sensor
- NodeMCU

### 6.3.2.1    Pulse oximeter and heart rate sensor

The sensor detects the pulse rate and level of oxygen saturation of the body. It uses two LEDs (emits infrared and red lights), optimized optics, photodetector, and low-noise analog signals. For detecting pulse rate, only the infrared LED is used and for oxygen saturation level, both red and infrared LEDs are used. The libraries MAX30100_PulseOximeter and Wire are used to read the data from MAX30100 and to communicate with MAX30100 using I2C protocol, respectively. The pulse oximeter and heart rate sensor are shown in Figure 6.5 (left).

### 6.3.2.2 ECG sensor

The sensor is used to determine the electrical movement of the human heart. It amplifies, extracts, and filters the biopotential signals in noisy conditions. It includes pins to connect the ECG electrodes and an LED to indicate the rhythm of heartbeat of a human. Figure 6.5 (right) shows the ECG sensor (AD8232).

### 6.3.2.3 Temperature sensor

The sensor detects the body temperature of the human body. It is a 1-wire interface sensor that requires only one digital pin to communicate to and from the micro-controller. It includes a unique 64-bit serial code that allows multiple DS18B20s to operate on the same 1-wire bus, making it easy for one microcontroller to control multiple distributed DS18B20s. The libraries OneWire and Dallas Temperature are used to communicate with DS18B20 and to access the registers of DS18B20 for reading temperature, respectively. Temperature sensor (DS18B20) is shown in Figure 6.6 (left).

MAX30100 sensor

AD8232 sensor

*Figure 6.5 Pulse oximeter and heart rate sensor (left) and ECG sensor (right)*

Temperature sensor      NodeMCU

*Figure 6.6 Temperature sensor (left) and NodeMCU board (right)*

#### 6.3.2.4   NodeMCU

NodeMCU is an open-source IoT firmware and development kit that is designed to develop IoT-based applications. It consists of multiple digital and one analog pin. It also has an inbuilt Wi-Fi that enables to communicate the detected data with the Internet. NodeMCU is shown in Figure 6.6 (right).

The circuit diagram of the system is represented in Figure 6.7. All the sensors are integrated together to the central coordinator which is NodeMCU in this scenario.

Hardware connections of the sensor module are given next:

1.   Connect VIN pin of MAX30100 to the 3.3V pin of NodeMCU.
2.   Connect INT pin of MAX30100 to the D0 pin of NodeMCU.
3.   Connect SCL pin of MAX30100 to the D1 pin of NodeMCU.
4.   Connect SDA pin of MAX30100 to the D2 pin of NodeMCU.
5.   Connect GND pin of MAX30100 to the GND pin of NodeMCU.
6.   Connect 3.3V pin of AD8232 to the 3v3 pin of NodeMCU.
7.   Connect GND pin of AD8232 to the GND pin of NodeMCU.
8.   Connect OUTPUT pin of AD8232 to the A0 pin of NodeMCU.
9.   Connect LO− pin of AD8232 to the D5 pin of NodeMCU.
10.   Connect LO+ pin of AD8232 to the D6 pin of NodeMCU.
11.   Connect the left pin of DS18B20 to the GND pin of NodeMCU.
12.   Connect the middle pin of DS18B20 to the 3v3 pin of NodeMCU.
13.   Connect the right pin of DS18B20 to the D4 pin of NodeMCU.

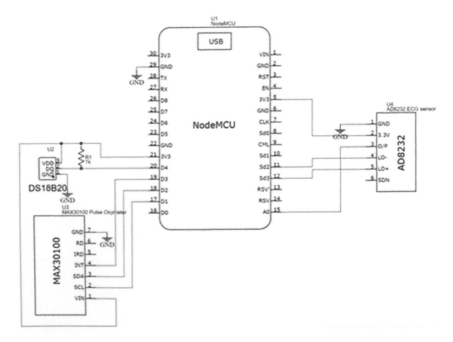

*Figure 6.7   Circuit diagram of the system*

### 6.3.2.5 IOTA

IOTA is an open, scalable distributed ledger that allows feeless transactions designed for an IoT ecosystem. It is based on tangle, a DAG. In tangle, every transaction points to two preceding transactions that are called as parents and get validated by the child transaction. Tangle grows in the direction of the paths that have the highest weights and the lightest branches never reach consensus. Figure 6.8 depicts the transactions in a tangle.

In IOTA, all the nodes issue and validate transactions, i.e., a node validates previous two transactions and then issues its own transaction. IOTA is asynchronous. A transaction takes different amount of time to reach different nodes and another node may be seeing a previous version of the tangle. The nodes always share new transactions with each other to increase their probability of getting verified and eventually reaching the consensus.

### 6.3.2.6 Masked-authenticated messaging

Masked-authenticated messaging (MAM) is an IOTA protocol-based module that permits sending and reading message flows through tangle. It allows to publish the sensor data on the IOTA tangle. Cryptography and authentication are applied to assure that the message will not be doctored and comes from an authenticated sender. MAM uses a Merkle signature scheme that provides more secure environment by resisting quantum computer attacks and short generating and verifying time period for signatures.

MAM has three modes of operation: public, private, and restricted. In public mode, root of the Merkle tree is taken as the address of a transaction. In private mode, the hash of the root is the address and in restricted mode, the address has to

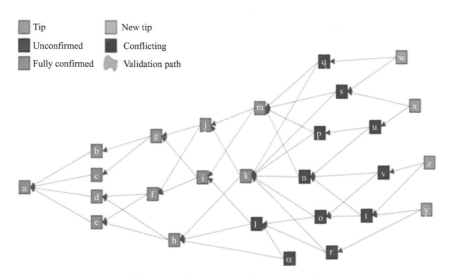

*Figure 6.8   Transactions in tangle*

be calculated from the root and search for masked messages (obtained using root and a sideKey). Figure 6.9 depicts the data stored in the public mode of MAM.

### 6.3.2.7   MongoDB

MongoDB is a document-oriented NoSQL database that is suitable for unstructured data. The data store is lightweight, easy to traverse, and allows fast execution. MongoDB Atlas is used to store the MongoDB database that is being used with the system. MongoDB Atlas is a cloud provider that lets users host their databases and related APIs. Integrating it into the system allows it to scale exponentially and also increases the availability of the system.

### 6.3.2.8   NodeJS

NodeJS is an open-source server platform based on JavaScript. It facilitates the creation of scalable and fast network applications. It provides a runtime environment and various JavaScript modules for the development of web applications. NodeJS is asynchronous (non-blocking) resulting in scalable and fast execution of code.

### 6.3.2.9   Express.js

Express.js is a web application framework based on NodeJS which provides robust APIs to build web apps and websites. Many modules are available in npm which can be plugged into Express making it flexible and pluggable. It helps to manage server and the various routes associated with it.

### 6.3.2.10   Storing the sensed data in IOTA

The health parameters are read using the sensors which is then fed into the NodeMCU. The NodeMCU sends the data to a NodeJS server which then processes

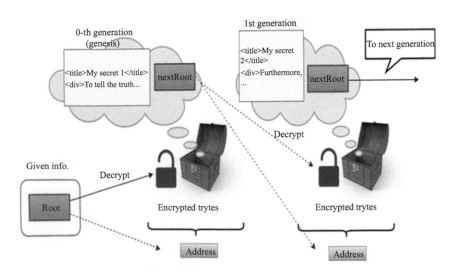

*Figure 6.9   Public mode of MAM*

the data to work with the other components in the workflow. The data is sent to the NodeJS server because the NodeMCU does not have enough power to directly write the data into the IOTA.

Express.js is used at the NodeJS server to further enhance the networking capabilities of the NodeJS server and also enable routing for the server. Express allows the processing of the incoming of the POST requests and also helps with the generation of the response and redirection of the data to other parts of the architecture. The extracted data is correlated with the base database hosted on the MongoDB Atlas, and if a match is found, the sensed data is written into the IOTA Devnet using the MAM package.

When the patient data is published for the first time, the root node will not be present in the MongoDB. In this case, the root is stored in the MongoDB and after storing the data, the latest state will be stored into a JSON file. The latest state will be an object that consists of the seed and the configurations of the state. The latest state is used to connect the transactions in the tangle. This means that all the data of a patient will be connected using the latest state. Figure 6.10 shows the data blocks stored in IOTA tangle using MAM.

### 6.3.2.11    Retrieving the data using web application

The process of retrieval of patient data is as follows. When patient ID is entered, all matching documents from MongoDB are retrieved. When the root file is fed into the mam.fetch() function, a set of callback functions is retrieved. The first callback function retrieves the data of each block and the second callback functions print all the data in the tangle. Each block of data holds the hash to access the next block. This hash can be given to the first callback function to retrieve the next block.

Using this technique, all blocks are retrieved and then stored into an array. When a block is received, the hash of the next block is taken and fed into the

*Figure 6.10   Data stored in IOTA using MAM*

*Figure 6.11    Fetching data from IOTA network using MAM*

callback function that was received. This process is done until the last block. Then the second callback function is used to display all this data. These data trytes are then converted to ASCII and then to JSON. Express.js is used to render this JSON data as a table. A user who is identified as a patient can only retrieve their own data. When a patient tries to retrieve the data by providing a patient ID, the requested ID and the patient ID are verified. If a match is found, the data is retrieved. Since this application is ran on development parameters, the public mode of MAM is used for better stability and predictability. Figure 6.11 represents fetching data from MAM explorer.

## 6.4    Conclusions

The proposed health monitoring and management system consists of a hardware module, blockchain module, and web application. The sensors incorporated with the NodeMCU detect the health data from a patient's body which can be used for determining their health conditions. The data is stored into an IOTA node with the help of a server and MAM. The patient ID is used to retrieve the stored data using the Web application. A patient can only retrieve his/her own data. After retrieving the data, the patient can consult with the doctor or a doctor can refer another doctor. When a doctor consults another doctor, the patient ID is shared using which the consulted doctor can access the patient's data. The advantages of the proposed system are as follows:

- Easier to track and analyze the vital parameters.
- Users can access their information and can use it to consult with a doctor.
- The overhead of paper-based records is eliminated.
- The process of consulting another doctor is made easier.
- More economical and optimum utilization of resources.

The future plans are to incorporate a device with more processing power in the hardware to eliminate the use of server and publish the data directly to IOTA tangle. Our next stage will try to publish the data blocks in the restricted mode of MAM and provide access control on the data stored on IOTA tangle.

# References

[1]   N. J. Kulkarni and J. W. Bakal, "Real Time Vital Body Parameter Monitoring," in *Fourth International Conference on Computing Communication Control and Automation (ICCUBEA)*, 2018.

[2]   G. Kalaiselvi, "A Comprehensive Study On Healthcare Applications using IoT, "*International Journal of Engineering Science Invention (IJESI)*, pp. 41–45, 2018.

[3]   H. S. Yeotkar and V. T. Gaikwad, "IoT Based Human Body Parameters Monitoring by Using Wearable Wireless Sensor Network," *International Research Journal of Engineering and Technology (IRJET)*, vol. 06, no. 07, pp. 2458–2466, 2019.

[4]   V. Ved, V. Tyagi, A. Agarwal, and A. S. Pandya, "Personal Health Record System and Integration Techniques With Various Electronic Medical Record Systems," in *IEEE 13th International Symposium on High-Assurance Systems Engineering*, Boca Raton, 2011.

[5]   M. Joshi, K. Joshi, and T. Finin, "Attribute Based Encryption for Secure Access to Cloud Based EHR Systems," in *IEEE 11th International Conference on Cloud Computing*, 2018.

[6]   X. Yang, T. Li, R. Liu, and M. Wang, "Blockchain-Based Secure and Searchable EHR Sharing Scheme," in *2019 4th International Conference on Mechanical, Control and Computer Engineering (ICMCCE)*, Hohhot, China, 2019.

[7]   R. Adlam and B. Haskins, "A Permissioned Blockchain Approach to the Authorization Process in Electronic Health Records," in *2019 International Multidisciplinary Information Technology and Engineering Conference (IMITEC)*, Vanderbijlpark, South Africa, 2019.

[8]   V. Mahore, P. Aggarwal, N. Andola, Raghav, and S. Venkatesan, "Secure and Privacy Focused Electronic Health Record Management System using Permissioned Blockchain," in *2019 IEEE Conference on Information and Communication Technology*, Allahabad, India, 2019.

[9]   I. Ahmed, Shilpi, and M. Amjad, "Blockchain Technology A Literature Survey," *International Research Journal of Engineering and Technology (IRJET)*, vol. 5, no. 10, 2018.

[10]  S. Tanwara, K. Parekha, and R. Evans, "Blockchain-Based Electronic Healthcare Record System for Healthcare Applications," *Journal of Information Security and Applications*, 2019.

[11]  S. Ramachandran, O. Obu Kiruthika, A. Ramasamy, R. Vanaja, and S. Mukherjee, "A Review on Blockchain-Based Strategies for Management of

Electronic Health Records (EHRs)," in *2020 International Conference on Smart Electronics and Communication (ICOSEC)*, Trichy, India, 2020.

[12]  C. Mary Subaja, M. A. Anigo, S. G. Partha, C. Priyanka, and M. Raj Kumari, "An Efficient Data Security in Medical Report using Block Chain Technology," in *2019 International Conference on Communication and Signal Processing (ICCSP)*, Chennai, India, 2019.

[13]  X. Liu, Z. Wang, C. Jin, F. Li, and G. Li, "A Blockchain-Based Medical Data Sharing and Protection Scheme," *IEEE Access*, vol. 7, pp. 118943–118953, 2019.

[14]  B. L. Radhakrishnan, A. Sam Joseph, and S. Sudhakar, "Securing Blockchain based Electronic Health Record using Multilevel Authentication," in *2019 5th International Conference on Advanced Computing & Communication Systems (ICACCS)*, Coimbatore, India, 2019.

[15]  R. Nuetey Nortey, L. Yue, P. Ricardo Agdedanu, and M. Adjeisah, "Privacy Module for Distributed Electronic Health Records (EHRs) Using the Blockchain," in *2019 IEEE 4th International Conference on Big Data Analytics (ICBDA)*, Suzhou, China, 2019.

[16]  J. Huang, Y. Wei Qi, M. Rizwan Asghar, A. Meads, and Y-C. Tu, "MedBloc: A Blockchain-Based Secure EHR System for Sharing and Accessing Medical Data," in *2019 18th IEEE International Conference On Trust, Security And Privacy In Computing And Communications/13th IEEE International Conference On Big Data Science And Engineering (TrustCom/BigDataSE)*, Rotorua, New Zealand, 2019.

[17]  J. W. Kim, A. R. Lee, M. G. Kim, I. K. Kim, and E. J. Lee, "Patient-Centric Medication History Recording System Using Blockchain," in *2019 IEEE International Conference on Bioinformatics and Biomedicine (BIBM)*, San Diego, CA, USA, 2019.

[18]  V. M. Harshini, S. Danai, H. R. Usha, and M. R. Kounte, "Health Record Management through Blockchain Technology," in *2019 3rd International Conference on Trends in Electronics and Informatics (ICOEI)*, Tirunelveli, India, 2019.

[19]  T. Mikula and R. H. Jacobsen, "Identity and Access Management with Blockchain in Electronic Healthcare Records," in *2018 21st Euromicro Conference on Digital System Design (DSD)*, Prague, 2018.

[20]  N. Živi, E. Kadušić, and K. Kadušić, "Directed Acyclic Graph as Tangle: An IoT Alternative to Blockchains," in *2019 27th Telecommunications Forum (TELFOR)*, Belgrade, Serbia, 2019.

*Chapter 7*

# Adaptive dictionary-based fusion of multi-modal images for health care applications

*Aishwarya Nagasubramanian[1], Chandrasekaran Bennila Thangammal[2] and Vasantha Pragasam Gladis Pushparathi[3]*

## 7.1 Introduction

Medical imaging has made significant advances in a variety of health-care uses in recent years, including research, diagnosis, and education. Various imaging modalities such as computed tomography (CT), magnetic resonance imaging (T1-MRI and T2-MRI), positron emission tomography (PET), and single-photon emission-computed tomography (SPECT) are used to provide more clinical data to medical practitioners, which reflects different information about the human body [1,2]. However, due to technical limitations, a single modality image cannot give enough information to meet specialists' clinical needs. Combining information from different modalities (CT-MRI, PET-MRI, SPECT-MRI, etc.) into a single image, which better identifies the region of interest and enhances diagnostic accuracy, is an effective way to overcome this problem. Despite the fact that there are numerous algorithms to conduct this operation [3,4], dictionary-based sparse representation (SR) techniques have grown in popularity in the field of image fusion. The first is a fixed dictionary that has been built using analytical models such as the discrete cosine transform (DCT), wavelet, etc. The second is a learned dictionary made from high-quality natural images. In image fusion, Yang and Li [5] were the first to introduce sparse representation. For multi-focus image fusion, they used a redundant DCT dictionary. Aharon *et al.* [6], on the other hand, demonstrated that an adaptive dictionary learned from input visuals beats a fixed dictionary. As a result, Yu *et al.* [7] suggest a fusion

[1]Department of Electronics and Communication Engineering, Amrita School of Engineering, Amrita Vishwa Vidyapeetham, Chennai, India
[2]Department of Electronics and Communication Engineering, R.M.D. Engineering College Kavaraipettai, Chennai, India
[3]Department of Computer Science and Engineering, Velammal Institute of Technology Panchetti, Chennai, India

strategy based on a joint sparsity model. The dictionary is trained by simply adding all of the source image patches, which takes a long time and renders the dictionary ineffective. For simultaneous fusion and denoising of multimodal pictures, Yin and Li [8] used a joint sparsity model. The experimental findings were adequate, although the proposed method's performance is significantly reliant on external data. For sparse coefficient estimation, Yang and Li [9] introduced the simultaneous orthogonal matching pursuit algorithm (OMP). The proposed method is tested on a variety of image types, and the dictionary used in this method is very sensitive on the input image. Wang *et al.* [10] combined non-subsampled contourlet transform (NSCT) with SR to perform image fusion. A major benefit of this strategy is that it produces comparable experimental findings with less computing time.

From the focus information map of multi-focus images, Nejati *et al.* [11] suggested a global dictionary learning approach. The dictionary input training data is created by randomly selecting an arbitrary number of patches, which may or may not result in a highly organized dictionary. Liu *et al.* [12] used multi-scale transforms (MSTs) and SR to offer an image fusion framework. For the dictionary learning process, a collection of 40 high-quality natural pictures is used. The same author later suggested an adaptive sparse representation (ASR) model for image fusion and denoising at the same time. The histogram of gradients is used to learn six compact sub-dictionaries. The disadvantage of this approach is that it has a higher computational cost. Kim *et al.* [13] suggested a dictionary learning strategy based on *K*-means clustering and principal component analysis to lower the computational cost of SR-based fusion approaches. The learnt dictionary is compact and informative, but with this method, the number of clusters must be preset.

As a result, existing SR-based fusion solutions either share a preconstructed vocabulary that requires previous knowledge of the external pre-collected data or utilize a learnt dictionary that requires prior knowledge of the external pre-collected data. The global dictionaries provided by Aishwarya and Bennila Thangammal [14] have been shown to have greater representation ability than existing SR-based approaches; nonetheless, there are still several key difficulties that need to be addressed. To begin, previous knowledge of the external data sets is required for the creation of the initial training samples. In reality, collecting appropriate training samples may not be achievable. Furthermore, the fusion performance is highly dependent on the original training data set's construction. Second, global dictionaries are built using the inherent structures of high-resolution images. As a result, dictionaries of this sort are more suited to single-sensor image fusion, such as multi-focus image fusion. Learning a dictionary adaptive to the relevant source images, on the other hand, can be more efficient in representing the complex, intrinsic structures of multi-sensor or multimodal fusion applications. As a result of these techniques, the need for a discriminative over-complete dictionary that reflects the complicated structures of given images has arisen.

The design of the dictionary, activity-level measurement of sparse coefficients, and the design of the optimum fusion rule are the significant elements that determine the ultimate fusion quality of SR-based techniques. Most SR-based fusion algorithms have focused on the former element so far, while the latter part has not been adequately addressed. Due to the aforementioned difficulties, this chapte proposes a multimodal medical fusion method based on adaptive dictionary learning. Because the adaptive dictionary is trained based on the modified spatial frequency (MSF) indicator and used for the fusion of medical images, the suggested method is called MIFMSF.

## 7.2   Learning a dictionary

The main goal of this work is to create a comprehensive and compact over-complete dictionary in order to improve fusion performance. An informative sampling strategy based on MSF is proposed to generate such a dictionary. Figure 7.1 depicts the detailed dictionary learning process. Assume the source images $I_A$ and $I_B$ are registered with size $N \times N$. To begin, each source image $I_A$ and $I_B$ is divided into image patches of size $n \times n$ using the sliding window approach. Let the patches be denoted by $P = \{p_c^t\}_{t=1}^{T}, c \in \{A, B\}$. Generally, only a significant percentage of medical image patches contain clinically valuable information. Using all of the image patches from the source images makes the dictionary very redundant and has a significant impact on the fusion result. The computing time is also increased as a result of this learning process. In order to address the aforementioned difficulties, only informative patches with higher structural information are chosen for dictionary learning.

First, any patch $p_c^t$ with an intensity variance of less than five $\left(\text{var}(p_c^t) < 5\right)$ will be eliminated. This preprocessing step removes all the meaningless patches of source images. The source image patches obtained after the preprocessing phase are denoted by $P_A = \{\overline{p}_A^j\}_{j=1}^{N_1}$ and $P_B = \{\overline{p}_B^k\}_{k=1}^{N_2}$. Training a dictionary with informative patches is widely known for allowing richer data representation than typical preconstructed dictionaries. The structural information of patches is

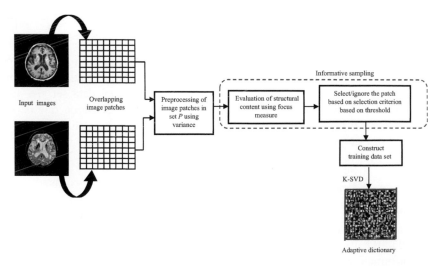

*Figure 7.1   Overall framework of proposed dictionary learning approach*

weighed using MSF to select such informative patches. *MSF* [15] is a useful metric for determining an image's overall edge strength in gradient directions. The *MSF* of an image $I$ with size $M_1 \times M_2$ is calculated as follows:

$$MSF = \sqrt{RF^2 + CF^2 + SDF^2 + MDF^2} \tag{7.1}$$

where *RF* and *CF* are the row and the column frequency which is given by

$$RF = \sqrt{\frac{1}{M_1 M_2} \sum_{x=1}^{M_1} \sum_{y=2}^{M_2} [I(x,y) - I(x,y-1)]^2} \tag{7.2}$$

$$CF = \sqrt{\frac{1}{M_1 M_2} \sum_{x=2}^{M_1} \sum_{y=1}^{M_2} [I(x,y) - I(x-1,y)]^2} \tag{7.3}$$

and frequencies along the main diagonal and secondary diagonal are given by

$$SDF = \sqrt{\frac{1}{M_1 M_2} \sum_{x=2}^{M_1} \sum_{y=1}^{M_2-1} [I(x,y) - I(x-1,y+1)]^2} \tag{7.4}$$

$$MDF = \sqrt{\frac{1}{M_1 M_2} \sum_{x=2}^{M_1} \sum_{y=2}^{M_2} [I(x,y) - I(x-1,y-1)]^2} \tag{7.5}$$

Equation (7.1) is used to calculate the edge strength of each patch in $P_A$ and $P_B$, which is indicated as $MSF_A = \{MSF_A^j\}_{j=1}^{N_1}$ and $MSF_B = \{MSF_B^k\}_{k=1}^{N_2}$. In (7.6), a cutoff threshold $T_c$, $c \in A, B$, is chosen to improve the efficiency of the dictionary learning process:

$$T_c = 0.1 \times \max(MSF_c), \quad c \in A, B \tag{7.6}$$

The threshold value is set low enough that both low- and high-frequency patches are selected for training with minimal redundancy. For the dictionary learning process, let $TD$, $\{TD_l | l = 1, 2, 3, \ldots, L\}$ indicate the training data set. To determine whether the patch contains enough spatial features, a selection rule is used. This is accomplished by comparing $MSF_A$ and $MSF_B$ of each patch in $P_A$ and $P_B$ with $T_c$. For example, if $MSF_A^j > T_A$, select $\vec{p}_A^j$. Otherwise ignore $\vec{p}_A^j$:

$$TD_l = \begin{cases} \text{Select } \vec{p}_A^j, & \text{if } MSF_A^j > T_A \\ \text{Ignore } \vec{p}_A^j, & \text{otherwise.} \end{cases} \tag{7.7}$$

According to the previous criteria, the patch with fine details and superior visual clarity is used in the dictionary learning process. This procedure is repeated until all of the useful patches in $P_A$ and $P_B$ have been retrieved. The mean value of each informative patch in the training data set is subtracted from zero before the dictionary learning process to guarantee that only the edge structures of the patches are included for training. Finally, the K-SVD method iterates between the sparse coding step and the dictionary update step D to learn an adaptive dictionary D.

## 7.3 Experimental setup and analysis

The size of the image patch used to create the training data is set to $8 \times 8$. The K-SVD algorithm is used to learn an adaptive dictionary with a size of 400 words and 50 iterations. Let us say each source image is having the size of $256 \times 256$. There will be 124,002 input patches for dictionary learning if the patch size is $8 \times 8$ and the step length is set to 1 pixel. According to the proposed method, the training data set TD contains about 40,000 patches, or about 32% of the total source image patches. Obtaining an adaptable dictionary takes around 1,500 s. As a result, processing time is reduced and memory utilization is optimized. Furthermore, the dictionary's redundant information is eliminated to a greater extent.

## 7.4 Overview of fusion scheme

Figure 7.2 shows a schematic diagram of the MIFMSF fusion scheme. The basic flow is comparable to standard SR-based fusion approaches, with the exception of sparse coefficient fusion. The input medical images are separated into overlapping image patches and lexicographically ordered into column vectors denoted by

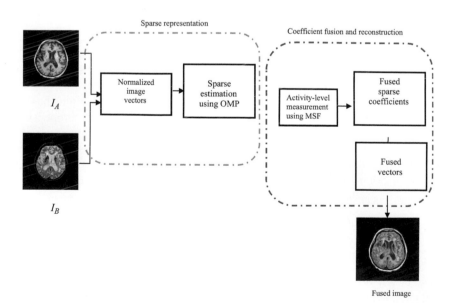

*Figure 7.2   Overview of MIFMSF fusion scheme*

$V_A = \{v_A^t\}_{t=1}^T$ and $V_B = \{v_B^t\}_{t=1}^T$. Before sparse coding, the DC component (mean value) of each patch is normalized to zero.

For sparse coefficient estimation, the batch-OMP technique is used to improve computing efficiency. In the fusion of sparse coefficients, there are two major challenges to consider. The first issue focuses on determining the activity level of source images, which aids in identifying their different features. The second issue focuses on the integration of sparse coefficients into fused image counterparts.

The former challenge is overcome in traditional SR-based fusion algorithms by using the L1-norm, which describes the detail information contained in the sparse vectors. The higher the value, the more energy the related image patch has. However, this metric ignores the image patch's spatial details, which are critical for preserving the source images' original visual clarity. Because SR is an approximation approach, measuring activity levels with a single measurement may not be possible. Due to the aforementioned issue, it has been suggested that the activity level of picture patches be measured in both the spatial and transform domains. MSF, as mentioned in the preceding section, describes the spatial features that an image contains. The higher the value, the more information it contains. The information from L1-norm and MSF is combined for each source image patch using scalar multiplication. The sparse coefficients of the $t$th patch in $I_A$ and $I_B$ are given by $\alpha_A^t$ and $\alpha_B^t$. The notion $\|\bullet\|_1$ denotes the L1-norm of sparse vectors and $MSF_A^t$ and $MSF_B^t$ are the corresponding MSFs. The proposed activity level measurement is calculated by

$$w_A^t = \|\alpha_A^t\|_1 \times MSF_A^t \tag{7.8}$$

$$w_B^t = \|\alpha_B^t\|_1 \times MSF_B^t \tag{7.9}$$

where $w_A^t$ and $w_B^t$ are the measurement results for the $t$th patch of source images $I_A$ and $I_B$.

Existing SR-based fusion approaches solve the latter issue by employing either a weighted average fusion rule or a maximum absolute (max-abs) rule. The first rule combines the input sparse vectors with certain user-defined weights based on the activity level to produce fused coefficients. This rule has the propensity to reduce the contrast of the fused image while suppressing the original texture of the input images. The other criterion chooses the sparse vector with the highest absolute value, allowing the fused image to capture the most important aspects of the source images. In general, a fusion rule should be designed to absorb all of the significant visual information from the input images into the fused image. In this chapter, the maximum weighted activity level is chosen as the fusion rule based on the aforementioned parameters. The proposed fusion rule is defined as follows:

$$\alpha_F^t = \begin{cases} \alpha_A^t, & \text{if } w_A^t > w_B^t \\ \alpha_B^t, & \text{otherwise} \end{cases} \tag{7.10}$$

The fusion coefficients are formed by selecting the sparse vector having maximum activity level both in spatial domain and transform domain. The fused vector for the $t$th patch is obtained as

$$v_F^t = D\alpha_F^t + m_F^t.1 \tag{7.11}$$

where the fused mean value of $t$th vector $m_F^t$ is given by

$$m_F^t = \begin{cases} m_A^t, & \text{if } \alpha_F^t = \alpha_A^t \\ m_B^t, & \text{otherwise} \end{cases} \tag{7.12}$$

## 7.5 Simulation results and discussion

Figure 7.3 shows five standard multimodal medical data sets that are used to evaluate the performance of the proposed MIFMSF fusion scheme. These data sets are divided into two categories. CT and MRI picture pairs make up the first group (image data sets 1, 2, and 3), while T1-weighted MRI (MR-T1) and T2-weighted MRI (MR-T2) image pairs make up the second group (image data sets 4 and 5). The photos are all the same size.

### 7.5.1 Results on standard multimodal medical data sets

Some recent SR-based methods, such as MST-based sparse representation (MST-SR) ASR model, and other state-of-the-art methods, such as NSCT proposed by Zhang and Guo [16], multilevel local extrema proposed by Hu [17], and guided filtering (GFF) based on guided filtering proposed by Li *et al.* [2], are compared to show the potency of the MIFMSF method.

Figure 7.4 shows the fusion findings of a CT and MRI image pair for subjective evaluation. The bone structure is visible in the CT picture without any loss of information. An MRI scan depicts the internal organs and soft tissues in great detail.

The MIFMSF approach, as shown in Figure 7.4, retains the complimentary information of source pictures with the best esthetic appearance and the fewest

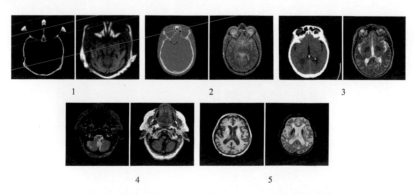

*Figure 7.3   Medical image data sets: 1–3—CT and MRI images; 4 and 5—MR-T1 and MR-T2 images*

artifacts. The NSCT method's fusion result in Figure 7.4(c) loses a lot of image features and has a contrast reduction problem. Figure 7.4(d) shows the blocking artifacts in the fusion outcome of multilevel local extrema. The outputs of GFF and MST-SR fusion are more visible; however, they do not maintain certain local information from the original images. Figure 7.4 shows that the fusion results of the ASR method and the MIFMSF approach cannot be separated easily. As illustrated in Figure 7.5, a particular portion of source pictures is expanded. Figure 7.5(c) shows that the NSCT approach has lost the edge and texture information of the original images, resulting in low contrast. The multilevel local extrema method has

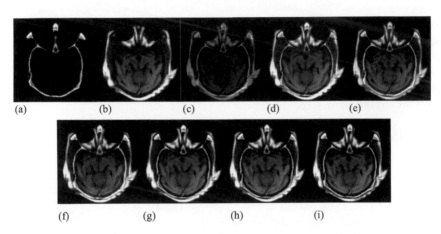

*Figure 7.4   Fusion results of CT and MRI image pair: (a) and (b) source images; fusion results of (c) NSCT, (d) multilevel local extrema, (e) GFF, (f) MST-SR, (g) ASR-128, (h) ASR-256, and (i) MIFMSF method*

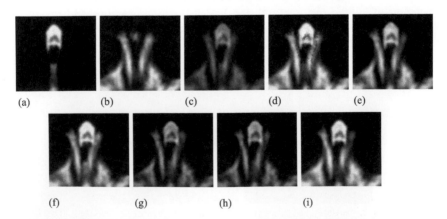

*Figure 7.5   The magnified details of fused image: (a) and (b) regions of source images. Fusion details of (c) NSCT, (d) multilevel local extrema, (e) GFF, (f) MST-SR, (g) ASR-128, (h) ASR-256, and (i) proposed method*

*Table 7.1* *Average statistical evaluation of five standard medical image pairs for different methodologies*

| Methods | $Q^{AB/F}$ | $Q_{CB}$ | $Q_{MI}$ | $Q_w$ | $Q$ | $Q_e$ | MG |
|---------|-----------|----------|----------|-------|-----|-------|-----|
| NSCT | 0.4547 | 0.5312 | 0.6965 | 0.4753 | 0.8098 | 0.3976 | 7.0088 |
| Multilevel local extrema | 0.602 | 0.566 | 0.9018 | 0.7427 | 0.8597 | 0.5669 | **9.7644** |
| GFF | 0.6509 | 0.5886 | 0.7177 | 0.6871 | 0.8489 | 0.5465 | 8.497 |
| MST-SR | 0.6382 | 0.6085 | 0.7426 | 0.7749 | 0.8491 | 0.621 | 9.673 |
| ASR-128 | 0.5849 | 0.583 | 0.6701 | 0.6426 | 0.8196 | 0.5312 | 7.8524 |
| ASR-256 | 0.5619 | 0.577 | 0.6673 | 0.6151 | 0.8158 | 0.4947 | 7.628 |
| MIFMSF method | **0.6606** | **0.6129** | **0.9056** | **0.7755** | **0.8762** | **0.6299** | 9.1806 |

substantial artifacts that blur the fused image's edge region (Figure 7.5(d)). Artificial traces (see the eye regions in Figure 7.5(e)–(h)) are introduced in the fused image since the GFF, MST-SR, and ASR algorithms fail to capture the original information of source images.

When compared to the input images, the MIFMSF technique produces output with greater sharpness, clarity, and information content. Furthermore, the proposed MIFMSF approach is free of undesired degradations and blocking artifacts, making it ideal for precise clinical diagnosis.

### 7.5.2 Objective analysis of standard medical image pairs

The average quantitative comparison of five standard multimodal medical image pairs are compared and reported in Table 7.1. The best results are indicated in bold.

Table 7.1 shows that, with the exception of mean gradient (MG), the suggested technique uses all of the highest quantitative results. The largest value of MG is found in the multilevel local extrema method, which could be attributed to undesirable artifacts in the fused image. Furthermore, the metric MG is only evaluated in terms of the final fused image. As a result, this statistic alone cannot determine the proposed method's fusion performance. The MIFMSF approach focuses on preserving source picture edge features and information content with maximum visual clarity. Higher value of $Q^{AB/F}$, $Q_{CB}$, $Q^{MI}$, $Q$, $Q_w$ and $Q_e$ demonstrates the effectiveness of proposed MIFMSF method to a greater extent.

## 7.6 Summary

The flaws of existing SR-based fusion schemes are investigated, and a discriminative dictionary with less computational effort is constructed without any prior knowledge about the external data sets. From the experimental analyses, the discriminative dictionary is constructed with approximately 32% of the total source image patches. The new fusion rule modifications ensure that all of the critical spatial information of the source images is well retained in the final fused image, resulting in the best visual appearance. As compared to state-of-the-art SR-based fusion schemes, the MIFMSF method shows approximately 4% improvement in quantitative analysis under noise-free condition. It has been experimentally verified that the MIFMSF technique shows promised results and competes with most of the mainstream techniques both visually and quantitatively.

# References

[1]   V. Barra and J. Y. Boire, A general framework for the fusion of anatomical and functional medical images, *NeuroImage* 13 (2001), 410–424.

[2]   S. Li, X. Kang and J. Hu, Image fusion with guided filtering, *IEEE Trans. Image Process.* 22 (2013) 2864–2875.

[3]   A. P. James and B. Dasarathy, Medical image fusion: a survey of the state of the art, *Inf. Fusion* 19 (2014), 14–19.

[4]   R. Singh, R. Srivastava, O. Prakash and A. Khare, Multimodal medical image fusion in dual tree complex wavelet transform domain using maximum and average fusion rules, *J. Med. Imaging Health Inf.* 2 (2012), 168–173.

[5]   B. Yang and S. Li, Multifocus image fusion and restoration with sparse representation, *IEEE Trans. Instrum. Meas.* 59 (2010), 884–892.

[6]   M. Aharon, M. Elad and A. Bruckstein, K-SVD: an algorithm for designing overcomplete dictionaries for sparse representation, *IEEE Trans. Signal Process.* 54 (2006), 4311–4322.

[7]   N. Yu, T. Qiu, F. Bi and A. Wang, Image features extraction and fusion based on joint sparse representation, *IEEE J. Sel. Top. Signal Process.* 5 (2011), 1074–1082.

[8]   H. Yin and S. Li, Multimodal image fusion with joint sparsity model, *Opt. Eng.* 50 (2011), 067007.

[9]   B. Yang and S. Li, Pixel-level image fusion with simultaneous orthogonal matching pursuit, *Inf. Fusion* 13 (2012), 10–19.

[10]  J. Wang, J. Peng, X. Feng, G. He, J. Wu and K. Yan, Image fusion with nonsubsampled contourlet transform and sparse representation, *J. Electron. Imaging* 22 (2013), 043019, 1–15.

[11]  M. Nejati, S. Samavi and S. Shirani, Multi-focus image fusion using dictionary-based sparse representation, *Inf. Fusion* 25 (2015), 72–84.

[12]  H. Liu, Y. Liu and F. Sun, Robust exemplar extraction using structured sparse coding, *IEEE Trans. Neural Netw. Learn. Syst.* 26 (2015), 1816–1821.

[13]  M. Kim, D. K. Han and H. Ko, Joint patch clustering-based dictionary learning for multimodal image fusion, *Inf. Fusion* 27 (2016), 198–214.

[14]  N. Aishwarya and C. Bennila Thangammal, An image fusion framework using morphology and sparse representation, *Multimedia Tools Appl.* 77 (2017), 9719–9736.

[15]  Y. Zheng, E. A. Essock, B. C. Hansen and A. M. Haun, A new metric based on extended spatial frequency and its application to DWT based fusion algorithms, *Inf. Fusion* 8 (2008), 177–192.

[16]  Q. Zhang and B. Guo, Multi-focus image fusion using the nonsubsampled contourlet transform, *Signal Process.* 89 (2009), 1334–1346.

[17]  Z. Hu, Medical image fusion using multi-level local extrema, *Inf. Fusion* 19 (2013), 38–48.

*Chapter 8*

# Artificial intelligence for sustainable e-Health

*Shrikaant Kulkarni[1]*

The study of exploring the improvement of efficiency in e-Health is done by means of regulating an access to electronic health records (EHRs). In the absence of appropriate apex bodies, EHR will continue to stay as lopsided and discrete network of lagging systems without much ability to attain accuracy and consistency, and thereby efficiencies. A multinational corporation (MNC) model is prescribed to cut down health-care (HC) expenses and execute a coherent system wherein data, technology, and training are consistently upgraded to remove any interoperability-related problems. The literature review reveals that EHR interoperability issues may be met by generating architectures that drive fragmented systems to interoperate on the guidelines of watch dog agencies. This chapter suggests a fundamental technology-driven model predicting the need to get over interoperability problems, and followed by suggesting an organizational model that would be the most suitable solution catering to the needs of a coherent system where data, technology, and training are consistently and regularly upgraded. Hence, an artificial intelligence (AI)-driven model is prescribed to facilitate the improvement in the efficiency of e-Health to standardize HER. This treatise deliberates on the research opportunities to provide sustainable e-health solutions particularly during pandemic like COVID-19 and keeping in view diabetes HC as a case study.

## 8.1 Introduction

This work is aimed at eliciting how an MNC organizational model can replace the UK National Health Services (UK-NHS) government model, in situations wherein a public-sector model is difficult to develop. Why and how the MNC model can offer solutions of its own kind to a viable and well-articulated EHR system. It is prescribed that the quality assurance of HC and efficiency with which it is accessed to EHRs can be enhanced if right solutions are derived to the interoperability issue among institutions, organizations, and computer systems. HC is in fact an area where rather than efficiency effectiveness is of paramount importance, the efficiency with which HERs are accessed is key because of the sensitivity of medical decision-making to time [1].

[1]Adjunct Professor, Faculty of Science & Technology, Vishwakarma University, Pune, India

One of the reasons for inadequate efficiency is regulated access to EHRs. In the absence of a supra organization, EHR systems will stay fragmented, leading to nonuniform networks of lagging and degraded systems, or subsystems that are not able to attain accuracy, consistency, and efficiencies in offering qualitative access to EHRs. Currently a supra organization of such a kind is found named UK-NHS (providing services to 6 crore people); few other nations too have alike organizations. However, these private or public umbrella organizations are not applicable across the board, like USA, having a population of 31 crore people. The MNC-based organizational model may be taken as a substitute to the nonprofit or for-profit NGO or MNC reply. Moreover, this model is driven by AI in order to facilitate EHRs interoperability on an e-Health platform [2].

This study defines EHRs and electronic patient records (EPRs), explaining the nature of interoperability issue, underscores certain constraints in executing a viable EHR system, and how to overcome these barriers. For addressing the interoperability problems, the organizational model prescribed is a typical MNC model associated with Internalization Theory, responsible for achieving efficiencies, economies of scale, and cut down HC expenses, which would be intrinsically more because of fragmentation and problems of interoperability. It means that the conclusions depending upon literature review are that most of the interoperability problems concerned with HER can be fulfilled by generating one or more infrastructures and architectures that facilitate fragmented systems to interact among themselves under supra organizations [3].

## 8.2    Reduction in margin of error in healthcare

HC is a service industry that expects abysmally low margin of error as against other services [4]. In HC, an error would prove fatal, and cannot be reversed, similar to an error from airline pilot, although redundant systems are inbuilt in an aircraft. In fact duplicate systems in HC may not be encouraged due to cost effectiveness problems, most important are accuracy, the framework of information architectures within data flow highways to assure quality of data, and technology, constancy in training and semantics for those feeding the data, information, and decisions. To attain such goals, it is indispensable that an organizational structure that is an umbrella for subsidiary units such as hospitals and HC units is required to coordinate and acquire efficiencies in health records entry and providing in an accurate and timely fashion. In the absence of such a supra organization, the subsidiary units will stay discrete, or fragmented, leading to critical interoperability problems and time lags in patient HC. The absence of suitable communication systems and information sharing among HC peers and with patients is also considered as a major challenge and is responsible for causing one in five medical errors due to access to inadequate information which is a barrier in effective decision-making. Another implication of fragmentation of computer systems is the duplication of procedures, which enhances costs, apart from discomfort to patients [5]. Earlier research shows that EPRs will check the medical errors to a large extent. However, studies have suggested that the efforts to employ EHR systems slow down procedures as the interface is user unfriendly, although the interface was done with care keeping in view professional users in perspective, and who evaluated it prior to use on a mass scale. There is still no solution in sight that takes care of the optimum utilization of latest information and communication technology (ICT) input/output systems [6].

EHRs- and ICT-associated problems have come to the fore. American Senator Hillary Clinton said "We have the highly sophisticated medical system in the world, still patient safety is compromised because of medical errors, duplication, and lack of efficiencies. Tapping the full potential of information technology will check errors and better quality in our health system." It is also found that electronic medical records should be favored over chapter-based ones [7].

## 8.3   EPRs, EHRs, and clinical systems

According to UK-NHS, EPR is a periodic record of patient care supplied by an acute hospital that provides HC treatment to the patient within a given time span, while EHR is a patient's life-long record consisted of numerous EPRs. According to International Standards Organization (ISO), an EHR is a bank of patient-centric health-related information that provides efficiency and integration of HC quality by offering plans, goals, and assessments of patient care. EHR is the compilation of discrete data of a patient [8]. A clinical record system should be put in place before EPR becomes functional, which will result into EPRs over time. Right clinical systems will link departments through a master patient index and the system will be integrated with an electronic clinical result reporting system. A clinical system, comprising a secure computer system, is a must for designing an EHR and EPR that enables hospital computer systems to communicate among themselves and allows physicians to secure patient data from various hospitals. The system in the entirety would be able to integrate with selective clinical modules and document imaging systems to offer key support. Generally, an EHR is enabled when state-of-the-art multimedia and telemedicine are hyphenated with a host of communication applications [9].

## 8.4   Barriers in an EHR system

Computer systems apart from fragmented or mutually exclusive cause inefficiencies, user unfriendliness, and obstructions to EHR systems in respect of [10]

- interfaces that demand betterment to better present HER;
- the way data is acquired;
- framing rules and regulations to acquire patient feedback and consent when sharing their data on HER;
- technology issues to deal with EHR execution because of large data transfers, their privacy supervision, and complexity of the system depending on existing ICT infrastructures;

- data quality, its availability and acceptability across nation by patients, medical practitioners, and health workers is a must for EHR development; and
- one more major bottleneck in EHR application is that medical professionals are not able to perform their jobs due to significant data entry needs to populate EHRs.

## 8.5    Getting over interoperability issues

Interoperability of EHR takes place when medical-record-enabled HC systems (patients, medical practitioners, nurses, and concerned HC-department-centric) can communicate among themselves. Interoperability is observed when one application receives data from other application and then does useful tasks [11]. Moreover, interoperability refers to IS that supports functions such as

- physical access to patient data;
- access in between suppliers of date in various care arrangements;
- access and conduct patient tests and medicines;
- access to computer-driven decision support system (DSS);
- access in a secured electrical-based communication among patients and physicians;
- administrative processes like scheduling automated;
- access for a patient to disease management tools, patient records, or health-related data;
- access to automated insurance claims; and
- access to database for safety of patients and efficiency in HC [12].

To a certain degree, interoperability issues have been removed by the ISO that has created structure- and function-related EHR standards and processing systems. The ISO has published 37 HC-related standards dealing with compatibility and interoperability. These standards are divided into three subsections:

- EHR content, structure, and context wherein it is employed and shared;
- technical-architecture-related specifications for fresh EHR standards to exchange EHR for designers called as open her; and
- standards to accomplish interoperability among HC applications and systems, in addition to messaging and communicating criteria for designers to enable reliable information transfer [13].

The interoperability issues have many bottlenecks, other than legal issues, ICT and EHR protocols, IT architectures, training, constancy in advancing technologies, entry accuracy, interpretation, etc. The organizational structure that tackles all issues need not be a government agency, preferably working either for profit or no profit such as UK-NHS and setup in nations like the United States. The objectives and goals would differ from one geographical area to another, although the organizational model could be alike. In the United States, a nonprofit organization or for-profit one would be acceptable similar to health insurance entities that are private companies and have networks either at local or national level of HC servers and facilities; however, only the insurance companies, the medical practitioners or the facility, and the patients are the repositories of their records and data. If an individual leaves an insurance company but not the doctor, then the doctor can make use of that EPR; however, on changing the doctor and if some other insurance company is involved, then there are a host of protocols to be followed to get records, which frequently are converted in terms of chapter records.

This happens mainly due to legal and privacy issues, and since there are non-automated or computerized systems that communicate with one another for seamless data transfer in between two doctors or facilities that are related to two different insurance firms. The interoperability issue in such a situation can be addressed only by proper coordination; however, another factor that often becomes a barrier is the legal system that governs the entities. The legal issues can vary from reluctance to share proprietary information, to leaking of information for either use or misuse of the EPR by the legal system, the lawyers of the patient, or of another company. Thus, fragmentation occurs not merely to the legal environment and the nonavailability of linked data architectures but also because of an organizational structure, either public or private, that can carry out all transactions with such a legal entity as like UK-NHS, and alike entities in other nations, but a best option is a supra organization in the NGO area or private sector would be encouraged preferably [14].

## 8.6   Barriers in EHR interoperability

The barriers in linking and executing EHR are as follows:

- Adaptability to novice systems and work procedure by clinicians.
- Costs toward HC savings, government requirements, and motivation.
- Networking vendors who are required to be forced to ensure interoperable systems.
- Standards that are required to be set to ensure communication.
- Legislation too is a concern and hence the US government has set up laws to regulate HC funding, which if breached would invite penal charges. Moreover, laws are in place that prevents interoperability. Lack of communication technology to promote interoperability, the United States is lagging from other countries in respect of technology to enable interoperability, although it is leading in per capita spending, with Germany ranked second, and France third [15].
- Lack of training, or proper implementation of the shared care concept which is innovative in patient HC, involves an integration of HC by a host of hospitals and doctors that demands well formulated and soundly designed interoperable IT systems, which will reduce patient HC quality, however, if systems are poorly designed [16].

## 8.7   UK-NHS model: characteristics and enhancements

This is one of the modern HC systems in the world which has dealt with a number of issues. However, since it belongs to public sector, it has some advantages, as well as limitations. There is a lot to learn from such supra organization, works using legislation with huge funds to spend. However, this model may be worth replicating in the public sector, a private-sector organization could come up with a coherent HC system, with or without the efficiency level attained by the UK-NHS. However, the model cannot be implanted in all countries because of variations in financial and legislative constraints prevailing in different countries.

The local and national NHS's IT systems require further upkeep or replacement of incumbent IT systems to

- integrate;
- implement innovative national systems;
- integrate NHS CRS with concerned HC-based products and services, like E-prescription, which enhances patient care by minimizing errors in prescriptions, redundancy of data, employee time, and cost; and
- provide right infrastructure (N3) to enable the NHS with smart network services and higher broadband connections to better patient care protocols by fetching patient care records from anywhere and anytime, thereby cutting down HC costs by offering patient care remotely and not only saving time but also by providing patient care expeditiously [17].

## 8.8    MNC/MNE characteristics

An alternative to UK-NHS organizational model has some characteristics that may not be applicable to HC but do so with things like interoperability across the countries and jurisdiction. An MNC is any company that owns, controls, and manages income creating assets across countries [18]. In this perspective, the parameters of interest are control and management of assets, or HC facility, across jurisdictions.

Following are MNC's representative characteristics as mentioned in literature:

- MNC's are popular for their capability in transferring technology, inducing the technology diffusion, and providing employee training and managing skill development. It means that it is a provider of HC with an ability of incorporating and implementing innovative ICT's and upskilling those concerned.
- They also have the ability to bridge the missing links in technology in between the overseas investor and the parent economy [19].
- There is intensive coaching for providers for quality assurance, managerial efficiency, and marketing. American MNEs emphasize upon formalization, while European MNEs stress on socialization of structure and process.
- Internalization theory describes the presence and functioning of MNE/MNC [20]. It adds up to comprehension of the boundaries of the MNE, interfacing it with the peripheral environment, and its organizational structure internally. Because of nonavailability of markets and inadequate contracts lead to opportunistic behavior from others, the company substitutes external contracts by direct ownership and internal hierarchies that promotes better transactional efficiencies [21].

- MNC—Internalization Theory has also been characterized in terms of company structures and advances its technology. The theory states that as the business transaction costs in other nations are more, an MNC can acquire both tangible and intangible savings as well as efficiencies by undertaking most of the activities, confined to its own organizational structure. Creating a control and accountability over both material and human assets protects against leakage in processes and intellectual capital and drives the MNC to attain cost efficiencies with the help of internal contractual accountability. If such activities are brought about via open market (through various companies, providers, etc.), particularly in different legal environments (such as states, nations, and cities) would open up many costly issues for small-scale companies, hospitals, because of compliance issues, and reliance on external agents having their own agenda.
- One more characteristic of an MNE is its transformation into an e-MNE, wherein the cyberspace is a global network of computers connected through high-speed data links and wireless systems and thereby enhancing national and global governance. Can an e-MNE be defined as an organization that has campuses in many countries and its management done through cyberspace? [22]. Most of the cyberspace MNCs have attained economies of scale and have capabilities or proficiency in cutting down costs.
- Currently the e-MNE is capable of controlling and managing income creating assets in many countries through a network across the world with an electronic base situated in every building or place [23].

According to the internalization theory, two parallels can be elicited: one refers to the circumstances and environment of the organization (as shown by UK-NHS model), and the other is external market (as system variations exhibited in interoperability issues). The UK-NHS is an umbrella for over 6 crore people as a supra organization which controls and accountable to the UK government legal authorities. The interoperability issues in United Kingdom are not within the ambit of legal jurisdictions, but in technology, data architectures, and human issues. Jurisdictional matters come to the fore when one shifts from the United Kingdom's legal environment, to USA, or other countries not at par.

## 8.9 UK-NHS model or the MNC organizational model

An EHR system tries to accomplish what the industries have already achieved. HC is complex and, thus, asks for a customizable model to fulfill its own and patient's needs. Moreover, lack or inadequate information in EHR prevents clinicians in making quality decisions. Hence, more efforts are to be taken for coordinating input and output. Therefore, an organizational model and structure fits into an environment where interoperability issues can be addressed when faced having two or more complex systems [24]. The UK-NHS is such a kind of organizational model that tries to get over interoperability problems via its writ of legislation and the law, which can enacted as it is a government organization. However, in spite of a healthy legal and political environment, there are host of interoperability problems that exist because of technology, training, and behavioral resistance. An alternative solution to the UK-NHS model depends primarily on an organizational model designed by MNC over many years and is relevant because they work across numerous boundaries and legal systems. Earlier literature on MNCs show that although these are private organizations working across several countries, they have to handle various types of interoperability problems and consequently have to get over the hurdles, which is attributed to their ability to address problems through access and deployment of huge resources. In addition, such MNC model can be put into effect in the e-Health sector enabled by AI.

## 8.10    e-Health and AI

Computing machines have transformed the HC sector in many dimensions, e.g., Internet of Things (IoT) [25] along with machine learning (ML) and AI as key technologies. The function of AI is expanding in its horizons with its application to the HC sector and has been emerging AI on the e-Health platform. AI is very vital as datasets and resources are readily available. AI is already working for the cause of HC sector: e.g., dermatology, oncology, radiology as representative examples. AI and ML are considered as support tools for knowledge-driven medical decision-making in patient care. AI is presently used where e-Health platforms transfer patient data on integration, e.g., EHRs obtained in different environments, e.g., in the patients' homes and clinical warn room too [26]. This is a novel and sound management information system that develops an AI-based DSS employable on e-Health platforms.

## 8.11    Sustainable healthcare

ANH-USA defined sustainable health as "A complex system with interacting strategies for restoring, managing and optimizing human health having an ecological foundation, environmentally, economically and socially viable for indefinite time, and works in a harmonious manner with both human and non-human environment, and which does not lead to unbalanced effects substantially on any factor of the HC system" [27]. Present COVID-19 pandemic, which has derailed the world crippling the best HC systems under its influence, directs strongly to all HC systems to be connected with sustainability principles and asks for a major shift in HC approach by nations for the betterment of society. Now it is time for the countries to put into practice sustainable HC for their people. Conventional and alternative medicines like Homeopathy, Ayurveda, Yunani, Chinese and Naturopathy about which questions were raised for their scientific basis by the practioners of modern medicines like Allopathy.

However, the alternative forms of medication have proved their potential particularly during testing times and are in practice since long. It requires strong desire to obtain, use, and analyze the data regarding conventional medication forms and its usefulness employing AI/ML tools.

## 8.12    Sustainable healthcare in the aftermath of COVID-19

Sustainability conceptually has benefited a lot various domains of business like energy, agriculture, forestry, construction, and tourism. It is gaining momentum in the advanced HC system which is prevalent in pharmaceutical drugs and products [28]. However, at times it has been proved time and again, that the contemporary medication was not effective against many infectious and chronic ailments.

## 8.13    Sustainability in staff and clinical practice during pandemic

To attain sustainability in terms of faculty and clinical practice particularly during pandemic situations like COVID-19, following recommendations are made:

- Tele-health technology helps clinicians to oversee patients at home and provide recommendations for treatment, a robust infrastructure for telemedicine is asked for.
- COVID-19 although has effectively lower death rate than SARS or MERS, still the pressure on HC systems across the globe is quite alarming [29]. The HC systems should have sound plan to protect HC employees from infection and fatigue during prolonged battle against COVID-19.
- Different HC offices are limited because of the lockdown timings, communication with policy makers as they formulate programs to provide necessary government relief and timely support.

## 8.14    Broadening health-care facilities at home during the COVID-19 pandemic

The HC environment can be expanded at home by using the following means:

- Hospital-at-home program can cut down HC expenses and mortality rate too.
- Hospital care-at-home can minimize the transmission risk of COVID-19, in particular for patients who are vulnerable.
- Hospital-at-home to be effective, interdisciplinary social and behavioral health services are demanded.
- Hospital-at-home and primary health services must include social and behavioral health necessities too.

## 8.15    Sustainable development groups

Group of experts can be formed for the development of sustainability in HC as well as in dealing efficiently and effectively pandemic situations in the following ways:

- The world wants to assure peace and prosperity for the mankind through collaborations (Governments–Private–NGOs–CSOs–Individuals) in all spheres. COVID-19 pandemic should be used for the cause of sustainable development in tandem with the SDGs.

- Medical council should carry on with furtherance of primary and hospital-at-home services in far flung areas too. The patients and HC teams should expand their services both before and post pandemia.
- The technical support is meant for long-term initiatives so as to facilitate heath service managers to maintain consistency and resource allocation during pandemic situations. This will assure that people carry on with care seeking adhering to public health recommendations [30].

## 8.16    Futuristic research directions

ML can create new opportunities for sustainable HC and the investigators can focus on automation in the following areas:

- analysis and prediction of COVID-19 cases;
- discovery of COVID-19 patients;
- current consolidated portal to support pandemics in the future;
- setting up of an innovative Pilot COVID-19 Data Warehouse for reference in future;
- upgraded tools for collecting, preparing, and storing data thoroughly; and
- platform to support for building up a community of medical professionals for pandemic situations.

## 8.17    Role of AI in diabetes care—a case study

AI is considered as a way wherein computers perform tasks that would otherwise demand human intelligence. Diabetes mellitus is a chronic, pervasive state, data rich and with a host of potential results. Therefore, diabetes is a strong case for introducing AI. Clinicians at times pose the following questions:

- How will a diabetic patient respond to a given medication?
- Who will be vulnerable to acquire diabetic retinopathy?
- How can we create a glucose control algorithm for developing a safe closed loop system?
- Which patients of mine are more vulnerable to influenza this fall?
- Of those with prediabetes, who are most likely to acquire diabetes and thereby get benefitted from preventive measures?

Most of the people are part of a vibrant ecosystem, where one's social, biological, and other variables are available to interested ones. Although privacy regulations regarding the access to such information by third parties will be put into place beyond doubt, once an individual allows to share his or her data, AI will result into better recommendations for a given individual. With advancements in ML and deep learning (DL) accompanied by enhanced natural language processing, AI should provide timely, quality, and validated advice [31].

The journey to HC future will cover advancements primarily in three areas:

1. HC technology,
2. HC delivery, and
3. computer science and information technology.

Advancements in HC technology cover breakthroughs in human genome project, pharmaceuticals, nutraceuticals, and medical devices. Novel methods in the HC have been devised for better disease control, evidence-enabled HC, and mind–body medicine. Novel computer science and information technology is facilitating to deal with and understand large amount of health information. Such developments are taking place in terms of speed, storage capacity, mobile personal computing and communication devices, cloud computing, AI, networking, and biometrics. The Internet, which is cutting across many networks in a broad spectrum of frontiers, has a substantial effect on all aspects of our lives. The generations to come of networks will make the use of a plethora of resources with substantial sensing and intelligent capabilities. These networks will cross physically connected computers to contain multimodal information right from biological, cognitive-to-semantic, and social networks. This major transition will have symbiotic networks of smart medical devices (implantable, injectable, on-body), and smart phones and communication devices. Such devices and the network will be consistently sensing, monitoring, and interpreting the environment, which is at times called as the IoT [32]. The IoT and social networks symbiosis is called the Internet of everything which will have major impacts in the manner HC is offered. The P4 medicine concept coined by Leroy Hood, Institute of Systems Biology, has been extended to the P7 concept by Sriram and Jain in 2017. P7 concept for the HC future covers the following elements:

1. Personalized: Personalized medicine consists of individualized treatment.
2. Predictive: Depending upon the information in the EHRs and genomic data, an individual's vulnerability to specific diseases can be determined.
3. Precise: On collecting data and information, the analytical tools can be employed to determine the cause of a disease and to suggest right therapeutic initiatives.
4. Preventive: Rather than treating a disease, ML and decision analytical tools can be made use of in employing strategies to prevent the start of disease.
5. Pervasive: The HC should be made available at all time, everywhere, and at all places.
6. Participatory: The patient should be actively involved in the diagnosis and the treatment.
7. Protective: Proper safety measures should be adopted to make sure that the patient data remains confidential.

## 8.18 Artificial intelligence and its area of applications

AI is related with ML, artificial neural network (ANN), DL, and knowledge-based systems as shown in Figure 8.1. AI is used in addressing different types of issues that surface in HC.

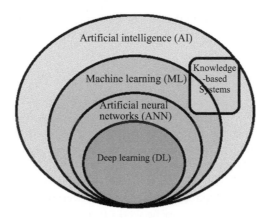

*Figure 8.1    Relation between AI, machine learning (ML), artificial neural network (ANN), deep learning (DL), and knowledge-based systems (KBS)*

### 8.18.1    Diagnosis

The diseases are made out depending upon potentially noisy data. The clinicians should be able to correlate the symptoms to the right disease(s). Such a task involves reasoning with inadequate and inexact data, defective sensors, etc. Diagnosis is normally followed by a treatment plan, which involves determination of a sequence of actions to treat the disease [33].

### 8.18.2    Interpretation

The collected data are analyzed to interpret. The data at times are unreliable, erroneous, or extraneous. Therefore, the system should have capability to remove outliers in the information.

### 8.18.3    Monitoring

Signals are constantly interpreted and alarms are put into effect as and when needed.

### 8.18.4    Control

Signals or data are interpreted, and the system is regulated, depending upon abnormalities in intended response [34].

### 8.18.5    Treatment planning

A program of actions is prepared to attain some goals. The actions initiated should be of such type that surplus resources are not consumed and with no violation of constraints.

### 8.18.6    Drug design

Drugs that fulfill specific requirements can be designed. Such type of problem covers meeting constraints from a host of sources. Design problems are normally addressed by breaking them into number of smaller ones. The designer must have ability to handle the relation between these smaller tasks appropriately [35].

## 8.19 Conclusion

The AI systems first of its kind were knowledge-enabled DSSs, using isolated static datasets. Such systems on connecting to electronic health data, AI became fruitful for teaching, though not prepared for clinical care. DL via multilayered connected ANNs has potential clinical applications. Google teams and New York University observed that DL models can improve accuracy in lung cancer diagnosis. Although our expectations of AI in clinical medicine and in diabetes are heightened, there have been incremental developments showcasing the applicability of AI.

AI can be useful in developing synthetic pancreas (closed-loop systems) and in comprehending the relation between social parameters and physiological bio-markers of health. Diabetes too produces a significant amount of retinal, renal, the taxonomy generated for diabetes with the help of root and rule-based method. End-stage renal disease, vascular, and other data are monitored over the time. Such pathophysiological data with other data will give new insights into diabetes management. An expert opinions and care can be accessed to patients from any part of the globe. A diabetes patient will have an access eye care from anywhere through the application of smart phone images. Glucose control algorithms can be individualized for the patients depending upon glucose consumption, insulin pharmacology, nutria-genomics, and exercise patterns. It is clear that we are on the verge of revolutionizing HC, with the ability to extract, analyze, the data for a timely and quality clinical advice. AI will play a key role in bringing about a paradigm shift in HC. It demands rapid progress in knowledge representation and reasoning.

The UK-NHS model has proved that it can manage HC of 6 crore people, by overcoming the interoperability issues and the countries that follow such public-sector-governed HC system can adopt the model, if they possess strong political and economic will power to follow. Countries, constitutions, legal and political systems, financial condition, etc. of which if are not suitable in employing a UK-NHS, or similar kind of model, can opt for an alternative in the form of MNC model irrespective of whether it is developed as a nonprofit NGO or a for-profit organization. Government sector organization gets the support from government and its legislators to pass laws that enables the working of an HC, EHR, and EPR system where interoperability issues are required to be made out and are to be overcome by the legislature. In private-sector corporation, the interoperability issues can be overcome by the generation of an internalized market under the aegis of an NGO or a corporation.

An MNC organizational model was designed in order to get over various inter-operability issues among countries. Therefore, an MNC model, having own inter-nalized market to control, is a fit case in overcoming EHR interoperability issues, integrating the internally related IS architectures, upgrading them, and training the

workers with certain consistency. Despite this nonuniformity in HC software applications throughout EHR systems may still be a problem concern [36].

Further, MNC model has dealt with software, privacy, jurisdictional, and a host
of other issues in the finance while dealing with largely confidential information in
financial matters, and offering people access worldwide to accounts of them.
Therefore, while problems are not much complex, the HC sector is complex to a
greater extent as it involves not mere card swipe and data recording, but substantial
volume of subjective interpretations and inferences are drawn by HC service providers of plethora of skills and then transferred it to other HC service providers.
Ultimately, it was brought to the notice that the UK-NHS model and the MNC
model operate by legislating laws, and the MNC model by reaching contracts with
people, who are held accountable through the legal system. Additionally, AI is
incorporated to lay emphasis on its application within the e-Health platform, so as
to facilitate the proposed MNC model across the globe. Making out the knowledge
hidden in the data is a quite challenging job in ML. This chapter focuses on the
measures to be taken for the sustenance of e-Health and can be employed for the
better HC of diabetic patients as well as during and post pandemic crisis.

# References

[1]   H. Almubarak, R. Stanley, W. Stoecker, and R. Moss, Fuzzy color clustering
      for melanoma diagnosis in dermoscopy images. *Information* 8(89) (2017).
[2]   A. Angulo, Gene selection for microarray cancer data classification by a
      novel rule-based algorithm. *Information* 9, 6 (2018).
[3]   Avon Health Authority, *Electronic Patient Records Electronic Health Records*,
      Avon Health Authority, Schofield, J, Bristol, Bristol 15, 389–406 (2000).
[4]   A.R. Bakker, The need to know the history of the use of digital patient data,
      in particular the EHR. *Int. J. Med. Inf.* 76, 438–441 (2007).
[5]   C.A. Bartlett and S. Ghoshal, *Managing Across Borders: The Transnational
      Solution*, Harvard Business School Press, Boston, MA (1989).
[6]   B. Baumann, Polarization sensitive optical coherence tomography: a review
      of technology and applications. *Appl. Sci.* 7, 474 (2017).
[7]   A. Begoyan, An overview of interoperability standards for electronic health
      records. In *Society for Design and Process Science. 10th World Conference
      on Integrated Design and Process Technology; IDPT-2007*. Antalya,
      Turkey, June 3–8 2007.
[8]   K. Chung, R. Boutaba, and S. Hariri, Knowledge based decision support
      system. *Inf. Technol. Manage.* 17, 1–3 (2016).
[9]   Commission on Systemic Interoperability, *Ending the Document Game*, U.S
      Government Official Edition Notice, Washington, DC (2005).
[10]  R.C. Deo, Machine learning in medicine. *Circulation* 132, 1920–1930
      (2015).
[11]  J. Dunning, *Multinational Enterprises and the Global Economy*, Addison-
      Wesley, Wokingham (pp. 3–4) (1992).

[12] S. Garde, P. Knaup, E.J.S. Hovenga, and S. Heard, Towards semantic interoperability for electronic health records: domain knowledge governance for open EHR archetypes. *Methods Inf. Med.* 11(1), 74–82 (2006).

[13] I. Guyon, J. Weston, S. Barnhill, and V. Vapnik, Gene selection for cancer classification using support vector. *Mach. Learn.* 46, 389–422 (2002).

[14] A. Harrison, The role of multinationals in economic development: the benefits of FDI. *Columbia J. World Bus.* 29(4), 6–11 (1994).

[15] D. Impedovo and G. Pirlo, Dynamic handwriting analysis for the assessment of neurodegenerative diseases. *IEEE Rev. Biomed. Eng.* 12, 209–220 (2018).

[16] S.M. Islam, D. Kwak, M.H. Kabir, M. Hossain, and K. Kwak, The Internet of Things for health care: a comprehensive survey. *IEEE Access* 3, 678–708 (2015).

[17] A. Jalal-Karım and W. Balachandran, The influence of adopting detailed healthcare record on improving the quality of healthcare diagnosis and decision making processes. In *Multitopic Conference, 2008 IMIC.* IEEE International, 23–24 (2008).

[18] A. Jalal-Karim and W. Balachandran, Interoperability standards: the most requested element for the electronic healthcare records significance. In *2nd International Conference–E-Medical Systems, 29–31 Oct 2008, EMedisys.* IEEE, Tunisia (2008).

[19] A. Kokko, Technology, market characteristics, and spillovers. *J. Dev. Econ.* 43(2), 279–93 (1994).

[20] Y. Li and L.S. Shen, lesion analysis towards melanoma detection using deep learning network. *Sensors* 18, 556 (2018).

[21] A. Massaro, V. Maritati, N. Savino, *et al.*, A study of a health resources management platform integrating neural networks and DSS telemedicine for homecare assistance. *Information* 9, 176 (2018).

[22] NHS National Program for Information Technology, *Making It Happen Information About the National Programme for IT.* NHS Information Authority, UK (nd), Michigan.

[23] W.P. Nunez, *Foreign Direct Investment and Industrial Development in Mexico*, OECD, Paris (1990).

[24] A. Razzaque and A. Jalal-Karim, The influence of knowledge management on EHR to improve the quality of health care services. In *European, Mediterranean and Middle Eastern Conference on Information Systems (EMCIS 2010).* Abu-Dhabi, UAE (2010).

[25] A. Razzaque and A. Jalal-Karim, Conceptual healthcare knowledge management model for adaptability and interoperability of EHR. In *European, Mediterranean and Middle Eastern Conference on Information Systems (EMCIS 2010).* Abu-Dhabi, UAE (2010).

[26] A. Razzaque, T. Eldabi, and A. Jalal-Karim, An integrated framework to classify healthcare virtual communities. In *European, Mediterranean & Middle Eastern Conference on Information Systems 2012.* Munich, Germany (2012).

[27] A. Razzaque, M. Mohamed, and M. Birasnav, A new model for improving healthcare quality using web 3.0 decision making. In *Making it Real:*

*Sustaining Knowledge Management Adapting for Success in the Knowledge Based Economy* ed. by A. Green, L. Vandergriff, A. Green, and L. Vandergriff, Academic Conferences and Publishing International Limited, Reading (pp. 375–368) (2013).

[28]    A.M. Rugman, *Inside the Multinationals: The Economics of Internal Markets*, Columbia University Press, New York, NY (1981) (Reissued by Palgrave Macmillan 2006).

[29]    O. Saigh, M. Triala, and R.N. Link, Brief report: failure of an electronic medical record tool to improve pain assessment documentation. *J. Gen. Int. Med.* 11(2), 185–188 (2007).

[30]    I. Sluimer and B. Ginneken, Computer analysis of computed tomography scans. *IEEE Trans. Med. Imaging* 25, 385–405 (2006).

[31]    D. Stacey, F. Légaré, K. Lewis, *et al.*, Decision aids for people facing health treatment or screening decision. *Cochrane Database Syst. Rev.* 4, CD001431 (2017).

[32]    O.E. Williamson, *Markets and Hierarchies, Analysis and Antitrust Implications: A Study in the Economics of Internal Organizations*, Free Press, New York, NY (1975).

[33]    G. Zekos, Foreign direct investment in a digital economy. *Eur. Bus. Rev.* 17 (1), 52–68 (2005).

[34]    M. Rigla, I. Martínez-Sarriegui, G. García-Sáez, *et al.* Gestational diabetes management using smart mobile telemedicine. *J. Diabetes Sci. Technol.* 12 (2), 260–264 (2018).

[35]    D. Grady, *A.I. Took a Test to Detect Lung Cancer. It Got an A*. New York Times, New York (2019). Available at: https://www.nytimes.com/2019/05/20/health/cancer-artificial-intelligence-ct-scans.html. Accessed: May 26, 2019.

[36]    G. Marcus and E. Davis. *Rebooting AI: Building Artificial Intelligence We Can Trust*. Pantheon, New York, NY (2019).

*Chapter 9*

# An innovative IoT-based breast cancer monitoring system with the aid of machine learning approach

*Bichitrananda Patra[1], Santosini Bhutia[1], Trilok Pandey[1] and Lambodar Jena[2]*

The increasingly revolutionary Internet of Things (IoT) grows rapidly in modern life with the intent of increasing the quality of life by integrating a variety of intelligent tools, technologies, and applications. The IoT Medical Devices will revolutionize the medical industry by creating an environment where patient data is transmitted to a cloud-based storage, processing and analysis network. This chapter provides novel tools for the continuous follow-up of breast cancer (BC) patient conditions—and iTBra that has incorporated sensors that monitor cell temperatures and transfer data on to a patient database in real time. An abnormal reading causes an alert to the patient and his doctor via smartphone. In reality, it is a big obstacle for medical professionals and researchers to detect BC early in their lives. In order to address the initial phase finding issue of BC has projected a machines-built diagnostic instrument that would identify malignancy and benign into IoT. For the implementation of our proposed method, a machine learning sequential minimal optimization (SMO) classification is used to distinguish malignant and benign of healthy citizens. We use support vector machine- recursive feature elimination (SVM-RFE) rank approach to improve the classification performance of BC systems by selecting all relevant features from the datasets. For preparing datasets, the process for training and evaluating the ranking integer aimed the finest prophetic model. In addition, concert assessment classification measures such as classified value of TP rate, FP rate, precision, recall, Matthews correlation coefficient (MCC), and ROC area were used to track classified results. The dataset "Wisconsin Diagnostic Breast Cancer (WDBC)" was employed in this study to check the proposed procedure. Experimental results show that the repeated algorithm for the choice of features selects the best subset and classification instead SMO achieves the highest result. In addition, we are proposing this system to diagnose BC

[1]Department of Computer Science and Engineering, Siksha 'O' Anusandhan (Deemed to be University), Bhubaneswar, India
[2]K L Deemed to be University, Vaddeswaram, Andhra Pradesh, India

effectively and in efficiently early stages. With this program, the reconstruction and treatment of BC would be more successful. Controller-assisted devices transmit all sensor values as packets to the mobile app via Bluetooth. We predicted and alerted the shift in patient status with the aid of the machine learning algorithm.

## 9.1    Introduction

BC has been the world's utmost severe and wide-ranging syndrome, with 2 million new cases occurring during 2018, according to the American Research Institute [1]. By improving clinical outcomes, and increasing cost-effectively patient care, the health-care sector contributes to two key objectives. In order to increase clinical results, real-time measurement and treatment of diseases are considered key features. Patient care needs to be improved to improve patients' quality of life and user experience. IoT offers a cost-efficient way of achieving the two objectives for the medical devices health industry. Connected health programs use scarce resources to enhance health quality, which results in better clinical results. Measurable associated advantages. Medical devices include reduced death rates, less visits to hospitals, and less medical devices.

Hospital and ambulance admissions include reduced bedding and hospital stay. Remote patient control results inefficient and prompt diagnosis and leads to improved health-care management [2]. In addition, patients (and their relatives) may become more visible and actively involved, by making them more visible in their current health conditions.

BC cells in BC tissue are growing abnormally and the rate of cell diminution, resulting in BC, is slowly increased. Typically, BC is a malignant cancer in the breast. Most dividing cells are tissues known as cancer (malignant) and non-cancerous (benign). Tumors are a piece of or build of tissue. In advanced medical research development nations, 5-year primary BC survival rate is 80%–90%, though secondary BC survival rate falls to 24% [3]. Specific invoice-based methods were used to diagnose BC. Breast tissues are collected for examination in the biopsy technique [4] and the result is highly accurate. Nevertheless, the patient has discomfort in taking a biopsy from the breast. Mammograms [5] are also used to treat BC and are used for BC diagnosis. Yet diagnosis of benign cancer is not easily rendered by the mammogram technique. Magnetic reasoning imaging [6], a very complex method that offers excellent outcomes with three-dimensional (3D) images and shows interactive features, is also an invoice-based technique for diagnosing the breast. Such methods for invoice-based diagnostics are highly difficult to implement and the tests do not diagnose BC efficiently and reliably.

Wearable technology offers continuous surveillance of BC women, unlike traditional invasive mechanisms. Basically, two solutions exist: traditional methods invasive in nature and one is the noninvasive method more frequently used. The use of IoT on devices like iTBra simplified monitoring for BC even further. Such IT devices monitor changes in a woman's metabolic profile overtime and distinguish between healthy and potentially cancerous profiles. The use of metabolic detection represents a global breakthrough in cancer screening over image-based technologies such as mammography or ultrasound [7]. In addressing these global health problems, a cost-efficient and time-consuming end-to-end approach needs to be given. A new, noninvasive approach such as the machine learning technique is more efficient and accurate in addressing these problems in invasive approaches for diagnosing BC. Machine learning methods were used in the literature to distinguish breast tissues these are either malignant or benign. This research briefly addresses the related literature on machinery for BC diagnosis.

The solution includes a method that measures signs like radius, textures, the perimeter, the area, smoothness, compactness, concavity, concave points, symmetry, and the fractal dimension in the proposed study. Such signs are important to any patient and the collected data will be used to avoid the patient's sudden increase/decrease. The main goal of this chapter is toward provide an IoT-built method of prediction grounded on machine learning for the successful analysis of patients with BC besides healthy individuals. The predictive master education SMO classical was applied to the classification of BC in malignant and benign persons. For selecting features improving SOM classification efficiency, the SVM-RFE feature selection (FS) algorithm has been adopted. In this chapter, we adopted SVM-RFE for correct selection because SVM-RFE FS-based system classification performance is good in comparison to other BC and safe people classification methods.

We begin with a brief overview of IoT on the iTBra framework and machine learning support for BC in Section 9.2, and Section 9.3 describes the iTBra concept, dataset preprocessing, SVM, SVM-RFE, SMO, and reforms of SMO algorithms are introduced with the BC forecast proposed predictive framework. Section 9.4 explains the experimental frame and performance. Finally, Section 9.5 introduces the conclusion and potential research.

## 9.2   Related works

As a new device, iTBra, demonstrates, the impact of IoT devices continues to grow. Associated bra is built for the early detection of BC, which will be put on sale globally in the first half of 2018 by Rob Royea [8]. Whereas mammograms are the primary form of recognizing BC, cancer cells in dense breast tissue are more difficult to detect as they have more tissue and less fat. According to Susan G. Komen, 40%–50% of females in the United States aged 40–74 have thick breasts. The iTBra from Cyrcadia Health comprises 16 sensors for breast tissue adjustments. The sensors are attached to the skin of the patient with a screw. The patient uses the iTBra for 2 h, and the information gathered is sent to the doctor for review. It is an alternative to the pain of mammograms, particularly for people with dense breast tissues like Royea's wife, Kelli Royea, who starred in the film. Royea has explained that the bra operates "through the prediction method of the algae" (artificial intelligence), all research is done at a cloud-based analytical venue. Screening tests are immediately sent to the customer, showing whether they are successful or you may want to see the doctor. The purpose of Royea was to make this established technology a portable product that could be sold as a wearable tool, so that millions of women could easily wear it and build an overall analytical database for early detection. This is modified by the iTBra. "Rob and his company have been able to attach sensors on the breast in search of cell-level changes in cancer and don't have to be seen by a doctor with his eye," explained Kramer.

This structure has their own advantages, but do not have an early symptom identification solution in terms of real-time predictions. The aim of this chapter is, therefore, to overcome this restriction in order to create a complete system that measures all BC characteristics necessary. In addition, the patient may be alerted before the disease worsens, thus decreasing the women beings mortality rate, by using the prediction algorithm on the real-time data. This inactive alternative is a good example to constantly track and avoid patient complications when combined with the real-time information allows prediction by the SMO classification with SVM-RFE FS and allows recommending suitable remedies.

Azar and El-Said [5] have suggested a BC screening technique. They employed three classification methods: radial basis function kernel (RBF), probabilistic neural network (PNN), and multilayer perceptron, respectively. The results of the classifiers were evaluated by applying performance assessment methods, including precision, specificity, and sensitivity. Precisely 97.80% and 97.66% of training and assessment classifications, respectively, were obtained and the accuracy was achieved. In addition to genetics, AliáźKović and Subasi proposed the two Wisconsin brain cancer datasets [9].

Using the fuzzy-genetic algorithm system that hits 97.36% accuracy, Akay [10] suggested using the *F*-score system for BC screening and endorsing the vector machine (SVM) and had strong output results. The *K*-means Zheng *et al.* [11] algorithm used for the aggregation and extraction properties and for the classification of brain and malignant breast tumors in combination with SVM. In classification and low processing time, the technology proposed achieved great precision [12]. Used in conjunction with various classifiers for Ramadevi Hybridized Primary Component Analysis (PCA) used in many datasets on BC and realized fair precision. Now [13] the writer suggested a Pareto-based mimetic strategy, the Naive Bayes Classifiers (NBC) Detection Network. The experimental results have shown that the technology proposed has achieved reasonable grading precision and very low machine time.

For feature extraction, the *K*-means and SVM were used for classification. Intelligent BC detection technique was developed by Onan [14]. For example, the floppy-through was used to pick and select functions based on consistency. In BC screening, he recycled the nearest neighbor algorithm. The technology for the optimization of swarm particles and nonparametric estimates for the kernel density of the BC density was developed by Sheikhpour *et al.* [15]. Rasti *et al.* [16] have developed a diagnostic technique of BC using a combination of convolutionary neural networks and have achieved 96.39% precision. Ani *et al.*'s IoT-built treatment and control [17] 93% accuracy has been reached by the ensemble classifier and system prediction process. Yang *et al.* [18] proposed a wearable ECG cloud-based intelligent IoT health system and proposed a very good system results for disease diagnosis.

This chapter's main goal is to implement an IoT-based approach for forecasting BC patients and healthy individuals by computer. In the BC classification of malignant and benign individuals, the predictive SMO model in master learning has been used. For selecting features improving SMO classification efficiency, the SVM-RFE FS algorithm has been adopted. In this chapter, we adopted SVM-RFE for correct selection because SVM-RFE FS-based system classification performance is good in comparison to other BC and safe people classification methods.

## 9.3 Proposed solution

### 9.3.1 Concept of iTBra

The gadget is covered with a woman's dress. Thermodynamic assessment will allow sensors that sit on the body, explain Royea [19], and experience metabolic change over time. Finally, he claims that the earliest symptoms of invasive cancer may be identified. The results are sent back to patients, the doctor, and the insurance provider. It is simple for patients to read results which essentially tell them "you're fine" or "call your doctor." The data is transmitted to a central laboratory in which artificial intelligence or predictive analysis is used in the cloud for determining the results.

Therefore, the iTBra appears to be a very early warning that may be essential to the cancer rather than a mammogram that cannot locate a tumor for years. The iTBra is a clinical trial in the United States with a clearance of FDA Class 2, but Royea claims that it operates on a clearance of Class 1, and it can be marketed over-the-counter. A company product could meanwhile be available in Asia by the end of the year, allowing iTBra to combine with a smartphone for performance.

### 9.3.2 Dataset

The data collection "WDBC" obtainable on machine learning source [20] has been developed by Dr William Wolberg from the University of Wisconsin. This was used as a dataset for the conduct of the proposed research to develop master training programs for diagnosing BC. The dataset includes 569 items, 32 attributes, and 30 characteristics are real-value characteristics. The diagnosis on the target performance label has two classes for the malignant or benign individual. Total 357 benign and 212 malignant individuals are classified in class. Therefore, the dataset is a matrix of 569×32.

#### 9.3.2.1 Preprocessing dataset

Information processing is required before applying the classification algorithms. The data processed [21] decreased classifier processing time and the efficiency of the classifier improved. The dataset is commonly used for methods like defective value recognition, regular scalar, and min–max scalar. Standard scalar guarantees the mean 0 of each function and the variance; thus, all features have one coefficient. For all functions, min–max scalar moves the data to 0–1. The vacant free function in the row is excluded from the dataset.

### 9.3.3    *Feature ranking with support vector machines*

#### 9.3.3.1    **Support vector machines**

We recycled an advanced classification technology to check the concept of using the sizes of a classifier to construct a function ranking: vector support engines (SVMs) [22]. SVMs have been researched and benchmarked intensively in recent years for a variety of techniques. Actually it is one of the most popular strategies for machine classification of their rivals.

While SVMs deal with arbitrary complexity's nonlinear decision limits, linear SVMs are common linear classifiers discriminating. A linear SVM is an extreme edge classifier for training dataset that is linearly separable. The decision-making boundary (a straight line for a level separation) is positioned so that the maximum distance on each side can be left. One advantage of SVMs is that the weights $w_i$ of the decision function $D(x)$ are only a small subset function of the "support vectors" training examples. These are the cases nearest to and on the edge of decision-making. The presence of such supporting vectors contributes to the computational properties of SVM and its efficient success in classification. Although SVMs base their decision function on borderline support vectors, they also base their decision function in the average case on other methods, including the approach used in the study of Guyon *et al.* [22].

Efforts: Preparation $\{x1, x2, \ldots xk, \ldots xl\}$ and class labels $\{y1, y2, \ldots yk, \ldots yl\}$. Reduce done $\alpha_k$:

$$J = \left(\frac{1}{2}\right) \sum_{hk} y_h y_k \alpha_h \alpha_h (x_h \cdot x_k + \lambda \delta_{hk}) - \sum_k \alpha_k$$

Subject to: $0 \leq \alpha_k \leq C$ and $\sum \alpha_k y_k = 0$
Productivities: Constraints $\alpha_k k$
The resultant assessment function of an input vector $x$ is

$$D(x) = w \cdot x + b$$

with $w = \sum_k \alpha_k y_k x_k$ and $b = (y_k - w \cdot x_k)$

#### 9.3.3.2    **SVM recursive feature elimination**

A function selection process can be used to remove terms that are statistically unrelated to class labels from the training dataset, thereby improving both efficiency and precise. The supervised method of dimensional reduction was provided by Pal and Maiti [7]. A mixed 0–1 integer program was used for the feature selection problem. The key characteristics are defined by the orthogonal arrays and the signal-to-noise ratio to create a reduced model scale. SVM-RFE is an algorithm created by SVM-based function selection. The selected key and important feature sets are used with SVM-RFE. In addition to reducing calculation time, the rating accuracy rate can be improved. In recent years, many scientists have enabled this method to improve the classification effect in medical diagnoses.

SVM-RFE is a recursive feature elimination program focused on the rating criteria of weight magnitude. The algorithm in the linear case can be represented in the following by using SVM-train.

Algorithm of SVM-RFE
$$\text{Training examples } X_0 = [x_1, x_2, \ldots x_k, \ldots x_l]^T$$
$$\text{Class labels } y = [y_1, y_2, \ldots y_k \ldots y_l]^T$$
Initialize:
  Subset of surviving features $s=[1,2,\ldots n]$
  Feature ranked list $r=[]$
  Repeat until $s=[]$
  Restrict examples of training to successful indices
$X=X_0(:,s)$
  Train the classification
$a=\text{SVM-train}(X, y)$
  Calculate the dimension length(s) weight vector
$$w = \sum_k a_k y_k x_k$$
  Calculate parameters of rating
$c_i=(w_i)^2$, for all $i$
  Find the function with the lowest classification criteria
$f=\text{argmin}(c)$
  Update feature ranked list
$r=[s(f)\cdot r]$
  Delete the function with the smallest classification criteria
$s=s(1: f-1, f+1: \text{length}(s))$
  Output:
  Feature ranked list $r$.

As described earlier, for speed reasons, more than one function can be removed by stage.

## 9.3.4   SMO algorithm

The SMO algorithm is now given in a short summary. The basic step is to select the index pair $(i_1, i_2)$ and only change $\alpha_{i_1}$ and $\alpha_{i_2}$ to maximize the dual objective. As the working set can be used to remove one of the two Lagrange multipliers only in size 2 and the equivalent restriction [23], the optimization problem in each step is quadratics in a single variable. A research solution for it is simple to write. All details need not be remembered at this point. We only create unique significant point about the function of the parameter threshold. In place of Platt, the productivity error in the $i$th pattern is defined as

$$E_i = F_i - \beta$$

Let us mark the indexes of the two multipliers chosen to optimize in one stage as $i_2$ and $i_1$ according to the Platt [8] pseudo code. An analysis of Platt's information (1998) shows that we just need to learn about $E_{i_1} - E_{i_2} = F_{i_1} - F_{i_2}$ to take a step from $\alpha_{i_1}$ and $\alpha_{i_2}$.

For an efficient solution to the problem, the method used for the choice of $i_1$ and $i_2$ at each stage is essential. Platt developed a strong set of heuristics, based on a variety of experiments. The two-loop method is used: the external loop is $i_2$, and the internal loop is $i_1$ for the chosen $i_2$. The external loop iterates over all patterns, violating the optimal conditions—first only over those with Lagrange multipliers at either the upper or lower boundary of optimality conditions to ensure that the problem has in fact been solved. Platt maintains and updates an $E_i$ cache for indices $i$ for no boundary multipliers for efficient implementation. The rest of the eggs are calculated as necessary.

Now let us see how $i_1$ is chosen by the SMO algorithm. The goal is to increase the objective function significantly. Because all the possible $i_1$ options to try to pick one that best enhances the target function are expensive, the $i_1$ index is chosen to optimize $| E_{i_2} - E_{i_1} |$. Since $E_i$ is available in cache for non-boundary multiplier indices, only the abovementioned $i_1$ indices are used initially. If the option of $i_1$ does not provide adequate improvement, the following steps are taken. All indexes of no bound multipliers, one by one, are evaluated as $i_1$ choices from a randomly selected set. If enough progress is not made, all indices are attempted, one at a time, from a randomly chosen index as $i_1$ options again. The random seed collection, therefore, affects SMO's running time.

### 9.3.5    Reforms of the SMO algorithm

Within this section, there are two updated SMO variants, both of which deal with the problems in the last paragraph. Well beyond the first SMO algorithm, almost all of the developments are much better and in most cases they are much better checked. Suppose $F_i$ is open to all at any time $i$.

Let *i_low* and *i_up* be indices s.t.

$$F_{i_{low}} = b_{low} = \max\{F_i : i \in I_0 \cup I_3 \cup I_4\}$$
$$F_{i\_up} = b_{up} = \min\{F_i : i \in I_0 \cup I_1 \cup I_2\}$$

Then it is easy to test a unique i for optimality. Suppose $i \in I_1 \cup I_2$ for instance. We just need to test if $F_i < F_{i\_low} - 2r$. If that is the case, the SMO takeStep process can also be applied to the index pair $(i, i\_low)$. For indices in the other sets, similar steps can be taken. Thus, as opposed to the original SMO algorithm, our solution involves searching for optimal $i_2$ and selecting the second index $i_1$ in hand. We will see later that through an efficient updating process, we calculate and use $(i\_low, b_{low})$ and $(i\_up, b_{up})$.

1.    We would like to be successful by using a great deal of the energy, as with the SMO algorithm $\alpha_i \in I_0$, to modify the $F_i$, $i \in I_0$ cache. Only if optimality is available, search for all the indicators for optimality.

2.    The takeStep protocol [23] involves a few additional steps. When the pair of indices $(i_2, i_1)$ is successfully used, let $\bar{I} = I_0 \cup \{i_1, i_2\}$. Notice that these extra steps are inexpensive, since $\{F_i, i \in I_0\}$ is available and updates of $F_{i_1}, F_{i_2}$ are simple to perform. A careful look reveals that each of the two sets,

$\bar{I} \cap (I_0 \cup I_1 \cup I_2)$ and $\bar{I} \cap (I_0 \cup I_3 \cup I_4)$, is nonempty; hence, the partially calculated (*i_low*, $b_{low}$) and (*i_up*, $b_{up}$) will not be zero elements, because $i_2$ and $i_1$
have only been involved with the effective move. Since in the next stage (see
element 1 earlier) I will take values from *i_low* and *i_up* and they will be used
as $i_1$ options, we also cache the $F_{i_1}$ and $F_{i_2}$ values.

3.  Only if the loop with examine All=0 is used with $\propto_i, i \in I_0$, it must be noted that
    if equation $b_{low} \leq b_{up} + 2\tau$ is maintained at some point, it implies optimality as
    far as $I_0$ is involved. (This is because the $b_{low}$ and $b_{up}$ choice is affected by all the
    indicators in $I_0$ as stated in item 2.) This makes it easy to leave this circuit.
4.  Two ways to enforce the loop with indices only in $I_0$ (examine All=0) are
    provided.
    
    **Process 1**. This is in line with SMO. Close all $i_2 \in I_0$. Search for optimal
    values for each $i_2$ and pick $i_1$ accordingly, when split. For instance, if
    there is a breach of ion $F_{i2} < F_{low} - 2\tau$, choose $i_1 = i\_low$ in this case.
    
    **Process 2**. Function always through the poorest violator couple, pick
    $i_2 = i\_low$ and $i_1 = i\_up$.
    
    The subsequent cumulative alteration of SMO, SMO—Alteration 1 and SMO—
    Modification 2, depends upon which one of these methodologies is used. SMO and
    SMO—Modification 1 are the same except for the test of optimality. SMO—
    Modification 2 can be viewed as an incremental upgrade to SMO—Modification 1,
    by efficiently using the cache to select a violation pair while examine All=0.

5.  When optimality is achieved with $I_0$, all indices (examineAll=1) are checked
    for optimal results. Here, we loop one by one across all indices. $I$ has been
    computed only partially using $I_0$ since. ($b_{low}$, *i_low*) and ($b_{up}$, *i_up*) we update
    the quantities each of them as they are examined. $F_i$ is first measured for a
    given $i$ and optimum control is rendered using the current ($b_{low}$, *i_low*) and
    ($b_{up}$, *i_up*); $F_i$ is used to change the amounts without any breach. There is an
    infringement, for example, when $i \in I_1 \cup I_2$ and $F_{i2} < F_{low} - 2\tau$ in which case
    we are making changes to the SMO algorithm of Platt.

### 9.3.6  Breast cancer prediction proposed predictive framework

The protocols for the new BC program (algorithm) are as follows. Figure 9.1 displays the flowchart of the device.

Algorithm for predictive method of BC

Start

Stage 1: Information preprocessing of BC using techniques of preprocessing

Stage 2: SVM-REF algorithm for attribute evaluation

Stage 3: Process of training and evaluating divisions for the data division

Stage 4: Prepare the training dataset SMO predictive model

Stage 5: SMO predictive model validation with test dataset

Stage 6: Computes models of assessment performance metrics such as TP rate,
FP rate, precision, recall, MCC, and ROC area.

End

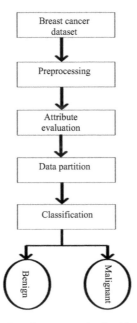

*Figure 9.1    Predictive method of breast cancer*

*Table 9.1    Confusion matrix*

|  | **BC subject predicated** | **Healthy subject predicated** |
|---|---|---|
| BC subject predicated | TP | FN |
| Healthy subject predicated | FP | TN |

Metrics performance evaluation: Assessment metrics used for evaluating the classifier's efficiency. Three methods of performance evaluation have been used in this study. Table 9.1 displays the binary classification problem uncertainty matrix. The following metrics and the equations are determined according to Table 9.1.

TP, when classified as BC Subject (true positive)

TN, if a good subject is considered healthy (true negative)

FP, if a healthy subject is classified as BC (false positive)

FN, if the BC is listed as safe (false negative)

Classification Accuracy $A_C$: The precision shows the total classification system output. Precision is the correct probability of diagnosis executed:

$$A_C = \frac{TP + TN}{TP + TN + FP + FN} \times 100\%$$

TP rate: True positive rate (correct classification of instances)

FP rate: False positive rates (fake class instances)

Precision: Proportion of cases that truly belong to a class separated by the whole class:

$$Precision = \frac{TP}{TP + FN} \times 100\%$$

Recall: Proportion of cases classified as a class separated by the actual class total (equivalent to the rate of TP):

$$Recall = \frac{TP}{TP + FN} \times 100\%$$

MCC: MCC is used to measure the quality of binary classifications (two classes) in machine learning. It takes real and false positive and negative considerations into account and is generally considered to be a balancing measure that can be used, even if the groups are very different:

$$MCC = \frac{TP \times TN - FP \times FN}{\sqrt{(TP + FP)(TP + FN)(TN + FP)(TN + FN)}} \times 100\%$$

ROC area: Area calculation of ROC (receiver operating properties): one of Weka's major output values. You get an understanding of how the classifiers function in general.

## 9.4    Study and discussion of experimental findings

Each section uses an algorithm for functionality selection to perform experiments for the prediction of BC. For the prediction of BC, the machine learning predictive model SVM was used. Dr. William Wolberg developed the dataset "WDBC," which can be downloaded from the UCI Machine Learning library [20]. The dataset is now accessible. This dataset is used in mobile and wireless communication.

For training and testing purpose, the dataset is divided into 70%. Varies performance assessment measures such as TP rate, FP rate, precision, recall, MCC, and ROC area are used to control the predictive model performance. All performance measurements are automatically calculated. Preprocessing methods are used on a dataset for data enhancement before implementing attribute evaluation algorithms and predictive analysis models. In addition, the tables show all these experimental findings and some graphics have also been developed to better explain them. Both tests have been performed on Weka.

### 9.4.1   Preprocessing for the dataset

Table 9.2 offers details and a summary of 569 instances with 32 dataset features and some statistical measures that are automatically measured [24]. The class distribution of the dataset consists of 357 benign and 212 malignant subjects.

*Table 9.2  Feature details and definition of certain Wisconsin Diagnostic Breast Cancer statistical indicators*

| Feature | Name of feature | Description | Min | Max | Mean | Standard deviation |
|---|---|---|---|---|---|---|
| 1 | id | Integer | | | | |
| 2 | radius_mean | Mean of distances from the center to points on the perimeter cell | 6.981 | 28.110 | 14.127 | 3.524 |
| 3 | texture_mean | The standard deviation of grayscale values | 9.710 | 39.280 | 19.290 | 4.301 |
| 4 | perimeter_mean | Perimeter of cell | 43.790 | 188.500 | 91.969 | 24.299 |
| 5 | area_mean | Area of cell | 143.500 | 2 501.00 | 654.889 | 351.914 |
| 6 | smoothness_mean | Local variation in radius lengths | 0.053 | 0.163 | 0.096 | 0.014 |
| 7 | compactness_mean | Perimeter²/area—1.0 | 0.019 | 0.345 | 0.104 | 0.053 |
| 8 | concavity_mean | The severity of concave portions of the contour | 0.000 | 0.427 | 0.089 | 0.080 |
| 9 | concave points_mean | Number of concave portions of the contour | 0.000 | 0.201 | 0.049 | 0.039 |
| 10 | symmetry_mean | Symmetry | 0.106 | 0.304 | 0.181 | 0.027 |
| 11 | fractal_dimension_mean | "Coastline approximation"—1 | 0.050 | 0.097 | 0.063 | 0.007 |
| 12 | radius_se | | 0.112 | 2.873 | 0.405 | 0.277 |
| 13 | texture_se | | 0.360 | 4.885 | 1.217 | 0.552 |
| 14 | perimeter_se | | 0.757 | 21.980 | 2.866 | 2.022 |
| 15 | area_se | | 6.802 | 542.200 | 40.337 | 45.491 |
| 16 | smoothness_se | | 0.002 | 0.031 | 0.007 | 0.003 |
| 17 | compactness_se | | 0.002 | 0.135 | 0.025 | 0.018 |
| 18 | concavity_se | | 0.000 | 0.396 | 0.032 | 0.030 |
| 19 | concave points_se | | 0.000 | 0.053 | 0.012 | 0.006 |
| 20 | symmetry_se | | 0.008 | 0.079 | 0.021 | 0.008 |
| 21 | fractal_dimension_se | | 0.001 | 0.030 | 0.004 | 0.003 |
| 22 | radius_worst | | 7.930 | 36.040 | 16.269 | 4.833 |
| 23 | texture_worst | | 12.020 | 49.540 | 25.677 | 6.146 |
| 24 | perimeter_worst | | 50.410 | 251.200 | 107.261 | 33.603 |
| 25 | area_worst | | 185.200 | 4 254.00 | 880.583 | 569.357 |
| 26 | smoothness_worst | | 0.071 | 0.223 | 0.132 | 0.023 |
| 27 | compactness_worst | | 0.027 | 1.058 | 0.254 | 0.157 |
| 28 | concavity_worst | | 0.000 | 1.252 | 0.272 | 0.209 |
| 29 | concave points_worst | | 0.000 | 0.291 | 0.115 | 0.066 |
| 30 | symmetry_worst | | 0.157 | 0.664 | 0.290 | 0.062 |
| 31 | fractal_dimension_worst | | 0.055 | 0.208 | 0.084 | 0.018 |
| 32 | diagnosis | | | | | |

Feature information:

(1)    id number
(2–31) Ten real-valued features are computed for each cell nucleus:
    (a)    radius (mean of distances from center to points on the perimeter)
    (b)    texture (standard deviation of grayscale values)
    (c)    perimeter
    (d)    area
    (e)    smoothness (local variation in radius lengths)
    (f)    compactness ($\text{perimeter}^2$/area—1.0)
    (g)    concavity (severity of concave portions of the contour)
    (h)    concave points (number of concave portions of the contour)
    (i)    symmetry
    (j)    fractal dimension ("coastline approximation"—1)
(32) Diagnosis (M=malignant, B=benign)

A digitized image of a fine needle aspirate of a breast mass is used to measure the characteristics. They define features of the cell nuclei that are present in the picture. Separating plane mentioned earlier was obtained using Multisurface System-Tree [25], a system of classification that uses linear programming to construct a decision tree. Related features were picked in the space and 1–3 separating planes using an exhaustive scan. In this section, we compiled ten 3D visualizations from Figures 9.2 to 9.11, each of which is calculated as *X*-axis, *Y*-axis, and *Z*-axis for every cell nucleus of mean, se, and worst. In respective pole, this includes the value from min to max.

## 9.4.2    Results of SVM-RFE experiment

In this reason, as with SVM-RFE, a risk of potential performance degradation may eliminate many functional variables per stage for computational efficiency. Therefore, it is important to normalize the values of each function variable across the samples in order to use SVM-RFE. Nevertheless, since the selection of functions is a step toward creating a good classification, if a better subset of functions is chosen, a computer-intensified way would be worthwhile.

For selection purposes, the weights of a linear discriminating classifier may be used. More specifically, one starts with all genes in a backward selection process and extracts the most informative gene iteratively. The gene which has the lesser effect on the costing role of the classification procedure is considered in deciding the feature to be removed in each iteration. The remaining features of the target mark are the most significant. Table 9.3 records the findings of the SVM-RFE algorithm.

## 9.4.3    Results of SMO classification

### 9.4.3.1    Tests of SMO (Normalized PolyKernel) classification

For prevision of the full range of features and on various ranked feature subset generated by SVM-RFE algorithms, and tabled in Table 9.3, the SMO

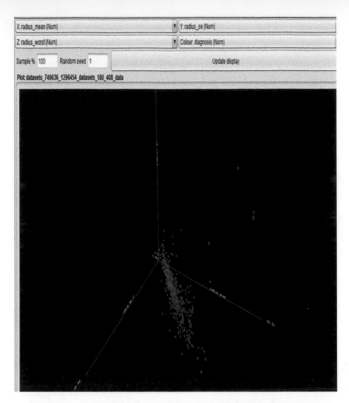

*Figure 9.2   Radius (mean of distances from center to points on the perimeter)—*
*range of X: 6.981–288.110, Y: 0.112–2.873, Z: 7.930–36.040*

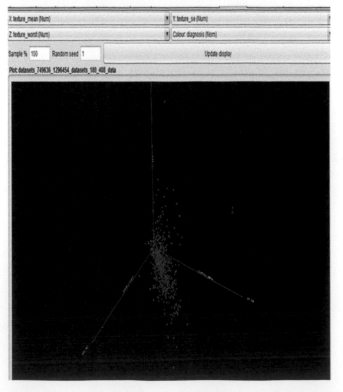

*Figure 9.3   Texture (standard deviation of grayscale values)—range of X:*
*9.710–39.280, Y: 0.360–4.885, Z: 12.020–49.540*

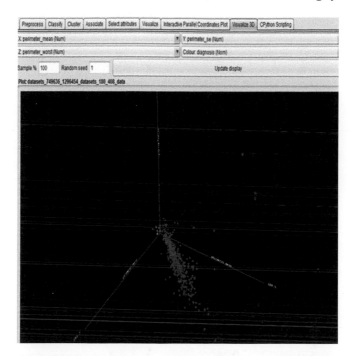

*Figure 9.4    Perimeter—range of X: 43.790–18.500, Y: 0.757–21.980, Z: 50.410–251.200*

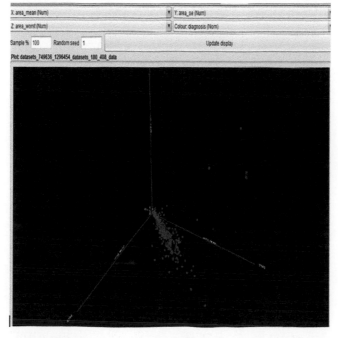

*Figure 9.5    Area—range of X: 143.500–2 501.000, Y: 6.802–542.200, Z: 185.200–4 254.000*

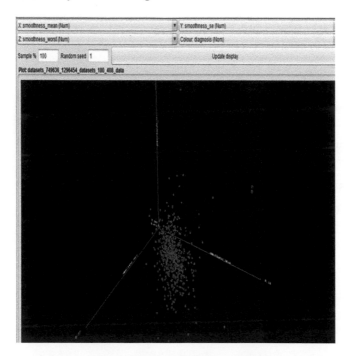

*Figure 9.6    Smoothness (local variation in radius lengths)—range of X:*
*0.053–0.163.110, Y: 0.002–0.031, Z: 0.071–0.223*

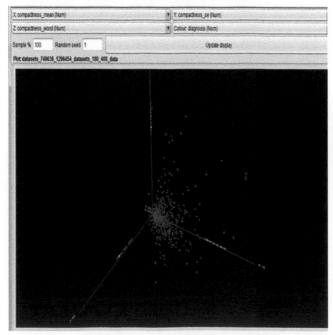

*Figure 9.7    Compactness (perimeter²/area—1.0)—range of X: 0.019–0.345, Y:*
*0.002–0.135, Z: 0.027–1.058*

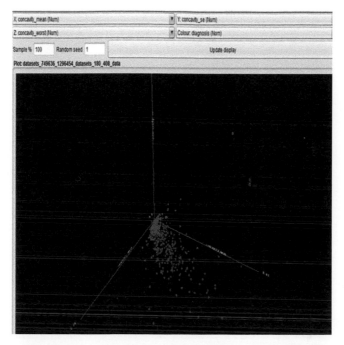

Figure 9.8 *Concavity (severity of concave portions of the contour)—range of X: 0.000–0.427, Y: 0.000–0.396, Z: 0.000–1.252*

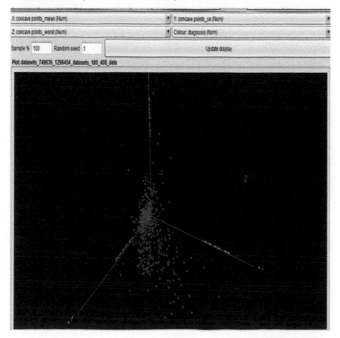

Figure 9.9 *Concave points (number of concave portions of the contour)—range of X: 0.000–0.201, Y: 0.000–0.053, Z: 0.000–0.291*

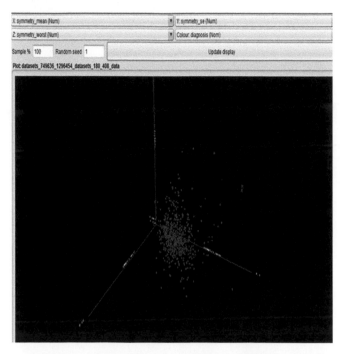

*Figure 9.10    Symmetry—range of X: 0.106–0.304, Y: 0.008–0.079, Z: 0.157–0.664*

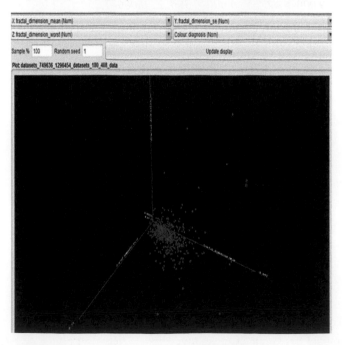

*Figure 9.11    Fractal dimension ("coastline approximation"—1)—range of X:*
*0.050–0.097, Y: 0.001–0.030, Z: 0.055–0.208*

*Table 9.3    Thirty features and their ranking created by SVM-RFE*

| Feature | Name of feature | Min | Max | Mean | Standard deviation |
|---|---|---|---|---|---|
| 1 | radius_worst | 7.93 | 36.04 | 16.27 | 4.83 |
| 2 | concave points_worst | 0.00 | 0.29 | 0.11 | 0.07 |
| 3 | perimeter_worst | 50.41 | 251.20 | 107.26 | 33.60 |
| 4 | texture_worst | 12.02 | 49.54 | 25.68 | 6.15 |
| 5 | concave points_mean | 0.00 | 0.20 | 0.05 | 0.04 |
| 6 | area_worst | 185.20 | 4 254.00 | 880.58 | 569.36 |
| 7 | symmetry_worst | 0.16 | 0.66 | 0.29 | 0.06 |
| 8 | radius_mean | 6.98 | 28.11 | 14.13 | 3.52 |
| 9 | smoothness_worst | 0.07 | 0.22 | 0.13 | 0.02 |
| 10 | area_mean | 143.50 | 2 501.00 | 654.89 | 351.91 |
| 11 | radius_se | 0.11 | 2.87 | 0.41 | 0.28 |
| 12 | texture_mean | 9.71 | 39.28 | 19.29 | 4.30 |
| 13 | perimeter_mean | 43.79 | 188.50 | 91.97 | 24.30 |
| 14 | concavity_mean | 0.00 | 0.43 | 0.09 | 0.08 |
| 15 | compactness_se | 0.00 | 0.14 | 0.03 | 0.02 |
| 16 | perimeter_se | 0.76 | 21.98 | 2.87 | 2.02 |
| 17 | fractal_dimension_mean | 0.05 | 0.10 | 0.06 | 0.01 |
| 18 | concavity_worst | 0.00 | 1.25 | 0.27 | 0.21 |
| 19 | area_se | 6.80 | 542.20 | 40.34 | 45.49 |
| 20 | symmetry_mean | 0.11 | 0.30 | 0.18 | 0.03 |
| 21 | compactness_mean | 0.02 | 0.35 | 0.10 | 0.05 |
| 22 | smoothness_mean | 0.05 | 0.16 | 0.10 | 0.01 |
| 23 | smoothness_se | 0.00 | 0.03 | 0.01 | 0.00 |
| 24 | fractal_dimension_se | 0.00 | 0.03 | 0.00 | 0.00 |
| 25 | fractal_dimension_worst | 0.06 | 0.21 | 0.08 | 0.02 |
| 26 | texture_se | 0.36 | 4.89 | 1.22 | 0.55 |
| 27 | concavity_se | 0.00 | 0.40 | 0.03 | 0.03 |
| 28 | concave points_se | 0.00 | 0.05 | 0.01 | 0.01 |
| 29 | symmetry_se | 0.01 | 0.08 | 0.02 | 0.01 |
| 30 | compactness_worst | 0.03 | 1.06 | 0.25 | 0.16 |

(kernel=Normalized PolyKernel) model performance predictive model was tested. All our experiments use SMO parameters as batchSize=100, buildCalibration Models=false, C=1.0, logistic calibrator, epsilon=1.0E−12, numDecmal Places=2, numFolds=−1, randomSeed=1, and toleranceParameter=0.001. Tables 9.4 and 9.5 record the performance of the SMO Normalized PolyKernel predictive model on a particular combination of features. SMO's Normalized PolyKernel has 95.08% correctly classified with TPRate of 95.1%, FPRate of 6.6%, precision of 95.1%, recall of 95.1%, 89.4% MCC, and ROC area (plotted in Figure 9.12) of 94.3%.

### 9.4.3.2    Tests of SMO (PolyKernel) classification

The SMO model performance predictive model (kernel=PolyKernel) was tested to provide the full range of features and identify feature subsets generated by SVM-

*Table 9.4    Correctly and incorrectly classification accuracy of SMO*

| Kernel | TP | FN | FP | TN | Correctly classified (%) | Incorrectly classified (%) |
|--------|-----|-----|-----|-----|--------------------------|----------------------------|
| Normalized PolyKernel | 193 | 19 | 9 | 348 | 95.08 | 4.92 |
| PolyKernel | 203 | 9 | 1 | 356 | 98.24 | 1.76 |
| PukKernel | 206 | 6 | 0 | 357 | 98.95 | 1.05 |
| RBFKernel | 178 | 34 | 1 | 356 | 93.85 | 6.15 |

*Table 9.5    Weighted average accuracy % of SMO classifier*

| Kernel | TPRate | FPRate | Precision | Recall | MCC | ROC area |
|--------|--------|--------|-----------|--------|-----|----------|
| Normalized PolyKernel | 95.3 | 6.1 | 95.3 | 95.3 | 89.8 | 94.6 |
| PolyKernel | 98.2 | 2.8 | 98.3 | 98.2 | 96.3 | 97.7 |
| PukKernel | 98.9 | 1.8 | 99.0 | 98.9 | 97.8 | 98.6 |
| RBFKernel | 93.8 | 10.2 | 94.3 | 93.8 | 87.1 | 91.8 |

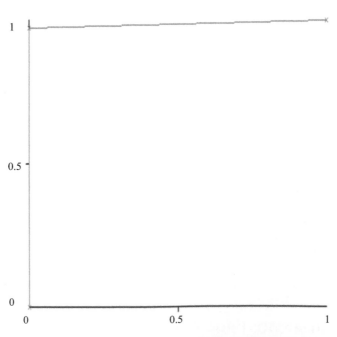

*Figure 9.12    ROC of Normalized PolyKernel SOM X: false-positive rate Y: true-positive rate*

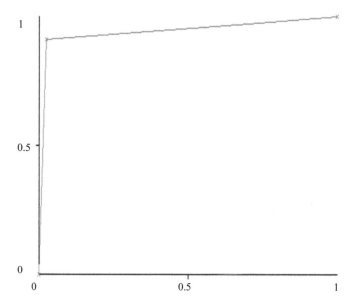

*Figure 9.13    ROC of Linear Kernel SOM X: false-positive rate Y; true-positive rate*

RFE algorithms and tabled in Table 9.3. All the experiments use SMO parameters like batchSize=100, buildCalibrationModels=false, C=1.0, epsilon=1.0E−12, numDecmalPlaces=2, numFolds=−1, randomSeed=1, and tolerance parameter=0.001. Tables 9.4 and 9.5 record the output in a specific feature combination of the SMO polykernel predictive model. The polykernel of SMO has 98.24% correctly classified with 98.2% TPRate, 2.8% FPRate, 98.3% precision, 98.2% recall, 96.3% MCC, and ROC area (plotted in Figure 9.13) of 97.7%.

### 9.4.3.3   Tests of SMO (Puk) classification

Tested to provide full feature sets and define feature subsets developed by SVM-RFE algorithms and tabled in Table 9.3, the SMO model performance predictive (kernel=PukKernel). For any experiment, SMO parameters are used, for example: batchSize=100, constructionCalibrationModels=false, C=1.0, epsilone=1.0E−12, numDecmalPlaces=2, numFolds=−1, RandomSeed=1, and parameter=0.001 for tolerance. The performance of the SMO PukKernel prediction model is shown in Tables 9.4 and 9.5 in a certain function combination. The SMO PukKernel contains 98.95% correctly classified with 98.9% of TPRate, 1.8% of FPRate, 99.0% of precision, 97.8% of recall, 98.6% of MCC, and 98.3% of the ROC area (plotted in Figure 9.14).

### 9.4.3.4   Tests of SMO (RBF) classification

The SMO model performance predictive (kernel=RBFKernel) is checked to provide complete feature sets and set feature subsets generated with SVM-RFE

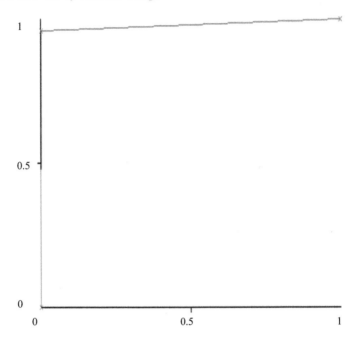

*Figure 9.14    ROC of PukKernel SOM X: false-positive rate, Y: true-positive rate*

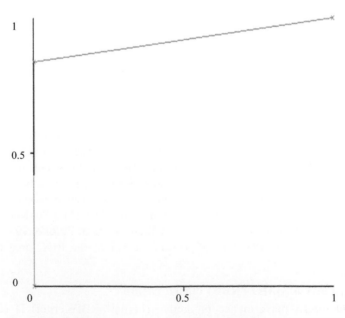

*Figure 9.15    ROC of RBFKernel SOM X: false-positive rate Y: true-positive rate*

algorithms and tabled in Table 9.3. SMO parameters, for example: batchSize=100, constructionCalibrationModels=false, C=1.0, epsilone=1.0E−12, numDecmalPlaces=2, numFolds=−1, RandomSeed=1, and parameter=0.001 tolerance shall be used for any experiment. A certain function combination is shown in Tables 9.4 and 9.5 to demonstrate the efficiency of the SMO RBFKernel prediction model. The RBFKernel SMO includes 93.85% correctly classified with 93.8% TPR, 10.2% FPR, 94.3% precision, 93.8% retrieval, 887.1% MCC, and 91.8% of the ROC area (plotted in Figure 9.15).

## 9.5 Conclusion

The IoT, which has become a means of processing both actual data and past knowledge by the evolving part of cloud computing and data mining, has seen the transition to life in recent years. A diagnostic method is built in this chapter analysis for the diagnosis of BC. SMO was used to detect BC in the design of the device computer prediction model. For the proper and relevant selection of the correct target type of malignant and benign persons, the SVM-RFE attribute assortment algorithm is used. New sets of characteristics from the Diagnostic BC dataset were developed by the SVM-RFE algorithm. The dataset was intended for training and validation. In addition for model performance assessment, techniques for measuring performance such as correctly and incorrectly classification accuracy, TP rates, fp rates, precision, retrieval, MCC, and ROC area were also used.

The WDBC dataset was developed to check the proposed program using 32 features with 30 existent importance features and 569 instances on the UC Irvine data mining depository. Weka machine learning libraries are used to incorporate and improve the proposed framework. The test results indicate that the method suggested efficiently classifies the malignant and benign. Various changes to the BC characteristics may result in an increase in malignant and benign predictions. These results indicate that the new diagnostic method can be used to assess BC reliably and to be incorporated into health care in addition. SVM classifications were evaluated on a rating subset of features using several kernels, such as the Normalized PolyKernel, linear, Puk, and RBF. SMO PukKernel-linear efficiency is higher than other SMO-kernels according to Tables 9.4 and 9.5 and Figure 9.16 graph also indicating. The novelty of the study is planned to distinguish BC and stable people as a diagnostic device. For the diagnosis of BC, the program used the FS algorithm SVM-RFE, SMO, training methods, and output assessment methods.

Machine-based decision-making is more effective for improved detection of BC. According to Table 9.5, the proposed device performance (SVM-RFE-SMO), compared with the classification results of other studies proposed, is excellent and achieves 98.9% classification accuracy. More technology will be used in future to boost the performance of BC diagnostic framework with the addition of assortment algorithms, optimization, and dedicated neural network classification approaches.

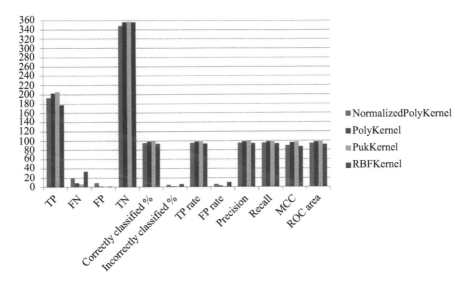

*Figure 9.16    Enactment appraisal of SMO-altered kernels for BC analysis*

*Table 9.6    Performance of other classification results %*

| Year [Reference] | Model | Results |
|---|---|---|
| 2017 [16] | Ensemble of CNN | 96.39 |
| 2017 [26] | SVM and KNN | 98.57 |
| 2018 [27] | IG-SVM | 98.83 |
| 2018 [28] | PCA-AE-Ada | 85 |
| 2018 [29] | Ensemble adaptive voting | 98.5 |
| 2018 [30] | SAE-SVM | 98.25 |
| Proposed | SVM-RFE-SMO | 98.9 |

# References

[1]  American Institute of Cancer Research, *"Breast Cancer Statistics,"* 2018, https://www.wcrf.org/dietandcancer/cancertrends/ breast-cancer-statistics.

[2]  A. J. Jara, M. A. Zamora, and A. F. G. Skarmeta, *An Internet of Things– Based Personal Device for Diabetes Therapy Management in Ambient Assisted Living (AAL)*. Springer, London (2011).

[3]  M. Islam, H. Iqbal, R. Haque, and K. Hasan, "Prediction of breast cancer using support vector machine and *K*-nearest neighbors," in *Proceedings of the IEEE Region 10 Humanitarian Technology Conference (R10-HTC)*, vol. 23, pp. 1–5, Dhaka, Bangladesh, 2017.

[4]  A. M. Ahmad, G. M. Khan, S. A. Mahmud, and J. F. Miller, "Breast cancer detection using Cartesian genetic programming evolved artificial neural

networks," in *Proceedings of the 14th Annual Conference on Genetic and Evolutionary Computation*, pp. 1031–1038, Philadelphia, PA, USA, 2012.

[5]   A. T. Azar and S. A. El-Said, "Probabilistic neural network for breast cancer classification," *Neural Computing and Applications*, vol. 23, no. 6, pp. 1737–1751, 2013.

[6]   E. Warner, M. Hans, C. Petrina, E. Andrea, S. Rene, and P. Donald, "Systematic review: using magnetic resonance imaging to screen women at high risk for breast cancer," *Annals of Internal Medicine*, vol. 148, no. 9, pp. 671–679, 2008.

[7]   S. K. Pal, T. Kesti, M. Maiti, *et al.*, "Geminate charge recombination in polymer/fullerene bulk heterojunction films and implications for solar cell function," *Journal of the American Chemical Society*, vol. 132, no. 35, pp. 12440–12451, 2010.

[8]   J. Platt, "Sequential minimal optimization: A fast algorithm for training support vector machines."

[9]   E. AliǎžKović and A. Subasi, "Breast cancer diagnosis using GA feature selection and rotation forest," *Neural Computing and Applications*, vol. 28, no. 4, pp. 753–763, 2017.

[10]  M. F. Akay, "Support vector machines combined with feature selection for breast cancer diagnosis," *Expert Systems with Applications*, vol. 36, no. 2, pp. 3240–3247, 2009.

[11]  B. Zheng, S. W. Yoon, and S. S. Lam, "Breast cancer diagnosis based on feature extraction using a hybrid of *K*-means and support vector machine algorithms," *Expert Systems with Applications*, vol. 41, no. 4, pp. 1476–1482, 2014.

[12]  G. N. Ramadevi, "Importance of feature extraction for classification of breast cancer datasets, a study," *International Journal of Scientific and Innovative Mathematical Research*, vol. 3, pp. 763–368, 2015.

[13]  H. A. Abbass, "An evolutionary artificial neural networks approach for breast cancer diagnosis," *Artificial Intelligence in Medicine*, vol. 25, no. 3, pp. 265–281, 2002.

[14]  A. Onan, "A fuzzy-rough nearest neighbor classifier combined with consistency-based subset evaluation and instance selection for automated diagnosis of breast cancer," *Expert Systems with Applications*, vol. 42, no. 15, pp. 6844–6852, 2015.

[15]  R. Sheikhpour, M. A. Sarram, and R. Sheikhpour, "Particle swarm optimization for bandwidth determination and feature selection of kernel density estimation based classifiers in diagnosis of breast cancer," *Applied Soft Computing*, vol. 40, pp. 113–131, 2016.

[16]  R. Rasti, M. Teshnehlab, and S. L. Phung, "Breast cancer diagnosis in DCE-MRI using mixture ensemble of convolutional neural networks," *Pattern Recognition*, vol. 72, no. 24, pp. 381–390, 2017.

[17]  R. Ani, S. Krishna, N. Anju, M. S. Aslam, and O. S. Deepa, "IoT based patient monitoring and diagnostic prediction tool using ensemble classifier," in *Proceedings of the 2017 International Conference on Advances in*

*Computing, Communications and Informatics (ICACCI)*, Udupi, India, 2017.

[18]  Z. Yang, Q. Zhou, L. Lei, K. Zheng, and W. Xiang, "An IoT cloud based wearable ECG monitoring system for smart healthcare," *Journal of Medical Systems*, vol. 40, p. 286, 2016.

[19]  R. Royea, K. J. Buckman, M. Benardis, *et al.*, "An introduction to the Cyrcadia Breast Monitor: A wearable breast health monitoring device," *Computer Methods and Programs in Biomedicine*, vol. 197, p. 105758, 2020.

[20]  W. H. Wolberg, *Wisconsin Diagnostic Breast Cancer (WDBC)*. University of Wisconsin School of Computer Science, UCI Machine Learning Repository, Madison, WI, USA (1995).

[21]  S. Kotsiantis, "Data preprocessing for supervised learning," *International Journal of Computer Science*, vol. 1, pp. 111–117, 2006.

[22]  I. Guyon, J. Weston, S. Barnhill, and V. Vapnik, "Gene selection for cancer classification using support vector machines," *Machine Learning*, vol. 46, pp. 389–422, 2002.

[23]  S. S. Keerthi, S. K. Shevade, C. Bhattacharyya, and K. R. K. Murthy, "Improvements to Platt's SMO algorithm for SVM classifier design," *Neural Computation*, vol. 13, no. 3, pp. 637–649, 2001.

[24]  M. H. Memon, J. Ping Li, A. Ul Haq, M. H. Memon, and W. Zhou., "Breast cancer detection in the IoT health environment using modified recursive feature selection," *Wireless Communications and Mobile Computing*, vol. 2019, p. 19, 2019, Article ID 5176705.

[25]  M. M. Islam, H. Iqbal, R. Haque, and K. Hasan, "Prediction of breast cancer using support vector machine and *K*-nearest neighbors," in *Proceedings of the 2017 IEEE Region 10 Humanitarian Technology Conference (R10-HTC)*, vol. 10, pp. 226–229, Dhaka, Bangladesh, 2017.

[26]  N. Liu, J. Shen, M. Xu, D. Gan, E.-S. Qi, and B. Gao, "Improved cost-sensitive support vector machine classifier for breast cancer diagnosis," *Mathematical Problems in Engineering*, vol. 2018, p. 13, 2018, Article ID 3875082.

[27]  D. Zhang, L. Zou, X. Zhou, and F. He, "Integrating feature selection and feature extraction methods with deep learning to predict clinical outcome of breast cancer," *IEEE Access*, vol. 6, pp. 28936–28944, 2018.

[28]  N. Khuriwal and N. Mishra, "Breast cancer diagnosis using adaptive voting ensemble machine learning algorithm," in *Proceedings of the 2018 IEEMA Engineer Infinite Conference (eTechNxT)*, pp. 1–5, New Delhi, India, 2018.

[29]  Y. Xiao, J. Wu, Z. Lin, and X. Zhao, "Breast cancer diagnosis using an unsupervised feature extraction algorithm based on deep learning," in *Proceedings of the 2018 37th Chinese Control Conference (CCC)*, pp. 9428–9433, Wuhan, China, 2018.

[30]  K. P. Bennett, "Decision tree construction via linear programming," in *Proceedings of the 4th Midwest Artificial Intelligence and Cognitive Science Society*, pp. 97–101, 1992.

*Chapter 10*

# Patient-centric smart health-care systems for handling COVID-19 variants and future pandemics: technological review, research challenges, and future directions

*Adarsh Kumar[1], Saurabh Jain[1], Keshav Kaushik[1] and Rajalakshmi Krishnamurthi[2]*

Information technology can play a vital role in future smart health-care systems. Using information technology, health-care services can be improved. This improvement includes shifting the specialization or department-centric health-care services to patient-centric health-care services. This shift is necessary to have better patient experiences and providing specialized health-care services to many patients with lesser resources. In information technology, the Internet of Things (IoT) is an advanced approach for ensuring this system. In IoT, industrial IoT (IIoT), Internet of nano things, Internet of robots, Internet of patients, and Internet of medical things (IoMT) are some of the concepts important to understand the functionality of smart health-care system. In addition to IoT or its variants, other IoT-associated solutions that include blockchain technology, parallel and distributed computing approaches (cloud/fog/edge), virtualization, cybersecurity, automated software development, and smart infrastructure development have shown great enhancements in recent times. The objective of this work is to explore different information-technology-based solutions that can make a patient-centric smart health-care system feasible in nearby times. In this work, recent developments of IoT that are used to interconnect health-care objects and made technical revolutions will be explored initially. Thereafter, IoT association with other technological approaches will be explored. IoT association with other technical aspects is necessary to understand the IIoT-based health-care solutions. The survey work will start with the integration of IoT technology with blockchain technology to keep the patient data confidential and transparent to authenticated parties. The IoT devices

[1]Department of Systemics, School of Computer Science, University of Petroleum and Energy Studies, Dehradun, India
[2]Department of Computer Science and Engineering, Jaypee Institute of Information Technology, Noida, India

integrated with the patient help in collecting the data which will be stored at some central repository. Here, blockchain maintains data security via cryptography primitives and protocols. The cryptography primitives will provide confidentiality, integrity, authentication, access control, and non-repudiation properties, whereas blockchain technology ensures immutability, transparency, distributed computing and ledger, and data security. In IoT networks, security is a major concern. IoT networks contain both resourceful and resource-constraint devices. Both types of the device-based networks require different security solutions. In any smart health-care system, both types of device-based solutions are required. This work will discuss feasible cybersecurity solutions for IoT networks useful in smart health-care systems that are developed in recent times. The feasible cybersecurity solutions will consider health-care infrastructure as cyberspace for collecting, storing, and analyzing data. In a similar but larger infrastructure, a vast amount of parallel and distributed computing approaches are required. In this work, we will be discussing various approaches that are used in recent times for parallel and distributed computing in health-care system. This includes cloud, fog, edge, and message passing interface (MPI)-based approaches. All these approaches are used in recent times at a large scale for IoT-based applications. These approaches will be required to understand and compute various healthcare-related tasks using IoT networks and provide efficient outcomes. Thereafter, data-related technological aspects that include the usage of artificial intelligence (AI), and machine learning (ML) will be explored. These aspects will address the recent developments that use AI- and ML-based approaches and are found to be useful in the smart health-care system. In this technological aspect, all associated approaches, including deep learning, reinforcement learning, federated learning, neural network, virtual reality (VR), and augments reality aspects, derived during recent times will be explored. Virtualization has played an important role in reducing the number of resources and improving the services. Thus, a few of the recent aspects in the direction that are associated with smart health-care systems are planned to be discussed here. In a smart health-care system or Healthcare 4.0-based technological solution, data privacy and security are other major concerns. The traditional security primitives and protocols are easily breakable with quantum computers. Post-quantum cryptography aspects are required to handle future security aspects. Thus, this will discuss the importance of quantum computations for IoT networks. Further, how post-quantum cryptography will be helpful, recent developments for the health-care system and applications to automated patient-centric services will be discussed. Lastly, robotics and drone-based technological solutions that are recently discussed in the scientific community and important for Healthcare 4.0 or smart health-care system will be explored. This study will briefly explain the recent medical operations and experimentations that are conducted successfully using robots and drones. All the information-technology-based solutions require smart infrastructure. Thus, requirements of smart infrastructure in the smart health-care system which include smart electric supply system, smartphone-based mobile applications, smart medical and pharmaceutical system, smart ambulance and other transportation systems, and smart medical appliances will be explained.

## 10.1   Introduction

Software systems with advanced technologies, including AI, ML, drones, cognitive computing, parallel and distributed processing, smart and intelligence processing, and interconnection of devices, have played important roles in various applications with different forms of their implementations. There are technological aspects like Healthcare 4.0, Industry 4.0, Agriculture 4.0, and Agriculture 5.0 that integrated major technological aspects under one umbrella for automation. Thus, the form and technological aspects vary from application to application. In a smart and intelligent health-care system, these technical aspects have played and will continuously play vital roles. The major advantaged that information-technology-based aspects can give to various applications include (i) health-care automation; (ii) patient-centric health-care services deployment rather than specialization or department-centric approaches; (iii) remote monitored, control, and analysis-based effective system; (iv) health-care datacenter creation for effective analysis and handling futuristic situations; (v) industrial health-care system with large-scale inter-connectivity; and (vi) secure and trustworthy health-care services. With these aspects taken into consideration, the major and important functionalities of healthcare-related applications are discussed in recent times concerning fast and secure processing approaches toward automation. The effective and efficient approaches can only be important to implement if a detailed analysis shows its prediction for a real-time system. The use of AI and ML approaches has made this possible with the help of advanced resources. Thus, there is a strong need to discuss and explore such recent advancements in the medical and health-care sector.

This work has surveyed the recent developments in the health-care sector for handling medical services to patients. In recent developments, technological aspects are covered in detail. Among technological aspects, those approaches are found which can handle the COVID-19 or its related situations effectively. The survey of the proposed system includes the interconnection of medical devices for patient-centric services. It has been observed that most existing health-care services are specialization-based services with the least interconnectivity. Lack of connectivity and automation make the medical services slower for patients. This increases the overall cost and time for health-care operations as well. Thus, there is a strong need to shift from a specialization-based health-care system to a patient-centric health-care system. In recent times, various initiatives have been taken using advanced technologies. This work discussed these technological systems briefly.

This work is organized as follows. Section 10.2 covers the healthcare-related advancements using IoT-based technology. Similarly, Section 10.3 covers the need and advancement of blockchain technological aspects for health-care systems and services. The interconnection of medical systems, patients, equipment, and processes needs data security. Section 10.4 covers health-care cyberspace and associated cybersecurity aspects. These aspects are necessary to handle a patient-related health-care system. Large-scale implementation of health-care services is not possible without the use of parallel and distributed computing architectures. Thus, important, and recently proposed parallel and distributed computing approaches for healthcare are discussed in Section 10.5. Section 10.6 discussed the recently proposed AI and machine-learning-based approaches for effectively handling health-care services and pandemic situations. Section 10.7 discusses the importance of virtualization for the effective utilization of resources in handling smart health-care systems. In the future, the quantum computational aspect is necessary for handling large health-care data and fast processing. Thus, Section 10.8 discusses the importance of quantum computation and its role in a smart health-care system. Post-quantum computing and cryptography is the solution to those problems that identify loopholes in quantum-based breakable solutions. In the health-care system, data privacy and security is very important. Thus, Section 10.9 discusses the role of post-quantum computing and cryptography to effectively handle futuristic pandemic situations. Section 10.10 discusses the recently implemented and/or proposed drone and robot-based approaches for medical and smart health-care services. Finally, the conclusion and futuristic aspects are drawn in Section 10.11.

## 10.2   Internet of Things (IoT) network for patient-centric health-care system

In recent COVID-19 timings, it has been observed that IoT networks played important roles in handling patients. Many wearable devices can help everyone to monitor their health-related activities and plan the future. Singh *et al.* [1] identified the integration of wearable devices and IoT networks to patient-centric smart health-care systems. It has been identified that the proposed wearable and IoT-network-based system can reduce the chances of medical mistakes that include doctor, medicine, and operational mistakes as well. Further, the proposed system is capable of handling patients with lesser expenses, efficient machinery for superior treatment, effective medical control, and enhanced medical diagnosis. An IoT-based system for handling medical situations (like COVID-19), the important processes include (i) health data monitoring in remote location, (ii) virtual management of meetings and conferences with sensor- and camera-based devices, (iii) data collection, storage, analysis, and visualization for effective control and monitoring, and (iv) case report preparation and presentation for effective display and handling at various levels. Kamal *et al.* [2] have discussed the importance of the patient health-care system in COVID-19 handling, its present situation, challenges, and opportunities. This is a small comprehensive survey explaining the systems of integrating wearable and sensor devices attached to a patient's body. With this integration, patient monitoring is much easier and automated. Likewise, the Internet of cameras can be constituted which constantly monitor the patient and hospital activities. In this monitoring, image-based analysis is possible which can constantly monitor patient movements, emergencies, remote monitoring, and surveillance. In similar cases, a camera-based interconnected system is helpful to handle hospital situations. The administration and surveillance are much easier and can be done with minimum manpower.

### 10.2.1    IoT and its applications for health-care sector

This section discusses the applications of IoT or its variants to smart health-care systems and services. There are various applications of IoT networks to health-care systems. Some of the popular applications are briefly explained as follows:

1.    Sensor-based biodegradable chips or implantable sensors can be attached to a patient's skin that continuously gives glucose monitoring and reading to the patient or his/her doctor over the phone. This way, it is very easy to self-monitor the regulation of sugar level in the human body.

2.    In activity-tracking-based applications, IoT sensors can help in adjusting the dietary and exercise plans as per his movements, habits, fatigue, etc. Thus, IoT is helpful to health-care professionals in effectively handling their patients with well-accepted data. With this feasibility, it is much easier to control overall health plans rather than focusing on overweight and age-based calculations only.

3.    Like blood sugar measurements, wearable IoT devices can be used for high blood pressure measurements as well. In this experimentation, the device will continuously monitor the variations in blood pressure. These measurements when made accessible to patients or health-care service providers, then it would be easy for them to monitor heart-related activities. For example, strokes, palpitations, and full-brown heart attacks. A well-connected system can arrange medical, ambulance, or doctor services on time whenever the chances of severity increase. Thus, the IoMT made it possible to monitor patients at a large scale and provide specialized services as and when they are required.

4.    A family-interconnected IoT system can help adults to monitor their family members and their health conditions. For example, if there are old people in the family and it is necessary to remotely monitor their health, an IoT-based system can help them a lot. As discussed earlier, they can monitor old people by looking at their health-related data variations, the system can give auto-generated signals, or a well-connected camera-based IoT network can send real-time images. With the help of these images, it is much easier to monitor patients and provide them with necessary services as and when it is required with remote accessibility only.

5.    IoT-network with the sensor-based system can help the patient to monitor their medicine dosages as well. It is much easier to check the quality and quality of medicines. Besides, analysis such as time of medicine effects of medicine over the body, right medication, etc. can be monitored using infectible sensors. In this way, it is much easier for any patient to handle their disease well on time rather it causes severe effects.

6.    The IoT-based monitoring system can help the patients or their family members to note the timings of their medicines and refill as and when it is necessary.

7.    The IoT-based system helps health-care service providers to monitor their equipment, medicines, and infrastructure-related status continuously with partial to full automation. This way, it is possible to reduce the efforts of manpower and increases the feasibility of everything work well on time and on a large scale.

8.    The IoT-based health-care system is effective for all stakeholders, including patients, doctors, hospitals, health-care service providers, and insurance

companies. This is because it creates a well-connected and trustworthy environment to share reliable information on time. The availability of this information ensures that it can be securely stored at the right locations and can be analyzed for timely treatment and diagnosis of diseases.

9.  Among other advantages, IoT-based health-care services provide cost reduction in health-care systems and improving medical operations and related services after analyzing reliable data.

Table 10.1 shows the comparative analysis of open-source IoT applications for health-care system proposed in recent times.

*Table 10.1   A comparative analysis of open-source IoT application for health-care system*

| Source | System | Description |
|---|---|---|
| [3] | IoT-healthcare for end-to-end connectivity, simulation, and reporting | In this implementation, a healthcare-related system is designed for reporting and monitoring. Using this system, end-to-end connectivity is possible. Additionally, item tracking, alert generation, remote medical assistance, and research are performed to understanding IoT-based health-care system. It has been observed that data privacy and security, system integration, overhead handling and cost are important parameters to design an effective health-care system |
| [4] | Raspberry Pi and Arduino-based patient's data reading system | In the proposed system, raspberry pi and Arduino-board-based patient data reading system is proposed for real-time health data collection from sensors. The proposed system sends collected data to the doctor and notifies the system. This sharing of information helps patients and doctors to continuously monitor patient's readings |
| [5] | IoT-based health-care system to collect heart rate | The proposed system collects heart rate data from 85 subjects. The data is collected with different features from subjects taken into consideration. The proposed system detects future heart rates using a random forest model |
| [6] | AWS-based IoT model for health-care services | The proposed health-care system integrated IoT options with cloud services for managing notifications. Here, notifications are immediately sent over to digital devices whenever a vital report is observed. The implemented push–pop model is effective in handling medical data sharing between different stakeholders |
| [7] | Health statistics application using JavaScript | The proposed health-care application is sponsored by Philips Healthcare. This application is developed for patient data collection and sharing with doctors. In this process, data is made continuously with web display and it is easy to understand and diagnose the patient |

## 10.2.2 Industrial IoT (IIoT) for smart health-care system

This section discusses a few of the recent and important developments in extending IoT networks to IIoT. In IIoT, sensor, wireless, and application-specific objects can be interconnected at a large scale for industrial applications. This connectivity is faster than response generation, data sharing, and service facility to a large scale. Some of the recent developments in IIoT and its health-care applications are discussed as follows.

Mumtaz *et al.* [8] discuss the importance of 5G and beyond networks for IIOT growth. In this discussion, the application-specific industrial level is on focus for vast and rapid industrial-level development. The health-care sector is one such major target that is achievable through IIoT. Using IIoT, health-care services can be extended to a large scale at a comparatively lesser cost. A chain of hospitals integrated with the IIoT network can focus its service on the patient-centric health-care system rather than specialization-based services. This way, it would be easier for patients to get his treatment under one umbrella. Further, it is easier for the health-care service provider or hospitals to provide their services as well. Rathee *et al.* [9] discussed the importance of integrating IIoT with blockchain technology. In this work, an IIoT framework is discussed and the importance of integrating blockchain technology with this framework is explored. It is recommended that if health-care services are required to be extended with IIoT network, there is a strong need to integrate blockchain technology as well because it can bring transparency, immutability, distributed computing, ledger, and cryptography-integrated security. All of these things are important for a patient-centric health-care system. In a patient-centric health-care system, if records are permanently stored, it would be much easier for any health-care service provider or doctor to see historical data. This data can be made available to any location in a secure way. Thus, this framework is good for those medical services, services of which are not easily available or they are rare.

## 10.2.3 Resourceful and resource constraint device-based smart health-care developments

IoT devices in the health-care sector can be resourceful or resource-constraint. The resourceful devices like laptops, desktops, display screens, cameras, and other large computational and storage-capable devices have an abundance of resources for computing cryptography primitives and protocols. On the other hand, resource constraint devices, including Radio Frequency Identification (RFID) tag, RFID reader, and sensors, have a scarcity of resources that cannot implement traditional cryptography primitives and protocols. To ensure security over these devices, lightweight cryptography primitives and protocols are required. Here, lightweight means lesser hardware resources in terms of XOR, OR, NAND, NOT, etc. gates. The RFID and sensor devices are useful in health-care applications in different scenarios. Medicines, equipment, machines, and patients can be identified with RFID easily.

## 10.2.4 Research challenges and future direction of IoT in patient-centric smart health-care system

In literature [7–9], it has been observed that there are many challenges to IIoT networks. For example, the Quality of Service (QoS) in the IIoT network is a major challenge for adopting it to large-scale application-specific usages. In QoS, throughput, delay, jitter, connecting topology, the number of secure connections, and more factors influence the IIoT network. Besides, developing patient-centric health-care services is not easier in real scenarios because of the lack of medical infrastructure in a large number of developing or underdeveloped countries. To handle these challenges, there is a need to integrate various information-technology-based recent developments into the health-care sector. For example, integrating AI and machine-learning-based technology in the health-care sector helps in faster data analysis. Thus, if a large amount of data is generated from every device of IoT or IIoT network, analyzing this much of data is difficult. The best solution is to apply ML, deep learning, AI, and cognitive computing aspects for faster and efficient analysis of results. Likewise, the IIoT network can be integrated with 5G and beyond network technologies for fast data accessibility and response generation. Availability of advanced Internet technologies ensures the availability of data as and when it is required. Thus, providing high QoS-based technologies for data sharing is important, which makes the real-time data available to health-care insurance, doctor, and health-care service providers. Similarly, blockchain and cryptography primitives can ensure the security of patient's data. Patient's data security and privacy is a major concern in the health-care sector. Ensuring these services can build trust in this system. To handle a large amount of data generated in IoT or IIoT networks, parallel and distributed computing approaches like cloud, fog, edge, and MPI-based computing should be integrated. To make faster the computational at an individual end, quantum computing can be used. This type of computing can faster the storage, transmission, and processing responses. To secure the data against quantum computing hacks, post-quantum cryptography mechanisms can be helpful. Thus, future challenges are (i) hoe to integrated IoT networks with advanced technologies such as blockchain, AI/ML, quantum computing, parallel and distributed computing, and post-quantum methodologies. Among all, patient data security and privacy are a prime concern. To achieve this target, cryptography primitives and protocols can be integrated at various levels. In traditional computing infrastructure, both resourceful and resource-constraint devices are available. Thus, traditional and lightweight cryptography solutions can be implemented. However, the advanced quantum-computing-based infrastructure required fast responding cryptography primitives and protocols. To handle traditional cryptography primitives and protocols against quantum computing attacks, post-quantum cryptography can be used.

## 10.3　Blockchain technology and IoT for patient-centric health-care system

There has been a rapid increase in health-care data in recent years since medical care has become the most common and necessary part of human lives. To make medical analysis and prescription comfortable and suitable for patients as well as doctors, the health sciences are now making their way toward the IoT. The implementation of the IoT in healthcare has made remote monitoring easy. Patients can now be monitored remotely without the need to visit hospitals periodically. All the data is shared directly with doctors, and the prescription can be made accordingly. But this personal data of patients needs protection as sharing and storing data using IoT is not secure and can be hacked easily. So, implementation of the blockchain in smart health-care systems can provide security to the data of the patients [10,11].

## 10.3.1   Need for the blockchain and IoT integration

Blockchain technology is one of the most emerging technologies nowadays. Blockchain is used almost in every field starting from healthcare, finance, education, and whatnot. The decentralized and autonomous nature of blockchain technology makes it suitable for integration with IoT networks. The blockchain-based approach can provide tangible solutions to various privacy and security issues in IoT. The integration of smart contracts into blockchain technology has made it possible to handle various possibilities in achieving reliable decentralization. The following is a list of features that make blockchain a unique technology [12,13].

- **Security:** In blockchain, data from IoT devices is stored as a transaction record in a block. Before data is stored in a block, each transaction is mined and validated by all other peer users using a consensus approach inside the blockchain. This guarantees information security.
- **Decentralization:** Decentralization means that there the power is not residing in a single authority which means that there is no such central authority. In a decentralized system, a group of authorities is held responsible for handling everything making it decentralized.
- **Scalability:** Scalability is the outcome of decentralization which improves fault tolerance.
- **Immutability**: Immutability means that once changes are done, they cannot be altered or changed after the changes are done making a blockchain an unaltered network. Immutability makes a blockchain corruption-free hence considered as a key feature of this.
- **Transparency**: Blockchain promises users regarding transparency and providing a pseudonymous system. Blockchain makes everything transparent making people argue that blockchain could be used as the new standard for transparency.

## 10.3.2   Role of Internet of Things in health-care system

HealthBank [14], a global Swiss digital health start-up, offers an approach to the transaction and sharing of personal health data. This start-up provides its users with a platform on which they can keep and manage their health records in a protected environment. Users can fully hold data sovereignty in their hands. As a next step, the HealthBank start-up applies blockchain technology to its underlying business model. With the help of blockchain technology, patients can get their health information such as eating habits, blood pressure, diabetes information, sleep patterns, and heart rate transparently and safely. Patients can use the health app or ask for information from doctors or hospitals. Today, using the HealthBank approach, not only patients are able to place their information on this platform, but it is also available for medical research purposes. This innovation has expanded a new direction of vulnerability and security for data from IoT-based networks. Implementation of traditional cryptographic solutions on IoT networks is not a future aspect as IoT devices have many constraints such as performance, memory, and computational power. In this work [15], the authors have proposed a novel structure, a unique architecture that integrates blockchain networks with IoT devices to achieve privacy and security threats to information integrity. Integration of smart contracts is very important in this work, by which we can handle authorization, access control, data management, and device authentication. The overall scalability of the network can be improved using an off-chain data storage mechanism in the framework, this model can be integrated into any existing IoT application with minimal modifications.

## 10.4    Cybersecurity and IoT for patient-centric health-care system

With the advancement in technology, interconnected smart devices are evolving. The domain of the IoT is giving various opportunities in the domain of healthcare. Various IoT-based health-care devices are assisting patients and doctors across the globe. These IoT-enabled smart devices are boon to the various medical practitioners and patients but on the other hand, if the security of such devices is not implemented properly, it can create some serious trouble. The growth of the IoT in healthcare is affecting people's lives. For people suffering from such illnesses, the use of new and advanced wearable devices makes life easier. With such functions, these wearable devices are produced that make them an appropriate portion of the human body. To provide the desired performance, wearables are also assisted by recent technologies such as edge computing. The role of wearables in IoT health-care, as well as the reference architecture of new wearable devices and various IoT communication protocols, is highlighted in [16]. Smart devices interpret data from their surroundings, make calculations on it, and then either save or transmit the data to a computer with similar capabilities. In this communication process, there are many security and trust concerns, which are really important to manage. These security and trust issues will pose potential challenges to the IoT environment, and the current architecture, framework, and technology need to be tackled. Several important security and confidence risks in the IoT and how they are handled by the new architecture are seen in [17].

### *10.4.1    IoT and cybersecurity*

Advances of medical care provision innovations are increasingly proliferating worldwide. In a plethora of new rules, policies, and legislation, these developments are being tackled piecemeal. Currently, these efforts frequently struggle to put the patient and his or her well-being at the center of changes in legislation, policy, and regulations. Rather, attempts are being made to balance patient results, financial benefits, and liability concerns. Increasingly, an increasingly acute danger to patients is the failure to recognize and handle cybersecurity problems associated with their own well-being. In [18], the argument for patient-centered approaches to not only medical treatment but also health-care cybersecurity is discussed. The development of the IoT is still in its infancy and it is important to solve several similar problems. The IoT is a coherent notion of combining all. IoT has a tremendous opportunity to make accessibility, honesty, availability, scalability, anonymity, and interoperability more available to the public. How to secure the IoT, however, is a difficult challenge. Device security forms the basis for IoT growth. In [19], IoT reviews cybersecurity. Protecting and incorporating heterogeneous smart devices and information technology systems are essential concerns (Information and Communications Technology). The architectural framework in relation to cybersecurity in IoT comprises various features and principles, some protocols related to the architecture, synchronization and wireless networking, heterogeneous and pervasive frameworks, lightweight technologies, authentication, etc. The architecture involves, from a technological perspective, integrity, scalability, reliability, secrecy, availability, and interoperability between heterogeneous smart devices.

Numerous risks are emerging in the IoT paradigm, including unauthorized or inappropriate operation, malicious code updates, control bypassing, and data integrity tampering. In IoT implementations, information may be revealed or lost. Consequently, safeguarding sensitive documents, passwords, and certificates is crucial. Provided that, unregulated IoT apps and systems reveal embedded patented algorithms that can easily be pirated or studied, intellectual property can be breached. To stop the discovery of hidden bugs, it is advised that hackers find it more difficult to reverse-engineer, study, or manipulate the code in general. To ensure continuity and authenticity of data, integrity processes are used. Hash functions and digital signatures are used to ensure the confidentiality of documents. In addition, at the storage level as well as on the network path in the IoT environment, data protection must be secured. The anonymity program is the concealment of sources of data. In addition, this program helps in the preservation of personal privacy and secrecy. In the IoT, non-repudiation [20] helps to guarantee that a bargaining side is unable to challenge on official papers the authenticity of its signature. Finally, freshness signifies the presence of facts and the lack of past texts. Figure 10.1 shows the integration of IoT and cybersecurity and related factors necessary to understand.

Device or network protection is a key issue, and best practices such as restricting external computer connections, restricting the usage of the Internet directly to some important endpoints and devices, ensuring that only designated networks are authorized, using keys for safe booting and safe firmware are used in numerous ways to secure them, enforcing device authentication at each link establishment. Virtual Private Networks are external networks that allow only partners to access them, which they pledge to, keep private and have assured honesty. This infrastructure, on the other hand, is not visible for dynamic global information sharing and is not safe for non-extranet third parties. DNS Security Extensions use asymmetric cryptography for asset

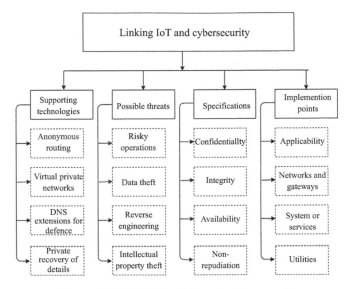

*Figure 10.1   Linking IoT and cybersecurity*

record signing to ensure the root validity and integrity of information received or delivered. Data is wrapped in multiple layers of encryption using the public keys of onion routers on the transmission network, for example, using onion routing technology to encrypt and mix the Internet traffic of several senders.

## 10.4.2   Recent developments in ensuring confidentiality, integrity, and availability (CIA) properties in IoT networks for smart health-care system

For those who require regular and real-time medical monitoring and therapeutic procedures, the integration of IoT with medical devices leads to promoting the consistency of health-care facilities and progress data on patient status. IoT accelerates early illness identification and facilitates the prevention and recovery process, such as exercise services, infectious illnesses, and caring for the elderly. With all the gains, IoT adoption is followed by the possibility of new security breaches and health-care system flaws. The following explanations are associated with this: (i) medical devices primarily capture and exchange confidential patient information, (ii) the design of IoT technologies causes problems of sophistication and incompatibility, and (iii) medical IoT system vendors do not pay attention to security features. Due to the abovementioned factors, confidentiality, integrity, and availability security [21] concerns are increasing. The apps and technologies that track and manage the vital signs of patients are some of the IoT solutions in healthcare. These technologies can, however, be subjected to security threats, such as authentication, permission, and privacy breaches. Cyber protection in the world of healthcare has been a major concern. Hackers can take the advantage of computer vulnerabilities and contribute to IoT system operational disturbance. More specifically, due to the limitations of medical equipment, including power usage, scalability, and interoperability, conventional security requirements for attack countermeasures are not applicable. Not only can unauthorized access to IoT components have detrimental implications for the running of processes, but also it more frequently presents a risk to human life and health. The intent of intruders may be to destroy some industrial facilities, copy records, intercept vital equipment systems maintenance, and other acts aimed at preventing the proper functioning of equipment. The inability of developers [22] to use simple techniques and methods of securing knowledge has resulted in various flaws and allegations of "hacking" IoT-solutions. Second, it should be remembered that suppliers at the design level of the systems do not take the classification of the data being handled into consideration. As a result, the established instruments deal with a wide variety of classified details, including personal information, business secrets, clinical secrets, and so on. The bulk of the bugs, on the other hand, could be removed by using safe data transfer methods. Many cloud links remain vulnerable to attack using transport-level encryption mechanisms like Secure Sockets Layer/Transport Layer Security.

IoT is basically a network of interconnected entities. Obviously, even though they have access to it, it is inexpedient to accept a group of objects that do not communicate within the network. Consequently, the data-sharing mechanism between objects is crucial. IoT enterprises also turn to automated message screening and review of transmitted data while embedding multiple technologies. Much of the time, these features are provided to make interacting with the device smoother, such as configuring incoming updates. Any of them, on the other hand, are intended to screen out potentially dangerous or faulty data transmitted from computers to humans. Personal medical devices patients will stay mobile and healthy for even longer, thus preventing the need for supportive housing. This type of gadget normally has a wireless interface that allows it to connect with a base station that can read medical data, monitor system status, change settings, or update the computer's firmware. This wireless software introduces the user to security dangers, raising the patient's security and privacy issues. The study also discovered that this system and its wireless interface are vulnerable to cyberattacks, placing healthcare, defense, and privacy at risk. Research teams have shown a number of attacks on medical devices, including snooping, message manipulation for security and reputation, and battery draining attacks to cause availability issues. Various countermeasures are proposed for these threats. When designing countermeasures for them, the cost constraints on medical devices for implementing protective measures are a major concern. Battery capacity is the most important consideration for implantable medical devices [23]. The batteries in computers are typically non-rechargeable and must be replaced every few years.

### 10.4.3    IoT cyberspace and data handling processes for information and network security

Because of their wide scope, openness, and comparatively high processing speed, IoT artifacts have been an ideal target for cyberattacks. Furthermore, since many

IoT nodes store and process private data, they are turning into a gold mine for cybercriminals. As a consequence, security, especially the ability to detect compromised nodes, as well as the ability to catch and preserve evidence of an attack or malicious activity, emerges as a top priority for effective IoT network deployment. In the IoT world [24], anonymity, access control, safe networking, and secure data storage are also becoming significant security issues. Furthermore, during an inquiry, every new device we develop, every new sensor we deploy, and every byte that is organized in an IoT environment can be scrutinized. The rapid growth of IoT devices and software has resulted in the introduction of various unstable and insecure nodes. Furthermore, traditional user-driven protection architectures are inefficient in object-driven IoT networks. Therefore, to protect IoT networks, obtain, store, and analyze residual information from IoT settings, we need advanced equipment, techniques, and procedures. Health programs and resources are more important, innovative, and linked than ever before. While enhancing clinical quality and changing patient delivery, thus improving human life, protection of health-care data and devices is becoming a growing concern. Health equipment and services have grown more intertwined, opening them to emerging cybersecurity risks. It makes the health-care industry the most vulnerable to serious safety threats. As mentioned earlier, the problem is compounded by the health-care services and infrastructures allowed by Cyber-Physical Systems (CPS)-IoT [25] that are vulnerable to a number of emerging cyberattacks. CPS-IoT systems are categorized as essential safety and protection systems and present extended attack surface characteristics of fragmentation, interconnectedness, heterogeneity, and cross-organizational existence. Cybersecurity threats have the ability to breach users' privacy, inflict bodily harm, financial losses, and pose a danger to human life, so avoiding them is vital. With millions of medical documents [26] stolen worldwide, studies illustrate the increase of attacks and the rise of medical identity fraud.

### 10.4.4   Research challenges and future direction of IoT in patient centric smart health-care system

The IoT movement involves linking a huge number of smartphones and wireless gadgets that are traditionally placed at the bottom of the Internet spectrum and capable of delivering large amounts of data at a high rate. The Internet data flow on its back has the potential to alter this trend. It is simply impractical or impossible to gather all of the data and send it to datacenters present remotely then wait for the reports to be transmitted back to the edge after large data processing. Essentially, two variables would preclude it. The first aspect [27] is the amount and speed at which the IoT devices collect the generated data. Data collection and transmission on a local basis is unavoidable. The second aspect is that many potential IoT technologies such as autonomous vehicles, VR, augmented reality, and involving AI have a low latency or rapid response requirement to make quicker decisions. In terms of technological developments, intelligent devices with high communication and data collection capacities are now possible, opening up a slew of new opportunities for IoT applications, particularly in healthcare. There are also a range of open topics with many of the benefits that discuss big IoT concerns, such as usability, portability, interconnection, data storage, and privacy. IoT provides a systemic basis for a range of high-tech health-care technologies, including real-time patient tracking, environmental and interior safety data, and ubiquitous and widespread access to information that helps both health professionals and patients while also providing essential features for health-care networks like usability, mobility, and extensibility. Continuous scientific advances allow IoT devices to be created by countless sensing, data fusion, and logging facilities, leading to many advances in better living environments (ELEs) [28]. To transfer data between sensors and servers, smart healthcare relies on a combination of short- and long-range communications networks. Wi-Fi, wireless metropolitan area network (WiMAX), Zig-Bee, and are the most popular Bluetooth short-range networking networks, which are mostly used for short smart health-care communications such as body area network. In smart healthcare, a series of technology such as mobile communication (global system for mobile communication) and General Packet Radio Service, Long-Term Evolution (LTE) Advanced, and LTE are used to relay data from a local server to a ground station. Security requires smart healthcare. Even though smart healthcare relies on the Internet to connect various devices, security is a major concern. Complex security mechanisms and algorithms are difficult to implement because of the restricted presence of IoT computers (limited processing and battery life). As a consequence, 70% of IoT applications [29], including intelligent health-care equipment, are vulnerable to cyberattacks. Consequently, there are regular threats and security and privacy concerns. From hospital to patient-centric healthcare, there is an increasing sense of urgency. IoT is designed to be a powerful enabler by ensuring that computers and cloud storage, as well as acting agents such as patients, hospitals, research laboratories, and emergency services, are all in harmony. Given the benefits of IoT eHealth [30], a variety of challenges must be resolved. Data storage, scalability, interoperability, device–network–human interfaces, usability, and privacy are among others. In terms of variety, length, and velocity, we can see that knowledge is getting more dynamic. Uniformity will allow for interoperability between different devices and records. All people, from children to the aged, should be able to use interfaces that are clear and genuine. Safe infrastructure, network protocols, less vulnerable to threats in the cloud, and adequate training for people handling secure data are all required to increase the security of devices, networks, clouds, and agents.

## 10.5  Parallel and distributed computing architecture using IoT network for patient-centric health-care system

This section discusses the parallel and distributed computing-based approaches proposed for the health-care system in recent times. Here, those frameworks are studied and explored in detail which is recent and found to be effective for handling pandemic situations. Details of recently proposed frameworks are discussed as follows.

### 10.5.1    Cloud computing architectures using IoT network for health-care system

Featherstone *et al.* [31] have surveyed the need for technologies in the health-care system and handling pandemic situations. In this survey, it has been identified that cloud computing and the web 2.0 framework are found to be very effective in educational institutions during COVID-19 pandemic times. Likewise, cloud-based infrastructure can be used for handling future pandemic situations as well. Cloud services can provide various services, including computation, storage, processing, and security. Nowadays a large number of applications are developed using cloud computing for different scenarios. In all of the scenarios, the performances are found to be better compared to old and present traditional computational approaches. Desai [32] discussed the need for software systems and Bigtech in pandemic situations. A large number of software systems are in usage for health-care services. All of these systems generate big data. This big data analysis is important for the health-care system. With the usage of cloud computing, it is much easier to analyze the data and evaluate the statistics. Cloud services are also very helpful in handling a large number of patients. In patient handling, their contract and historical data are required to be maintained which is possible easily using cloud services. This service adds remote accessibility and fast response time. All of these services make it possible for software-based health-care systems to handle COVID-19 situations as well. The software systems are found to categorize the patients easily and isolate them. This way it is possible to take care of them and their medical requirements more carefully. With the addition of cloud computing services, it can be implemented at an industrial scale. Thus, handling pandemic situations would be much easier. Gupta *et al.* [33] have developed communities for effectively handling the COVID-19 situation. This is a different approach where smart and intelligence solutions are proposed to effectively handle COVID-19 situations. In this chapter, a detailed survey is performed to explain the need for such community development. Kumar *et al.* [34] have proposed a drone-based solution to effectively handle the COVID-19 pandemic situation. In this approach, thermal imaging is applied to collect the patient's data. This data helps in provide sanitization and medication services. All of these services use the cloud, fog, and edge computing aspects. To implement these computing services, different environments are created that made the COVID-19 handling and integration with the health-care system possible. Table 10.2 shows the other parallel and distributed computing approaches for smart and intelligent health-care system proposed in recent times.

## 10.6    Artificial intelligence and machine learning approaches in IoT for smart health-care system

Artificial intelligence and ML are integral parts of any system nowadays. The important features of this technology include data analysis with the least error and fast processing, learn from the data and predict future trends, the ability to generate

*Table 10.2    Comparative analysis of parallel and distributed computing approaches for smart and intelligent health-care systems*

| Author | Year | A | B | C | D | E | F | Remarks |
|---|---|---|---|---|---|---|---|---|
| Featherstone *et al.* [31] | 2012 | N | Y | N | Y | Y | N | This is a survey article to identify the current pandemic situation and future aspects. This article discussed various challenges in medical and IT-based systems useful for health-care services |
| Desai [32] | 2020 | N | Y | N | Y | Y | Y | This article discusses the need for software and system to handle COVID-19 and pandemic systems. The designed systems can be useful for future pandemic handling and treatments. Using this software, it is much easier to classify the pandemic-affected patients and their handling |
| Gupta *et al.* [33] | 2021 | N | Y | N | Y | Y | Y | This article addresses the development of communities and handling of COVID-19 pandemic situations using a community-based approach. In a community-based approach, similar features or functionality-based groups can be performed to handle the current or future pandemic scenarios |
| Kumar *et al.* [34] | 2021 | N | Y | N | Y | Y | Y | This article addressed the usage of drones and robotic systems for medical treatment. Here, a major concentration is drawn toward the use of contactless approaches that are safe for medical treatments. Flying multiple drones in a geographical region without collision and maximum energy utilization for health-care service is the prime concern of the proposed system |

A: Patient centric, B: specialization or department centric, C: large-scale deployment using Cloud/Edge/Fog/MPI, D: helpful in data collection, processing, analysis, or visualization, E: able to handle COVID-19 situation, F: able to handle futuristic pandemic situations.

or support data visualization for interpretation, and many more are important for any system. In health-care systems, AI and ML have played vital roles and it is expected to continue as well. This section will explore the recent advancement of the use of AI and associated technologies for COVID-19 and its variants. Figure 10.2 shows the important technical aspects that will be explored in detail.

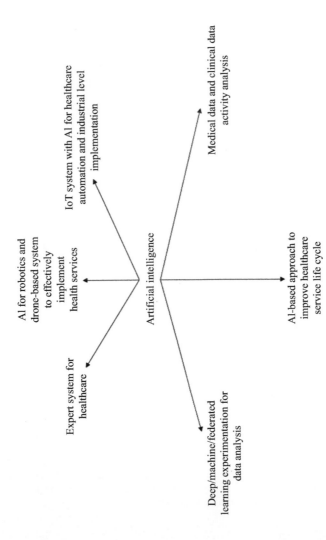

*Figure 10.2 AI-based technological aspects for the smart health-care system*

All of these technical aspects are associated with AI-based developments. In brief, the use of AI-integrated technological aspects is explained as follows.

- AI technology with robotics is used to perform various experimentations in the sanitization, thermal imaging, monitoring, and surveillance. All of these activities are contactless and important to handle pandemic situations. In past pandemic situations, these activities helped to identify the patients with COVID-19 symptoms, sanitization, and other healthcare-related activities. A large number of developments in developed and developing countries are made to address the challenges of handling COVID-19-related situation handling using drones. Likewise, robotics is equally important. In the past decade, efforts are made to integrate human intelligence behavior to machines using robotics for performing health-care operations.
- IoT system generates a lot of data as well. The best way to handle this data is using AI and ML. The classification or categorization of data, its interpretations, and visualizations are easily possible using ML approaches.
- Medical data analysis can be performed in various sections, including clinical trials, patient records, operations success rate, and susceptible, infectious, recovery model. This analysis and their observations are important to respective sectors. All of this creates more important when there is a need to speed up the clinical trials and obtain the results in comparatively lesser time duration. For example, it has been observed that to successfully obtain COVID-19 medicine, the clinical trials are performed at a much fast rate.
- In healthcare, the patient service life cycle starts from symptoms identification to post-discharge treatments. All of these aspects need constant monitoring and inspection that is not possible using manual processing. Automated processes with the use of technology can make this feasible. In this aspect, AI technology is very useful.

## 10.6.1   *Healthcare, COVID-19, and future pandemic-related datasets for smart health-care systems*

In this section, important COVID-19 and pandemic-related datasets are identified and explored. Table 10.3 shows the various recently prepared datasets. These datasets are compared using various parameters, including COVID-19 image dataset, COVID-19 text dataset, COVID-19 audio dataset, other health-care datasets, other pandemic datasets, medicine dataset, and patient-related. Results show that a large number of studies are performed prepared in recent times to study the impacts of COVID-19 in society. Most of these datasets are based on patient's symptoms (cough, fever, headache, etc.) or image-based scanning. However, there is a strong need to study the hidden factors in COVID-19 variants and future pandemic identification or its chances.

## 10.6.2   *Artificial intelligence in smart health-care system*

Technology like AI provides the ability to interpret complex medical data, analyze images, video, audio, and text records, and help the doctor to treat the patient in

*Table 10.3    Comparative analysis of datasets available for healthcare, COVID-19, and pandemics*

| Dataset | A | B | C | D | E | F | G | Remark |
|---------|---|---|---|---|---|---|---|--------|
| [35] | Y | N | N | N | N | N | N | This is an image-based dataset to study the impact of COVID-19 in recent times. Here, a comparative analysis of COVID-19 and the non-COVID-19 dataset is made to have a better analysis. This dataset consists of X-ray and CT chest images |
| [36] | Y | N | N | N | N | N | N | This is a dataset of COVID-19 X-ray dataset. This dataset is divided into training and test datasets. This dataset is useful for COVID-19 virus detection, preliminary diagnosis, and contributes toward virus control progress |
| [37] | Y | N | N | N | N | N | N | This dataset is image-based one in which images are classified into six categories: viral, bacterial, fungal, lipoid, aspiration, and unknown. Each of these categories includes further classification. For example, viral images are classified as COVID-19 (SARS-CoV-2), SARS (SARS-CoV-1), MERS-CoV, Varicella, Influenza, and Herpes. Likewise, other categories are classified |
| [38] | Y | N | N | N | N | N | N | This dataset contains augmented X-ray images. In this dataset, images are classified as all augmented images and COVID-10 X-ray-augmented images |
| [39] | Y | N | N | N | N | N | N | This dataset contains CT images of a large number of COVID-19 patients. This dataset has the classification of images with COVID-19 and non-COVID-19 patients. These images are used by Tongji Hospital, Wuhan, China for diagnosis and treatment of patients |
| [40] | Y | Y | N | Y | N | N | N | This dataset contains X-ray images with detailed symptoms. Some of the symptoms are used to calculate the COVID-19 score. This analysis is performed to identify the chances of COVID-19. Dataset is divided into three major categories: training, validation, and testing. Using these categories, the whole dataset is |

*(Continues)*

*Table 10.3    (Continued)*

| Dataset | A | B | C | D | E | F | G | Remark |
|---------|---|---|---|---|---|---|---|--------|
|  |  |  |  |  |  |  |  | divided into two parts. The first part contains information about those images that are X-ray images for distribution. On the other hand, the second part contains those X-ray images that are collected to classify patient distribution |
| [41] | Y | Y | N | Y | N | N | N | This is another dataset over COVID-19 and non-COVID-19 symptoms. This dataset is regularly updated and the last update was performed on January 28, 2021. This dataset also contains CXR images having positive and negative COVID-19 cases. Here, pneumonia is the most common feature considered for analysis that can indicate COVID-19 as well. Here, chest radiography is applied to identify COVID-19 cases with different patients. This image-based analysis helps in identifying critical factors necessary to understand COVID-19 |
| [42] | Y | Y | N | Y | N | N | N | This is another image-based dataset that contains categories like left lung, right lung, cardiomediastinum, airways, ground-glass opacities, consolidation, pleural effusion, pneumothorax, endotracheal tube, central venous line, monitoring probes, nasogastric tube, chest tube, and tubings. Images of all these categories are used in experimentation to identify the COVID-19 symptoms |
| [43] | Y | N | N | N | N | N | N | This is another image-based dataset that contains lung images for identifying COVID-19-affected patients |
| [44] | Y | Y | N | Y | N | N | N | This image-based dataset focuses on multiple symptoms for identifying COVID-19 cases. Here, the dataset is divided into normal patients' images, COVID-19-affected images, pneumonia symptom images, lung opacity images, and metadata of all categories. Thus, this data is very useful in COVID-9 case identification and treatments |

*(Continues)*

*Table 10.3    (Continued)*

| Dataset | A | B | C | D | E | F | G | Remark |
|---|---|---|---|---|---|---|---|---|
| [45] | Y | N | N | N | N | N | N | This is another sort dataset with COVID-19 symptom identification using comparative analysis of pneumonia and normal patient |
| [46] | Y | N | N | N | N | N | N | This dataset contains CT images that can be more than 40 COVID-19 patient's data for analysis and study |
| [47] | Y | N | N | N | N | N | N | This dataset is not publically available for study |
| [48] | Y | N | N | N | N | N | N | This dataset contains COVID-19 feature-based images that were used in past for identifying COVID-19 patients with observable features |
| [49] | Y | Y | N | Y | N | N | N | This is an image-based dataset that classifies the COVID-19 symptoms into various categories, including common, less common, and rare. In the common category, symptoms include fever, cough, anosmia, fatigue, sputum, and shortness of breath. Among less common features, myalgia/arthralgia, headache, sore throat, chills, Pleuritic pain, and diarrhea are taken for identification. Likewise, nausea, vomiting, abdominal pain, GU bleeding, nasal congestion, palpitation chest tightness, hemoptysis, and stroke are taken in the rare category. In conclusion, this data is very useful for image and feature-based analysis |
| [50] | Y | N | N | N | N | N | N | This image-based dataset is labeled with COVID-19 CT scans with left, and right lungs, and infections. Dataset is prepared to have a comparative analysis of COVID-19 and non-COVID-19 symptoms with lung disease features |
| [51] | Y | N | N | N | N | N | N | This dataset is prepared with lung and infection segmentation with limited annotations, segment COVID-19 CT scans from non-COVID-19 scans, and both COVID-19 and non-COVID-19 scans. The annotation and labeled dataset is useful for easy classification |
| [52] | Y | N | N | N | N | N | N | This is ultrasound-based dataset for COVID-19 patient identification. |

*(Continues)*

*Table 10.3* (*Continued*)

| Dataset | A | B | C | D | E | F | G | Remark |
|---|---|---|---|---|---|---|---|---|
| | | | | | | | | The dataset is helpful for noninvasive, cheap, portable and available for almost all medical facilities compared to other challenging and time-consuming options for COVID-19 identification |
| [53] | Y | N | N | N | N | N | N | This is a chest CT-scan-based dataset for COVID-19 identification and adds a provision to apply artificial intelligence in radiology for data analysis based on advanced innovative technologies |
| [54] | Y | N | N | N | N | N | N | This is another CT scan image-based public dataset available for SARS-CoV-2 CT scan. This dataset contains 1,252 images for SARS-CoV-2-infected COVID-19 patients and 1,230 non-SARS-CoV-2-infected COVID-19 patients. All of this data is collected from Sao Paulo, Brazil hospitals. This dataset can be used for COVID-19 identification and comparative feature analysis with non-COVID-19 patient data |
| [55] | Y | N | N | N | N | N | N | BIMCV-COVID-19+ is a large dataset with chest X-ray and CXR (CR, DX), and computed tomography images. In this image-based analysis, COVID-19 patients can be identified with radiographic findings, pathologies experimentation, polymerase chain reaction (PCR) prediction, immunoglobulin (IgG), and immunoglobulin M (IgM) diagnosis. In addition to this, various other test data is available for analysis. In this dataset, high-resolution images are stored with the medical imaging data structure that includes semantic segmentation of radiographic findings. In addition to images, patient's demographic evolution, method of projection, and acquisition are also available for studies |
| [56] | Y | N | N | N | N | N | N | This dataset is labeled chest X-ray and CT-images-based dataset for COVID-19 identification. This dataset is weakly labeled. This dataset is |

(*Continues*)

*Table 10.3    (Continued)*

| Dataset | A | B | C | D | E | F | G | Remark |
|---------|---|---|---|---|---|---|---|--------|
|         |   |   |   |   |   |   |   | a collection of medical images and can be used for comparative analysis of clinical symptoms and clinical findings of COVID-19 and other influenza demonstrations |
| [57]    | Y | N | N | N | N | N | N | This dataset is not publicly available but is used with AI and machine-learning-based systems for identifying COVID-19 patients |
| [58]    | Y | N | N | N | N | N | N | In this work, deep learning is applied for an image-based dataset for identifying COVID-19 patients |

A: COVID-19 image dataset, B: COVID-19 text dataset, C: COVID-19 audio dataset, D: other health-care datasets, E: other pandemic datasets, F: medicine dataset, G: patient dataset.

many efficient ways. The use of technology can help in reducing the medical treatment costs that are increasing day by day. The costly medical treatments are difficult to select for many especially people living below the poverty line. In the case of scarcity of resources, and higher medical costs, an AI-based system can help the patient to self-monitor themselves and reduce the cost to a certain extent. AI-technology can behave like human intelligence, pattern recognition, data analysis, anomaly, and outlier detection and prediction. These features can help the medical system to handle more complex challenges that a human can handle. AI technology is much rich in handling the problem and finding the solutions. For example, AI-technology can widely be used for analyzing the COVID-19 symptoms in recent times, accelerate the scientific discovery processing to handle COVID-19, its variants, and future pandemics. Usage of AI technology is not just helpful for medical staff but it helps administrative staff as well. To administrative bodies, this system can automate the administrative jobs, accelerate and amplify the system transparency to staff roles and responsibilities, and remove fabricated services. In the medical system, data is very important. To handle the data efficiently, error detection and removal methods need to be focused upon. This error can occur in data collected for diagnosis, prognosis, and therapy. In medical diagnosis, patient data collection, and interpretation using doctor's knowledge and experience formulate it to a proper diagnosis and therapeutic plans for a patient. In the present system, all of these plans are prepared by a physician. However, it is expected that this system can be automated with AI in nearby times. This automation can help the patients to give their inputs and get the diagnosis in output. An expert system is a well-known example of this type of treatment. An expert system's inference engine can handle complex problems with multiple If-then type rules and transform the input to actionable outputs. Thus, expert systems are very much useful to doctors in clinical decision-making. To handle COVID-19 patients, infectious disease knowledge can be represented in the form of production rules. The conditional statements in production rules can help to emphasize overdiagnosis and management of COVID-19-infected patients.

### 10.6.3  *Machine learning aspects in smart health-care system*

Sujath *et al.* [59] applied the linear regression algorithm to identify the ailment and pace of COVID-19 cases in India. This analysis has experimented with over Kaggle dataset and multilayered perceptron and vector autoregression is used for this experimentation. In the analysis, it has been observed that the main symptoms of COVID-19 are cold, cough, and fever. COVID-19 can cause respiratory ailment with manifestations as well. In this experimentation, definition and data combination is kept persistently for analysis. Figure 10.3 shows an example of a machine- and deep-learning-based system that can be used for COVID-19 diagnosis and treatment. This system is picked from the real-life observations and it is divided into three layers (patient-level, hospital-level, and national level analyses). The roles of ML at different layers are briefly explained as follows:

- National-level ML usages are important for performing randomized clinical trials and observations. To analyze the success of new medicines, clinical trials are performed in a randomized fashion over a different set of populations. Randomized experiments in medical observation, patient monitoring, medical services, and other healthcare-related systems generate a large amount of data. This data analysis can easily be performed through the machine and deep learning models. In health-care systems, ML models take input from EMR and image-based medical data and give clinical trials recommendation as output.

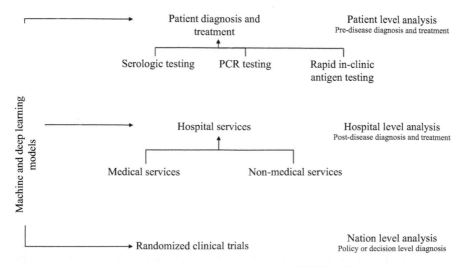

*Figure 10.3   A machine- and deep-learning-based COVID-19 treatment system*

Over the clinical set of data, natural language processing can be applied for generating more medical data that can be further analyzed. This is an iterative cycle that operates until the desired output is achieved.

• Hospital-level analysis includes hospital services (medical and nonmedical) that can also generate a large amount of data for analysis. The medical services include the type of treatment, medicines, operations, equipment, and other medical support. Among nonmedical operations, administration, payment, insurance, patient monitoring, and other duties are counted. To automate the complete medical setup, both medical and nonmedical services have to be precise that is possible with the least error-based ML approach. For example, the medicine supplier system should have a record of how, which, and what medicines are delivered to different hospitals. Analysis of this data can indicate the future requirements, hospital practices in experimenting with the medicines and their success ratio, a list of authentic medicine suppliers and distributors in a specific geographical region, and many more.

• In the patient-level analysis, patient diagnosis and treatments can be analyzed for a depth study. In this analysis, patient test records that include serology, PCR, and rapid in-clinic antigen tests data are recorded for COVID-19. This analysis if analyzed through machine- and deep learning aspects then it is very much useful for patients to get timely diagnosis and treatment.

## 10.7    Virtualization and IoT in IoT for smart health-care system

Virtualization technology is important in the future because of the increase in the number of working people and advancements in technology. Using virtualization, there is no need for a patient to visit a doctor instead physician or doctor can attend to the patient through an online video call. Likewise, the experimentations can be extended to a large scale for the virtual hospital. Thus, virtualization can help to handle a large number of patients and it is also useful in providing specialized doctor services on a large scale. The concept of virtual healthcare is surfacing the market due to the increasing number of working people and advancements in technology. Virtual healthcare can be defined as virtual visits to physicians through video calls, chats, or phones. And this is all possible because of the audio and video connectivity enabling virtual meeting from anywhere. Sometimes a patient is away from the city, or unable to reach the clinic due to various surrounding factors. In these cases, videoconferencing with an off-site health-care practitioner is the most convenient option.

### 10.7.1    *Operating system and storage virtualization for desktop- and mobile-based smart health-care applications*

Ambigai *et al.* [60] discussed the smart health-care application to improve the quality of life of urban people. The medical records of patients stored securely in case they for virtual machine migration. Smart health-care applications store patient's medical records, analyze these records, and monitor the patient's condition regularly. Integration of cloud services made the availability of patient records easy, fast, and to a longer distance. This work has used the Ant colony optimization algorithm to improve the virtual machine selection for generating a sequence of random optimized solutions. Here, a large number of iterations are performed that execute the medical record processing at a much faster rate. Virtual machine migration using particle swarm optimization and virtual machine selection algorithm minimized the number of virtual machines to be migrated and reduces energy consumption. The objective of smart health-care application development and integration with virtualization is to minimize the number of virtual machine requirements to be migrated, reduce energy consumption, and minimize response time by handling a large number of users. Demirkan [61] has proposed a framework to include three-layer architecture for a smart health-care system. In the proposed framework, three-layer architecture is having an option of the service-oriented framework to include virtualization of resources. The conceptualized data have driven model in mobile and cloud-enabled smart health-care system with virtualization give better performance compared to other approaches. The health-care organization provides cost-effective solutions to health-care services with IT setup costs and reduced risks. Figure 10.4 shows the smart health-care system blocks with virtualization. In this system, inputs can be provided through health-care service providers with different specializations. These specializations include services to handle patients, patient data, equipment suppliers, and other services like medicines distribution and staff arrangements. In an IT-based smart health-care system, services operate with different data, applications, and software. In service-oriented

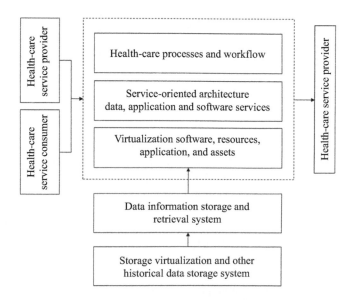

*Figure 10.4 A smart health-care system with virtualization*

architecture, data, application, and software can be divided into two categories: software services and components. In software services, all technical aspects related to individual software execution can be explored, whereas components include the integration of one or more software services to achieve health-care objectives. For example, patient treatment requires a historical data retrieval system and a patient monitoring system. In another example, data may be required to share with multiple systems. This feature can be achieved through storage virtualization. In storage virtualization, medical records can be transferred easily and at a higher rate. Further, if application virtualization is shared with storage, the advantage of a complete system can be taken. A smart health-care system with virtualization can give various advantages. Some of the advantages are explained as follows:

- Big-data-enabled intelligence and acknowledgment management systems and services are very useful to the health-care system because the health-care sector can collect, analyze, share, and visualize the medical structured or unstructured data for patient treatment and actionable decisions.
- The patient-centric or electronic-record-centric health-care system is useful for the future in keeping the data secure and safe. This data can be utilized for better medical treatments and patient monitoring. This data can be used for preparing patient profiles and can be interrelated for symptom-related experimentation in medical treatment.
- Data linked with ambulance and other medical services can help the patients to arrive and leave the hospital as per his/her needs. Availability of such data can automate the patient arrival and discharge system.
- Availability of data can reduce medical costs, shorten patient stays, and can implement medical treatments much easily. All this is possible when medical staff is educated with advanced technology to handle the medical treatments and can see and understand the variations in medical data.

In the area of integrating virtualization technology with healthcare, very few initiatives have been taken. This area can be explored with the objective of (i) identifying the direct and indirect risks associated with the collection, storage, sharing, processing, and analysis of data at various levels; (ii) apply ML and AI principles in prior identification of medical operations with the highest potential of improving the patient's condition; (iii) to understand the challenges in enhancing the successful medical practices to the industry or large-scale implementations; (iv) focus on research in smart health-care systems that offer opportunities to study the different environments and propose models, frameworks, and methods to improve and automate the health-care services.

## 10.8    IoT and quantum computing for smart health-care system

This section explores the IoT and quantum computing operations integration for the smart health-care system. Abd EL-Latif *et al.* [62] explained the importance of IoT and quantum computing integration and proposed a two-phase cryptosystem for security against quantum computing. Quantum computation and quantum algorithms developed in recent times are mathematically very strong compared to traditional cryptography primitives and protocols. Thus, quantum walks is the term used for computational models incorporating quantum algorithms and cryptography. In [63], a quantum-walks-based privacy-preserving mechanism is proposed for IoT used in the health-care system. The proposed system is a two-phase system in which substitution and permutations are computed using quantum walks. These computations provide security and safety. The simulation results show that there is enough evidence to prove the robustness of image encryption and experimentation done for quantum walks. These experiments are conducted for protecting patient's data and ensuring privacy. Fernández-Caramés [63] identified the threats to traditional cryptography primitives and protocols. Quantum computing is important for cryptography due to its ability in solving key distribution problem and high security in insecure communication channels. Quantum computing provides high security to email exchange, financial transactions, digital signed documents, medical data, and military secret information exchanges. Traditional cryptography mechanisms such as Rivest, Shamir, Adleman (RSA), Elliptic Curve Cryptography (ECC), Hyper ECC, ElGamal, and Diffie–Hellman algorithms are integral part of network-based communication. These algorithms are in use over both resourceful and resource-constraint devices [65,66]. However, long-term usage against quantum computing challenges is not feasible for resource constraint IoT devices. In [67], quantum computing survey is performed. Thereafter, need of post-quantum cryptosystem is discussed. The need of IoT architecture and challenges are discussed with future trends to secure both resourceful and resource-constraint devices and networks. The survey article provides a wide range of survey over post-quantum cryptography, IoT secure, need to integrated quantum computing with traditional cryptography system for security analysis and important instruction to handle the future network against quantum computing challenges.

## 10.8.1 Introduction to IoT and quantum computing

Quantum technology with low power IoT devices is a major challenge for designing and developing a secure IoT network having security against quantum attacks. Quantum technology has various associated terminologies, including (i) quantum networks; (ii) quantum simulators; (iii) post-quantum cryptography; (iv) quantum sensors and particle generators atomic clocks; (v) quantum cloud computing; (vi) quantum memories, quantum repeaters, quantum chips; (vii) quantum software; (viii) quantum computing, and quantum annealers; (ix) quantum materials; and (x) quantum key distribution. All of these terminologies are important for quantum computations.

## 10.8.2 Quantum computing and smart health-care system

Smart health-care system requires fast and easy processing results. Among these results, quantum computing can play important roles, including (i) ensuring security to end devices. Patient's data security is prime concern in futuristic health-care systems. Quantum-computation-based security system in smart healthcare can ensure this at a minimum cost. (ii) Analyzing large data with minimum time duration. Health-care system needs patient's data to be analyzed at much faster rate compared to traditional systems. This analysis can predict the disease at an early stage and helps in patient-centric treatments as well. Quantum computing plays transformative effects in many ways. For example, quantum computing can help in developing supersonic drug design at much faster rate. In pharmaceutical industry, pharmaceutical developments are lengthy and costly. Here, IT-technologies like artificial intelligence, human organs-on chip, and silico trials play important roles. For example, the treatment in the case of Ebola virus, and developing new drugs with smart algorithm. According to [64], the important use cases of quantum computing in healthcare include the following: (i) it is helpful in diagnostic assistance. Quantum computing can diagnose the patients at early stage with more accuracy and effi-ciency. This is possible because of the use of advanced technology and fast com-putations; (ii) it is helpful in people healthy with personalized interventions and precision medicine; and (iii) the careful analysis and processing can optimize insur-ance premiums and price. Quantum computing can play important role in health-care sector by analyzing the medical images, detecting edges in images and image matching algorithms. Thus, quantum computing is very helpful in fast image analysis and image-aided diagnostics. Using quantum computing, it is much easier to com-bine multiple datasets, perform analysis, and give results at much higher rate. Quantum support vector machine is very helpful in enhancing the classification and performing diagnosis that classify cancerous cells from normal easily.

### 10.8.3   Challenges of quantum computing to health-care data and data security

The major challenges of quantum computing architecture in health-care domain include (i) its feasibility in real scenario for applications like healthcare. So far, very few quantum computing machines are in practice. Most of the quantum computing implementations are mathematical in present scenario. (ii) Quantum computers are required to have interdependencies and correlations among con-tributions that optimize treatment effectiveness. (iii) To provide precision centric health status and intervention, transition from umbrella treatment to patient-centric precision health status and interventions are necessary to be focused. (iv) Optimizing pricing is another major challenge for quantum computing. In quantum computation, risks to patients, their health conditions, risk model analysis, and importance of pricing models are important to understand and realize.

## 10.9   Post-quantum cryptography solutions for futuristic security in smart health-care system

This section explores the usage of post-quantum in the health-care sector. To secure the cyberattacks against quantum computing, various post-quantum approaches are proposed. In literature [67–73], various post-quantum cryptography-based approaches are proposed to secure IoT network that is useful to the health-care system. In [67], post-quantum cryptography aspects are discussed for IoT networks that can secure health-care applications and data. This work has discussed the limitation and future applications of quantum cryptography in the health-care system. It has been realized that quantum computation can revolutionize the health-care system and ways of handling patients. Quantum computations are capable of providing the processing power to forecast futuristic health-care malfunctioning. The existing health-care industry in a developed or developing country is storing data securely. However, the biggest threat to this industry is the breach of information which is possible through quantum computing. To protect the system from quantum attacks, post-quantum cryptography can play an important role. In healthcare, an attacker can eavesdrop, modify, spoof, and intercept the information. Post-quantum cryptography can be classified into various forms. These forms and their importance to the health-care sector are explained as follows.

### 10.9.1   Code-based cryptography for health-care data and system

In [71–74], cryptography approaches suitable for health-care systems are discussed. However, most of the cryptography approaches use traditional encryption/decryption and authentication algorithms for security. However, code-based cryptography can be an effective approach for securing a smart health-care system. In code-based cryptography, the use of a code-based encoding and decoding system is useful. Numerical and polynomial-based encoding and decoding procedures can make the breaching job tough for attackers. Thus, this area needs exploration. Further, integration of already developed code-based cryptography mechanisms with health-care systems needs experiment. The chances of higher security are expected as the post-quantum cryptography mechanisms are difficult to break because of their complexity.

### 10.9.2   Lattice-based cryptography for health-care data and system

In [75,76], lattice-based cryptography is explored for the health-care system. There are various lattice-based cryptography mechanisms like encryption/decryption (NTRUEncrypt, GGH encryption, Peikert's Ring), the hash function (SWIFFT, LASH), homomorphic encryption, and signature-based approaches (GGH, NTRUSign, Learning with Errors). All of these approaches are helpful in health-care systems. For example, NTRUEncrypt [77] is used for application and data-level security in healthcare. The use of encryption/decryption is explored but other lattice-based cryptography is yet needed to experiment for health-care services.

### 10.9.3   Hash-based cryptography for health-care data and system

In [67,75–78], the importance of post-quantum cryptography mechanisms for health-care data and application is studied. In these studies, quantum computation is tried to be integrated with IoT networks and blockchain for providing healthcare-related services. Quantum computations integrated with blockchain technology need the implementation of hash computations. In a blockchain network, the hash function provides security to the network using consensus algorithms. The concept of Hash-cash is also relevant for integrating immutability and transparency to transactions.

### 10.9.4    Multivariate cryptography for health-care data and system

In [79], the importance of multivariate post-quantum cryptography mechanism is discussed for different applications, including healthcare. In this work, a proxy signature mechanism to delegate signature to other is discussed. The requirement of ensuring secure delegation is used of authentic servers. The use of proxy signature approaches protects against various quantum adversaries. The multivariate public-key cryptography, its heuristic proofs, and signature approaches are explored. The authors have implemented the proxy signature scheme and results are analyzed. In observations, it has been found that distributed approach using multivariate cryptography can give security to various potential applications including healthcare.

### 10.9.5    Supersingular cryptography for health-care data and system

In supersingular cryptography, the use of discrete mathematics adds potential challenges to attackers. For example, Menezes, Okamoto, and Vanstone approach for supersingular curves provides higher security compared to traditional cryptosystem. The proposed approach provides a significant improvement in performance (e.g., bandwidth) and higher security. The use of discrete mathematics in a supersingular cryptosystem increases the complexity and security that can be useful for medical data as well.

### 10.9.6    Post-quantum cryptography application and research challenges for smart health-care system

The major challenges of integrating post-quantum cryptography aspects with the smart health-care system are as follows [80–82]: (i) implementation issues that are impossible to handle in the present scenario. A large number of post-quantum aspects are theoretical and the lack of sufficient platforms to test in real scenario is not possible in nearby times. (ii) Post-quantum cryptography aspects are considered to be more complex than can cause major disruption to systems and stakeholders as compared to prior migrations. (iii) The transition from existing security infrastructure to post-quantum cryptography-based infrastructure will be costly and can cause more disruptive changeover. (iv) Existing security infrastructure is developed over a long time in consideration with challenges evolved. The major challenge is the orderly transition from existing application-based scenarios to advanced applications (like smart healthcare)-based application scenarios. This transition also expects an orderly follow-up that does not look feasible in nearby times.

## 10.10 Drone and robotics operation management using IoT network for smart health-care system

This section explores the usage of drone networks in health-care operations. Recently, various drone and robot-based applications are proposed for COVID-19 operations [83–86]. Among these applications, drone-based medication, sanitization, surveillance, and monitoring are popularly used. The use of robots in the health-care sector is largely observed for surgical operations and hospitality. The research in drone networks and robotics for healthcare is not new. Over the last two decades [34,87–90], various advancements are observed in this sector that can be used in the health-care sector effectively. The recent usages of drones and robotics are explained as follows.

### 10.10.1 Medical robots and recent developments

This section explores the usage of robots in the medical and health-care domain. In recent times, various advancements are made in this sector. Some of the recent developments are discussed as follows.

Lum *et al.* [87] proposed an IoT-network-integrated surgical drone. Here, medical equipment, kits, and medicines are remotely arranged with minimum human efforts. This experimentation is performed in a remote area to successfully execute surgical operations. Here, drones are also used to capture the live environment and broadcast it to the remote control system. Authors claim successful execution of the medical operation. However, it has been observed that delay in signal transmission has affected surgical activities. These activities and corresponding results are important to observe and analyze. Zhang and Lu [91] have surveyed recent advancements in the field of bionics, flexible actuation, sensing, and intelligent control systems. This study has prepared a detailed limitation analysis of various relevant studies performed flexible, secure, and application-specific research directions for the usage of drones in real-time scenarios. The clinical medical applications are very useful in ensuring the potential capabilities of medical robots. In these clinical applications, medical robots are found to be flexible for usage especially power, intelligent control, and stiffness in medical operations and services. These three factors are also considered as important influence factors in soft medical robot history. Siegfarth *et al.* [92] discussed the usage of 3D-printed hydraulic actuators for medical operations with medical robots. Such sensors and actuators in the medical sector help in collecting real-time patient data and helpful for immediate observations and treatment as well.

### 10.10.2 Drone and IoT network for health-care operations

This section discusses the usage of drone devices for health-care operations. There are many approaches proposed in recent times for providing medical services [34,87,88]. Internet of Drones (IoDs) in the case of multi-drone movement or IoD and robot devices is necessary to successfully perform medical operations [34,87,88]. Some of the recent development in this area is explained as follows.

Kumar *et al.* [34] proposed a drone-based system for thermal imaging, sanitization, monitoring, surveillance, and medication. In the proposed system, data can be collected and processing at local and remote places before to share with the hospital. Here, a drone-based system is designed and used for health-care operations. To avoid collision among multi-drone flying strategies, single and multilayer drone flying approaches are proposed. Here, an analysis of the proposed approach is made using simulators. Results show that the proposed approach is efficient in drone flying and handling health-care operations. Lum *et al.* [87] proposed a drone and robot integrated system for surgical operation. Here, a drone device is used to move to a remote area where it is difficult to provide health-care service. There, a robot is an instruction to operate and perform medical surgery. Here, a drone device is used to signal and arrange the medical facilities necessary for medical operations. Câmara *et al.* [88] have discussed the importance of drones in disaster scenarios. In such scenarios, drone devices are very useful in remote monitoring and surveillance. Drone devices can collect the live on-ground status that can help in arranging necessary services especially medical and first aid kits. In today's scenario, drone devices are available for touchless screens and secure reporting. These services can make pandemic handling much easier and simpler. The usage of such devices can reduce the cost of monitoring and extending the health-care service for needful compared to costs observed during COVID-19 times. Kim *et al.* [89] addressed the issue of providing medication and test kits to chronic disease patients. This experimentation has used drones for this service and it has been found that drones are very useful in this case. Here, drones are used for two major purposes: (i) identifying the optimal number of drones required for handling medical services and (ii) how to reduce the cost of drone-based medical operations where medication is provided to the patient and test kits (that include blood and other samples) are collected. In this approach, optimization approach is used for cost–benefit analysis. Results show that drone-aided health-care services are very powerful for health-care services and easy to apply. Graboyes and Skorup [90] explored medical drones. Here, technical and policy challenges are discussed in detail. Flying drones and collecting data can breach privacy and security. Thus, flying drones in many countries are not allowed. Besides, the lack of drone-related policies does not provide easy and effective solutions for integrating this technology with the real-time application such as healthcare. Here, the solution is proposed to have an initial step to make it feasible on-ground. In conclusion, implementing the proposed approach in the real-time application needs to solve large challenges that are difficult to achieve in the present scenario. To address this challenge, infrastructure level changes and transparent policies are required.

### 10.10.3  *Robot, drone, and IoT network integrations for health-care applications*

In [87–90], it has been observed that drone usages can be observed from independent flying or observational planning. In [93–101], drones can be used in an interconnected environment using IoT concepts. The use of IoT or constituting

IoDs help in preparing a collaborative support environment with partial or full automation. IoD can be controlled either through fixed cellular infrastructure or privately governed policies. In private IoD, Internet governance principles are required to successfully implement it. In Internet governance principles, application-specific nomenclature, addressing, interconnection, access control, and security primitives are required to be clarified. For example, there are a large number of small- to large-size medical equipment available for surgical operations [102]. Identification of equipment, their operations (to maximum possibilities), patient monitoring, live image capturing, contactless medication, and medical services can be extended with drones and their collaboration. IoD is a concept that can ensure maximum security as well. Presently, drone noise, large size, battery constraints, and lesser security are major constraints to apply in real scenarios. However, outdoor drone services to rural and remote areas can fulfill the need for lack of infrastructure and manpower to handle health-care services. The major challenges in implementing drone-based strategies in medical or health-care operations include the following: (i) air-space awareness is required. For an electromechanical device, it is difficult to identify the space where it has to execute its operations. Thus, a preplanned strategy is required and its mapping in the drone devices is equally important. (ii) Non-line-of-sight control is another major challenge. In this challenge, controlling the drones across the boundaries is considered at large. In the case of IoD, the same challenge exists as well. In IoD, drones in line-of-sight of each other can work collaboratively and are controllable as well. It is difficult to successfully move, control, and operate the drones in non-line-of-sight of control. (iii) Location of drone movement is equally important. In a large number of countries, flying drones in open space are not allowed because of security and privacy issues. Thus, it is always better to preplan and take the government's approval by ensuring that flying will be safe and secure from every aspect. (iv) Finally, a collision-free environment is required for drones to fly and operate. Collisions can be drone to drone, and drone to object. Drone-to-drone collision avoidance comes in collaborative flying strategy in IoD. On the other hand, drone-to-object collision avoidance is part of awareness of the area and preplanned flying strategy. In real time, collisions can be avoided with LiDAR.

## 10.10.4   Recent developments and future directions

Kumar *et al.* [103] proposed a drone-based approach for handling the COVID-19 pandemic. This approach has proposed a single and multiplayer drone movement strategy. In this preplanned strategy, multiple drones can fly without collision. To avoid collisions, either the LiDAR approach can be used or a preplanned drone movement strategy can be followed. With this approach, it is possible to provide health-care services on a large scale as well. It has been observed that COVID-19 patients are increasing day by day. To handle a large number of patients with minimum contact is possible through drones and robotics. Thus, a collision-free drone movement environment is useful for handling COVID-19 and pandemic situations. In the future, it is required to have drone-based data collection and real-time ML experimentation. ML experimentation would be the first step to automate the drones for medical operations. Thereafter, it can be extended to have a surgical drone or doctor drone. These drones can have collaborative efforts to successfully perform multi-organ and multispecialty surgical operations. For example, Li *et al.* [104] proposed multi-vehicle detection in a congested environment. With this approach, multi drone-based multi-objective detection will be useful for health-care operations as well. McRae *et al.* [105] prepared the case study to apply drones for complex high altitude search and rescue operations. Here, the people and object detection approach can be applied to collect the data in real time. This data can later be analyzed for process improvement and removing the lags in observations. In pandemic situations, drones can be used at a large scale for delivering blood, medicines, samples, and organs. Applying contactless organ delivery would be a major challenge for drones but if it is found to be experimentally successful, it would be the fastest and best way of saving lives. In the present scenario, it has been observed that the lack of medical services in rural and remote areas was a major hurdle to handle COVID-19 pandemic situations. With drones, this can be made possible easily. In the present scenario, the drone market is increasing day by day. A huge investment is expected to be prepared with multi-drone multi-application planning. With this approach, drones can be effectively used on a large scale.

## 10.11    Conclusion and future scope

This work has surveyed and explored the usage of information technology and its recent developments in the health-care sector. Various technological advancements made the usage of technology important for various applications, including health-care and medical services. This work has explored the recent proposal in AI, ML, drone, robotics, cryptography, and IoT to the health-care sector. This survey and various comparative analyses drawn in this work are useful to analyze the factor necessary while taking the advantage of technology in the health-care sector. Some technologies (such as drones) require infrastructure level changes to accommodate a collision-free and safe environment without which it would be difficult to adapt in real-time application.

## References

[1]  Singh, R. P., Javaid, M., Haleem, A. and Suman, R., 2020. Internet of things (IoT) applications to fight against COVID-19 pandemic. *Diabetes & Metabolic Syndrome: Clinical Research & Reviews*, 14(4), pp. 521–524.
[2]  Kamal, M., Aljohani, A. and Alanazi, E., 2020. IoT meets COVID-19: Status, challenges, and opportunities. arXiv preprint arXiv: 2007. 12268.
[3]  Amit Kumar M., 2019. IoT Healthcare, GitHub, https://github.com/mishracodes/IOT-Healthcare.

[4] Sharath S., HealthCareSystem IoT, GitHub, https://github.com/sharath29/Health-Care-System-IOT.

[5] Drupad K., 2018. HealthCare IoT, GitHub, https://github.com/dkhublani/Healthcare-IOT.

[6] Kien N., 2020. IoT HealthCare GitHub, https://github.com/Nyquixt/iot-healthcare.

[7] Ritvik, 2017. IoT HealthCare GitHub, https://github.com/ritvik91/IoT-healthcare.

[8] Mumtaz, S., Bo, A., Al-Dulaimi, A. and Tsang, K. F., 2018. Guest editorial 5G and beyond mobile technologies and applications for industrial IoT (IIoT). *IEEE Transactions on Industrial Informatics*, 14(6), pp. 2588–2591.

[9] Rathee, G., Sharma, A., Kumar, R. and Iqbal, R., 2019. A secure communicating things network framework for industrial IoT using blockchain technology. *Ad Hoc Networks*, 94, p. 101933.

[10] Simić, M., Sladić, G. and Milosavljević, B., 2017, June. A case study IoT and blockchain powered healthcare. In *Proc. ICET*.

[11] McGhin, T., Choo, K. K. R., Liu, C. Z. and He, D., 2019. Blockchain in healthcare applications: Research challenges and opportunities. *Journal of Network and Computer Applications*, 135, pp. 62–75.

[12] Panarello, A., Tapas, N., Merlino, G., Longo, F. and Puliafito, A., 2018. Blockchain and IoT integration: A systematic survey. *Sensors*, 18(8), p. 2575.

[13] Reyna, A., Martín, C., Chen, J., Soler, E. and Díaz, M., 2018. On blockchain and its integration with IoT. Challenges and opportunities. *Future Generation Computer Systems*, 88, pp. 173–190.

[14] Nichol, P. B., Blockchain applications for healthcare, March 2016 [online]. Available: http://www.cio.com/article/3042603/innovation/blockchain-applications-for-healthcare.html.

[15] Satamraju, K. P and Malarkodi, B., 2020. Proof of concept of scalable integration of internet of things and blockchain in healthcare. *Sensors*, 20(5), p. 1389.

[16] Singh, K., Kaushik, K., Ahatsham and Shahare, V., 2020. "Role and impact of wearables in IoT healthcare," in *Advances in Intelligent Systems and Computing*, 1090, pp. 735–742. Singapore: Springer. doi: 10.1007/978-981-15-1480-7_67.

[17] Kaushik, K. and Singh, K., 2020. "Security and trust in IoT communications: Role and impact," in *Advances in Intelligent Systems and Computing*, vol. 989, pp. 791–798. Singapore: Springer. doi: 10.1007/978-981-13-8618-3_81.

[18] Brantly, A. F. and Brantly, N. D., 2020. Patient-centric cybersecurity. *Journal of Cyber Policy*, 5(3), pp. 372–391, doi: 10.1080/23738871.2020.1856902.

[19] Lu, Y. and Da Xu, L., 2019. Internet of things (IoT) cybersecurity research: A review of current research topics. *IEEE Internet of Things Journal*, 6(2), pp. 2103–2115, doi: 10.1109/JIOT.2018.2869847.

[20]   Yaqoob, I., Ahmed, E., Muhammad Habib ur Rehman, *et al.*, 2017. The rise of ransomware and emerging security challenges in the Internet of Things. *Computer Networks*, 129, pp. 444–458, doi: 10.1016/j.comnet.2017.09.003.

[21]   Nasiri, S., Sadoughi, F., Tadayon, M. H. and Dehnad, A., 2019. Security requirements of internet of things-based healthcare system: A survey study. *Acta Informatica Medica*, 27(4), pp. 253–258, doi: 10.5455/aim.2019. 27.253-258.

[22]   Usmonov, B., Evsutin, O., Iskhakov, A., Shelupanov, A., Iskhakova, A. and Meshcheryakov, R., 2017. The cybersecurity in development of IoT embedded technologies. In *2017 International Conference on Information Science and Communications Technologies, ICISCT 2017*, vol. 2017 (pp. 1–4), doi: 10.1109/ICISCT.2017.8188589.

[23]   Mohan, A., 2014. Cyber security for personal medical devices internet of things. In *Proceedings – IEEE International Conference on Distributed Computing in Sensor Systems, DCOSS 2014* (pp. 372–374), doi: 10.1109/ DCOSS.2014.49.

[24]   Conti, M., Dehghantanha, A., Franke, K. and Watson, S., 2018. Internet of Things security and forensics: Challenges and opportunities. *Future Generation Computer Systems*, 78, pp. 544–546, doi: 10.1016/j.future.2017.07.060.

[25]   Abie, H., 2019. Cognitive cybersecurity for CPS-IoT enabled healthcare ecosystems. In *International Symposium on Medical Information and Communication Technology, ISMICT*, vol. 2019, doi: 10.1109/ ISMICT.2019.8743670.

[26]   Coventry, L. and Branley, D., 2018. Cybersecurity in healthcare: A narrative review of trends, threats and ways forward. *Maturitas*, 113, pp. 48–52, doi: 10.1016/j.maturitas.2018.04.008.

[27]   Pan, J. and Yang, Z., 2018. Cybersecurity challenges and opportunities in the new 'edge computing + IoT' world. In *SDN-NFVSec 2018 – Proc. 2018 ACM Int. Work. Secur. Softw. Defin. Networks Netw. Funct. Virtualization, Co-located with CODASPY 2018*, vol. 2018 (pp. 29–32), doi: 10.1145/3180465.3180470.

[28]   Marques, G., Pitarma, R., Garcia, N. M. and Pombo, N., 2019. Internet of things architectures, technologies, applications, challenges, and future directions for enhanced living environments and healthcare systems: A review. *Electronics*, 8(10), p. 1081, doi: 10.3390/electronics8101081.

[29]   Ahad, A., Tahir, M. and Yau, K. L. A., 2019. 5G-based smart healthcare network: Architecture, taxonomy, challenges and future research directions. *IEEE Access*, 7, pp. 100747–100762, doi: 10.1109/ACCESS.2019.2930628.

[30]   Farahani, B., Firouzi, F., Chang, V., Badaroglu, M., Constant, N. and Mankodiya, K., 2018. Towards fog-driven IoT eHealth: Promises and challenges of IoT in medicine and healthcare. *Future Generation Computer Systems*, 78, pp. 659–676, doi: 10.1016/j.future.2017.04.036.

[31]   Featherstone, R. M., Boldt, R. G., Torabi, N. and Konrad, S. L., 2012. Provision of pandemic disease information by health sciences librarians: A

multisite comparative case series. *Journal of the Medical Library Association: JMLA*, 100(2), p. 104.

[32] Desai, B. C., 2020. Pandemic and big tech. In *Proceedings of the 24th Symposium on International Database Engineering & Applications* (pp. 1–10).

[33] Gupta, D., Bhatt, S., Gupta, M. and Tosun, A. S., 2021. Future smart connected communities to fight Covid-19 outbreak. *Internet of Things*, 13, p. 100342.

[34] Kumar, A., Sharma, K., Singh, H., Naugriya, S. G., Gill, S. S. and Buyya, R., 2021. A drone-based networked system and methods for combating coronavirus disease (COVID-19) pandemic. *Future Generation Computer Systems*, 115, pp. 1–19.

[35] El-Shafai, W. and El-Samie, F. A. (12 June 2020), Extensive COVID-19 X-Ray and CT Chest Images Dataset, Mendeley Data. https://data.mendeley.com/datasets/8h65ywd2jr/3

[36] Khoong, W. H., (March 2020) COVID-19 Xray Dataset (Train & Test Sets), Kaggle, https://www.kaggle.com/khoongweihao/covid19-xray-dataset-train-test-sets/version/1

[37] Cohen, J. P., Morrison, P., Dao, L., Roth, K., Duong, T. Q. and Ghassemi, M. COVID-19 Image Data Collection: Prospective Predictions Are the Future. Retrieved from https://github.com/iece8023/covid-chestxray-dataset, 2020, arXiv:2006.11988.

[38] Alqudah, A. M. and Qazan, S. (26March 2020), Mendelcy Data https://data.mendeley.com/datasets/2fxz4px6d8/4

[39] Zhao, J., Zhang, Y., He, X. and Xie, P., 2020, COVID-CT-Dataset: a CT scan dataset about COVID-19, Github, https://github.com/UCSD-AI4H/COVID-CT

[40] Mangal, A., Kalia, S., Rajgopal, H., Rangarajan, K., Namboodiri, V., Banerjee, S. and Arora, C., 2020, CovidAID: COVID-19 Detection Using ChestX-Ray, Github, https://github.com/arpanmangal/CovidAID

[41] Wang, L., Lin, Z. Q. and Wong, A., 2020, COVID-Net: a tailored deep convolutional neural network design for detection of COVID-19 cases from chest X-ray images, https://doi.org/10.1038/s41598-020-76550-z

[42] General Blockchain, 2021, covid-19-chest-xray-segmentations-dataset, https://github.com/GeneralBlockchain/

[43] Sajid, N., 2020, COVID-19 Patients Lungs X Ray Images 10000, Kaggle, https://www.kaggle.com/nabeelsajid917/covid-19-x-ray-10000-images

[44] Rahman, T., 2020, COVID-19 Radiography Database, Kaggle, https://www.kaggle.com/tawsifurrahman/covid19-radiography-database

[45] Khoong, W. H., (March 2020) COVID-19 Xray Dataset (Train & Test Sets), Kaggle, https://www.kaggle.com/khoongweihao/covid19-xray-dataset-train-test-sets

[46] Jenssen, H. B., 2020, COVID-19 CT segmentation dataset, https://medium.com/@hbjenssen/covid-19-radiology-data-collection-and-preparation-for-artificial-intelligence-4ecece97bb5b

[47]    Rahman, T., 2020, COVID 19 Detection with X-Ray & COVID19 - Pytorch, Kaggle, https://www.kaggle.com/portgasray/covid-19-detection-with-x-ray-covid19-pytorch

[48]    Società Italiana di Radiologia,2020, covid-19 Database, https://sirm.org/category/senza-categoria/covid-19/

[49]    Dr Daniel J. Bel , 30 Oct 2021, COVID-19 radiopaedia, https://radiopaedia.org/articles/covid-19-4?lang=us

[50]    Ma, J.; 2020, COVID-19 CT Lung and Infection Segmentation Dataset, zendo, https://zenodo.org/record/3757476#.YX2FOlVBzIW

[51]    Ma, J. *et al.*, 2021, MP-COVID-19-SegBenchmark, gitee, https://gitee.com/junma11/COVID-19-CT-Seg-Benchmark

[52]    Born, J. *et al.*, 2021, Accelerating Detection of Lung Pathologies with Explainable Ultrasound Image Analysis ,GitHub, https://github.com/jannis-born/covid19_pocus_ultrasound

[53]    Stanislav E. S., 2020, Artificial intelligence in radiology, MosMedData, https://mosmed.ai/en/

[54]    Eduardo, P., 2020, SARS-COV-2 Ct-Scan Dataset, Kaggle, SARS-COV-2 Ct-Scan Dataset

[55]    BIMCV-COVID19,2020, BIMCV-COVID19, Datasets related to COVID19's pathology course, BIMCV, https://bimcv.cipf.es/bimcv-projects/bimcv-covid19/

[56]    Yang H. and Sohn E. Expanding Our Understanding of COVID-19 from Biomedical Literature Using Word Embedding. *Int J Environ Res Public Health*. 2021; 18(6): 3005. doi: 10.3390/ijerph18063005. PMID: 33804131; PMCID: PMC7998313

[57]    Banerjee, I., Sinha, P., Purkayastha, S., *et al.*, 2020. Was there COVID-19 back in 2012? Challenge for AI in Diagnosis with Similar Indications. arXiv preprint arXiv: 2006. 13262.

[58]    Ahsan, M. M., Gupta, K. D., Islam, M. M., Sen, S., Rahman, M. and Hossain, M. S., 2020. Study of different deep learning approach with explainable AI for screening patients with COVID-19 symptoms: Using CT scan and chest x-ray image dataset. arXiv preprint arXiv: 2007. 12525.

[59]    Sujath, R., Chatterjee, J. M. and Hassanien, A. E., 2020. A machine learning forecasting model for COVID-19 pandemic in India. *Stochastic Environmental Research and Risk Assessment*, 34, pp. 959–972.

[60]    Ambigai, S. D., Manivannan, K. and Shanthi, D., 2018. An efficient virtual machine migration for smart healthcare using particle swarm optimization algorithm. *International Journal of Pure and Applied Mathematics*, 118(20), pp. 3715–3722.

[61]    Demirkan, H., 2013. A smart healthcare systems framework. *IT Professional*, 15(5), pp. 38–45.

[62]    Abd EL-Latif, A. A., Abd-El-Atty, B., Abou-Nassar, E. M. and Venegas-Andraca, S. E., 2020. Controlled alternate quantum walks based privacy preserving healthcare images in internet of things. *Optics & Laser Technology*, 124, p. 105942.

[63]    Fernández-Caramés, T. M., 2019. From pre-quantum to post-quantum IoT security: A survey on quantum-resistant cryptosystems for the Internet of Things. *IEEE Internet of Things Journal*, 7(7), pp. 6457–6480.

[64]    Flöther, F., Murphy, J., Murtha, J. and D. Sow, Exploring quantum computing use cases for healthcare. Accelerate diagnoses, personalize medicine, and optimize pricing, IBM Report, URL: https://www.ibm.com/downloads/cas/8QDGKDZJ [LastAccessed on: 31October,2021].

[65]    Kumar, A., Gopal, K. and Aggarwal, A., 2013. Lightweight trust propagation scheme for resource constraint mobile ad-hoc networks (MANETs). In *2013 Sixth International Conference on Contemporary Computing (IC3)* (pp. 421–426). IEEE.

[66]    Kumar, A., 2013. Performance & probability analysis of Lightweight Identification Protocol. In *2013 International Conference On Signal Processing And Communication (ICSC)* (pp. 76–81). IEEE.

[67]    Kumar, B., Prasad, S. B., Pal, P. R. and Pathak, P., 2021. Quantum security for IoT to secure healthcare applications and their data. In *Limitations and Future Applications of Quantum Cryptography* (pp. 148–168). Hershey, PA: IGI Global.

[68]    Fernández-Caramés, T. M. and Fraga-Lamas, P., 2020. Towards post-quantum blockchain: A review on blockchain cryptography resistant to quantum computing attacks. *IEEE Access*, 8, pp. 21091–21116. Piscataway, NJ.

[69]    Chaudhary, R., Jindal, A., Aujla, G. S., Kumar, N., Das, A. K. and Saxena, N., 2018. LSCSH: Lattice-based secure cryptosystem for smart healthcare in smart cities environment. *IEEE Communications Magazine*, 56(4), pp. 24–32. USA.

[70]    Li, Z., Wang, J. and Zhang, W., 2019. Revisiting post-quantum hash proof systems over lattices for Internet of Thing authentications. *Journal of Ambient Intelligence and Humanized Computing*, pp. 1–11. Germany.

[71]    Alhadhrami, Z., Alghfeli, S., Alghfeli, M., Abedlla, J. A. and Shuaib, K., 2017, November. Introducing blockchains for healthcare. In *2017 International Conference on Electrical and Computing Technologies and Applications (ICECTA)* (pp. 1–4). USA: IEEE.

[72]    Yi, H., Li, J., Lin, Q., *et al.*, 2019. A rainbow-based authentical scheme for securing smart connected health systems. *Journal of Medical Systems*, 43(8), pp. 1–10.

[73]    Sepulveda, J., Zankl, A. and Mischke, O., 2017, September. Cache attacks and countermeasures for NTRUEncrypt on MPSoCs: Post-quantum resistance for the IoT. In *2017 30th IEEE International System-on-Chip Conference (SOCC)* (pp. 120–125). Munich: IEEE.

[74]    Zhao, W. and Sampalli, S., 2020. *Sensing and Signal Processing in Smart Healthcare*. Switzerland.

[75]    Imran, M., Abideen, Z. U. and Pagliarini, S., 2020. An experimental study of building blocks of lattice-based NIST post-quantum cryptographic algorithms. *Electronics*, 9(11), p. 1953. Switzerland.

[76]    Li, C., Tian, Y., Chen, X. and Li, J., 2021. An efficient anti-quantum lattice-based blind signature for blockchain-enabled systems. *Information Sciences*, 546, pp. 253–264.

[77]    Akleylek, S., Goi, B. M., Yap, W. S., Wong, D. C. K. and Lee, W. K., 2018. Fast NTRU encryption in GPU for secure IoP communication in post-quantum era. In *2018 IEEE SmartWorld, Ubiquitous Intelligence & Computing, Advanced & Trusted Computing, Scalable Computing & Communications, Cloud & Big Data Computing, Internet of People and Smart City Innovation (SmartWorld/SCALCOM/UIC/ATC/CBDCom/IOP/SCI)* (pp. 1923–1928). USA: IEEE.

[78]    Bellini, E., Caullery, F., Hasikos, A., Manzano, M. and Mateu, V., 2018, May. You shall not pass!(once again) an IoT application of post-quantum stateful signature schemes. In *Proceedings of the 5th ACM on ASIA Public-Key Cryptography Workshop* (pp. 19−24). USA.

[79]    Chen, J., Ling, J., Ning, J., *et al.*, 2020. Post-quantum proxy signature scheme based on the multivariate public key cryptographic signature. *International Journal of Distributed Sensor Networks*, 16(4), p. 15501477 20914775.

[80]    Gill, S. S., Kumar, A., Singh, H., *et al.*, 2020. Quantum computing: A taxonomy, systematic review and future directions. arXiv preprint arXiv: 2010. 15559. UK: Software Practice and Experience, Wiley.

[81]    Kumar, A., Elsersy, M., Darwsih, A. and Hassanien, A. E., 2021. "Drones combat COVID-19 epidemic: Innovating and monitoring approach," in *Digital Transformation and Emerging Technologies for Fighting COVID-19 Pandemic: Innovative Approaches*, p. 175. Cham: Springer.

[82]    Kumar, A. and Sharma, K., 2021. "Digital transformation and emerging technologies for COVID-19 pandemic: Social, global, and industry perspectives," in *Artificial Intelligence and Machine Learning for COVID-19*, p. 73. Cham: Springer.

[83]    Kumar, A., Sharma, K., Singh, H., Srikanth, P., Krishnamurthi, R. and Nayyar, A., 2021. "Drone-based social distancing, sanitization, inspection, monitoring, and control room for COVID-19," in *Artificial Intelligence and Machine Learning for COVID-19*, p. 153. Cham: Springer.

[84]    Krishnamurthi, R., Gopinathan, D. and Kumar, A., 2021. "Wearable devices and COVID-19: State of the art, framework, and challenges," in *Emerging Technologies for Battling COVID-19: Applications and Innovations*, p. 157. Cham: Springer.

[85]    Kumar, A. and Jain, S., 2021. "Drone-based monitoring and redirecting system," in *Development and Future of Internet of Drones (IoD): Insights, Trends and Road Ahead*, p. 163. Cham: Springer.

[86]    Sharma, K., Singh, H., Sharma, D. K., Kumar, A., Nayyar, A. and Krishnamurthi, R., 2021. "Dynamic models and control techniques for drone delivery of medications and other healthcare items in COVID-19," in *Emerging Technologies for Battling Covid-19: Applications and Innovations*, p. 1. Cham: Springer.

[87] Lum, M. J., Rosen, J., King, H. H., *et al.*, 2007. Telesurgery via unmanned aerial vehicle (UAV) with a field deployable surgical robot. In *MMVR* (pp. 313–315). Netherlands.

[88] Câmara, D., 2014, November. Cavalry to the rescue: Drones fleet to help rescuers operations over disasters scenarios. In *2014 IEEE Conference on Antenna Measurements & Applications (CAMA)* (pp. 1–4). Antibes Juan-les-Pins, France: IEEE.

[89] Kim, S. J., Lim, G. J., Cho, J. and Côté, M. J., 2017. Drone-aided healthcare services for patients with chronic diseases in rural areas. *Journal of Intelligent & Robotic Systems*, 88(1), pp. 163–180.

[90] Graboyes, R. F. and Skorup, B., 2020. *Medical Drones in the United States and a Survey of Technical and Policy Challenges*. USA: Mercatus Center Policy Brief.

[91] Zhang, Y. and Lu, M., 2020. A review of recent advancements in soft and flexible robots for medical applications. *The International Journal of Medical Robotics and Computer Assisted Surgery*, 16(3), p. e2096.

[92] Siegfarth, M., Pusch, T. P., Pfeil, A., Renaud, P. and Stallkamp, J., 2020. Multi-material 3D printed hydraulic actuator for medical robots. *Rapid Prototyping Journal*.

[93] Gharibi, M., Boutaba, R. and Waslander, S. L., 2016. Internet of drones. *IEEE Access*, 4, pp. 1148–1162.

[94] Lin, C., He, D., Kumar, N., Choo, K. K. R., Vinel, A. and Huang, X., 2018. Security and privacy for the internet of drones: Challenges and solutions. *IEEE Communications Magazine*, 56(1), pp. 64–69.

[95] Lv, Z., 2019. The security of Internet of drones. *Computer Communications*, 148, pp. 208–214.

[96] Kumar, A., Gopal, K. and Aggarwal, A., 2014. Design and analysis of lightweight trust mechanism for accessing data in MANETs. *KSII Transactions on Internet & Information Systems*, 8(3).

[97] Kumar, A., Gopal, K. and Aggarwal, A., 2013. Outlier detection and treatment for lightweight mobile ad hoc networks. In *International Conference on Heterogeneous Networking for Quality, Reliability, Security and Robustness* (pp. 750–763). Springer, Berlin, Heidelberg.

[98] Kumar, A., Krishnamurthi, R., Nayyar, A., Sharma, K., Grover, V. and Hossain, E., 2020. A novel smart healthcare design, simulation, and implementation using healthcare 4.0 processes. *IEEE Access*, 8, pp. 118433–118471.

[99] Kumar, A., Srikanth, P., Nayyar, A., Sharma, G., Krishnamurthi, R. and Alazab, M., 2020. A novel simulated-annealing based electric bus system design, simulation, and analysis for Dehradun Smart City. *IEEE Access*, 8, pp. 89395–89424.

[100] Kumar, A., Aggarwal, A. and Gopal, K., 2018. A novel and efficient reader-to-reader and tag-to-tag anti-collision protocol. *IETE Journal of Research*, pp. 1–12.

[101] Kumar, A., Rajalakshmi, K., Jain, S., Nayyar, A. and Abouhawwash, M., 2020. A novel heuristic simulation-optimization method for critical

infrastructure in smart transportation systems. *International Journal of Communication Systems*, 33(11), p. e4397.

[102]   Kumar, A., Gopal, K. and Aggarwal, A., 2016. Simulation and cost analysis of group authentication protocols. In *2016 Ninth International Conference on Contemporary Computing (IC3)* (pp. 1–7). IEEE.

[103]   Kumar, A., Krishnamurthi, R., Nayyar, A., Luhach, A. K., Khan, M. S. and Singh, A., 2021. A novel Software-Defined Drone Network (SDDN)-based collision avoidance strategies for on-road traffic monitoring and management. *Vehicular Communications*, 28, p. 100313.

[104]   Li, W., Li, H., Wu, Q., Chen, X. and Ngan, K. N., 2019. Simultaneously detecting and counting dense vehicles from drone images. *IEEE Transactions on Industrial Electronics*, 66(12), pp. 9651–9662.

[105]   McRae, J. N., Gay, C. J., Nielsen, B. M. and Hunt, A. P., 2019. Using an unmanned aircraft system (drone) to conduct a complex high altitude search and rescue operation: A case study. *Wilderness & Environmental Medicine*, 30(3), pp. 287–290.

## Chapter 11

# Application of intelligent techniques in health-care sector

*Niharika Singh[1], Richa Choudhary[1], Thipendra Pal Singh[1]
and Anshika Mahajan[1]*

Artificial intelligence (AI) is more important in today's technological world. It is a cacophony of technology. AI has been instrumental in transforming several aspects of healthcare and has proven to be more efficient than human caregivers. The dynamic increase in the number of population of the world provides excess pressure over the health-care system. Hence, AI provides new technologies for delivering the benefits to human health and well-being. Thus, this chapter focuses on the importance of AI, health-care system in India followed by the future scope and the challenges.

## 11.1  Introduction

AI is the emulation of human intelligence processes by computers. It is a term used to characterize computing technologies that are analogous to human intelligence processes, including "learning and adaptation," "sensory understanding and interaction," "reasoning and planning," "searching and optimization," and "autonomy and creativity" [1]. Depending upon the domains, AI is classified as weak or strong. Weak AI is a type of AI that is developed and educated for a specific job, such as voice-activated assistants. It can either respond to your inquiry or carry out a preprogrammed order, but it cannot function without human contact. Strong AI is a type of AI that has generalized human cognitive skills, which means it can solve problems and discover answers without the need for human interaction. A self-driving automobile is an example of powerful AI that utilizes a mix of computer vision, image recognition, and deep learning to steer a vehicle while keeping in a specified lane and avoiding unforeseen hazards such as pedestrians.

Healthcare, education, finance, law, and manufacturing are just a few of the areas where AI is being used to benefit both businesses and customers. Automation, machine learning (ML), machine vision, natural language processing, and robotics

[1]School of Computer Science, University of Petroleum and Energy Studies, Dehradun, India

are just a few of the technologies that use AI. The use of AI presents legal, ethical, and security problems. Empower new technology to enhance human health and well-being in areas such as "primary care, service delivery, medical data integration and analysis, and disease outbreaks and other medical crises." Projects are intended to offer 1 billion additional individuals with improved healthcare and well-being AI applications [2].

One of the driving forces behind the rise of AI is the data economy [3]. It relates to how much data has grown in recent years and how much more can be added in the future. The proliferation of data has spawned a new economy, and there is a continual struggle for data ownership among businesses seeking to profit from it. The increase in data volume has given rise to big data, which aids in the management of massive volumes of data. Data science aids in the analysis of the data. As a result, data science is moving toward a new paradigm in which robots may be taught to learn from data and provide a range of useful insights, giving rise to AI. AI refers to artificial intelligence that mimics human and animal intelligence. It incorporates intelligent agents, which are self-contained creatures that sense their surroundings and take actions to improve their chances of achieving a certain objective. AI is a method for computers to imitate human intellect through reasoning. It is a program with the ability to perceive, reason, and act. AI is redefining industries by providing greater personalization to users and automating processes.

ML is at the heart of AI. The first part of ML involves using algorithms to discover meaning in random and unordered data, and the second part involves using learning algorithms to identify a link between that knowledge enhance the learning process. As a result, the ultimate objective of ML is to enhance the computers' performance on a given job, such as diseases diagnosis, prediction of drugs, and automation of healthcare services.

The causes for the rapid development may be ascribed to: an ageing population need more health care services; an increase in chronic illnesses necessitating more long-term healthcare services; and many older individuals prefer to live in residential care facilities or in their own homes. These are not insignificant reasons for the need for additional nurses, but the robotic revolution powered by AI will be able to address them [4]. To alleviate this deficit in the medical area, nursing robots [5] are already in use medical treatments that are more effective and safer.

## 11.2    Evolution of AI in health-care informatics

Patient safety has long been a major concern in public health across the world. There is a good possibility that a patient may experience nonessential damage while undergoing therapy. About half of them could have been avoided. It is one of the major contributors to the worldwide illness burden. Diagnostic errors are common throughout medical care, according to the Institute of Medicine research, and there is no effective way to reduce them. AI systems can give differential diagnosis and helpful testing suggestions as a useful tool for identifying various diseases. Medical providers and patients can benefit more from the huge medical data of physiology, behavior, laboratory, and medical imaging, which is combined with the development of ML technology.

Today, hospitals generate abundant data that provides analytics in order to assist patients in the future which is extremely challenging. AI is a wide phrase that refers to a large-scale endeavor to develop nonhuman intelligence. AI allows using data from tens of thousands of patients to anticipate what will happen to a specific patient and prevent it from occurring. To do so, researchers may utilize data from tens of thousands of patients to predict who is at danger and intervene to prevent it from happening. In healthcare, humans are dealing with an enormous quantity of data, and the only way it can be evaluated is via the use of machines. The ultimate objective of this type of technology is to reduce the cost, improve efficiency, and ensure the safety of the service provided. The importance of early therapy in enhancing outcomes cannot be overstated. Another area where it is beneficial is in solving the global shortage of medical knowledge. AI's contribution to healthcare is that it can aid in the scaling up of some of these complicated and vital jobs. When extra labor is necessary, which is common in the medical profession, AI models work ceaselessly, which is a problem.

Another difficult deep learning topic with much more complicated data is pathology [6]. Being able to visually distinguish between hundreds of diseases is quite difficult. Additionally, field that has benefited greatly from deep learning is genomics [7]. Medical data processing is demanding and hard to perform data modeling. This may be accomplished by correcting bias in the training data as well as bias in the model architecture and issue formulation. If none of this applies, researchers may test and guarantee that equitable results and resource allocations are achieved at the conclusion of AI model deployment. When it comes to public health, epidemiological models are highly useful, but there are other aspects to consider, such as climate change, flood forecasts for public health warnings, land stability, and climate restrictions.

## 11.3   Healthcare in India

AI has brought a change in industries all around the world and one among those in the health-care industry. AI is a superset of various concepts and technologies like deep learning, ML, and natural language processing and integration of these technologies in digital healthcare can help doctors all around the world to achieve great accuracies and better results. Moreover, discussions over digital healthcare have increased due to the global pandemic COVID-19.

From predicting health problems in patients by processing and analyzing their previous health data, to smart wearable fitness watches, AI plays a vital role in the health-care sector. Governments of various countries and also major tech giants are investing huge amounts into digital health. Earlier in the 1990s, Food and Drug Administration (FDA)-approved algorithms were used to detect cancers in medical images but now new AI solutions and image detection techniques have made these efforts much easier. The use of various ML techniques to train the models from labeled data where inputs and outputs both are known and then based upon the learning, the model predicts output feature for new test data. The model keeps on learning and increases its efficiency to give better results. This automation in the health industry can change the facet of the health industry by many folds. To provide this automation, one needs to process the health-care datasets for a well-defined research problem and the system can be trained for automation.

## 11.4    Health-care dataset

Health-care data means any type of data related to the overall health and wellness of an individual. Due to the huge advancement in computational techniques and devices, a huge set of data is generated daily which can be analyzed to predict/ diagnose the current health issues. Table 11.1 shows the various forms of medical data and its types along with how this data can be preprocessed to be able to feed to the AI algorithm.

Health-care data is varied in nature and is difficult to process as it comes from multiple sources and a variety of data types and forms. Implementing an AI algorithm to predict or diagnose a particular health issue needs huge datasets which can be converted into various labeled classes to detect the problem. Currently, available

*Table 11.1    Different types of medical data*

| | Medical data | Data type | Data preprocessing |
|---|---|---|---|
| 1 | X-rays | Image | Image is converted into pixel for processing |
| 2 | Computed tomography (CT) | Image | Image is converted into pixel for processing |
| 3 | Magnetic resonance imaging (MRI) | Image/video | Image is converted into pixel for processing |
| 4 | Positron emission tomography (PET) | Image | Image is converted into pixel for processing |
| 5 | Ultrasound | Image/video | Image is converted into pixel for processing |
| 6 | Medical reports (blood/urine tests) | Textual | Normalization of data |
| 7 | ECG/EEG/PPG | Signals | Signal to image and pixels |
| 8 | Clinical trials (treatments) | Textual | Normalization of data |
| 9 | Health and fitness device | Textual/signals/ numerical | Normalization of data for processing |
| 10 | Health insurance and claims | Textual | Normalization of data for processing |
| 11 | Health surveys | Textual | Normalization of data for processing |

health-care datasets/databases are small and cannot fulfill the variety of cases that exist across the huge population in India.

## 11.4.1    Electronic medical records

Electronic medical records (EMRs) include X-rays, ultrasounds, medicinal prescriptions, lab records, etc., and these are being collected in mass volumes everyday. Record of patients is an important factor, as it is used to learn about the health of the patient and improve the type of treatment and medicines that the patient requires. Various AI techniques are used in analyzing EMRs and provide adequate information to doctors.

Large amounts of data stored in these EMRs are used to train various AI algorithms. While training, these algorithms try to find some patterns in the data and then generate certain rules, so that when next time new data of any patient is provided, then the algorithm can evaluate the output using its experience from the previous data. Data processing and its challenges are how to acquire, transform, storage, and security of data. One of the biggest concerns while using health-care data is acquiring the data itself. There are three major challenges while acquiring a high-quality health-care dataset.

## 11.4.2    Reluctant to adopt EMR/digitalization of medical procedures

In India, there are guidelines to collect EMR but no policy due to which many of them are reluctant to start with EMR. Due to this, the practice of EMR is very limited.

**Variety in data:** No single standards or policies are in place for the medical fraternity due to which available data is heterogeneous, complex, and difficult to integrate.

**Privacy and security concerns:** Health is a personal thing so is the data related to it. This belongs to the individuals. Harnessing this data has privacy and security concerns, which is also a big challenge to address.

Indian Government is working in this direction and few initiatives are starting to tackle these issues. One such initiative is open-source websites that collect and maintain health-related data of Indian citizens by the health ministry of India. It is called the Open Government Data platform of India. Such initiatives can provide a baseline to improve the research in health-care field.

AI is amalgam of many other techniques and technologies, to effectively use AI in health-care data processing, the following steps can be taken:

1.   defining research question;
2.   acquiring health-care dataset to be analyzed;
3.   selecting AI algorithm (from plethora of AI algorithms) to be used for the decided problem statement;
4.   code to implement AI algorithm; and
5.   analyzing, validating, and identifying future work.

## 11.5    AI in healthcare

AI is a technology where machines analyze and process the data in way much similar to human brain mechanism. AI is a big term that includes many other techniques and technology to simulate the capabilities of human brain. This is a promising technology that holds the key to the future of humanity [8,9]. It has huge potential in all domains of life. Healthcare is one of the domains where AI is most sought after technology due to the global pandemic—COVID-19 the world is currently facing. Scientists and researchers are decoding AI to answer the medical research questions that cannot be answered by any other technologies.

AI can change the landscape of healthcare and is coloring the dream image of revolutionizing healthcare and help address some of the challenges in the field. Many countries are investing huge amount in health-care research using AI. India is also investing in this field since 2012, which has also given rise to many health-care startups in India [3]. India is a country that provides some of the best hospitals and highly qualifies medical experts and staff; but still it lacks in proper health-care infrastructure. There are many initiatives in collaboration with government, big health-care companies, and hospitals to improve the health-care infrastructure in India using AI techniques. Currently, there are many firms that are using AI techniques to help in diagnosis and prediction of diseases. One such example is a startup based in Bangalore which is using ML to diagnose cancer; few examples are there who are trying to provide primary care and early detection of diseases based on patients' previous EMR. Seeing the huge potential of AI in health-care technology giants Google, Microsoft, IBM, and many others are collaborating with govt. and health service providers to design software and tools to aid in health-care services. AI in healthcare around the globe has many success stories and holds promising results. Figure 11.1 shows the various medical fields where AI can be used.

The applications mentioned earlier, some are already in use or in their early phases of commercialization around the globe. But there are few misconceptions about this high end technology—one of the most prevailing is—it will kill human jobs or in terms of healthcare it will replace the medical staff or doctors. It is a misconception, as there are still many areas of AI which have many challenges. It is very far from replacing doctors or medical staff [4].

Currently, AI algorithms are lacking to fulfill the requirements of processing any type of health-care data. It needs lot of efforts and big initiatives to build a self-learning model that should be able to treat and manage diseases and can help in clinical decision-making, it needs human intervention at many stages [5]. But collaborative efforts of govt. big firms and medical fraternity can produce the promising results in coming years.

The promising application of AI in health-care sector in current years is in imagery detection, for example, cancer detection from the images and retinal diseases detection where it provides great accuracy and very quick and precise results.

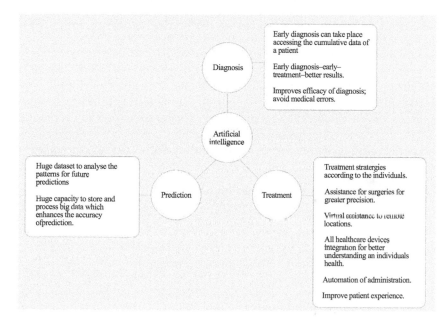

*Figure 11.1   Applications of AI in health-care domain*

Another example is IBM Watson—it has healthcare-related question–answering computer system, which has health-care applications. IBM Watson helps medical practitioners in making decisions by using natural language processing, hypothesis creation, and evidence-based learning.

## 11.5.1   What could be achieved using AI in healthcare?

AI is making strides into the public health sector, and it has a significant impact on all aspects of primary care. Primary care providers can better identify patients who require extra attention and give tailored treatments for each one, owing to AI-enabled computer tools [11,12].

1. **Drug discovery:** Discovery and the development of drugs takes several years and costs a lot of money, but these efforts, time, and money can be reduced by using various AI techniques. AI cannot complete the whole process of drug discovery but can help in discovering new compounds and medicine formulas that may form the desired drug. AI solutions can also help in determining more and more applications of drugs that have been discovered and tested earlier [8]. New AI solutions are even being developed to determine new therapies of medicines from databases related to medicines.

2. **Dermatology:** Deep learning that is a subset of AI mainly focuses on image detection techniques and has contributed a lot in image processing. Dermatology mainly depends upon images, and convolutional neural networks

have achieved very high accuracies in determining skin cancer as well as other skin diseases from various contextual, micro- and macro images [9].

3. **Designing treatment plans and diagnosis:** AI can help in designing prescriptions and treatment plans for patients. AI can analyze data from other patients and suggest strategies for treating other patients. From medical images such as X-rays, MRIs, and ultrasounds, AI has higher capability to detect signs of disease based upon various algorithms that suggest ways to diagnose them as well. For example, the use of support vector machines (SVM) to detect heart cancer based upon details of cell and use of neural networks to detect lung cancer.

Following are ML techniques that are used [13]:

1. **Supervised learning:** In this kind of learning, model is provided with labeled data. Inputs and outputs both are known, and the model tries to learn through the given data. This data used to train the model is known as train data. After learning the model tries to predict output values and if they are wrong, model tries to improve the accuracy.

2. **Un-supervised learning:** In this kind of learning, input to the model is fed with unlabeled data. The model is not provided with any relation between inputs and outputs. This learning technique is very complex as model has to learn itself. Unsupervised learning is mainly used for cluster analysis, anomaly detection, etc.

The most immediate need for AI in healthcare is disease diagnosis. Early diagnosis of common diseases such as breast cancer, diabetes, coronary artery disease, and tumors can help patients control and minimize their chances of dying from these illnesses. With the advancement in ML and AI, several classifiers and clustering algorithms, including SVM, logistic regression/linear regression, *K*-nearest neighbor, decision trees, Naïve Bayes, random forest, and adaptive boosting, are used for the prediction of the abovementioned diseases and gain unprecedented insights into diagnostics [11].

As discussed earlier, health-care dataset comes in the form of image/video and text/signals which is quite challenging to process and predict patterns. The AI algorithms need to classify the available dataset into different classes. These classes serve as training dataset to effectively recognize medical events or patterns in the data. These algorithms need to be trained for any outliers as well for better efficacy.

## 11.5.2    Challenges of using AI and possible solutions

In domains such as imaging and diagnosis, risk analysis, lifestyle management and monitoring, health information management, and virtual health help, all kinds of AI are being intensively explored for innovative health-care applications [10]. And the expected proximate benefits of AI in these fields are numerous. Despite the potential benefits of faster and more customized treatment and services, as well as cheaper health-care costs, AI technologies also carry with them complex organizational problems and long-term societal consequences. In the realm of healthcare, the potential negative effects of AI on society, whether they are magnifying human biases and injustice or the potential dangers of over-automation, cannot be ignored since they directly impact decision-making about people's health. AI-based health-care technology, for example, might open up a plethora of new scenarios in which generally held values and ethical standards are challenged. The reliance on enormous volumes of health-related data is one of the most obvious characteristics of AI in healthcare. Patient data acquired through wearable devices or other types of surveillance to aid in the development of more customized and individualized therapies might have a significant influence on consent procedures such as notifying patients, asking for their preferences, and getting their agreement [14]. Consent is critical when it comes to developing trustworthy connections between patients/clients, physicians, and health institutions. To reflect the evolving nature of health information and its consequences for patients/clients, consent processes and documentation may need to be revised. To overcome this barrier, both health institutions and technology firms must be open and honest about the AI.

A large set of challenges involves privacy and ethical data processing [15], as well as the unclear future applications of health information beyond basic clinical treatment. Diagnoses and prognoses may improve in accuracy and information quality as a result of the insights gained from patient data. However, data misuse, whether through cyber-hacking or by governing bodies, is a risk that can sway patients' opinions, hopes, and fears. To address developing privacy and data handling problems, health organizations and practitioners may need to familiarize themselves with new future rules for information security and data management as well as provide employee training and create awareness about the issues. These challenges must be solved if AI-driven technologies are to complement human thinking and decision-making.

Integrating AI into health-care demands contact between AI and a broad set of people, yet it can be expected to have some prejudice from AI users due to popular culture's notion of "scary AI." The answer to this problem will be to raise public knowledge of AI, dispel common misconceptions about the technology, and be able to communicate concepts to governments in a simple and compelling manner so that they understand the significance of adopting the technology.

## 11.5.3   Future scope

AI will play an important role in future health-care solution. It is a critical capacity that underpins the development of precision medicine, which is widely recognized as a much-needed breakthrough in healthcare. Most radiology and pathology pictures are likely to be examined by a computer at some point in the future, thanks to substantial advances in AI for imaging analysis [16,17]. Speech and text recognition are already being utilized for patient communication and clinical note recording, and this trend is expected to grow. In many health-care disciplines, the most challenging obstacle for AI is ensuring its acceptability in everyday clinical practice, rather than whether the technology will be capable enough to be beneficial. These challenges may look daunting, but they might be an opportunity for growth for organizations wanting to embrace exemplary responses to the clinical and ethical problems raised by a tough but promising set of AI-based healthcare practices. Rapid advances in AI research, as well as government and private-sector funding, make it extremely probable that AI will be widely used in healthcare delivery, with significant cost-cutting and service-quality-improvement potential. In current scenario, huge amount of work needs to be done in the realm of AI in health-care. Government needs to lay down guidelines in terms of privacy and security, law and responsibility, psychological and ethical issues as far as AI in healthcare is concerned. AI will become a strong tool for saving lives and improving their quality of life if humans develop on all of these areas.

## 11.5.4    Current status of AI in healthcare

AI research in medicine is quickly expanding, and several attempts to create and market AI-based medical devices have been launched. Furthermore, prominent global information technology (IT) companies like Samsung, Google, Apple, Microsoft, and Amazon, as well as a slew of competing startups, have demonstrated significant research accomplishments in the application of AI in healthcare [18,19]. These initiatives by industry and medicine are assisting regulatory agencies in licensing AI-based medical devices. The FDA in the United States initially allowed the use of AI-based medical devices in 2017, while the Ministry of Food and Drug Safety in Korea has approved the use of AI-based medical devices since 2018.

*Table 11.2    Current applications of AI in healthcare [12]*

| Technology | Description | Application area |
| --- | --- | --- |
| Machine learning | It predicts the patterns in medical data to give tailored made treatment, reduces the ambiguity in patient treatment, empowers decision-making by using self-learning model to evaluate huge data of medical images | Disease diagnosis |
| Robotics | Helps to perform surgeries with better precision and accuracy | Medical tools and devices |
| Natural language processing | Converts text data, such as medical charts, into something that can be read and understood quickly | Medical device, health IT |
| Big data analysis | By analyzing large quantities of data maintained by health-care organizations, provides individualized recommendations to patients and medicines | Medicine, health IT |
| Image processing | Processes vast numbers of medical images quickly and uses the data to determine disease kind, as well as negative and positive test results | Diagnostic medical image, health IT |

AI is a game changer in the medical field. It effectively analyzes data, medical records, and systems, as well as improving digital automation to produce faster and more trustworthy outcomes. AI has a significant capability in the medical business to complete required activities with minimum human interaction. AI enables a computer to comprehend human speech and writing in order to operate a business. It gives doctors, surgeons, and physicians real-time advice on how to improve results and perfect the skill [20,21]. AI provides step-by-step guidance and additional analysis to the surgeon in order to improve and get better results. For clinical judgment, analysis, and training, AI looks to be the most successful tool. Moreover, a number of research on the application of AI-based technologies in healthcare are presently underway (Table 11.2).

# References

[1] Secinaro, S., Calandra, D., Secinaro, A., *et al.* The role of artificial intelligence in healthcare: a structured literature review. *BMC Medical Informatics and Decision Making* 2021; 21: 125. https://doi.org/10.1186/s12911-021-01488-9.

[2] Mead, L. *Global Summit Focuses on The Role of Artificial Intelligence in Advancing SDGs.* SDG knowledge hub 2018. [accessed 10 August 2019]. Available at: http://sdg.iisd.org/news/global-summit-focuses-on-the-role-of-artificial-intelligence-inadvancing-sdgs/.

[3] Vijai, C and Wisetsri, W. Rise of artificial intelligence in healthcare startups in India, *Advances in Management*, 2021; 14(1): 48–52.

[4] Pepito, J. A. and Locsin, R. Can nurses remain relevant in a technologically advanced future? *International Journal of Nursing Sciences* 2019; 6(1): 106–110 [accessed 20 November 2019]. Available at: https://www.sciencedirect.com/science/article/pii/S2352013218301765.

[5] Väänänen, A., Haataja, K., Vehviläinen-Julkunen, K. and Toivanen, P. AI in healthcare: a narrative review [version 1; peer review: 1 not approved]. *F1000Research* 2021; 10: 6. https://doi.org/10.12688/f1000research.26997.1.

[6] Yu, K.-H., Beam, A. L. and Kohane, I. S. Artificial intelligence in healthcare. *Nature Biomedical Engineering* 2018; 2: 719–731. www.nature.com/natbiomedeng.

[7] Kohli, P. S. and Arora, S. Application of machine learning in disease prediction. *2018 4th International Conference on Computing Communication and Automation (ICCCA)*, 2018. 978-1-5386-6947-1/18/$31.00 ©2018 IEEE.

[8] Claire Muñoz P. and Aneja, U. Artificial Intelligence for Healthcare: Insights from India, ISBN: 978 1 78413 394 8, 2020. [Accessed 27 July 2021]. Available at: https://www.chathamhouse.org/2020/07/artificial-intelligence-healthcare-insights-india.

[9]    Teneva, M. Debunking 10 Misconceptions about AI 2019. [Accessed 25 July 2021]. Available at: https://365datascience.com/trending/debunking-misconceptions-ai/.

[10]   Rong, G., Mendez, A., Assi, E. B., Zhao, B. and Sawan, M. Artificial intelligence in healthcare: review and prediction case studies. *Engineering* 2020; 6(3): 291–301. ISSN 2095-8099, https://doi.org/10.1016/j.eng.2019.08.015. (https://www.sciencedirect.com/science/article/pii/S2095809919301535).

[11]   Manne, R. and Kantheti, S. C. Application of artificial intelligence in healthcare: chances and challenges. *Current Journal of Applied Science and Technology* 2021; 40(6): 78–89 67947 ISSN: 2457-102.

[12]   Paul, D., Sanap, G., Shenoy, S., Kalyane, D., Kalia, K. and Tekade, R. K. Artificial intelligence in drug discovery and development. *Drug Discovery Today* 2021; 26(1): 80.

[13]   Mantzaris, D. H., Anastassopoulos, G. C. and Lymberopoulos, D. K. Medical disease prediction using artificial neural networks. *2008 8th IEEE International Conference on BioInformatics and BioEngineering*, 2008. doi:10.1109/bibe.2008.4696782.

[14]   Racine, E., Boehlen, W. and Sample, M. Healthcare uses of artificial intelligence: Challenges and opportunities for growth. *Healthcare Management Forum* 2019; 32: 272–275. doi:10.1177/0840470419843831.

[15]   Schönberger, D. Artificial intelligence in healthcare: a critical analysis of the legal and ethical implications. *International Journal of Law and Information Technology* 2019; 27: 171–203. doi:10.1093/ijlit/eaz004.

[16]   Jiang, F., Jiang, Y., Zhi, H., *et al.* Artificial intelligence in healthcare: past, present and future. *Stroke and Vascular Neurology* 2017; 2: e000101. doi:10.1136/svn-2017-000101.

[17]   Iiashenko, O., Bikkulova, Z. and Dubgorn, A. Opportunities and challenges of artificial intelligence in healthcare. *E3S Web of Conferences* 2019; 110: 02028. doi:10.1051/e3sconf/201911002028.

[18]   Park, S. Y., Kuo, P.-Y., Barbarin, A., *et al.* Identifying challenges and opportunities in human-AI collaboration in healthcare. *Conference Companion Publication of the 2019 on Computer Supported Cooperative Work and Social Computing – CSCW '19*, 2019. doi:10.1145/3311957.3359433.

[19]   Reddy, S., Fox, J. and Purohit, M. P. Artificial intelligence-enabled healthcare delivery. *Journal of the Royal Society of Medicine*; 112(1) 1–7. doi:10.1177/0141076818815510.

[20]   Panesar, A. (2021). Machine Learning and AI for Healthcare. doi:10.1007/978-1-4842-6537-6.

[21]   Brinker, T. J., Hekler, A., Utikal, J. S., *et al.* Skin cancer classification using convolutional neural networks: systematic review. *Journal of Medical Internet Research* 2018; 20(10): e11936. Published 2018 Oct 17. doi:10.2196/11936.

*Chapter 12*

# Managing clinical data using machine learning techniques

*V. Diviya Prabha[1] and R. Rathipriya[1]*

Analyzing clinical data is a great challenge in today's digital data world. This perspective imposes the need of machine learning (ML) algorithms to extract useful patterns in clinical data. This chapter improves patient care by diagnosing disease accurately. It also helps to study the importance of clinical data and managing into PySpark environment. Various disease datasets are trained to ML techniques (MLT) to identify the best model. It ensures the collection of clinical data from different sources, integrating and extracting the useful patterns with less time consumption. This approach improves the understanding of clinical data and improves patient care.

## 12.1 Introduction

The promising approach of ML in health-care data is improving day by day. It is an important technique that drives to the advancement of artificial intelligence. Maintaining the history of patient's data improves the health-care populations and minimizes cost of healthcare. Nevertheless, the ability to manage huge datasets is difficult for human knowledge and it is not reliable to convert or analyze medical data. Converting the data into useful sights and attaching to real-time data is tedious.

Managing clinical data information and achieving a good decision is difficult in health-care scenario. Extracting useful information to make a decision with traditional man-made analysis is not sufficient. Medical data analysis is moved to efficient analysis to promote a useful information and diagnose meaningful information. The objective of this chapter is to understand that MLT concepts are suitable for clinical data analysis. The prediction of disease might be different based on features. This targets the improvement of individual patient care and suggests the supporting features. For transforming clinical data [1] to useful data, this approach is suitable. A novel ML algorithm [2] is developed for diagnosing disease. The main objective of this chapter is to develop and classify MLT for

[1]Department of Computer Science, Periyar University, Salem, India

different diseases. The histories of patient records of various diseases such as diabetes, kidney and heart disease are diagnosed through MLT.

The objective of this work is to analyze clinical data and make all the models run in pipeline process for datasets. Section 12.2 discusses the related work about clinical data analysis in MLT. Section 12.3 comprises the results of clinical datasets validation and results. Section 12.4 concludes the chapter.

## 12.2  Related work

Different ML algorithms are used for classification, which help to predict the diagnosis of different diseases. Different disease benchmark datasets are taken from the UCI and trained using ML algorithm [3] to get better and more reliable prediction. Running one algorithm and not comparing with any other algorithm does not show us the best result. Finding a best classifier depends on comparing the algorithm with more than one algorithm. It must be trained and tested with different datasets in a health-care scenario. Ebola virus disease [1] prediction using ML is trained with several predictors to qualify the best model. Also in predicting hospitalization, ML plays an important role [4] to improve the clinical data as early prediction reduces the patient risk. MLT is integrated into certain parts of health-care sectors to assist health-care providers and patients [5]. It provides solution for challenging health-care problems. However, complex use of methods [6] and opportunities are discussed. It highlights to deal with clinical data toward technology. Addressing the usage [7] of MLT in disease predictions suggests methods to improve patient care. With the rapid progress of large amount of data [8–12], these techniques decrease the patient risk. EHR (Electronic Health Record) [13] prediction model suggests MLT for clinical decision for better patient outcome (Table 12.1). Table 12.1 describes the detail description about the clinical dataset collected from UCI repository.

## 12.3  Clinical data analysis

The main objective of this chapter is to extract meaningful patterns from clinical datasets collected from UCI repository. It helps us to take a better decision in choosing the model and leverage to real-time data. The coding is developed in PySpark. Figure 12.1 represents the flow of clinical records applied to MLT approach using traditional techniques.

*Table 12.1    Datasets details*

| Datasets | Features | Instances |
|---|---|---|
| Pima Diabetes [14] | 9 | 769 |
| Heart Disease [15] | 14 | 304 |
| Diabetes 130 US Hospital Dataset [16] | 55 | 100 000 |
| Kidney Disease [17] | 26 | 401 |

Clinical Records

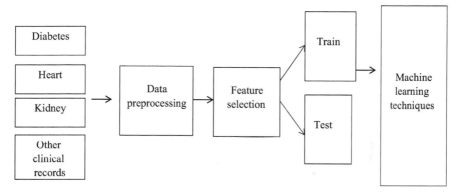

*Figure 12.1    Clinical data analysis using MLT*

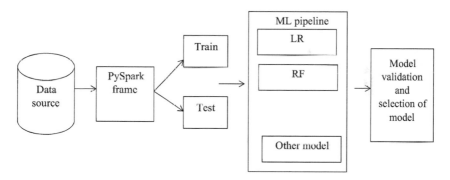

*Figure 12.2    PySpark clinical data analysis*

Figure 12.2 represents the flow of clinical data analysis in PySpark framework; the data source is divided into training and testing. To develop a spark environment [18] create a Spark Context to connect with clusters. Using the one hot encoding method converts the categorical data into numerical data, String Indexer transforms the string features into numerical form, for example, "M" represents that the male is converted into 0 and similarly "F" represents the female as 1. Certain techniques are used for preprocessing. The data is transformed to the pipeline to run the algorithm simultaneously to achieve better results.

### 12.3.1    Dataset 1

Pima dataset is collected from UCI repository consists of nine features that are calculated with PySpark approach. Table 12.2 represents the accuracy of different MLT and their accuracy level: logistic regression (LR), decision tree (DT), random forest (RF), support vector classifier (SVC) and gradient boosting (GBT). High accuracy is achieved in RF classifier model with 81 percentage of accuracy and

Table 12.2    Pima dataset MLT details

| Machine learning techniques | Accuracy | Test error | Time (s) |
|---|---|---|---|
| LR | 0.76 | 0.24 | 34 |
| DT | 0.71 | 0.25 | 56 |
| RF | 0.81 | 0.19 | 39 |
| SVC | 0.76 | 0.24 | 40 |
| GBT | 0.73 | 0.27 | 41 |

Table 12.3    Raw prediction and probability of LR method

| Age | Raw prediction | Probability |
|---|---|---|
| 22 | 1.9 | 0.87 |
| 22 | 3.93 | 0.98 |
| 22 | 2.51 | 0.92 |
| 21 | 3.48 | 0.97 |
| 21 | 2.31 | 0.90 |
| 25 | 1.63 | 0.83 |
| 25 | 1.35 | 0.79 |
| 24 | 3.43 | 0.96 |
| 23 | 2.6 | 0.93 |
| 28 | 0.51 | 0.62 |

Table 12.4    Raw prediction and probability of DT method

| Age | Raw prediction | Probability |
|---|---|---|
| 22 | 179.0,57.0 | 0.75 |
| 21 | 43.0,13.0 | 0.76 |
| 24 | 83.0,1.0 | 0.98 |
| 25 | 179.0,57.0 | 0.75 |
| 23 | 43.0,118.0 | 0.27 |
| 28 | 179.0,57.0 | 0.75 |
| 26 | 83.0,1.0 | 0.98 |
| 31 | 179.0,57.0 | 0.75 |
| 41 | 43.0,118.0 | 0.26 |
| 30 | 83.0,1.0 | 0.98 |

minimum test error of 0.19. The time consumption for running the algorithm is low in LR model and it is high in GBT model.

Table 12.3 statistics explains the raw prediction and probability of age feature. The value increases and decreases on the basis of age. It is high at age 25, 22 and 31; only the first 10 rows are listed in the table.

Tables 12.4–12.7 describe the prediction and probability values of different methods. The value is increasing and decreasing based on the age factor. Based on

*Table 12.5   Raw prediction and probability of RF method*

| Age | Raw prediction | Probability |
| --- | --- | --- |
| 22 | 16.03 | 0.80 |
| 22 | 10.14 | 0.50 |
| 21 | 16.64 | 0.83 |
| 21 | 15.38 | 0.76 |
| 25 | 14.96 | 0.74 |
| 25 | 13.80 | 0.69 |
| 24 | 13.87 | 0.69 |
| 24 | 16.75 | 0.83 |
| 23 | 9.17 | 0.48 |
| 28 | 14.27 | 0.74 |

*Table 12.6   Raw prediction and probability of SVC method*

| Age | Raw prediction | Probability |
| --- | --- | --- |
| 22 | 16.12 | 0.80 |
| 22 | 15.1 | 0.75 |
| 21 | 17.23 | 0.86 |
| 21 | 16.7 | 0.83 |
| 21 | 14.6 | 0.73 |
| 24 | 16.72 | 0.83 |
| 24 | 16.74 | 0.81 |
| 24 | 15.06 | 0.70 |
| 25 | 11.27 | 0.56 |
| 25 | 16.5 | 0.82 |

*Table 12.7   Raw prediction and probability of GBT method*

| Age | Raw prediction | Probability |
| --- | --- | --- |
| 22 | 1.08 | 0.89 |
| 22 | 1.36 | 0.93 |
| 21 | 0.80 | 0.83 |
| 21 | 1.02 | 0.88 |
| 25 | 0.54 | 0.74 |
| 24 | 1.02 | 0.88 |
| 24 | 1.21 | 0.91 |
| 23 | 0.08 | 0.49 |
| 28 | 0.81 | 0.88 |
| 31 | 1.21 | 0.91 |

age, the probability value cannot be concluded in different MLT. It is purely based on the prediction and training results of the algorithm.

## 12.3.2    Dataset 2

Heart disease data is collected from [15] UCI repository consisting of 303 instances and 14 features. This data is divided into train and testing and given as input to ML pipeline process. Table 12.8 summarizes the accuracy of different MLT, where RF attains high accuracy rate.

Table 12.9 shows the age value of heart disease dataset with raw prediction and probability. The value of raw prediction is high at the age of 54 and minimum at the age of 57. Similarly, the probability is maximum at the age of 58 and low at the age of 57. So, the prediction value is obtained from these statistics value. This table concludes that if raw prediction value increases, the probability value decreases.

Tables 12.10–12.13 describe clinical dataset 2 manipulated using different MLT raw predictions and probability value. The value increases and decreases on the basis of the age factor. In DT method, the values are similar for raw prediction. Considering RF method at age of 52, the prediction value is maximum and at the age of 54, the probability value is high. In SVC and GBT, the value is high at the age of 64. The higher the age value, the prediction value is high.

*Table 12.8    Heart disease dataset MLT details*

| Machine learning techniques | Accuracy | Test error | Time (s) |
| --- | --- | --- | --- |
| LR | 0.86 | 0.3 | 36 |
| DT | 0.88 | 0.4 | 32 |
| RF | 0.92 | 0.08 | 36 |
| SVC | 0.90 | 0.1 | 30 |
| GBT | 0.85 | 0.15 | 29 |

*Table 12.9    Raw prediction and probability of LR method*

| Age | Raw prediction | Probability |
| --- | --- | --- |
| 58 | 4.60 | 0.99 |
| 57 | 0.85 | 0.29 |
| 54 | 6.04 | 0.99 |
| 59 | 3.00 | 0.95 |
| 52 | 4.09 | 0.98 |
| 51 | 2.34 | 0.91 |
| 44 | 2.99 | 0.95 |
| 64 | 2.5 | 0.92 |
| 41 | 2.17 | 0.89 |
| 53 | 1.10 | 0.75 |

*Table 12.10  Raw prediction and probability of DT method*

| Age | Raw prediction | Probability |
|-----|---------------|-------------|
| 58 | [0.0,1.0] | 1.0 |
| 57 | [5.0,17.0] | 0.22 |
| 54 | [42.0,1.0] | 0.97 |
| 59 | [49.0,16.0] | 0.75 |
| 52 | [49.0,16.0] | 0.75 |
| 51 | [49.0,16.0] | 0.75 |
| 44 | [42.0,1.0] | 0.97 |
| 67 | [3.0,53.0] | 0.05 |
| 65 | [3.0,53.0] | 0.05 |
| 40 | [16.0,7.0] | 0.69 |

*Table 12.11  Raw prediction and probability of RF method*

| Age | Raw prediction | Probability |
|-----|---------------|-------------|
| 58 | 13.92 | 0.69 |
| 57 | 7.88 | 0.39 |
| 54 | 17.77 | 0.88 |
| 59 | 10.20 | 0.51 |
| 52 | 16.75 | 0.83 |
| 51 | 15.56 | 0.77 |
| 62 | 11.46 | 0.57 |
| 44 | 17.03 | 0.85 |
| 60 | 4.77 | 0.32 |
| 40 | 13.30 | 0.66 |

*Table 12.12  Raw prediction and probability of SVC method*

| Age | Raw prediction | Probability |
|-----|---------------|-------------|
| 58 | 1.45 | 0.33 |
| 58 | 1.34 | 0.43 |
| 57 | 0.10 | 0.10 |
| 54 | 2.32 | 0.52 |
| 52 | 1.95 | 0.27 |
| 51 | 0.17 | 0.19 |
| 44 | 0.77 | 0.20 |
| 60 | 0.80 | 0.27 |
| 64 | 2.44 | 0.57 |
| 62 | 1.09 | 0.47 |

Table 12.13    Raw prediction and probability of
GBT method

| Age | Raw prediction | Probability |
|---|---|---|
| 58 | −1.34 | 0.06 |
| 54 | 1.40 | 0.94 |
| 52 | 0.25 | 0.62 |
| 51 | 0.59 | 0.76 |
| 62 | 0.68 | 0.79 |
| 44 | 0.58 | 0.76 |
| 60 | 1.05 | 0.89 |
| 64 | 1.41 | 0.94 |
| 55 | 0.53 | 0.74 |
| 40 | 1.01 | 0.88 |

Table 12.14    Diabetes disease dataset MLT details

| Machine learning techniques | Accuracy | Test error | Time (s) |
|---|---|---|---|
| LR | 0.93 | 0.3 | 148 |
| DT | 0.92 | 0.4 | 130 |
| RF | 0.94 | 0.29 | 112 |
| SVC | 0.93 | 0.3 | 142 |
| GBT | 0.90 | 0.5 | 148 |

## 12.3.3    Dataset 3

Diabetes dataset is collected and consists of 100 000 instances. Using feature selection [19], only 11 features are selected to divide to test and train. This data is given as input to pipeline MLT observe Table 12.14 results. The accuracy obtained by RF model is high compared to other models.

Table 12.15 summarizes the raw prediction and probability value based on age. The prediction value is high at the age of 35 and is minimum at age 65. The probability value is low at the age of 65.

Tables 12.16–12.19 describe the various raw prediction and probability values for diabetes dataset. For certain age value, the value is high, which means percentage of predicted probability is high.

## 12.3.4    Dataset 4

Chronic kidney disease dataset is collected from UCI repository [17] and consists of 400 patient details. Feature consists of a combination of string, integer and double value. The data is preprocessed using techniques in PySpark. Table 12.20 describes the accuracy and test error values. RF technique obtained high value and minimum time consumed for classifying the algorithm.

*Table 12.15   Raw prediction and probability of LR method*

| Age | Raw prediction | Probability |
|-----|----------------|-------------|
| 25  | 2.12           | 0.10        |
| 35  | 1.95           | 0.12        |
| 35  | 2.47           | 0.07        |
| 45  | 2.13           | 0.10        |
| 55  | 1.32           | 0.19        |
| 65  | 0.4            | 0.39        |
| 65  | 1.14           | 0.2         |
| 45  | 1.73           | 0.14        |
| 55  | 1.20           | 0.23        |
| 65  | 1.12           | 0.24        |

*Table 12.16   Raw prediction and probability of DT method*

| Age | Raw prediction | Probability |
|-----|----------------|-------------|
| 25  | [5 066.0,11 742.0] | 0.30    |
| 35  | [5 066.0,11 742.0] | 0.30    |
| 45  | [5 066.0,11 742.0] | 0.30    |
| 65  | [5 066.0,11 742.0] | 0.30    |
| 65  | [5 066.0,11 742.0] | 0.30    |
| 75  | [5 066.0,11 742.0] | 0.30    |
| 75  | [5 066.0,11 742.0] | 0.30    |
| 75  | [5 066.0,11 742.0] | 0.30    |
| 85  | [5 066.0,11 742.0] | 0.30    |
| 95  | [5 066.0,11 742.0] | 0.30    |

*Table 12.17   Raw prediction and probability of RF method*

| Age | Raw prediction | Probability |
|-----|----------------|-------------|
| 35  | 8.21           | 0.41        |
| 35  | 5.76           | 0.28        |
| 45  | 5.79           | 0.28        |
| 45  | 7.42           | 0.37        |
| 45  | 8.44           | 0.42        |
| 55  | 5.79           | 0.28        |
| 55  | 7.20           | 0.36        |
| 55  | 8.31           | 0.41        |
| 55  | 5.79           | 0.28        |
| 55  | 5.79           | 0.28        |

*Table 12.18    Raw prediction and probability of SVC method*

| Age | Raw prediction | Probability |
| --- | --- | --- |
| 25 | 1.09 | 0.21 |
| 25 | 1.16 | 0.26 |
| 35 | 1.04 | 0.27 |
| 35 | 1.09 | 0.26 |
| 45 | 1.05 | 0.21 |
| 45 | 1.03 | 0.22 |
| 45 | 0.86 | 0.01 |
| 55 | 0.96 | 0.1 |
| 55 | 0.95 | 0.12 |
| 55 | 0.92 | 0.10 |

*Table 12.19    Raw prediction and probability of GBT method*

| Age | Raw prediction | Probability |
| --- | --- | --- |
| 25 | 7.9 | 0.39 |
| 25 | 5.70 | 0.28 |
| 35 | 5.76 | 0.28 |
| 35 | 7.74 | 0.38 |
| 45 | 5.79 | 0.28 |
| 45 | 8.26 | 0.422 |
| 55 | 7.02 | 0.35 |
| 55 | 8.16 | 0.40 |
| 65 | 7.20 | 0.36 |
| 65 | 8.35 | 0.41 |

*Table 12.20    Chronic kidney disease dataset MLT details*

| Machine learning techniques | Accuracy | Test error | Time (s) |
| --- | --- | --- | --- |
| LR | 0.97 | 0.03 | 38 |
| DT | 0.96 | 0.04 | 39 |
| RF | 0.98 | 0.02 | 37 |
| SVC | 0.95 | 0.05 | 36 |
| GBT | 0.94 | 0.06 | 37 |

Table 12.21 summarizes the kidney disease raw prediction and probability value. The raw prediction value is high at the age of 72 and minimum at 63. The probability value is maximum at the age of 59 and minimum at age 33.

*Table 12.21   Raw prediction and probability of LR method*

| Age | Raw prediction | Probability |
|-----|----------------|-------------|
| 72 | 14.85 | 0.8 |
| 63 | 0.02 | 0.50 |
| 70 | 4.7 | 0.90 |
| 63 | 0.02 | 0.54 |
| 59 | 5.4 | 0.9 |
| 33 | 3.41 | 0.03 |
| 41 | 1.2 | 0.5 |
| 72 | 7.08 | 0.2 |
| 43 | 5.90 | 0.2 |
| 54 | 4.97 | 0.90 |

*Table 12.22   Raw prediction and probability of RF method*

| Age | Raw prediction | Probability |
|-----|----------------|-------------|
| 53 | 14.66 | 0.99 |
| 72 | 15.01 | 0.99 |
| 62 | 4.89 | 0.99 |
| 30 | 5.13 | 0.99 |
| 38 | 1.84 | 0.86 |
| 50 | 2.4 | 0.91 |
| 39 | −3.5 | 0.02 |
| 62 | −3.73 | 0.02 |
| 80 | −8.36 | 2.31 |
| 46 | −4.27 | 0.01 |

*Table 12.23   Raw prediction and probability of DT method*

| Age | Raw prediction | Probability |
|-----|----------------|-------------|
| 53 | [145.0,3.0] | 0.97 |
| 40 | [4.0,98.0] | 0.03 |
| 44 | [145.0,3.0] | 0.97 |
| 69 | [145.0,3.0] | 0.97 |
| 30 | [145.0,3.0] | 0.97 |
| 55 | [145.0,3.0] | 0.97 |
| 74 | [145.0,3.0] | 0.97 |
| 38 | [145.0,3.0] | 0.97 |
| 60 | [145.0,3.0] | 0.97 |
| 69 | [145.0,3.0] | 0.97 |

Tables 12.22–12.25 show the raw prediction and probability value of chronic disease dataset. The probability and raw prediction based on age factor increases and decreases.

*Table 12.24    Raw prediction and probability of SVC method*

| Age | Raw prediction | Probability |
|-----|----------------|-------------|
| 25  | 1.09           | 0.21        |
| 25  | 1.16           | 0.26        |
| 35  | 1.04           | 0.27        |
| 35  | 1.09           | 0.26        |
| 45  | 1.05           | 0.21        |
| 45  | 1.03           | 0.22        |
| 45  | 0.86           | 0.01        |
| 55  | 0.96           | 0.1         |
| 55  | 0.95           | 0.12        |
| 55  | 0.92           | 0.10        |

*Table 12.25    Raw prediction and probability of GBT method*

| Age | Raw prediction | Probability |
|-----|----------------|-------------|
| 25  | 7.9            | 0.39        |
| 25  | 5.70           | 0.28        |
| 35  | 5.76           | 0.28        |
| 35  | 7.74           | 0.38        |
| 45  | 5.79           | 0.28        |
| 45  | 8.26           | 0.422       |
| 55  | 7.02           | 0.35        |
| 55  | 8.16           | 0.40        |
| 65  | 7.20           | 0.36        |
| 65  | 8.35           | 0.41        |

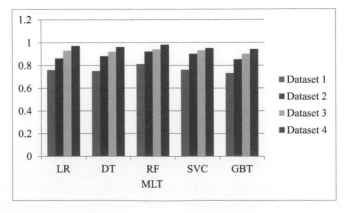

*Figure 12.3    MLT accuracy calculation of different clinical datasets*

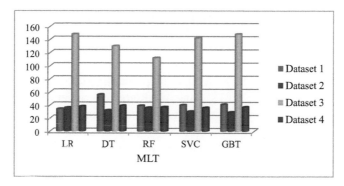

*Figure 12.4   Time consumption of ML*

Figure 12.3 explains the different datasets with various MLT. Among the models, RF model that acquires high accuracy is the best for clinical data analysis. The second highest accuracy is DT. Figure 12.4 describes the time consumed to train and test the algorithm. The RF acquires minimum time in seconds for large dataset.

## 12.4   Conclusion

This chapter discusses three different aspects of clinical data. First step is to ana-lyze the data, integrate the model using pipeline and validate the results. Among the different benchmark datasets, RF works better in accuracy and time. It also works best in raw prediction based on age. This helps us to define the usage of MLT and their scope of clinical data from small to large dataset. Comparison with other model diagnosis disease better and improve the patient care. For different features, managing clinical data using MLT gives better results.

## References

[1]   A. Colubri, T. Silver, T. Fradet, K. Retzepi, B. Fry, and P. Sabeti, Transforming clinical data into actionable prognosis models: machine-learning framework and field-deployable app to predict outcome of Ebola patients. *PLoS Negl Trop Dis.* 2016; 10(3): e0004549.

[2]   S. Dagdanpurev, S. Abe, G. Sun, *et al.*, A novel machine-learning-based infection screening system via 2013–2017 seasonal influenza patients' vital signs as training datasets. *J Inf Secur.* 2019; 78(5): 409–421.

[3]   C. Verdonk, and F. Verdonk, How machine learning could be used in clin-ical practice during an epidemic. *Critical Care*, 24(1). doi:10.1186/s13054-020-02962-y.

[4]   S. J. Patel, D. B. Chamberlain, and J. M. Chamberlain. (2018). A machine learning approach to predicting need for hospitalization for pediatric asthma exacerbation at the time of Emergency Department Triage. *Academic Emergency Medicine*, 2018; 25(12): 1463–1470. doi:10.1111/acem.13655.

[5]   M. A. Ahmad, and C. Eckert, Interpretable machine learning in healthcare, *BCB'18 Proceeding of the 2018 ACM International Conference on Bioinformatics, Computational Biology and Health Informatics*, August 2018, pp. 559–560.

[6]   M. Ghassemi, and T. Naumann, Opportunities in machine learning for Healthcare. *DeepAI*. (2018, June 1). Retrieved November 1, 2021, from https://deepai.org/publication/opportunities-in-machine-learning-for-healthcare.

[7]   S. F. Weng, J. Reps, J. Kai, J. M. Garibaldi, and N. Qureshi, Can machine-learning improve cardiovascular risk prediction using routine clinical data? *PLoS One*. 2017; 12(4): e0174944.

[8]   A. Callahan, and N. H. Shah, Machine learning in Healthcare. *Key Advances in Clinical Informatics*, 2017; 279–291. doi:10.1016/b978-0-12-809523-2.00019-4.

[9]   A. Salcedo-Bernal, and M. P. Villamil-Giraldo, Clinical, Data analysis: an opportunity to compare machine learning methods, *Conference on ENTERprise Information Systems/International Conference on Project MANagement/Conference on Health and Social Care Information Systems and Technologies, Procedia Computer Science* 100, 2016.

[10]  T. Jiang, Supervised machine learning: a brief primer. *Behav Ther*. 2020.

[11]  A. V. Lebedev, and E. Westman, Random forest ensembles for detection and prediction of Alzheimer's disease with a good between-cohort robustness. *Neuroimage Clin*. 2014; 6(4): 115–25.

[12]  P. H. C. Chen, and Y. Liu, How to develop machine learning models for healthcare. *Nat Mater*. 2019.

[13]  A. Ashfaq, Predicting clinical outcomes via machine learning on electronic health records (Licentiate dissertation). 2019. Retrieved from http://urn.kb.se/resolve?urn=urn:nbn:se:hh:diva-39309.

[14]  D. Johnson, PySpark tutorial for beginners: Learn with examples. *Guru99*. 2021. Retrieved from https://www.guru99.com/pyspark-tutorial.html.

[15]  A. Rajkomar, J. Dean, and I. S. Kohane, Machine learning in medicine. *N Engl J Med*. 2019; 380(14): 1347–1358.

[16]  UCI Machine Learning Repository: Data Set. Retrieved from https://archive.ics.uci.edu/ml/datasets/heart%C3%BEDisease.

[17]  V. Diviya Prabha, and R. Rathipriya, Readmission prediction using hybrid logistic regression. *Innovative Data Communication Technologies and Application*, 2020; 702–709. doi:10.1007/978-3-030-38040-3_80.

[18]  P. P. Sengupta, and S. Shrestha, Machine learning for data-driven discovery. *JACC: Cardiovascular Imaging*, 2019; 12(4), 690–2. doi:10.1016/j.jcmg.2018.06.030.

[19]  D. A. Clifton, K. E. Niehaus, P. Charlton, and G. W. Colopy. Health informatics via machine learning for the clinical management of patients. *Yearbook of Medical Informatics*. 2015; 24(01): 38–43.

## Chapter 13

# Use of IoT and mobile technology in virus outbreak tracking and monitoring

*Marimuthu Narayanan Saravana Kumar[1], Ravi Bharath[2], Balasubramani Yogeshwaran[2], Rajendiran Ranjith[2] and Krishnamoorthy Santhosh Kumar[2]*

## 13.1 Introduction

The Internet of Things (IoT) has proven useful in the field of electronic-health (E-Health) management as a network of sensors gathering data both locally and remotely. The collection of patient vitals and the provision of essential track and trace services for pandemic management have been made possible thanks to a combination of body area networks and field monitoring devices. Health data such as blood pressure (BP), temperature, and heart rate can be collected by locally based E-Health mechanisms. This data can be saved locally and accessed by a health-care provider. Local systems can also be used to notify patients when they need to consult with medical staff to take medicine. Remote-based E-Health is critical for health-care providers because it allows them to access patients and patient data from afar. Patient vitals and location may be sent to local or faraway medical facilities at regular intervals for monitoring purposes. In the event of a global pandemic, such as the 2019 coronavirus (COVID-19), it is important to follow social distance guidelines and track and trace patients successfully. These two factors play an important role in limiting the virus's global spread. IoT services' ability to provide remote data collection and monitoring of patients in quarantine has made them a key component in the fight against virus pandemics. To manage a rapidly spreading respiratory pandemic, health workers and authorities need data. In the case of COVID-19, data can be used to begin the diagnosis of infection as well as track the spread of the virus in the community. Body temperature, location, and travel history are the most important pieces of information. These parameters can alert officials as to whether or not more investigation and

[1]Department of Electronics and Instrumentation Engineering, Erode Sengunthar Engineering College, Anna University, Erode, India
[2]Department of Biomedical Engineering, Erode Sengunthar Engineering College, Anna University, Erode, India

testing are needed. Initially, health workers relied on manual methods such as infrared thermometers to measure temperatures and verbal interrogation of people about their backgrounds and locations. Because of the increased contact with potentially infected subjects, this posed a risk to health workers. As infection rates reached the millions, it had also become a more difficult approach.

## 13.2    IoT in healthcare

IoT applications, in addition to IoT services, deserve more attention. It is worth noting that services are used to create applications, while applications are used directly by users and patients. As a result, services are developer-focused, while applications are user-focused. Various gadgets, wearables, and other health-care devices currently available on the market are discussed in addition to the application covered in this section. These products can be thought of as IoT technologies that could lead to a variety of health-care solutions. The following sections cover a variety of IoT-based health-care applications, including single- and clustered-condition applications. One of the most important aspects of the IoT in healthcare is the IoT health-care network, also known as the IoT network for healthcare (or simply "the INTERNET"). It provides access to the IoT backbone, as well as the transmission and reception of medical data and the use of healthcare-specific communications.

## 13.3    IoT health-care applications

### 13.3.1    Glucose level sensing

Diabetes is a group of metabolic diseases characterized by persistently high blood glucose (sugar) levels. Individual patterns of blood glucose changes are revealed by blood glucose monitoring, which aids in the planning of meals, activities, and medication times. An m-IoT setup method for real-time noninvasive glucose sensing measuring device. Patients' sensors are connected to relevant health-care providers through IPv6 connectivity in this method. The utility model reveals a transmitting device based on IoT networks for the transmission of collected somatic data on blood glucose. A generic IoT-based medical acquisition detector that can be used to monitor glucose levels is another similar innovation.

### 13.3.2    Electrocardiogram monitoring

Monitoring the electrocardiogram (ECG), or the electrical activity of the heart as recorded by electrocardiography, involves determining the fundamental rhythm and measuring the simple heart rate, as well as diagnosing multifaceted arrhythmias, myocardial ischemia, and prolonged QT intervals. The IoT is being used in a variety of ways. ECG monitoring has the potential to provide a wealth of data and can be used to its full potential. IoT-based ECG monitoring has been debated in a number of studies. Cardiac function can be detected in real time thanks to the system's integration of a search automation method for detecting abnormal data. At the application layer of the IoT network, there is a comprehensive ECG signal detection algorithm for ECG monitoring.

### 13.3.3    Blood pressure monitoring

The issue of how a blood pressure (BP) meter kit combined with a near field communication (NFC)-enabled mobile phone becomes part of IoT-based BP monitoring is resolved. The communication structure between a health post and the health center is used to present a motivating scenario in which BP must be periodically controlled remotely. The question of how the Withings BP device works in conjunction with an Apple mobile computing device is discussed. This device is for data collection and transmitting the BP data over an IoT network was proposed. A BP apparatus body and a communication module make up with this device carrying on with BP tracking and location-aware terminal.

### 13.3.4    Blood temperature monitoring

Because body temperature is a crucial vital sign in the maintenance of homeostasis, body temperature monitoring is an important part of health-care services. A body temperature sensor embedded in the TelosB mote is used to validate the IoT concept, and the results of a typical sample of achieved body temperature variations are presented, demonstrating the successful operation of the developed m-IoT system. It is proposed to use an IoT-based temperature measurement system based on a home gateway. With the assistance of infrared detection, the home gateway transmits the user's body temperature.

Another temperature monitoring system based on the IoT is proposed. The radio frequency identification (RFID) module and the module for monitoring body temperature are the principal system components responsible for temperature recording and transmission.

### 13.3.5    Oxygen saturation monitoring

Pulse oximetry is a noninvasive, continuous monitoring system for blood oxygen saturation. For technology-driven medical health-care applications, the integration of the IoT with pulse oximetry is beneficial. The potential of IoT-based pulse oximetry is discussed in a survey of CoAP-based health-care services. The Nonin WristOX2 wearable pulse oximeter is demonstrated in action. This device uses a Bluetooth health device profile for connectivity, and the sensor connects directly to the Monterey platform. It is proposed to develop an IoT-optimized low-power/low-cost pulse oximeter for remote patient monitoring. Over an IoT network, this device can be used to continually monitor the patient's health. The author describes an integrated pulse oximeter system for telemedicine applications. A wireless sensor networks (WSN)-enabled wearable pulse oximeter for health monitoring can be adapted to an IoT network.

### 13.3.6    Rehabilitation system

Physical medicine and rehabilitation are important branches of medicine because they can improve and restore functional ability and quality of life in people who have physical impairments or disabilities. The IoT has the potential to improve rehabilitation systems by addressing issues such as ageing populations and a shortage of health professionals. For IoT-based smart rehabilitation systems, an ontology-based automating design method is proposed. This design successfully illustrates how the IoT can be a useful platform for linking all relevant resources and providing real-time information interactions. IoT-based technologies have the potential to create a valuable infrastructure for remote consultation in comprehensive rehabilitation. Many IoT-based rehabilitation systems are available, including an integrated application system for prisons, hemiplegic patient rehabilitation training, a smart city medical rehabilitation system, and a language-training system for children with autism.

### 13.3.7   Medication management

Noncompliance with prescription poses a serious threat to public health and wastes a lot of money all over the world. The IoT provides some promising solutions to this problem. A smart packaging method for medicine boxes is proposed for IoT-based medication management. This approach involves building a prototype I2Pack and iMedBox system and testing it in the field. This packaging technique uses delamination materials that are controlled by wireless communications to provide controlled sealing. The IoT network is used to present an eHealth service architecture based on RFID tags for a medication control system. This ubiquitous medication control system is designed specifically for providing acute lymphoblastic leukemia solutions, and the prototype implementation is demonstrated here.

### 13.3.8   Wheelchair management

Many researchers have worked to create fully automated smart wheelchairs for disabled people. The IoT has the potential to speed up the pace of work. On the basis of IoT technology, a health-care system for wheelchair users is proposed. Wireless body area networks are integrated with various sensors, functions of which are tailored to IoT requirements in the design. A peer-to-peer and IoT medical support system is introduced. This system can detect the status of the wheelchair user and control chair vibration. The linked wheelchair, developed by Intel's IoT department, is another notable example of IoT-based wheelchair development. This progression eventually demonstrates how commonplace "things" can evolve into data-driven connected machines. This device can monitor the user's vitals and collect data on the user's surroundings, allowing for the assessment of a location's accessibility.

### 13.3.9   Imminent health-care solutions

There are a variety of other portable medical devices available. There is no explicit demonstration of how those devices can be integrated into IoT networks. That is, it will only be a matter of time before these devices are equipped with IoT capabilities. The growing demand for IoT-based services around the world has resulted in an increase in the number of medical health-care applications, devices, and cases. Hemoglobin detection, peak expiratory flow, abnormal cellular development, cancer therapy, eye disorder, skin infection, and remote surgery are some of the health-care areas where IoT integration appears imminent. The majority of today's devices are portable diagnostic devices with traditional connectivity.

## 13.3.10    Health-care solutions using smartphones

In recent years, there has been an increase in the number of electronic devices with a smartphone-controlled sensor, highlighting the rise of smartphones as a driver of the IoT. To make smartphones a flexible health-care device, various hardwire and software products have been developed. A thorough examination of health-care apps for smartphones is given, including a discussion of apps for patients and general health-care apps, as well as medical education, training, information search apps, and others (collectively referred to as auxiliary apps). Furthermore, there are a plethora of new apps that serve similar functions. Figure 14 shows a classification diagram of auxiliary apps based on these sources. This figure does not include general health-care apps or patient-facing apps, which are discussed later in this section. Diagnose and therapy information can be accessed via diagnostic apps. Reference to a drug name, indications, dosages, prices, and identifying characteristics are commonly provided by apps. Apps for searching biomedical literature databases make it easier to discover relevant medical information. Tutorials, training, various surgical demonstrations, color illustrations of various photographs, and medical books are all common topics in medical education apps. Calculator apps include a variety of medical formulas and equations that can be used to calculate different parameters of interest (e.g., the body surface burn percentage). Clinical collaboration apps make it easier for doctors to communicate inside a hospital. A number of image analysis algorithms for smartphones are presented that allow for noncontact measurements in health-care applications. This is a nice (but not exhaustive) list of smartphone apps that provide health-care solutions. Smartphones are capable of diagnosing and/or tracking the following medical conditions: Asthma, chronic obstructive pulmonary disease, cystic fibrosis, choking, allergic rhinitis, and nose-related symptoms can all be detected. In advanced diabetic patients, the respiratory tract, heart rate, BP, blood oxygen saturation, melanoma, and wound analysis are all examined. Smartphone health-care apps have a significant advantage in terms of delivering low-cost solutions, in addition to their pervasive deployment capabilities and availability for consumers. Many difficulties, such as computational complexity, power consumption, and noisy environments around smartphones, exist, but they should be simple to overcome. In addition, there are a variety of health and fitness accessories for smartphones that can assist people in getting in the best shape possible. Fitbit Flex, for example, is a fitness wristband that keeps track of steps taken, distance travelled, and calories burned. Existing commercial health-care products that can be considered as a foundation for IoT health-care devices are discussed in greater detail in a separate section of this paper.

## 13.4    **Benefits**

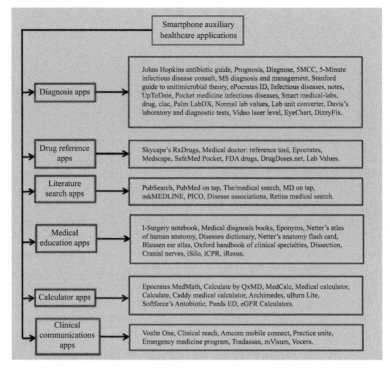

Smartphone auxiliary healthcare applications

**Diagnosis apps** → Johns Hopkins antibiotic guide, Prognosis, Diagnose, 5MCC, 5-Minute infectious disease consult, MS diagnosis and management, Stanford guide to anitimicrobial theory, ePocrates ID, Infectious diseases, notes, UpToDate, Pocket medicine infectious diseases, Smart medical-labs, drug, clac, Palm LabDX, Normal lab values, Lab unit converter, Davis's laboratory and diagnostic tests, Video laser level, EyeChart, DizzyFix.

**Drug reference apps** → Skycape's RxDrugs, Medical doctor: reference tool, Epocrates, Medscape, SafeMed Pocket, FDA drugs, DrugDoses.net, Lab Values.

**Literature search apps** → PubSearch, PubMed on tap, The/medical search, MD on tap, askMEDLINE, PICO, Disease associations, Retina medical search.

**Medical education apps** → I-Surgery notebook, Medical diagnosis books, Eponyms, Netter's atlas of human anatomy, Diseases dictionary, Netter's anatomy flash card, Blausen ear atlas, Oxford handbook of clinical specialties, Dissection, Cranial nerves, iSilo, iCPR, iResus.

**Calculator apps** → Epocrates MedMath, Calculate by QxMD, MedCalc, Medical calculator, Calculate, Caddy medical calculator, Archimedes, uBurn Lite, Softforce's Antobiotic, Paeds ED, eGFR Calculators.

**Clinical communications apps** → Voalte One, Clinical reach, Amcom mobile connect, Practice unite, Emergency medicine program, Tradassan, mVisum, Vocera.

### 13.4.1    *Simultaneous reporting and monitoring*

In the event of a medical emergency such as heart failure, diabetes, or asthma attacks, real-time monitoring through connected devices will save lives. The IoT device gathers and transmits health information such as BP, oxygen, and blood sugar levels, as well as weight and ECGs. These data are stored in the cloud and can be shared with an approved person, such as a physician, your insurance company, a participating health firm, or an external consultant, who can access the information regardless of their location, time, or device.

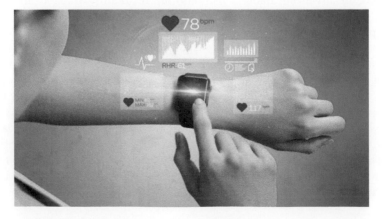

### 13.4.2    Data assortment and analysis

When a health-care device's real-time application sends a large amount of data in a short period of time, it is difficult to store and handle if cloud access is inaccessible. Even for health-care providers, manually collecting data from various devices and sources and analyzing it is a risky proposition. IoT devices can gather, report, and analyze data in real time, reducing the need for raw data storage. This will all be done in the cloud, with providers only seeing the final reports with graphs.

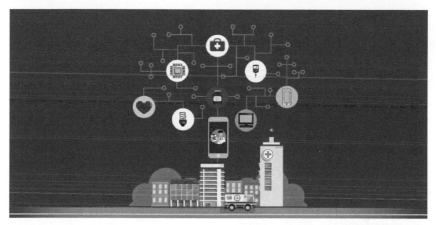

### 13.4.3    Tracking and alerts

In the event of a life-threatening situation, prompt notification is essential. Medical IoT devices collect vital data and send it to doctors in real time for monitoring, as well as sending out alerts to people about critical components via mobile apps and other connected devices. As a result, IoT provides real-time alerting, tracking, and monitoring, allowing for hands-on treatments, improved accuracy, and appropriate doctor intervention, as well as improved overall patient care delivery results.

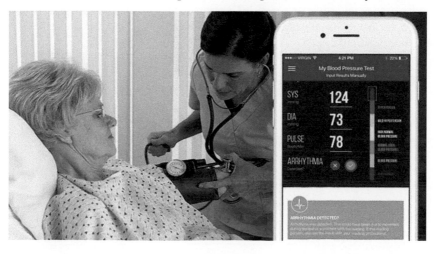

## 13.5    Challenges

### 13.5.1    *Data security and privacy*

Data security and privacy are two of the most serious threats posed by IoT. Data is captured and transmitted in real time by IoT devices. All of these considerations make the data extremely vulnerable to cybercriminals who can hack into the system and compromise both patients' and physicians' personal health information (PHI). Cybercriminals may use patient information to produce fake IDs in order to purchase drugs and medical equipment that they will later sell. Hackers will also file a false insurance claim in the name of a patient.

### 13.5.2    *Cost*

You would be surprised to learn that cost factors are included in the challenge parts. I know most of you are, but the bottom line is that IoT has not yet made healthcare more accessible to the average person. The rise in health-care costs is a cause for concern for everyone, particularly in developed countries. The situation has led to the development of "medical tourism," in which patients with critical illnesses use health-care facilities in developed countries for a fraction of the cost. The principle of IoT in healthcare is a fascinating and promising one.

### 13.5.3    *Data overload and accuracy*

Data aggregation is impossible due to the use of various communication protocols and standards, as previously mentioned. IoT sensors, on the other hand, continue to collect a large amount of data. The information gathered by IoT devices is used to make important decisions.

## 13.6 Use of IoT in virus outbreak and monitoring

### 13.6.1 Using IoT to dissect an outbreak

IoT would have many more applications during an epidemic because of the myriad and varied datasets gathered by mobile devices. The IoT should be used to track down the source of an epidemic. Researchers at Massachusetts Institute of Technology (MIT) recently used aggregated mobile phone data to track the spread of dengue fever in Singapore during 2013 and 2014, down to granular details of short distances and time periods. As a result, using a geographic information system to overlay IoT mobile data from infected patients will accomplish two goals. It can aid epidemiologists in their search for patient zero upstream, and it can aid in the identification of all those who have come into contact with infected patients and may, thus, be infected downstream.

### 13.6.2 Using IoT to manage patient care

The scalability of IoT is also useful for keeping track of all the patients who are high-risk enough to require quarantine but not severe enough to require in-hospital care. Patients are already checked on a daily basis by health-care professionals who go door-to-door. A health-care worker had patients stand on their apartment balconies so he could fly a drone up and take their temperatures with an infrared thermometer, according to one report. Patients should have their temperatures taken and then upload the data to the cloud via their mobile devices for analysis using IoT. This allows health-care professionals to gather more data in less time while also reducing the risk of cross-infection among patients. In addition, IoT will provide relief to the hospital's overworked staff. The IoT has already been used to track in-home patients with chronic conditions like hypertension and diabetes. In hospitals, telemetry has been used to track a large number of patients with limited staff by transmitting biometric measurements such as heartbeat and BP from wearable, wireless instruments on patients to central monitoring. IoT should be used to decrease the workload and improve the productivity of medical personnel while also lowering the risk of infection among health-care workers.

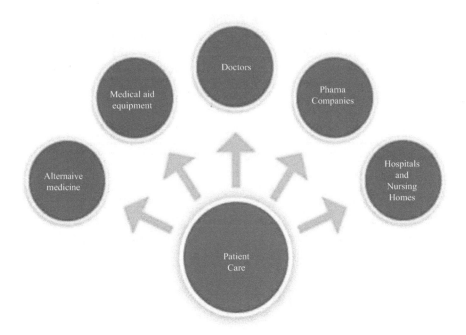

## 13.7    Use of mobile apps in healthcare

### 13.7.1    *Mobile report*

Patient reports can be mobilized with the assistance of health mobile apps. Not only can the patient keep track of his or her progress through frequent updates, but also can the doctor and other hospital officials at any time and from any location.

### 13.7.2    *Saving human resources*

Allocating resources to monitor and retain patient physical data, as well as other health-care expenditures and earnings, accounts for the majority of the cost. Once you have got your mobile app up and running, you will be able to save a lot of time and effort. The same human resources can be put to use in putting other good thoughts into action in order to better serve the patients.

## 13.8 Healthcare IoT for virus pandemic management

When IoT technology is used to combat a global virus pandemic, it creates a well-defined ecosystem of hardware, software, and policies. Based on findings from surveyed studies, this section delves into identifying the components of this particular health-care ecosystem. The philosophy of using IoT technology to handle a pandemic results in a unique set of well-integrated components. These elements work together as part of a virus-fighting ecosystem to stop or slow the spread of a virus.

Other benefits of using IoT to combat a pandemic like COVID-19 include improved patient management accuracy, lower costs, efficient control, accurate diagnosis, and the ability to provide superior treatment. As characterized by different research contributions, an ecosystem like this can be divided into the following primary components.

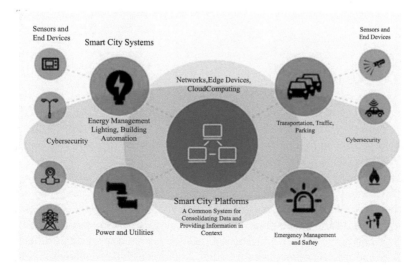

## 13.9    Evolution of healthcare (pandemic)-based IoT

Several research efforts were invested in "urban intelligence" in the aftermath of World War II to bring scientific principles into urban activities. As a result, several of these efforts culminated in the concept of the "smart city." Indeed, the principle of urban intelligence outlines three key know-hows: municipal information resources, science data handling capabilities, and executive power for pandemic preparedness and response. Skills like data sensing and mining, as well as information integration, modeling, interpretation, and visualization, have all been used to respond to a pandemic. In its most basic form, urban intelligence refers to the use of data science frameworks and computing methods to solve domain-specific urban challenges. In recent years, research in the field of the Internet of Medical Things (IoMT) has suggested a new health-care paradigm known as smart healthcare or intelligent healthcare (health-care IoT). The earlier research and development activities in WSN sparked interest in health-care IoT. IoMT primarily deploys Internet-enabled digitally connected devices with embedded identification, sensing, and data-sharing capabilities. This would help to close the gap between patients and health-care providers. Using advances in the management of the health-care system is, without

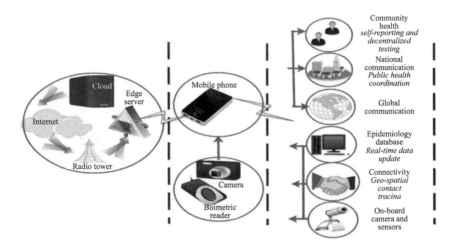

a doubt, the goal of clever healthcare. Intelligent healthcare, for example, uses wearable devices, a flexible web, and IoT to collect data from people, equipment, and agencies involved in health-care services and then uses that data to oversee and respond to health-care needs in a thoughtful manner. Take COVID-19, for example. By gathering, incorporating, and analyzing exact, appropriate, and high-quality data in real-time, intelligent healthcare can prevent the virus's transmission and spread. To track new COVID-19 cases, intelligent healthcare will gather data through patient-centered health-based apps. In addition, instead of encounter-based care, wearable technology (bodyworn-sensors) can be used to provide healthcare to COVID-19 patients via constant linked care. Additionally, through continuous data stream and growth, potential COVID-19 hotspots can be proactively identified and tracked. This makes the virus's prevention and spread easier. In addition, by combining several data sources, intelligent healthcare will increase community safety. We examine existing business developments and how they are applied to healthcare to gain a better understanding of health-based IoT. We have divided the IoT-based health-care evolution into two categories based on our results. To begin, consider the use of H-IoT prior to COVID-19. Second, how has the IoT in healthcare react to the COVID-19 pandemic.

## 13.10    Increase availability of social networks

Physicians would use mobile technology to consult with other doctors for a second opinion on their patients. These devices are also beneficial to doctors who work in different offices in different towns that are relatively far apart. Doctors will use mobile technology to communicate with patients and coworkers, exchange medical data, communicate through voice, video, and chat and maintain their workspace. Doctors will now reach out to more people and assist more patients in more places thanks to mobile technology.

### 13.10.1    Improve efficiency of health services

In a variety of ways, mobile technology has aided patients in saving money. Patients have spent less time in hospitals and have made less visits to their physicians as a result of mobile technology. When doctors offer their personal information instead of using the hospital's phone directory, patients can contact their doctors much more quickly and effectively. Doctors should speak to their patients over the phone for a few minutes instead of leaving calls with their receptionist to follow up if there is not a physical involvement.

Patients' independence has improved as a result of mobile technology's ability to help them improve their health. Patients have benefited from Equated Monthly Installment's (EMIs) continuous monitoring of their health conditions. This device has enabled patients to take responsibility for their health and reduce their reliance on doctors and nurses. The EMIs have given patients information about their symptoms and what they need to do about their newly diagnosed disease. EMIs, according to the author, provide information on barriers that prevent patients from quitting smoking and losing weight by showing progress after the device has been used daily. Having a device to keep track of the improvements that need to be made to achieve one's personal health goals instead of visiting physicians, nurses, and/or nutritionists is a fantastic benefit for patients.

### 13.10.2    Improve patients health condition

The primary reason why mobile technology has become so prevalent in hospitals is that it has improved the lives of many patients. According to Avancha (2012), mobile technology has enabled doctors to keep track of their patients more regularly, increase the quality of health care, and make it easier for patients to take care of their own. Doctors have been able to better serve their patients in a timely fashion thanks to mobile technology. According to Heron (2010), equated monthly installment (EMI) has aided in the treatment of a variety of disorders, including obsessive-compulsive disorder, generalized anxiety disorder, panic disorder, and social phobia. There are a slew of other ailments for which mobile technology has made a difference in people's lives.

### 13.10.3    Enhances physician efficiency

Physicians who are well-functioning are the foundation of a well-functioning health-care system. However, it is a high-stress position. Approximately 60% of emergency medicine physicians, according to the American Medical Association, are burnt out. Physicians often lament the amount of time they spend on data entry and other administrative activities. Only 27% of their time is spent caring for patients. To combat this issue, service providers are looking for ways to make the medical profession less stressful. Doctors are using phones and tablets to fix problems quicker and with less stress.

Physicians should record patient history on mobile devices with zero errors. These devices give users easier access to the most up-to-date drug information, allowing them to make better choices. They automate a lot of paperwork, freeing up time for doctors. It also means that doctors now have access to all of their patients' information, allowing them to spend less time delivering the same level of care. Overall, the use of mobile devices in healthcare has increased physician productivity and improved patient care.

## 13.11    Data privacy and security is a significant concern

Data privacy and security have long been a source of concern for health-care institutions. This was the case before smartphones and other devices, such as notebooks, tablets, and portable hard drives, allowed information to freely travel outside their facility walls. If a smartphone is lost or stolen and does not have adequate security, the data stored on it and available via apps can be viewed and potentially downloaded. A situation like this might have serious legal and financial ramifications for a company and its clinicians.

### 13.11.1    Lack of information control

Many hospitals have expressed fears about the lack of control over how an individual would gain access to some information and who may possibly gain access to other people's information. Technology has progressed to the point where someone might potentially gather significant quantities of data without anyone's knowledge. Many people are concerned about the confidentiality of their personal information as a result of this problem. Passwords restrict the confidentiality of information on mobile technology. Anyone might accidentally tap into someone's phone, which could cause a slew of issues. The primary problem with mobile technology is that it is difficult for health administrators to use it, and the hospital must adhere to numerous privacy regulations. Software is used by 65% of businesses to block websites. However, 35% of businesses are not adhering to medical privacy regulations, which may cause a slew of issues for patients and their families. Patients may not want certain people in their lives, such as their boss, to know about their health conditions because it may put them at a disadvantage at work, or family members who may profit from the information that the patient does not want to share. Strong regulations, such as the Health Insurance Portability and Accountability Act (HIPAA), mandate patient–doctor secrecy. HIPAA also stresses protecting PHI from health-care providers and mandates that health information in electronic form be protected, monitored, and controlled through organizational access protection, monitoring, and control.

## *13.11.2    Digital divide among patients*

Hospitals should be available to all patients, regardless of their socioeconomic status. There are also people who do not have a smartphone or even a computer to contact via e-mail for more frequent updates. Hospitals with a high proportion of poor patients lag behind in creating digital technologies, and administrators find it impossible to change their systems to become more digital. This problem of the digital divide has the potential to result in inequalities in healthcare.

## **13.12    Conclusion**

We suggest a model for IoT-based health-care systems in this chapter, which can be used for both general systems and systems that monitor special conditions. Then, for each component of the proposed model, we submitted a detailed and systematic overview of the state-of-the-art works. Several nonintrusive, wearable sensors were demonstrated and evaluated, with a focus on those that monitor vital signs, BP, and blood oxygen levels. The suitability of short-range and long-range communication requirements for health-care applications was then compared. For short-range and long-range communications in healthcare, bilateral lower extremity and Narrow Band-Internet of Things (NB-IoT) emerged as the most suitable standards. Recent cloud-based data storage research was introduced, demonstrating that the cloud is the best option for storing and coordinating big data in healthcare. Several studies have also found that data processing in the cloud is much better than data processing on wearable devices with their limited resources. The most important disadvantage of using the cloud is that it adds security risks; as a result, we introduced several works aimed at enhancing cloud security. Access control policies and encryption were discovered to substantially improve security, but no known standard is suitable for immediate implementation in a wearable, IoT-based health-care system. We found several important areas for future study based on our analysis of state-of-the-art technologies in the fields of wearable sensors, communication standards, and cloud technology. Machine learning and the development of a secure but lightweight encryption scheme for cloud storage are the two areas where researchers looking to make substantial changes in the field of IoT-based healthcare have the most opportunities.

## Further reading

[1]   M.U. Ahmed, S. Begum, and J.-B. Fasquel (Eds.) *4th International Conference*, HealthyIoT 2017, Angers, France, 2017, pp. 3–9.

[2]   K. Govinda *Contemporary Applications of Mobile Computing in Healthcare Settings*, VIT University, Vellore, India, 2018, pp. 51–57. Copyright: © 2018.

[3]   A.K. Singh, R.S. Singh, A.K. Pandey, S. Udmale, and A. Chaudhary ISBN: 9780128214725, 11th November 2020, pp. 36–59.

[4]   C. Chakraborty, A. Banerjee, A. Kolekar, H. Maheshkumar, and B. Chakraborty *Internet of Things for Healthcare Technologies*, March 2020 Pages: 21–43. ISBN: 978-981-15-4111-7.

[5]   A. Gantait, J. Patra, and A. Mukherjee Defining Your IoT Governance Practices, January 19, 2018. Updated January 20, 2018.

[6]   P. Sharma How Edge Computing in Healthcare Is Transforming IoT Implementation. Apc.com, December 12, 2017.

[7]   Edge Computing for IoT in Buildings. Navigant Research, Q4 2018.

[8]   Global Smart Healthcare Products Market Will Reach USD 66.7 Billion by 2024, Zion Research, January 2019.

[9]   Gartner, IT Glossary, Internet of Things http://www.gartner.com/it-glossary/internet-of-things/.

[10]  Gartner, Press release, 2013, online at http://www.gartner.com/newsroom/id/2636073.

[11]  ITU Internet Reports, The Internet of Things, November 2005 http://www.itu.int/osg/spu/publications/internetofthings/InternetofThings_summary.pdf.

[12]  IERC – European Research Cluster on the Internet of Things, "Internet of Things – Pan European Research and Innovation Vision", October, 2011.

[13]  L. Adori, A. Iera, and G. Morabito The Internet of Things: A Survey, *Computer Networks*, 54 (2010) 2787–2805.

[14]  H. Jun-Wei, Y. Shouyi, L. Leibo, Z. Zhen, and W. Shaojun A Crop Monitoring System Based on Wireless Sensor Network, *Procedia Environmental Sciences*, 11 (2011) 558–565.

[15]  A.M. Vilamovska, E. Hattziandreu, R. Schindler, C. Van Oranje, H. DeVries, and J. Krapelse *RFID Application in Healthcare – Scoping and Identifying Areas for RFID Deployment in Healthcare Delivery*, RAND, Europe, 2009.

[16]  P. Pande Internet of Things – A Future of Internet: A Survey, *International Journal of Advance Research in Computer Science and Management Studies*, 2(2), 2014.

[17]  Internet of Things: From Research and Innovation to Market Deployment – IERC 2014. http://www.internet-of-things-research.eu/pdf/IERC_Cluster_Book_2014_Ch.3_SRIA_WEB.pdf.

[18]  Proteus, Digital health feedback system, http://www.proteus.com/technology/digital-health-feedback-system.

[19] Proteus, Digital Medicine, http://www.proteus.com/future-products/digital-medicines/.

[20] D. Christin, A. Reinhardt, P. Mogre, and R. Steinmed "Wireless Sensor Networks and the Internet of Things: Selected Challenges," in *Proceedings of the 8th GI/ITG KuVS Fachgespräch "Drahtlose Sensornede"*, 2009, pp. 31–33.

[21] C. Li, A. Raghunathan, and N. Jha "Hijacking an Insulin Pump: Security Attacks and Defenses for a Diabetes Therapy System," in *IEEE 13th International Conference on e-Health Networking, Applications and Services*, Columbia, MO, 2011, pp. 150–156.

[22] Wikipedia, Personalized medicine http://en.wikipedia.org/wiki/Personalized_medicine.

[23] IEEE Newsletter, P. Desikan, R. Khare, J. Srivastava, R. Kaplan, J. Ghosh, L. Liu, and V. Gopal Predictive Modeling in Healthcare: Challenges and Opportunities http://lifesciences.ieee.org/publications/newsletter/november-2013/439-predictive-modeling-in-healthcare-challenges-and-opportunities.

[24] M. Abo-Zahhad, S. M. Ahmed, and O. Elnahas A Wireless Emergency Telemedicine System for Patients Monitoring and Diagnosis. https://www.who.int/gho/mortality_burden_disease/life_tables/situation_trends_text/en/24.

[25] S. Gotadki, R. Mohan, M. Attarwala, and M.P. Gajare "Intelligent Ambulance".

[26] C. Li, X. Hu, and L. Zhang "The IoT-Based Heart Disease Monitoring System for Pervasive Healthcare Service," in *International Conference on Knowledge Based and Intelligent Information and Engineering Systems, KES2017*, Marseille, France, 6–8 September 2017.

[27] L. Yu "Smart Hospital based on Internet of Things".

[28] D.S. Abdul Minaam and M. Abd-ELfattah Smart Drugs: Improving Healthcare Using Smart Pill Box for Medicine Reminder and Monitoring System, *Future Computing and Informatics Journal*, 3(2018) 443–456.

[29] P. Deepika Mathuvanthi, V. Suresh, and Ch. Pradeep IoT Powered Wearable to Assist Individuals Facing Depression Symptoms, *International Research Journal of Engineering and Technology (IRJET)*, 6 (2019) 1676.

[30] A. Haleem, M. Javaid, and I.H. Khan Internet of Things (IoT) Applications in Orthopaedics, *Journal of Clinical Orthopaedics and Trauma* (2019), doi: https://doi.org/10.1016/j.jcot.2019.07.003.

[31] M. AboZahhad, S.M. Ahmed, and O. Elnahas A Wireless Emergency Telemedicine System for Patients Monitoring and Diagnosis, *International Journal of Telemedicine and Applications*, 2014 (2014) 380787.

## Chapter 14

# Video-based solutions for newborn monitoring

*Veronica Mattioli[1], Davide Alinovi[1,*], Francesco Pisani[2], Gianluigi Ferrari[1] and Riccardo Raheli[1]*

Efficient monitoring of vital signs is a fundamental tool in disease prevention and medical diagnostics. Main physiological parameters to monitor are not only heart rate, blood pressure, respiratory rate and body temperature, but motion analysis may also provide essential information about the clinical status of a patient. Very specific pathological movements can indeed be signs of important or potentially threatening disorders. Besides being almost exclusively performed in hospital settings, conventional monitoring often requires a contact with the body of the patient that makes traditional systems possibly invasive and uncomfortable, especially if applied on newborns. To make home care more accessible and comfortable, novel methods for remote and contactless monitoring have been developed in the recent years. Among others, appealing solutions that have received recent research attention are based on video processing techniques that allow to capture and analyze the movements of a patient in a contactless fashion.

## 14.1 Introduction

Early diagnosis of neonatal disorders may be crucial for timely intervention and treatment. As some rare but potentially harmful diseases in newborns that can manifest themselves with clinical symptoms, such as seizures and apneas, affect the movements of the patient, movement monitoring and analysis may be an effective diagnostic tool. In particular, some types of seizures can be characterized by jerky periodic movements of one or more body parts, usually limbs and head. On the other hand, apneas are associated with the absence of periodic breathing movements [1].

A seizure can be defined as an age-dependent clinical event characterized by a neurological dysfunction caused by paroxysmal alterations of neurological, behavioral and/or automatic functions [2]. One of the most common outward effects is an uncontrolled shaking due to involuntary and rapidly contraction and relaxation

[1]Department of Engineering and Architecture, University of Parma, Parma, Italy
[2]Department of Medicine and Surgery, University of Parma, Parma, Italy
*Deceased on 16 September 2020

of one or more muscle groups. Preterm and at-term newborns are more likely to suffer from a seizure within 28 days after birth or 44 weeks of conceptional age, respectively [2]. The estimated incidence is 2.6% for overall newborns, 2.0% for term neonates, 11.1% for preterm neonates and 13.5% for infants weighing less than 2 500 g [3]. Hypoxic–ischemic encephalopathy and stroke are not only two of the more frequent etiologies, but brain malformation and infection can also be triggers [4]. As reported in [4,5], several classifications have been proposed, but usually four main types of clinical manifestations are considered indicative of neonatal seizures: subtle, clonic, tonic and myoclonic [2]. Each clinical type of seizure is characterized by distinguishable features and requires focused analysis and diagnostic approach. Clonic seizures, for instance, are associated with rhythmic and slow movements.

On the other hand, apneas can be defined as sudden interruptions of the respiratory airflow. In newborns, these episodes are considered to be significant if lasting longer than 20 s or less if associated with other symptoms, i.e., bradycardia and cyanosis [6]. As reported in [1], among the main causes of neonatal apneas, we recall seizures, cerebrovascular events [7] and congenital disorders, such as congenital central hypoventilation syndrome (CCHS) [8,9]. CCHS, in particular, is a rare life-threatening disease caused by a defect in the PHOX2B homeobox gene [9]. It mainly occurs during sleep and is responsible of alveolar hypoventilation. It is usually associated with cyanosis, apnea or cardiorespiratory arrest [10]. Finally, three main categories of apneas can be identified, i.e., central, obstructive and mixed, according to the presence or the lack of an obstruction of the upper airway [6].

Due to the severity of these neonatal disorders, early treatments are needed to prevent life-threatening episodes as well as lifelong consequences. To this purpose, efficient monitoring tools must be deployed. The investigation of modern monitoring systems based on video processing solutions can be considered a promising and effective alternative to conventional equipment. Motion analysis plays a key role to detect anomalous movements related to the aforementioned disorders and will be discussed in the next sections.

## 14.2    Vital signs monitoring

Conventional systems for monitoring vital signs are often intrusive and not suitable for home care. The main standard tool for the diagnosis of sleep-related disorders, such as seizures and apneas, is the polysomnogram that allows to record the sleep of a patient and includes several monitoring systems, i.e., electro-encephalogram (EEG), electrooculogram, electromyogram and electrocardiogram [11]. Each of these measurement techniques requires wired sensors to be directly attached to different body parts of the patient. In particular, electrodes placed on the scalp, near the eyes, under the chin and on the chest are employed to record brain activity, eyes movements, muscle activity and heart rate, respectively. Additional information is acquired through elastic belt sensors placed around the chest, nasal flow meter and pulse oximeter to measure the amount of effort to breathe, the airflow and the oxygen saturation of the blood, respectively [11]. Cameras can also be employed for simultaneous traditional monitoring. A schematic overview of the polysomnogram test is shown in Figure 14.1(a) and an example of recorded data is reported in Figure 14.1(b) where the first four traces are the EEG channels, and the subsequent traces are, from top to bottom, snoring noise, nasal flow, thoracic movements and oxygen saturation. The abnormal breathing pattern is characterized by recurrence of central apneas (closed boxes), in the absence of airway obstruction and snoring. Central apneas determine severe oxygen desaturations.

Besides being expensive and moderately invasive, especially for newborns, these techniques are almost exclusively deployed in clinical settings and require trained medical staff who may not be available full time. To make home care more accessible, various monitoring systems have been developed, e.g., smart bed [12] and wearable-sensor-based systems [13], but they still require contact with the body of the patient. Contactless solutions, on the other hand, may be devised for the automatic detection of anomalous activities potentially related to neonatal disorders. To this purpose, digital cameras can be used to frame the movements of a patient to be analyzed through proper video processing algorithms. The integration of these novel approaches allows to enhance both hospital and home constant monitoring by providing low-cost preliminary alert signals to be possibly further investigated by conventional diagnostic tools, i.e., the EEG.

## 14.3 Video processing systems for neonatal disorder detection

Early work on video-based solutions for newborn monitoring was mainly focused on seizure detection and was based on motion extraction algorithms such as optical flow [14] and block matching [15]. Neural networks for anomalous event detection and motion classification were also investigated. The implementation of all these methods may be complex, expensive and not suitable for real-time monitoring. However, in [1] a fast and reliable approach for the real-time analysis of newborns' movements is proposed on the basis of preliminary contributions [16–18]. This method is based on the extraction of motion signals acquired with single or multiple cameras and ultimately relies on the well-known maximum likelihood (ML) estimation criterion [19]. Besides being presented for clonic seizures and apneas detection, it is valid for any disorder characterized by the presence or the absence of periodic movements.

In Sections 4.3.1 and 14.3.2, the motion estimation algorithm presented in [1] will be briefly introduced for single- and multiple-sensor analysis, respectively. The performance in the latter case is improved by the different viewing angles that allow to capture movements that may be occluded for a single camera, hence undetectable. In particular, models to describe motion signals acquired from properly preprocessed video sequences are discussed. The specific procedures for the extraction of motion information related to seizures and apneas will be presented in Sections 14.4 and 14.5, respectively. Since the disorders under investigation are characterized by the presence or absence of periodic movements, motion signals will be modeled as

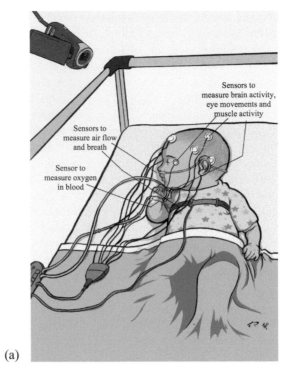

(a)

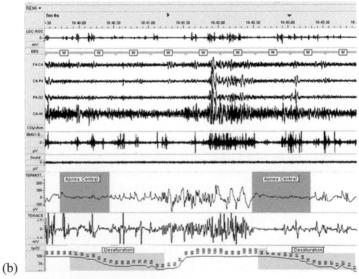

(b)

*Figure 14.1    Polysomnography during wakefulness: (a) schematic overview and*
*(b) example of recorded data. Image by Francesca and Andrea*
*Pisani*

periodic signals, where the fundamental frequency represents the main unknown parameter to be estimated.

In the following analysis, we will consider video sequences with sampling period, $T$, where frames have dimension $W \times H$ and are sampled at time instants $iT$, $i$ being the frame number.

## 14.3.1   Single sensor

Let $\bar{L}[i]$ be the average luminance signal extracted at frame $i$ of a considered video sequence. We define it as

$$\bar{L}[i] = \frac{1}{WH} \sum_{x=1}^{W} \sum_{y=1}^{H} I[x,y,i] \tag{14.1}$$

Where $I[x,y,i]$ represents the $[x,y]$ entry of matrix $I[i]$ that describes the $i$th frame after a proper processing procedure. The motion signal in (14.1) can be modeled as

$$\bar{L}[i] = c + A\cos(2\pi f_0 iT + \varphi) + n[i] \tag{14.2}$$

Where $c$ is a continuous component and $n[i]$ are samples of independent identically distributed zero-mean Gaussian noise. The unknown parameters $A$, $f_0$ and $\varphi$ represent the amplitude, phase and frequency, respectively, of the periodic signal and may be collected in a vector $\theta = [A, f_0, \phi]$. The ML approach can now be exploited to estimate the vector $\theta$. In particular, observing a window of $N$ frames and following standard methods described in [20], an estimator of the fundamental frequency can be obtained and expressed as

$$\widehat{f}_0 = \operatorname*{argmax}_f \left| \sum_{i=0}^{N-1} \bar{L}[i] e^{-j2\pi fiT} \right|^2. \tag{14.3}$$

Similarly, an expression of the amplitude estimator can be written as

$$\widehat{A} = \frac{2}{N} \left| \sum_{n=0}^{N-1} \bar{L}[n] e^{-j2\pi \widehat{f}_0 iT} \right|. \tag{14.4}$$

The presence of a significant periodic component can be finally declared if the following constraint is verified:

$$N\widehat{A}^2 > \eta \tag{14.5}$$

Where the value of the threshold $\eta$ may be determined by trial and error.

## 14.3.2   Multiple sensors

The method described in Section 14.3.1 can be extended to multiple sensors to achieve better performance. Multi-camera systems can indeed detect movements that may be occluded for a single camera. Considering $S$ sensors, a set of motion signals is defined as in (14.1):

$$\bar{L}_s[i] = \frac{1}{WH} \sum_{x=1}^{W} \sum_{y=1}^{H} I_s[x, y, i], \quad s = 1, 2, \dots, S. \tag{14.6}$$

Where the processed $i$th frame for the $s$th sensor is described by matrix $I_s[x, y, i]$. The model in (14.2) can be generalized as

$$\bar{L}_s[i] = c_s + A_s \cos(2\pi f_0 iT + \varphi_s) + n_s[i] \tag{14.7}$$

Where the sampling period $T$ and the fundamental frequency $f_0$ are assumed to be identical for each capturing device; where present, the subscript $s$ refers to the $s$th sensor. Following the same procedure of the single-sensor analysis and exploiting now data fusion techniques to combine data acquired by different sensors, an estimator of the fundamental frequency can now be formulated as

$$\widehat{f}_0 = \operatorname{argmax}_f \sum_{s=1}^{S} \left| \sum_{i=0}^{N-1} \bar{L}_s[i] e^{-j2\pi fiT} \right|^2. \tag{14.8}$$

Likewise, assuming that different values of amplitude are associated to each sensor, a set of amplitude estimators is:

$$\widehat{A}_s = \frac{2}{N} \left| \sum_{n=0}^{N-1} \bar{L}_s[n] e^{-j2\pi \widehat{f}_0 iT} \right|, \quad s = 1, 2, \dots, S. \tag{14.9}$$

Finally, the constraint to be satisfied in order to detect a significant periodic component is now

$$\frac{N}{S} \sum_{s=1}^{S} \widehat{A}^2 > \eta. \tag{14.10}$$

To improve the performance of both single- and multi-sensor analyses, interlaced windows can be considered, as the selected detection algorithm may indeed fail when pathological movements manifest across two consecutive disjoint windows [16].

## 14.4    Seizure detection

In order to extract the average motion signals defined in (14.1) and (14.6), each frame of a considered video sequence needs to be properly processed. A schematic overview of the preprocessing algorithm exploited in [1,16] for seizure detection is presented in Figure 14.2, where four phases are highlighted: grayscale conversion, difference filtering, binarization and erosion. A generic red, green and blue (RGB) video sequence $X[i]$ is considered the input of the processing system and initially converted to gray scale. The difference of frames (DoF) is then performed on consecutive frames as a

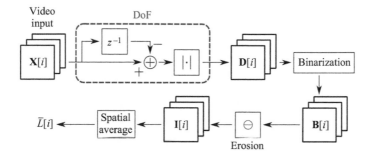

*Figure 14.2   Seizure detection preprocessing algorithm*

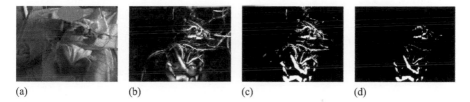

(a)                    (b)                    (c)                    (d)

*Figure 14.3   Results of each processing step: (a) gray-scale, (b) difference filtering, (c) binarization and (d) erosion*

basic image filtering operation and the result is threshold to obtain a binary mask, where white pixels correspond to foreground regions. Finally, the erosion morphological operation [20] is implemented to reduce noise as discussed in [16]. Examples of frames at each processing step are shown in Figure 14.3. Eventually, an example of periodic movements induced by a clonic seizure and extracted according the procedure illustrated in Figure 14.2 is shown in Figure 14.4, where the extracted average motion signal is plotted against the frame number along with a corresponding EEG signal [16]. The two signals exhibit a comparable periodicity.

## 14.4.1   Performance in seizure detection

The performance of the described detection method has been evaluated in terms of sensitivity and specificity over $n$ tests, respectively, defined as

$$\alpha = \frac{n_{TP}}{n_{TP} + n_{FN}} \tag{14.11}$$

$$\beta = \frac{n_{TN}}{n_{TN} + n_{FP}} \tag{14.12}$$

where $n_{TP}$, $n_{TN}$, $n_{FP}$ and $n_{FN}$ are the numbers of true positives, true negatives, false positives and false negatives in the considered sequence. In particular, positives and negatives are classified when a seizure is detected or undetected, respectively. Performance of single- and multi-sensor systems have been investigated and the

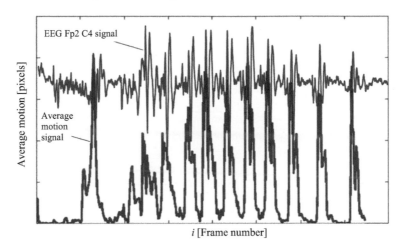

*Figure 14.4    Average motion signal [16]*

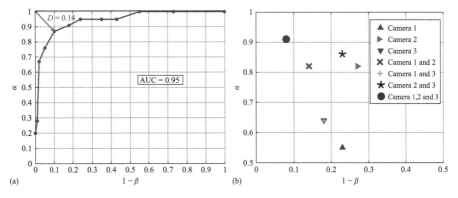

*Figure 14.5    Performance analysis for (a) single RGB camera (ROC curve); (b) different RGB camera configurations [1]*

results obtained using a single RGB sensor are illustrated in Figure 14.5(a), where the receiver operating characteristic (ROC) [21] curve is plotted as a function of $\alpha$ and $1 - \beta$ for various values of the threshold $\eta$. We recall that an optimal predictor is characterized by $\alpha = 1$ and $\beta = 1$, i.e., all seizures are correctly detected when present, and an area under the curve (AUC) is equal to 1. In the presented example, the minimum Euclidean distance $D$ from the ideal configuration is 0.14 and the AUC is 0.95, which indicates high reliability [21]. In Figure 14.5(b), sensitivity and specificity values are plotted for optimal values of $\eta$ and different RGB cameras configurations. The best performance is achieved when all three sensors are employed, i.e., $S = 3$ in (14.6)–(14.10). Depth sensors could also be employed to better distinguish pathological movements from background noise or random movements [1].

## 14.5   Apnea detection

Breathing-related movements are often subtle and difficult to detect, especially for newborns. To make the detection algorithm efficient also in the presence of small movements, a motion magnification algorithm can be applied to amplify the considered motion signals. In particular, the Eulerian video magnification (EVM) method presented in [22] can be exploited and its schematic representation is illustrated in Figure 14.6, where the input signal $\mathbf{X}[i]$ is processed through four main phases. Initially, each frame of the considered video sequence is decomposed into different spatial frequency bands by spatial decomposition. The obtained outputs are then filtered through a pixel-wise temporal operation and the frequency bands of interest are extracted. Multiplications by proper gains are now performed to amplify the filtered signals and a video frame reconstruction is finally implemented to obtain a new output signal where small changes at the input are enhanced. The motion extraction algorithm shown in Figure 14.2 can be applied after the EVM processing.

An example of an extracted motion signal is plotted in Figure 14.7(a), where the normal periodic behavior of a respiratory signal can be easily observed. The corresponding periodogram is shown in Figure 14.7(b), where the estimated

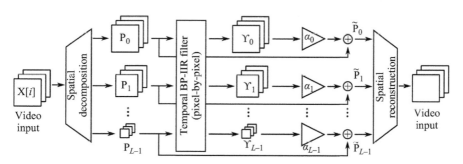

*Figure 14.6   EVM algorithm [18]*

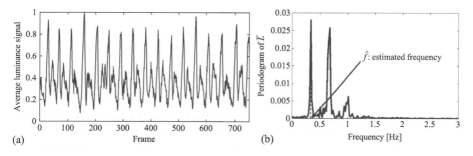

*Figure 14.7   (a) Periodic motion signal example and (b) periodogram*

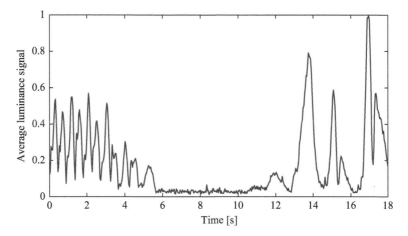

*Figure 14.8    Anomalous motion signal related to an apnea event in a newborn*

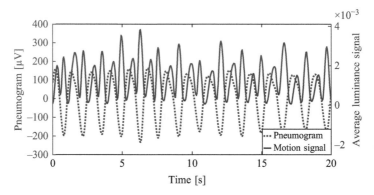

*Figure 14.9    Extracted motion signal and correspondent pneumographic signal*

fundamental frequency is highlighted at the peak of the function. On the other hand, an example of an anomalous motion signal is illustrated in Figure 14.18, where the sudden interruption of the respiration caused by an apnea episode is visible in the flat central part of the plot.

Finally, for the sake of comparison, an instance of an extracted motion signal is shown in Figure 14.9 along with the equivalent signal obtained from a pneumograph, where every period of the pneumographic signal corresponds to a complete respiratory act of the patient. Considering that a respiratory act is composed by two phases, i.e., inhalation and exhalation, a good match of the two signals can be observed.

A number of improvements are possible with reference to the method described in Figure 14.6. Among them, we mention [23] where the computationally intensive reconstruction of the video stream is avoided and the sublevel signals are directly combined in a multidimensional effective estimator. Direct application of

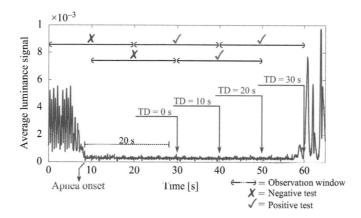

*Figure 14.10    Detection of a long apnea episode*

multidimensional ML estimator to the video stream was also investigated and showed very good performance, provided proper processing is performed to select a suitable region of interest [24]. We also remark that these methods could be applied to seizure detection as well. However, the subtle respiration movements specifically require these more sensitive (and complex) solutions.

### 14.5.1    Performance in apnea detection

To evaluate the performance of the apnea detection algorithm, sensitivity and specificity coefficients are still considered but slightly differently defined as

$$\alpha = \frac{T_{TP}}{T_{TP} + T_{FN}} \tag{14.13}$$

$$\beta = \frac{T_{TN}}{T_{TN} + T_{FP}} \tag{14.14}$$

where $T_{TP}$, $T_{TN}$, $T_{FP}$ and $T_{FN}$ represent now the total duration of time intervals when an apnea episode is correctly detected (time true positives), correctly undetected (time true negatives), incorrectly detected (time false positives) and incorrectly undetected (time false negatives), respectively. An interval of tolerance, i.e., tolerance delay (TD), is allowed to declare that an apnea episode is detected. As an illustrative example, the motion signal related to a long apnea episode is shown in Figure 14.10, where half interlaced observation windows are highlighted in the upper part of the plot and different TD values are considered. The apnea detection fails for TD = 0 s, while it succeeds for TD = 10, 20 and 30 s.

## 14.6    Conclusion

In this chapter, novel techniques for newborn monitoring based on video processing solutions have been proposed. Considering that disorders such as seizures and apneas are characterized by specific pathological movements, proper algorithms for motion analysis have been presented. In particular, as clonic seizures trigger jerky movements of some human body parts and apneas cause sudden interruptions of the rhythmical respiration movements, periodicity is the fundamental parameter to be investigated. Motion signals extracted from video sequences can indeed be modeled as periodic signals, where the fundamental frequency can be ultimately estimated by standard probability theory techniques. The main goal is the integration of reliable, noninvasive and contactless systems with conventional equipment to provide clinical support to enhance early diagnosis of potentially life-threatening diseases.

# References

[1]   Cattani L, Alinovi D, Ferrari G, *et al.* Monitoring infants by automatic video processing: A unified approach to motion analysis. *Computers in Biology and Medicine*. 2017; 80: 158–165.

[2]   Volpe JJ. *Neurology of the Newborn*. 5th ed. Philadelphia, PA, USA: Saunders Elsevier; 2008.

[3]   Ronen GM, Penney S, and Andrews W. The epidemiology of clinical neonatal seizures in Newfoundland: A population-based study. *The Journal of Pediatrics*. 1999; 134(1): 71–75.

[4]   Pellegrin S, Munoz FM, Padula M, *et al.* Neonatal seizures: Case definition and guidelines for data collection, analysis, and presentation of immunization safety data. *Vaccine*. 2019; 37(52): 7596–7609.

[5]   Riviello JJ. Classification of seizures and epilepsy. *Current Neurology and Neuroscience Reports*. 2003; 3: 325–331.

[6]   Mishra S, Agarwal R, Jeevasankar M, *et al.* Apnea in the newborn. *Indian Journal of Pediatrics*. 2008; 75: 57–71.

[7]   Tramonte J and Goodkin H. Temporal lobe hemorrhage in the full-term neonate presenting as apneic seizures. *Journal of Perinatology*. 2004; 24: 726–729.

[8]   Rand CM, Patwari PP, Carroll MS, *et al.* Congenital central hypoventilation syndrome and sudden infant death syndrome: disorders of autonomic regulation. *Seminars in Pediatric Neurology*. 2013; 20(1): 44–55. Pediatric Autonomic Disorders.

[9]   Healy F and Marcus CL. Congenital central hypoventilation syndrome in children. *Paediatric Respiratory Reviews*. 2011; 12(4): 253–263.

[10]  Cielo CM and Marcus CL. Central hypoventilation syndromes. *Sleep Medicine Clinics*. 2014; 9(1): 105–118.

[11]  Martin RJ, Block AJ, Cohn MA, *et al.* Indications and standards for cardiopulmonary sleep studies. *Sleep*. 1985; 8(4): 371–379.

[12]  Spillman Jr WB, Mayer M, Bennett J, *et al.* A smart bed for non-intrusive monitoring of patient physiological factors. *Measurement Science and Technology*. 2004; 15(8): 1614–1620.

[13]  Pantelopoulos A and Bourbakis NG. A survey on wearable sensor-based systems for health monitoring and prognosis. *IEEE Transactions on Systems,*

Man, and Cybernetics, Part C (Applications and Reviews). 2010; 40(1): 1–12.

[14] Karayiannis NB, Varughese B, Tao G, *et al.* Quantifying motion in video recordings of neonatal seizures by regularized optical flow methods. *IEEE Transactions on Image Processing.* 2005; 14(7): 890–903.

[15] Karayiannis NB, Sami A, Frost JD, *et al.* Automated extraction of temporal motor activity signals from video recordings of neonatal seizures based on adaptive block matching. *IEEE Transactions on Biomedical Engineering.* 2005; 52(4): 676–686.

[16] Ntonfo GMK, Ferrari G, Raheli R, *et al.* Low-complexity image processing for real-time detection of neonatal clonic seizures. *IEEE Transactions on Information Technology in Biomedicine.* 2012; 16(3): 375–382.

[17] Cattani L, Kouamou Ntonfo GM, Lofino F, *et al.* Maximum-likelihood detection of neonatal clonic seizures by video image processing. In: *2014 8th International Symposium on Medical Information and Communication Technology (ISMICT)*; 2014. p. 1–5.

[18] Cattani L, Alinovi D, Ferrari G, *et al.* A wire-free, non-invasive, low-cost video processing-based approach to neonatal apnoea detection. In: *2014 IEEE Workshop on Biometric Measurements and Systems for Security and Medical Applications (BIOMS) Proceedings*; 2014. p. 67–73.

[19] Kay SM. *Fundamentals of Statistical Signal Processing: Estimation Theory.* 1st ed. Upper Saddle River, NJ, USA: Prentice Hall; 1993.

[20] Solomon C and Breckon T. *Fundamentals of Digital Image Processing.* 1st ed. Croydon, UK: Wiley-Blackwell; 2011.

[21] Swets J. Measuring the accuracy of diagnostic systems. *Science.* 1988; 240 (4857): 1285–93.

[22] Wu HY, Rubinstein M, Shih E, *et al.* Eulerian video magnification for revealing subtle changes in the world. *ACM Transactions on Graphics.* 2012; 31(4).

[23] Alinovi D, Cattani L, Ferrari G, *et al.* Spatio-temporal video processing for respiratory rate estimation. In: *2015 IEEE International Symposium on Medical Measurements and Applications (MeMeA) Proceedings*; 2015. p. 12–17.

[24] Alinovi D, Ferrari G, Pisani F, *et al.* Respiratory rate monitoring by maximum likelihood video processing. In: *2016 IEEE International Symposium on Signal Processing and Information Technology (ISSPIT)*; 2016. p. 172–177.

## Chapter 15

# IoT sensor networks in healthcare

## *Rinki Sharma[1]*

Over the past few years, there have been numerous advances in the health-care industry. Incorporation of Internet of Things (IoT) in the health-care applications has unlocked numerous possibilities in the way healthcare operates now. This chapter concentrates on IoT sensor networks in healthcare. The suitability of sensor networks in healthcare is presented. The applications in which IoT sensor networks play a crucial role, and thus related sensors are presented. Key sensors, and their applications in healthcare, are presented. The most common and popular use cases of IoT sensor networks in healthcare are discussed. The wireless communication technologies used in IoT sensor networks for healthcare are described along with their characteristics. Even though health-care IoT (H-IoT) networks have been in use for some time, and their incorporation in health-care services is only expected to increase further over the years, their implementation and adoption is still a challenge. This chapter discusses those challenges in detail. The potential contemporary technologies that help in overcoming these challenges are explained.

## List of abbreviations

| | |
|---|---|
| 3D | three dimensional |
| EHR | electronic health record |
| GPS | global positioning system |
| H-IoT | health-care Internet of Things |
| IoT | Internet of Things |
| IR | infrared |
| IrDA | Infrared Data Association |
| LAN | local area network |
| MEMS | microelectromechanical systems |
| NFC | near-field communication |
| NFV | network function virtualization |

[1]Department of Computer Science and Engineering, Ramaiah University of Applied Sciences, Bengaluru, India

QoS        quality of service
RFID       radio frequency identification
SDN        software-defined networking
UWB        ultra-wideband
WBAN       wireless body area network
Wi-Fi      wireless fidelity
WSN        wireless sensor networks

## 15.1    Introduction

In the past decades, the interaction of doctors with their patients remained limited to the patients physically visiting the doctors/nurses and vice versa. With advances in communication technologies and ease of communication, this interaction was advanced to the form of tele- and text communications. The health-care technology evolved further with the introduction of electronic health records (EHRs) that made it possible for the hospitals to store and access the patient-centric information. The portal technology allowed patients to log in to the health-care service provider's website taking a more active role by keeping a check on their health, accessing their medical records and tracking their appointments. The cloud computing and big data technologies are driving the innovation into this field. However, the solution to attain constant remote monitoring of the patient's health and vital parameters was made possible through the Internet of Things (IoT) technology that is powered by the wireless sensor networks (WSN). Sensors convert physical parameters into signals that can be processed further by other devices. When used in the form of wearable devices, these sensors can be used to check and monitor the physiological parameters of the patient. The values of these parameters include body temperature, heartbeat, pulse rate, blood pressure, oxygen saturation and blood sugar. With the help of these sensor-based IoT devices, real-time patient health monitoring and clinical feedback have become a possibility. The rising adoption of wearable devices, emergence of connected care solutions and implementation of digital technologies for healthcare are the main factors causing the surge in the demand for digital health-care solution and the expansion of the digital health-care market. The IoT-based health-care market is segmented into medical devices, system and software and medical services. The medical devices can be wearable external devices or implanted medical devices, as well as stationary or mobile medical devices used in the hospitals or health-care centers.

The WSN and IoT-based devices are majorly used for remote patient monitoring, telemedicine, telesurgery, medical imaging, health-care apparatus and medication management, smart health-care equipment, connected devices and clinical operations. According to the survey carried out by Global Market Insights, the global digital health market is increasing exponentially and is predicted to be a 500 billion dollar industry by the year 2025 [1]. According to the report published by the "Data-Driven Investor" [2], the estimates show that the inclusion of WSN and IoT-based devices in the health-care industry has saved the health-care industry up to 300-billion dollars, as the patients can now be monitored remotely decreasing the hospital admission costs, need for space, beds and other necessary equipment and staff to serve the visiting patients. According to the same report, 70% of the best-selling wearables are meant for health and fitness tracking of the present IoT device market share, and 40% of the IoT devices and applications are being used for health-care applications in the year 2020. Companies such as Microsoft, Apple, Phillips, General Electrical (GE), Wipro and many startups have invested in IoT-based health-care research and development. Microsoft Azure's cloud platform facilitates numerous health-care applications and services. Smart health monitoring and tracking devices and solutions developed by Apple, Philips and Wipro such as smart watches, smart beds/mattresses ARE used for monitoring of vital parameters, diagnostic imaging and medical implants.

This chapter presents the impact of IoT sensor network on present-day health-care systems and solutions. The advantages and issues of incorporating IoT technology in healthcare are discussed. The sensors used for health-care applications, use cases, supporting technologies, popular architectures, solutions/products, research opportunities, challenges (security in particular) are also discussed.

## 15.2 Wireless sensor networks (WSN) and Internet of Things (IoT)

Over the past few decades, the embedded computing platforms have evolved and emerged into integrated processing, storage and communication units that support wireless communication. The need for low-cost, low-powered and small-sized computing systems in the medical field has witnessed the surge of WSN-based applications and equipment in healthcare. The benefits of using sensor-based IoT networks for health-care applications are presented in Figure 15.1.

These sensor-based devices can be worn, implanted or fixed on the stationary or mobile medical devices. These sensor-based devices/systems have been proven highly efficient in providing smart, reliable and real-time care by monitoring of patient's health and sharing their health records with the medical professionals. These

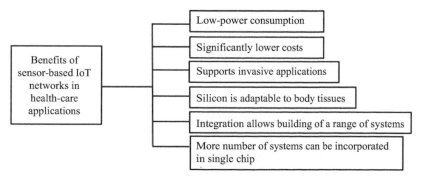

*Figure 15.1   Benefits of sensor-based IoT networks in health-care applications*

devices can be embedded in a variety of medical equipment not only at hospitals and clinics but also at homes. Sensors meant for medical applications are used to monitor physical and physiological parameters of the patient for detection, diagnosis, treatment and posttreatment monitoring and management of patient's health [3,4]. Some of the popularly used sensors for medical applications are presented in Table 15.1.

Apart from the sensors, encoders are used in magnetic resonance imaging machines, surgical robots, medical imaging, tomography, X-ray machines and other critical/noncritical medical devices.

While these sensing devices have become popular for use in medical equipment, they are constrained in resources such as computation and processing power, battery power, storage/memory and supporting data rate/bandwidth [5]. The distinct features that have led to the rise of wireless sensing and communication technology in healthcare are as follows:

1.  Microelectromechanical systems (MEMS):
    Advances in the MEMS technology have made it possible to implement and deliver inexpensive remote patient monitoring and diagnostic capabilities. This has made the early detection and curing of critical medical conditions. This has

*Table 15.1   Key sensors and their applications in healthcare*

| Key sensors | Applications |
| --- | --- |
| Pressure sensors | Oxygen concentrators, anesthesia delivery machines, ventilators, insulin pumps, blood-flow analyzers, respiratory and blood pressure monitoring equipment, surgical fluid maintenance, infusion pumps and pressure-based dental instrument |
| Temperature sensors | Medical incubators, neonatal ICUs, humidified oxygen heaters, patient temperature monitoring units and digital thermometers |
| Flow sensors | Anesthesia delivery machines, ventilators, gas mixing and electrosurgery wherein high-frequency electric current is passed to destroy the malignant tissues |
| Image sensors | Endoscopy, radiography, fluoroscopy, dental imaging, mammography, retinal therapy and ocular surgery |
| Accelerometers | Heart pacemakers, blood pressure monitors, defibrillators and other integrated health-monitoring equipment |
| Biosensors | Testing of cholesterol, blood glucose levels, pregnancy, drug abuse and infectious diseases |
| SQUIDs (semiconductor quantum interface devices) | Comprise sensitive magnetometers and are used in magnetoencephalography (MEG) and magnetocardiography (MCG) systems used for analyzing neural activity inside the brain |
| Implantable medical sensors | Brain implants for treatment of neuropsychiatric disorders, electrotherapeutic treatments, immunomodulatory implantable, bioresorbable medical devices for repairing and regeneration of damaged cells and organs and bioactive and drug-releasing surgical implants |

also made personalized care of patients by constantly monitoring their health conditions and providing personalized treatment.

2. Small size and low cost:

The recent advances in MEMS, computing and processing technologies have made real-time and reliable exchange of patients' vital parameters and medical records possible. The wearable, portable and ambulatory medical sensors have made constant/frequent measurement of physiological parameters possible without visiting the hospitals and health-care centers. The devices, mainly wearable ones, are targeted toward fitness enthusiasts.

Implantable medical sensors are required to be small in size and are equipped with radio frequency identification (RFID) or near-field communication (NFC) communication modules to enable wireless communication and charging.

3. Connectivity and communication:

With the advances in communication technology, protocols, standards and antenna design, the medical sensor motes are capable of communicating wireless to other nearby devices or cloud. For short-range communication, these devices are equipped with modules supporting technologies such as Bluetooth, Zigbee, Infrared (IR) RFID and NFC. For long-distance communication, wireless fidelity (Wi-Fi), cellular and cloud-computing services are used.

While supporting wireless, mobile and short/long-distance communication, these medical sensors are also capable of recording the parameters/signals in non-volatile memory and share it later when wireless connection is available. These devices are also capable of communicating and uploading the recorded information over cloud that can be accessed by the authorized personal over time while maintaining patient history.

Existing medical sensor devices make use of 8- or 16-bit microcontrollers having tens of kilobytes of random-access memory and hundreds of kilobytes of read-only memory. These devices have small duty cycles and go to sleep mode when not operational. They are equipped with low-power radios capable of transmitting at the rates of up to 250 kbps and consume 20–60 mW of power for short-distance (up to 10 m) communication.

## 15.3   Role of Internet of Things (IoT) sensor networks in healthcare

Over the past decade, machine-to-machine and device-to-device communication technologies have given networking and connectivity a different meaning by enabling and establishing communication between devices. As the name suggests, with IoT, things/devices are able to communicate with little or no human intervention. With the level of automation achieved through IoT, this technology has found numerous applications in the wide range of technologies such as healthcare, emergency services, smart cities, vehicular networks, home and industrial automation, waste management and structural health monitoring. In this section, we are going to concentrate on the applications of IoT in healthcare.

The IoT sensor network-based health-care market is expected to rise with a compound annual growth rate of 30.2% over the period of 2018–23. Some of the key causes driving this industry are as follows:

1.  advances in communication technologies and wireless communication in particular,
2.  wireless communication technologies with high data rates supporting reliable and real-time communication,
3.  advances in MEMS technology and biosensors related to health-care applications,
4.  availability of cloud/fog/edge devices for efficient processing and storage,
5.  digitization of medical services and records such as EHRs,
6.  advances in wearable health devices,
7.  increasing geriatric population,
8.  increasing need and demand for advanced health-care information systems.

Before the introduction of IoT sensor networks in healthcare, availability of an efficient, reliable, responsive and remote health-care system was the challenge for the health-care industry. With the rise in geriatric population and increasing prevalence of lifestyle and chronic diseases, the demand for advanced health-care systems has increased. To cater to the demand of increasing population that needs healthcare, the presently existing health-care system needs transformation. Digitizing of the healthcare system, from consultations (patient–health-care professional interaction) to maintenance of health records and management of health-care equipment, stocks and the fleet (such as ambulance) [6] is the way to go for handling these demands.

Figure 15.2 presents the health-care IoT (H-IoT) use cases. This section discusses the use cases of H-IoT. H-IoT is gaining popularity to provide remote health-care services such as diagnosing, monitoring and remote surgeries over the Internet [7]. Smart rehabilitation is used to take care of the aged. H-IoT connects health-care resources and assistive devices with doctors, nurses, caretakers, hospitals and rehabilitation centers. Some of the popular H-IoT applications as presented in Figure 15.2 are as follows:

1.  **Remote patient monitoring:** Wearable devices and sensors are used to monitor the vital parameters of the patient. This information can be transmitted wirelessly to the doctor's/nurse's device or to the cloud from where it can be read by the medical staff involved in taking care of the patient. Such a facility allows the patient to move around instead of sitting at one place and allows doctors to monitor patient's vitals without requiring to visit the patient often [8].
2.  **Fitness and activity trackers:** People wearing fitness and activity trackers mounted on wrist, ankle or belt is a common sight these days. These trackers check the physical activity of the user such as steps taken, stairs climbed and vital health parameters such as pulse, heartbeat, body temperature and other basic physiological parameters. This data is stored on the cloud and users can study it over time to track their fitness and activity levels [9].

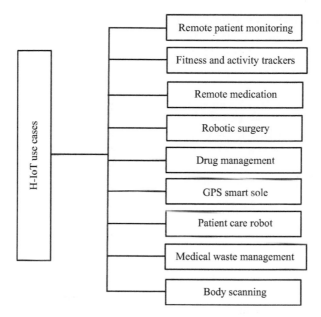

*Figure 15.2 Health-care IoT (II-IoT) use cases*

3. **Remote medication through ingestible sensors:** Ingestible sensors coated with magnesium and copper are used to trigger a signal if medication is not taken by a patient within appropriate time [10].
4. **Robotic surgery:** To perform surgical operations with enhanced control and precision, surgeons use IoT-enabled robotic surgery devices. Surgeons can also perform surgery in remote locations using these devices. However, this calls for real-time response over a high bandwidth communication channel [11].
5. **Drug management:** Drug supply, distribution, management and monitoring are carried out by using RFID. This helps in achieving enhanced supply chain management and reduced overall production costs. In the case of wrong distribution, reports can be sent to the regulatory bodies through cloud [12].
6. **Global positioning system (GPS) smart sole:** A smart insole embedded with GPS can be used to monitor the movement and location of the patient. This application of H-IoT can be particularly useful to monitor the movement of aged people or Alzheimer patients [13].
7. **Body scanning:** Smart body scanner is used for regular fitness checks as well as to check the vitals of a person. A weight scale, also known as the turntable, spins the body of the concerned person for 15 s. Three dimensional (3D) cameras are used to capture 360-degree images of the person to develop a 3D model of the person's body. A body fat, circumference, vitals and weight scan are sent on the mobile devices. A comparison of new readings with old values of the parameters is also made available [14].

8. **Medical waste management:** Medical waste disposal, monitoring and management are critical issues in healthcare. Automated medical waste management uses sensors embedded in dustbins located at different locations in the hospital to notify the quantity of waste. When the waste needs to be cleared, an automated robot is used to collect the waste and dump it in an appropriate place. This avoids any human interaction with hazardous medical waste and keeps the environment clean [15].

9. **Patient care robot:** These robots are used to provide care and support to the patients in the hospital. They are used to deliver medication, food and necessary items to the patient. Equipped with onboard sensors, these robots navigate using built-in maps and communicate over wireless medium [16].

Some of the key health-care applications based on IoT are tabulated in Table 15.2.

With the incorporation of IoT in healthcare, some of the expected transformations are as follows:

1. **Constant patient monitoring:** Continuous monitoring of the vital parameters of a patient even from remote locations is possible. The need for doctors/nurses going on rounds or them meeting the patient in person is reduced. Need for patients to take appointments from the doctors and waiting for doctor's availability for consultation is not there anymore. Wireless body area networks (WBAN) measure various vital parameters of the patient through concerned sensors and transmit this information over the network to the smart devices through which the concerned can monitor these parameters remotely and take appropriate actions.

2. **Auto patient access:** Intelligent personal devices such as smartphones, wearable watches and personal digital assists equipped with healthcare-related sensors facilitate the patient to keep a track of vital parameters and store the information for future analyses.

3. **Customized remote treatment:** Customized treatment plans can be shared by the doctors with the patients remotely, accessing the EHR of the patients and information of the patient's vitals over time.

4. **Virtual care:** Real-time information and notifications can be sent to the patients regarding their medication, exercise and diet as part of virtual consultation. This helps the health-care centers to advance treatment and achieve improved outcomes from the treatment of their patients.

5. **Remote retail centers:** Medicines and other necessary medical equipment can be ordered and paid for automatically without the need to visit the medical store. Automation provided by IoT can be used to identify the medicines required to be ordered based on need/requirement.

6. **Connected care:** The vitals measured by the biosensors are shared and stored over cloud, the consultations provided by the health-care personal.

7. **Health insurance:** The cost of healthcare can be eased through easy and reliable health insurance system that can be established for easy risk assessment, pricing and claim handling, with transparency.

*Table 15.2 IoT-based healthcare*

| Medical condition | Sensors and connections | Operation |
|---|---|---|
| Body temperature | Wearable body temperature sensors and WBAN-connected smart devices | These devices transmit the measured temperature to the cloud through an appropriate gateway. This information can be accessed remotely through the cloud |
| Heart rate monitoring | Capacitive electrodes on a PCB connected to the wireless transmitter in real time | |
| Blood pressure monitoring | Wearable blood-pressure-monitoring sensors, automatic inflation and measurement data are collected, analyzed and transmitted through connected smart devices | |
| Oxygen saturation monitoring | Wearable pulse oximeter sensor measures pulse rate and does pulse-by-pulse oxygen saturation measurement | |
| ECG self-monitoring | Device/application registers ECG data to the inbuilt ECG self-check software | |
| Eye disorders | Visual inspection and pattern-matching devices comprising a standard library of images used to check eye disorders | Cloud-aided applications and related software platforms used for monitoring and diagnosis |
| Skin allergies/ infection | Smartphone cameras, pattern matching and remote visual inspection | |
| Pulmonary infections | Calculation of air-flow rate, flow-time, volume-time and flow-volume graphs. Built-in microphones in the smartphone are used for this | |
| Cough and bronchial infections | Analysis of spectrograms and their classification through machine learning algorithms. Built-in microphones in the smartphone are used for this | |
| Allergic rhinitis | Speech recognition and classification using machine learning techniques. Built-in microphones in the smartphone are used for this | |
| Carcinoma melanoma detection | Smartphone camera used to capture images. Pattern matching through a library of images of cancerous skin | |
| Wound analysis | Smartphone camera used to capture images that are observed remotely to analyze the wounds and suggest corrective action | |

*(Continues)*

*Table 15.2    (Continued)*

| Medical condition | Sensors and connections | Operation |
|---|---|---|
| Rehabilitation | WBAN-connected smart devices used for measuring patient's vital parameters, patient tracking, monitoring, event detection, notification and reporting | Interactive wireless network technologies used through remote locations to interact with the patient and for consultation |
| Drug management | Diagnosis and prognosis of the vitals measured and transmitted through the WBAN sensors and stored in the cloud through wireless communication | Accessing the vitals of the patient and consultation and suggestion for medication are done from remote location |
|  | Medicines can be identified through RFID and their quantity monitored through sensors. Alert/notification generated for refill Alert/notification generated to inform the patient about right time and dosage of the medicine |  |
| Wheelchair navigation | Proximity sensors, location monitoring, LIDAR/RADAR, object detection, avoidance and navigation, lane detection and navigation. Alert/notification/alarm generated in unavoidable circumstances | Heterogeneous wireless communication and network technologies used for navigation and monitoring |
| Remote robotic surgery | High-definition video streaming, assistance robots, smart sensors and wearables and connected ambulance communicate with paramedics at the hospital premises | High data rate wireless communication technologies such as 5G, robotics and automation used to make this a reality |

## 15.4    Communication technologies for health-care IoT sensor networks

The healthcare-related IoT communications require reliable and, in many applications, real-time communication. To support such communication, there is a need for tested and reliable technologies that are capable of supporting communication with varying data rates, communication range, operating frequency, transmission power, communication power and security. Based on the application requirement and services provided by the communication technologies, appropriate technology is used for H-IoT sensor networks. The health-care applications related to communications vary from personal area network that is popularly used by sensor network technologies, local area network (LAN), metropolitan area network to wide-area-network-based wireless communication technologies. This section discusses the communication technologies used for H-IoT applications. These technologies and their characteristics are presented in Table 15.3.

*Table 15.3  Communication technologies used for H-IoT sensor networks*

| | Wi-Fi | Zigbee | Bluetooth | RFID | IrDA | UWB |
|---|---|---|---|---|---|---|
| International Standard | IEEE 802.11a/b/g/n | IEEE 802.15.4 | IEEE 802.15.1 | ISO 18047 | – | IEEE 802.15.3a |
| Data rate | 1–450 Mbps | 20–250 kbps | Up to 3 Mbps | 106–424 kbps | 14.4 kbps | 53–480 Mbps |
| Frequency band of operation | 2.4 GHz, 5 GHz | 868 MHz, 2.4 GHz | 2.4 GHz | 13.56 MHz | 850–900 nm | 3.1–10.6 GHz |
| Communication distance | 200 m | 10–20 m | 20–200 m | 20 cm | 0–1 m | 0–10 m |
| Communication type | Point to multipoint | Point to multipoint | Point to point | Point to point | Point to point | Point to point |
| Security | SSID, WEP, WPA | AES | AES, ECDH | AES | – | AES |
| Power (mW) | >1 000 mW | 100 mW | 1–100 mW | <1 mW | 1 μW | <1 mW |

By using **Wi-Fi** technologies, the medical and IoT devices all over the campus can be connected for reliable communication by virtue of their communication range and supported data rate. Wi-Fi supports device mobility over the network, thus providing a dynamic network environment.

**Zigbee** is a popular WSN technology that uses unlicensed wireless spectrum. Various medical sensors make use of Zigbee for communication. In H-IoT, the most common use of Zigbee is in remote patient monitoring. Body sensor network is used for patient health monitoring, and fitness and activity trackers make the use of Zigbee sensors. Zigbee provides an appropriate balance of parameters such as data rate, communication range and transmission power to make it the chosen technology for these applications.

**Bluetooth** technology supports both voice and data, provides 1 Mbps of data rate and uses unlicensed spectrum for communication. These features of Bluetooth make it suitable choice for H-IoT. In a hospital campus, Bluetooth devices can be identified and visitors can be informed about the floor plan, doctors on duty and appointment scheduling through Bluetooth beacons. Bluetooth can be used for automated patient check-in and checkout, optimized patient flow, scheduling appointments with doctors, compliance tracking and recording, asset tracking and wayfinding.

**RFID** is a short-distance, noncontact communication technology, which does not require a direct line of sight communication. It is an economical and reliable technology used for location and identification of objects. In H-IoT applications, RFID is extensively used to identify, locate and track medical equipment.

**Infrared Data Association (IrDA)** is a very short-distance, point-to-point, line of sight, which involves very low bit rate wireless optical communication technology. This is used to carry out physically secured data transmission. IR technology is used in remote control of appliances such as television, projector, air conditioner and such other devices. In healthcare, IrDA can be used for remotely controlling different medical devices.

**Ultra-wideband (UWB)** is a short-distance communication technology that provides data rates of up to 450 Mbps. This uses low-power pulses for communication and generates low electromagnetic radiation, thus making it suitable for medical applications. UWB radar is used for the monitoring of patient's motion over short distances, real-time exchange of medical images (such as X-rays, cardiology-, pneumology-, obstetrics-, ear, nose, throat-imaging) and data over a distance of up to 10 m.

## 15.5    Challenges in the implementation of H-IoT and related research

With constant increase in the need for H-IoT applications and uses, the integration of H-IoT in health-care organizations and other related areas/applications has risen. However, though there are numerous benefits of integrating IoT sensor networks with healthcare, it faces numerous challenges also, that need to be overcome. This section discusses the challenges involved in the integration of H-IoT sensor network in healthcare.

1. **Massive data generation:** IoT sensor networks in healthcare involve thousands of devices involved in various healthcare-related applications and generate huge amounts of data that mostly needs to be stored and processed in real time. This calls for the development of a large-scale health-care IoT infrastructure that requires financial investment, time and effort. Solutions provided in [17,18] deal with handling big data generated by health-care applications.

2. **Need for updated infrastructure:** With continuous upgradation of IoT devices, the IT infrastructure also needs to be upgraded constantly. Out-of-date infrastructure and software become incompatible with new and upgraded devices. This requires the health-care organizations to constantly upgrade their IT and software infrastructure so that it is compatible with changing IoT-based health-care technology. Authors in [19] have developed a software-based IoT health-care infrastructure using technologies such as network virtualization, cloud and blockchain.

3. **Need for upgraded network technologies:** The rise of communicating IoT devices has led to exponential rise in the network traffic. To deal with this exponential rise of data and maintain the quality of service (QoS) required by real-time and reliable health-care applications, there is a need for high network bandwidth, computation and storage. As these devices mostly communicate over wireless networks, when the density of the IoT devices increases within a given area, the network performance may drop due to node mobility and interference among neighboring devices. Traditional network architectures are not considered to be appropriate for these IoT sensor-based mobile networks. To support the high data rate and bandwidth requirements of these networks, dual polarized directional antenna-based protocols presented in [20–22] can be used.

4. **Heterogeneous networks:** Implementation of IoT sensor networks for healthcare involves a variety of networks and requires devices implemented on varying hardware, operating systems and programming languages to coexist and interoperate. The communication technologies used cover short range such as Bluetooth, IrDA, UWB and Zigbee, as well as long range such as Wi-Fi and global system for mobile communication/long-term evolution. Long-range communication leads to the device battery draining out faster. It is necessary that despite this heterogeneity in implementation and communication, these devices should be able to interoperate by identifying and discovering each other. To deal with the issues arising due to IoT network heterogeneity, authors in [23] have developed a framework to decompose the IoT applications into smaller operations that can be handled independently. Authors in [24] have developed semantic interoperability model to ensure interoperability between heterogeneous IoT devices and technologies.

5. **Quality of service (QoS):** IoT sensor networks are characterized by low-latency, low-power operation with high reliability. As H-IoT deals with critical issues involving a patient's health, they are bound to be time-critical by

nature. Therefore, minimal delays should be incurred in transmission and processing of H-IoT signals. This can be achieved by the availability of high bandwidth networking resources. Reliable network connectivity is essential in IoT sensor network for health-care applications that require real-time interaction and data access, such as remote surgery. To maintain QoS of health-care sensor network, it is required to maintain sufficient bandwidth and data rate. The solutions are presented in [20–22]. An adaptive QoS aware algorithm is presented in [25] for QoS computation of different IoT-based health-care applications.

6. **Scalability:** The growing popularity of H-IoT has led to exponential increase in the number of H-IoT devices. It is important to maintain consistent performance and QoS in the H-IoT network even as the new devices are added to the network. To support a large-scale deployment of H-IoT networks, this issue needs to be addressed effectively to avoid system downtime particularly in crucial H-IoT networks. A fault-tolerant and scalable architecture for IoT-based health-care networks is presented in [26] that is capable of handling situations such as node malfunction and traffic bottleneck due to high node density and data.

7. **Data collection and management:** IoT sensor devices generating digital health-care data face numerous data collection and management challenges. As the state of a human body changes constantly, thousands of bytes of data are generated every minute. A connected health-care network comprises heterogenous network technologies, devices and systems, leading to large data volumes, variety, velocity and veracity. Managing and analyzing this data requires data-driven learning techniques. Also, the data collection and management techniques need to be standardized for health-care applications. For health-care applications, data integrity also plays an important role; therefore, robust authentication systems are required to be in place for health-care systems. Authors in [27] have presented an architecture for integration of WSN with cloud service for efficient collection of IoT sensor network data and sharing.

8. **Security and privacy:** Security and privacy of the patients and their data is of paramount importance in H-IoT. In many cases, H-IoT data is communicated for long distances over heterogeneous networks and stored in the cloud, making it vulnerable to attacks. Therefore, robust encryption and authentication techniques for security and privacy of data are essential. However, while designing these techniques, it has to be taken into consideration that the devices used for H-IoT are resource constrained; hence, the developed solutions too should be lightweight and energy efficient. A survey of security and privacy issues in H-IoT is presented in [28]. Advanced technologies such as learning-based Deep Q-Networks are used to develop solutions to attain security and privacy in health-care networks [29].

9. **Increased attack surfaces:** IoT sensor networks give rise to numerous vulnerable security areas. This is risky for medical/health-care applications, as hackers can hack the medical devices, log in to these devices and steal/modify

the information, which can lead to life critical situations. An entire hospital network can be hacked through the infamous ransomware attack. Authors in [30] have developed a framework to test the security of IoT devices. An intrusion detection system for H-IoT networks is presented in [31].

10. **Cost:** While going digital and using technology in healthcare has brought down the cost of physical visits for both patients and health-care professionals, as well as providing ease of interaction/consultation, and patient health observation, the IoT sensor network technology is still out of reach for many. While IoT-based healthcare is fascinating and promising, its implementation is yet to overcome the cost considerations. The successful development, implementation and optimization of these technologies are still an issue and require setting up a costly infrastructure to ensure reliable connectivity and communication. Some of the low-cost smart health-care solutions are presented in [32,33].

## 15.6    Contemporary technologies to overcome the challenges on IoT sensor networks for healthcare

With the evolution of IoT and other mobile and wireless communication technologies, traditional computer networking technologies also need to be evolved, in order to cater to the demand of contemporary applications such as IoT sensor networks for healthcare. This section presents some of those contemporary technologies being used extensively in IoT sensor networks for healthcare.

### 15.6.1    Cloud/fog/edge computing for H-IoT sensor networks

The H-IoT devices produce massive amounts of data by a minute. This data needs to be processed efficiently and reliably. In applications such as robotic surgery, wheelchair navigation, constant patient monitoring and live consultations, the data needs to be processed in real time with high reliability, high efficiency and least delay. Over the years, cloud computing has been the go to technology for IoT devices to store and process the data. In such cases, the IoT data is transmitted all the way to the cloud and processing and storage. When stored in the cloud, the data can also be accessed/downloaded for future reference. From the IoT perspective, the massive data generated by these devices is stored and computed securely and efficiently over the cloud and is accessible seamlessly over multiple devices [34]. Amalgamation of cloud with network function virtualization (NFV) further reduces the capital and operation expenses of the H-IoT sensor networks [35,36]. The data transmitted to the cloud and stored over it is end-to-end encrypted. However, cloud computing for H-IoT requires availability and access to the massive data centers located in remote locations. These data centers can become inaccessible due to unavailability of proper Internet connectivity and cause delay in communication and processing of the IoT data due to distance between the IoT devices' cloud/data centers. Such delays can lead to poor quality of experience and slow data processing, thus adversely affecting the performance of real-time H-IoT applications, which is unacceptable and critical for life health-care applications in particular.

For efficient, reliable and real-time processing of delay-sensitive H-IoT data, edge and fog computing technologies are used. Both edge and fog computing are the extensions of cloud computing. While cloud computing allows the health-care organizations such as hospitals, nursing homes and rehabilitation centers to not spend on storage and processing infrastructure, it is observed over the years a combination of edge, fog and cloud computing benefits through efficient usage of end-user IoT devices and faster computing and processing of the health-care data. Better distribution of data for storage and processing achieves better performance by reducing the network traffic to the cloud, thus enhancing its operational efficiency. The edge and fog computing networks enhance network performance and optimize usage of cloud-computing resources by performing computations at the edge/fog nodes themselves, reducing network traffic and thus reducing the risk of network connection bottleneck [34,37,38]. It also increases network security by encrypting the data closer to the network devices.

Both edge and fog computing bring the location of computation and processing closer to the end nodes, thus drastically reducing the delays involved in delay-sensitive health-care applications. The edge computing places processing and computation power on the edge devices such as embedded controllers on the health-care devices, while fog computing places the computation and intelligence power on the network gateways and devices in the LAN.

**Edge computing** in H-IoT is powered by the fact that there are numerous edge devices in an IoT network, generating a massive amount of data in the network that leads to challenges in processing this data over a data center located remotely. In edge computing, the data is sent to the edge device, and it is processed on the edge device itself. Edge computing comprises thousands of nodes, wherein each device is capable of acting as the server in edge network. Edge network is a consolidation of voluntary compute devices that are located one to two hops away from the sensor nodes. These devices support high mobility but have low compute power. Therefore, edge computing is the least vulnerable form of decentralized processing and storage. Some of the advantages of edge computing are as follows:

1.  faster data processing
2.  reduced network traffic
3.  real-time data analysis
4.  reduced network operating cost
5.  decentralized data processing and storage
6.  reduced network vulnerability

While there are advantages of edge computing, it is not possible to run all the applications in intelligent endpoints as the endpoints face challenges regarding security, reliability, modularity, storage, processing power and environment. Therefore, there is a need for fog and cloud computing (Figure 15.3).

**Fog computing** is useful in the case of intermittent network connectivity. In fog computing, the delay-sensitive requests are transmitted directly to the fog computing devices and are processed within the LAN. The data from applications that are not/less delay sensitive is sent to the cloud data centers for processing. The

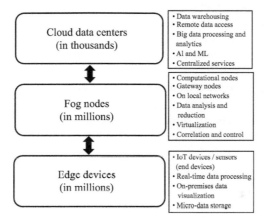

*Figure 15.3 Edge, fog and cloud for H-IoT sensor networks*

devices in the fog network have high compute power compared to the edge network devices. These are installed as a backbone to the cloud networks. These devices are located five to six hops away from the sensor nodes and support high-speed connectivity and guaranteed connectivity to the edge devices. Some of the advantages of fog computing are as follows:

1. faster data computing and processing
2. reduced latency
3. enhanced data security
4. setter network and data control
5. support for online and offline data access
6. decentralized data storage and processing

By adding layers of edge and fog nodes, the network load is partitioned to run at the optimal network level.

**Cloud computing** provides enhanced scalability and performance to the IoT networks. As the end H-IoT devices generate huge amounts of data every second, it is difficult for the enterprises and health-care organizations to store such huge data for future access. Due to the issues such as node mobility, node's geographic location, latency, network bandwidth and reliability, it is neither efficient nor advisable to run all the applications in the cloud. That is where edge and fog computing play an important role. Cloud comprises data centers that are capable of data warehousing, big data processing and making the data available for future remote access. Cloud provides Infrastructure as a Service for better H-IoT scalability, storage and processing power. Some of the benefits of cloud computing for H-IoT networks are as follows:

1. data storage,
2. access to data remotely for future use,
3. remote data processing,

4.  data security,
5.  reduced infrastructure cost at the organization,
6.  present-day cloud solutions capable of applying artificial intelligence, machine learning and big data techniques on the IoT data.

## 15.6.2    *Software-defined networking for H-IoT sensor networks*

Software-defined networking (SDN) separates the control plane (the decision-making plane, mostly implemented in software) from the data plane (the data transfer plane, mostly implemented in hardware). The application plane comprises the applications configured by the network operator such as load balancer, access control and bandwidth allocation [39]. The SDN network controller has the global view of the network and is capable of making decisions about resource allocation based on changing network requirements. The traffic forwarding policies are defined by the network operator, while the centralized network controller facilitates automated network management. To handle the increasing network demand, network resources can be virtualized. NFV in association with SDN brings in numerous advantages to network performance while achieving reduced capital expenditure and operational expenditure [36]. The communication between network devices and applications takes place through the network controller. As the networks scale up, the number of network controllers incorporated into the network could be increased to maintain the network performance with increasing traffic load.

An example of SDN-based H-IoT [40] system is presented in Figure 15.4. The system is divided into three following planes:

**Data plane:** The data plane comprises the network devices and infrastructure used to forward the data over the network. This plane is also called the forwarding plane. The network routers and switches fall in this plane. As shown in Figure 15.4,

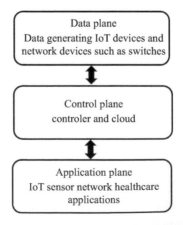

*Figure 15.4    SDN for H-IoT sensor networks*

the data is acquired from sensors and other IoT devices through the wireless/wired network infrastructure. The received data is routed and forwarded to the network controller (in the control plane) through the data plane.

**Control plane:** Control plane is the decision-making plane. The main entity of this plane is the network controller that comprises the logic written for traffic control such as routing, load balancing and traffic engineering. The controller fetches, maintains different network information, such as network state, topology and statistics, and makes network infrastructure control decisions based on this information. The network controller receives application requirements from the application layer and makes decision regarding QoS and dynamic bandwidth allocation. It has an abstract view of the network, the events in the network and network statistics.

The SDN can be combined with the cloud for better network management and network data access. This removes the barrier associated with network hardware access and builds the network implementation cost-effective and agile. As seen from Figure 15.4, the data from the network controller is uploaded onto the cloud. Similarly, the network controller also fetches the data from the cloud and transmits it to the end devices.

**Application plane:** Application plane presented in Figure 15.4 comprises all the healthcare-related applications that work with the H-IoT data. The application plane comprises the receiving applications that obtain the data originated at the patient. This data is used for diagnosis, analytics, generate statistics and makes appropriate decisions. As seen from Figure 15.4, the decisions made or messages can be conveyed back to the patient through the cloud and network controller.

## 15.7   Conclusion

This chapter presents the role, significance, applications, supporting technologies, challenges faced and contemporary technologies to overcome those challenges in IoT sensor network for healthcare. IoT sensor networks play a significant role in healthcare and have become popular in the health-care industry over the past few years. According to different surveys and estimates, the use of IoT sensor networks in healthcare will grow exponentially in the future. This chapter discusses the sensors used in different healthcare-related applications. The communication technologies facilitating the H-IoT networks and their characteristics are discussed. Despite growing popularity of IoT sensor networks in healthcare, there are numerous challenges in the implementation and realization of H-IoT. These challenges are discussed in detail and the role of contemporary technologies such as edge/fog/cloud computing and SDN to overcome some of these challenges is highlighted.

## References

[1]    https://www.businessinsider.in/science/news/iot-healthcare-in-2020-compa-nies-devices-use-cases-and-market-stats/articleshow/74126142.cms: accessed on 7 January 2021.

[2]    https://medium.com/datadriveninvestor/7-staggering-stats-on-healthcare-iot-innovation-fe6b92774a5c: accessed on 7 January 2021.

[3]    Sharma R., Gupta S.K., Suhas K.K. and Kashyap G.S., 2014, April. Performance analysis of Zigbee based wireless sensor network for remote patient monitoring. In *2014 Fourth International Conference on Communication Systems and Network Technologies* (pp. 58–62). IEEE.

[4]    Al-Khafajiy M., Baker T., Chalmers C., *et al.*, 2019. Remote health monitoring of elderly through wearable sensors. *Multimedia Tools and Applications*, 78(17), pp. 24681–24706.

[5]    Sharama R., Shankar J.U. and Rajan S.T., 2014. Effect of number of active nodes and inter-node distance on the performance of wireless sensor networks. In *2014 Fourth International Conference on Communication Systems and Network Technologies* (pp. 69–73). IEEE.

[6]    Juneja S., Juneja A. and Anand R., 2020. Healthcare 4.0-digitizing healthcare using big data for performance improvisation. *Journal of Computational and Theoretical Nanoscience*, 17(9–10), pp. 4408–4410.

[7]    Tarouco L.M.R., Bertholdo L.M., Granville L.Z., *et al.*, 2012. Internet of Things in healthcare: interoperability and security issues. In *2012 IEEE International Conference on Communications (ICC)* (pp. 6121–6125). IEEE.

[8]    Marakhimov A. and Joo J., 2017. Consumer adaptation and infusion of wearable devices for healthcare. *Computers in Human Behavior*, 76, pp. 135–148.

[9]    Philip V., Suman V.K., Menon V.G. and Dhanya K.A., 2017. A review on latest internet of things based healthcare applications. *International Journal of Computer Science and Information Security*, 15(1), p. 248.

[10]   Lomotey R.K., Pry J. and Sriramoju S., 2017. Wearable IoT data stream traceability in a distributed health information system. *Pervasive and Mobile Computing*, 40, pp. 692–707.

[11]   Shabana N. and Velmathi G., 2018. Advanced tele-surgery with IoT approach. In *Intelligent Embedded Systems* (pp. 17–24). Springer, Singapore.

[12]   Liu L. and Jia W., 2010, September. Business model for drug supply chain based on the internet of things. In *2010 2nd IEEE International Conference on Network Infrastructure and Digital Content* (pp. 982–986). IEEE.

[13]   Wilden J., Chandrakar A., Ashok A. and Prasad N., 2017. IoT based wearable smart insole. In *2017 Global Wireless Summit (GWS)* (pp. 186–192). IEEE.

[14]   Muneer A., Fati S.M. and Fuddah S., 2020. Smart health monitoring system using IoT based smart fitness mirror. *Telkomnika*, 18(1), pp. 317–331.

[15]   Raundale P., Gadagi S. and Acharya C., 2017. IoT based biomedical waste classification, quantification and management. In *2017 International Conference on Computing Methodologies and Communication (ICCMC)* (pp. 487–490). IEEE.

[16]   Patel A.R., Patel R.S., Singh N.M. and Kazi F.S., 2017. Vitality of robotics in healthcare industry: an Internet of Things (IoT) perspective. In *Internet of*

*Things and Big Data Technologies for Next Generation Healthcare* (pp. 91–109). Springer, Cham.

[17] Chen M.Y., Lughofer E.D. and Polikar R., 2018. Big data and situation-aware technology for smarter healthcare. *Journal of Medical and Biological Engineering*, 38, pp. 845–846.

[18] Manogaran G., Lopez D., Thota C., Abbas K.M., Pyne S. and Sundarasekar R., 2017. Big data analytics in healthcare Internet of Things. In *Innovative Healthcare Systems for the 21st Century* (pp. 263–284). Springer, Cham.

[19] Salahuddin M.A., Al-Fuqaha A., Guizani M., Shuaib K. and Sallabi F., 2017. Softwarization of internet of things infrastructure for secure and smart Healthcare. *Computer*, 50(7), pp. 74–79. doi:10.1109/MC.2017.195.

[20] Rinki S., 2014. *Simulation studies on effects of dual polarisation and directivity of antennas on the performance of MANETs* (Doctoral dissertation, Ph.D. thesis, Coventry University, UK).

[21] Sharma R., Kadambi G.R., Vershinin Y.A. and Mukundan K.N., 2015. Multipath routing protocol to support dual polarised directional communication for performance enhancement of MANETs. In *2015 Fifth International Conference on Communication Systems and Network Technologies* (pp. 258–262). IEEE.

[22] Sharma R., Kadambi G.R., Vershinin Y.A. and Mukundan K.N., 2015. Dual polarised directional communication based medium access control protocol for performance enhancement of MANETs. In *2015 Fifth International Conference on Communication Systems and Network Technologies* (pp. 185–189). IEEE.

[23] Jha D.N., Michalák P., Wen Z., Ranjan R. and Watson P., 2019. Multiobjective deployment of data analysis operations in heterogeneous IoT infrastructure. *IEEE Transactions on Industrial Informatics*, 16(11), pp. 7014–7024.

[24] Ullah F., Habib M.A., Farhan M., Khalid S., Durrani M.Y. and Jabbar S., 2017. Semantic interoperability for big-data in heterogeneous IoT infrastructure for healthcare. *Sustainable Cities and Society*, 34, pp. 90–96.

[25] Sodhro A.H., Malokani A.S., Sodhro G.H., Muzammal M. and Zongwei L., 2020. An adaptive QoS computation for medical data processing in intelligent healthcare applications. *Neural Computing and Applications*, 32(3), pp. 723–734.

[26] Gia T.N., Rahmani A.M., Westerlund T., Liljeberg P. and Tenhunen H., 2015. Fault tolerant and scalable IoT-based architecture for health monitoring. In *2015 IEEE Sensors Applications Symposium (SAS)* (pp. 1–6). IEEE.

[27] Piyare R. and Lee S.R., 2013. Towards Internet of Things (IoTs): integration of wireless sensor network to cloud services for data collection and sharing. *International Journal of Computer Networks & Communications*, 5(5), pp. 59–72.

[28] Hathaliya J.J. and Tanwar S., 2020. An exhaustive survey on security and privacy issues in Healthcare 4.0. *Computer Communications*, 153, pp. 311–335.

[29]    Shakeel P.M., Baskar S., Dhulipala V.S., Mishra S. and Jaber M.M., 2018. Maintaining security and privacy in health care system using learning based deep-Q-networks. *Journal of Medical Systems*, 42(10), p. 186.

[30]    Lally G. and Sgandurra D., 2018. Towards a framework for testing the security of IoT devices consistently. In *International Workshop on Emerging Technologies for Authorization and Authentication* (pp. 88–102). Springer, Cham.

[31]    Thamilarasu G., Odesile A. and Hoang A., 2020. An intrusion detection system for internet of medical things. *IEEE Access*, 8, pp. 181560–181576.

[32]    Gia T.N., Jiang M., Sarker V.K., *et al.*, 2017. Low-cost fog-assisted health-care IoT system with energy-efficient sensor nodes. In *2017 13th International Wireless Communications and Mobile Computing Conference (IWCMC)* (pp. 1765–1770). IEEE.

[33]    Ganesh G.R.D., Jaidurgamohan K., Srinu V., Kancharla C.R. and Suresh S. V., 2016, December. Design of a low cost smart chair for telemedicine and IoT based health monitoring: an open source technology to facilitate better healthcare. In *2016 11th International Conference on Industrial and Information Systems (ICIIS)* (pp. 89–94). IEEE.

[34]    Dang L.M., Piran M., Han D., Min K. and Moon H., 2019. A survey on internet of things and cloud computing for healthcare. *Electronics*, 8(7), p. 768.

[35]    Ananth M.D. and Sharma R., 2017. Cost and performance analysis of net-work function virtualization based cloud systems. In *2017 IEEE 7th International Advance Computing Conference (IACC)* (pp. 70–74). IEEE.

[36]    Ananth M.D. and Sharma R., 2016. Cloud management using network function virtualization to reduce CAPEX and OPEX. In *2016 8th International Conference on Computational Intelligence and Communication Networks (CICN)* (pp. 43–47). IEEE.

[37]    Ray P.P., Dash D. and De D., 2019. Edge computing for Internet of Things: a survey, e-healthcare case study and future direction. *Journal of Network and Computer Applications*, 140, pp. 1–22.

[38]    Paul A., Pinjari H., Hong W.H., Seo H.C. and Rho S., 2018. Fog computing-based IoT for health monitoring system. *Journal of Sensors*, 2018.

[39]    Sharma R. and Reddy H., 2019. Effect of load balancer on software-defined networking (SDN) based Cloud. In *2019 IEEE 16th India Council International Conference (INDICON)* (pp. 1–4). IEEE.

[40]    Sharma R. 2021. 11 Software-defined networking for healthcare Internet of Things. In *Applications of Machine Learning in Big-Data Analytics and Cloud Computing* (pp. 231–247). River Publishers.

*Chapter 16*

# Machine learning for Healthcare 4.0: technologies, algorithms, vulnerabilities, and proposed solutions

*Saumya[1] and Bharat Bhushan[1]*

Healthcare 4.0 is motivated from Industrie 4.0. It is a boon to the present health-care system due to its widespread applications that have boosted its efficiency and enhanced its services. Healthcare 4.0 is a vision that integrates all the leading technologies together given that each technology has different benefits to offer to the system. Various technologies such as big data, Health Cloud (HC), Health Fog (HF), Internet of Things (IoT), blockchain, and machine learning (ML) are incorporated in Healthcare 4.0. There are many applications of Healthcare 4.0 for patients, health-care professionals, resource management, etc. This chapter aims to study ML with respect to Healthcare 4.0 and highlights different ML algorithms and its applications for healthcare in different phases such as prognosis, diagnosis, treatment, and clinical workflow. ML provides many solutions for Healthcare 4.0 which have applicability for patients, health-care professionals, as well as health-care facilities. However, there is some vulnerability for ML in healthcare that needs to be checked. This chapter highlights these vulnerabilities and presents the recently proposed solutions in this regard.

## 16.1 Introduction

Healthcare today is covered with many challenges and difficulties such as the high cost of health-care services, lack of skilled professionals, demands of high-quality services, lack of collaboration among different health-care service providers, and high competition among them [1]. These things are raising questions on the reliability of the system for the patients and their satisfaction. Therefore, there is a need to look for new solutions to overcome these challenges [2]. The need of the hour is to evolve the health-care system, one such sector evolving is Industry Sector 4.0 which is developed from Industries 1.0, 2.0, and 3.0. The goal of Industry 4.0 is to build on automated smart machines that make the system cost-effective, enhance operation,

[1]School of Engineering and Technology (SET), Sharda University, Greater Noida, India

and increase quality of services. These principles taken from Industry 4.0 are applied to the health-care system and gave birth to Healthcare 4.0, without any existence of Healthcare 1.0, 2.0, and 3.0. It aims to enhance the efficiency of health-care services, including new technologies to increase the quality of services and still being cost-effective for the patients. The benefits of Healthcare 4.0 are numerous such as improve flexibility, reliability, scalability, and cost-effectiveness [3]. Apart from this, it will also help in better management and response to health pandemics like COVID-19 [4]. Despite its benefits, building such a versatile system for healthcare is challenging and complex within itself. Many factors are needed to be considered. But, once built, it will boost its efficacy. Healthcare 4.0 is built on the integration of human resources, expertise with technologies like blockchain, ML, HC, big data, IoT, deep learning (DL), and artificial intelligence (AI).

The chapter discusses ML, its algorithms, and its applicability to Healthcare 4.0. ML is a vast field, which is growing every day. It has already transformed many systems such as governance, transportation, and manufacturing. The use of these technologies is carried in people's day-to-day life either knowingly or unknowingly. ML is now being incorporated into the field of healthcare, which is influencing this system to provide various advantages [5]. Using ML models in healthcare has many benefits like it will make the system less dependent on human resources, fewer chances of errors and thus, increase in efficiency without manual support. It can assist medical professionals through AI in learning information from medical books, texts, etc. Medical tasks like monitoring, analyzing, and managing reports of patient become efficient when embedding of ML with IoT devices is done [6]. ML can also lead to the discovery of novel therapeutics through analyzing of large biological databases and finding patterns within them. In near future, the ML model will also support the radiologists as well as physicians and will boost medical research and practice [7]. Kumari *et al.* [8] presented the transition of ML toward cloud toward the fog and IoT-based healthcare. Multan *et al.* [9] also discussed growth in fog computing in the healthcare IoT domain. Mohanta *et al.* [10] discussed shifting of paradigm toward healthcare using AI, IoT, and 5G technologies. Rong *et al.* [11] reviewed some of the applications using epileptic seizures and filling of a dysfunctional urinary bladder by the use of AI. With increasing availability of clinically relevant databases, ML is applied to Healthcare 4.0 for diagnostic/identification tasks and prediction tasks [12,13]. In recent years, ML is gaining importance across several disciplines and led to emerging breakthroughs in Healthcare 4.0 and machine translation [14,15]. In summary, the major contributions of this chapter are enumerated as follows.

- This work provides an overview of Healthcare 4.0 and the major technologies used in it.
- This work categorizes and discusses different applications of Healthcare 4.0.
- This work presents an in-depth analysis of ML algorithms with the main focus on their applications for healthcare.
- This work presents security and other vulnerabilities involved in adopting ML for healthcare.

- Finally, this work presents different solutions that can be used for ensuring the security and efficacy of ML systems in Healthcare 4.0.

The remainder of the chapter is organized as follows. Section 16.2 presents Healthcare 4.0 and the technologies involved in it, Section 16.3 presents an overview of different algorithms involved in ML that are used in healthcare, Section 16.4 presents ML applicability in healthcare and different functions. Section 16.5 presents the challenges faced during the deployment of ML in Healthcare 4.0. Section 16.6 concerns with the solutions to enhance the security for ML-based systems in Healthcare 4.0. Finally, Section 16.7 concludes the work.

## 16.2 Healthcare 4.0

When technologies such as blockchain, the Internet of Health Things (IoHT), HC, big data, medical cyber-physical systems (MCPS), and other smart algorithms are integrated together to be deployed in order to provide a new vision to the health-care industry, it is known as Healthcare 4.0. It aims to provide better, cost-effective, and reliable services to the patients with enhanced efficiency and effectiveness of the health-care system. The main principles of Healthcare 4.0 are taken from Industry 4.0 [16–20]. Thus, Industry 4.0 inherits the 4.0 version of healthcare; however, there has been no existence of Healthcare 1.0, 2.0, and 3.0. Healthcare 4.0 in spite of providing many advantages to the system is complex to build and achieve. These complexities can be solved by adopting an advanced service-oriented middleware framework. This will not only help us to integrate different advanced technologies that will be incorporated with real-time data collections, enhanced AI, and interactive virtual interfaces facilitating advanced inquisitive solutions but, it will also increase the use of current services and their platforms. The main aim of Healthcare 4.0 is to create a health-care value chain with a smart health-care network of patients, hospitals, clinics, medical devices, and suppliers [21].

### 16.2.1 Main technologies of Healthcare 4.0

Here is the summarized description of the major technologies used in Healthcare 4.0.

- **Internet of Things (IoT):** Also known as the IoHT, which enables the connection of the medical devices in the network [22]. Some examples are virtual hospitals/wards, insulin pens, wearable biosensors, smart thermometers, low-cost IoT sensor systems for real-time remote monitoring [23], etc. Qadri *et al.* [24] have shown the impact of IoT on the advancement of the health-care industry.
- **Internet of Services (IoS):** These medical services and health-care devices are provided on well-integrated interfaces and software over the Internet [25]. These services are essential for automation and collaboration.
- **Health cloud:** It is a health information technology customer relationship management system that incorporates the relationship of doctor–patient and

includes record management services. It is the cloud-based technology that provides data storage, various software resources, and applications, which requires high storage and rigorous computations [26]. The HC also provides advantages in cost, security, scalability, and collaboration. For example, cloud-based health-care monitoring system using IoT [27], cloud-based approach in designing electronic health records (EHRs), which can be interoperable [28]. Gorp *et al.* [29] discussed that EHRs should be the lifelong property of patients and they can share these any time with virtual machines via cloud technology. Cloud computing with other technologies reduces the cost and also helps in the timely diagnosis of patients [30]. However, there are certain challenges for cloud technology to be adopted in healthcare. Idoga *et al.* [31] discussed some factors affecting the attitude of health-care consumers toward adopting cloud-based health centers.

- **Health big data analytics:** Big data is the huge volume of information on various digital technologies that collects records of patients. It helps in managing the hospital's performance. Big data analytics is used to discover mechanisms and processes to find the correlations and insights of the data. Analysis of this big data provides advantages in health-care systems like enhanced healthcare and cost-effectiveness. Examples of big data in healthcare are big data for personalized healthcare [32], big data analytics used in optimizing EHRs [33], etc. Li *et al.* [34] presented a case study of China for applying big data governance to regional health information networks. Lin *et al.* [35] did a survey that targets chronic diseases and health monitoring big data technologies.

- **Medical cyber-physical systems (MCPS):** It is integration for a network of medical devices to the cyber world through computer networks via physical processes. This helps in fulfilling the vision of continuous availability of high-quality health-care services [36]. Wireless sensors are critical parts of these MCPS systems. Some examples of CPS include medical monitoring, implantable medical devices [37] like, cardiac pacemakers, coronary stents, implantable insulin pumps, and hip implants. Qiu *et al.* [38] have proposed secured data storage and sharing using MCPS system.

- **Health fog:** HF is basically fog computing which is a mediator layer between the cloud and the end user that provides on-demand computation, software resources, and different services of health-care applications [39]. It is efficient in reducing extra cost incurred for the communication in related systems. It has the capability of collaborating data from various sources, maintaining proper security, and privacy concerns. In [40], fog-assisted IoT-enabled patient health monitoring is presented.

- **Mobile communication networks (5G):** The 5G communication network provides a far higher level of performance in terms of communication speed. It contributes to the health-care system by supporting high-speed data transmission for health-care applications, real-time sharing of data, facilitating real-time consultations, and decision-making across the network [41]. Overall, this would foster health-care transformation and delivery innovations.

- **Blockchain:** The concept is used to denote record in the form of blocks and is very sensitive to any change in the whole chain that is formed using combination of blocks. Blockchain can facilitate various applications in Healthcare 4.0 such as protecting medical data, sensitive personal patients' symptoms stored in the form of data, EHRs data management, etc. Blockchain also provides security in sharing of data and protection of the patient's privacy [39,42]. There are numerous applications of blockchain in healthcare. Wang *et al.* [43] discussed a framework of parallel health-care systems based on the artificial systems, including computational experiments together with parallel execution (ACP) approach. Zarour *et al.* [44] discussed the impact of blockchain models for Secure and Trustworthy Electronic Healthcare Records.

## 16.2.2   Health 4.0 objective

There are many objectives of Healthcare 4.0 but, broadly it can be divided into two. First one is by enhancing the quality of services with cost effectiveness. Second one by more efficient and effective systems. Other than this, there are also other benefits like secure data collection and transmission with efficient management, management of patient's records, enhanced rate of automation, etc. Healthcare 4.0 has many capabilities within itself, which are when utilized to the full potential will help to achieve desired abovementioned objectives. This section discusses the objective that can be achieved in Healthcare 4.0.

- **Efficient management of patient's databases:** Healthcare 4.0 involves technologies like HC, big data, and HF which ease out the management task of the patient's record as these are large databases that require intensive administration.
- **Less dependency on humans and more on machines:** The technologies like MCPS help in efficient automation in Healthcare 4.0 which provides better efficiency and accuracy, thus, reducing the reliability of staff or workers.
- **Better synchronization and administration of health-care staff/workers and professionals:** Improved resource allocation in health-care staff with better scheduling by analyzing the current and past data of each professional will result in a better yielding team in the system and will increase the satisfaction from the patients.
- **The enhanced doctor–patient relationship and customer satisfaction:** Healthcare 4.0 technologies when put together provide people with a better and efficient overall system in a cost-effective manner. If Healthcare 4.0 is able to utilize its capabilities to a complete extent, the trust between patient and doctor relation will increase many folds. As a result, the system will be more reliable for everyone.
- **Improved services in remote areas:** Healthcare 4.0 and its technology helps to make healthcare accessible in the remote areas with virtual appointments and conferencing with health professionals provided in a cost-effective way. Also, technologies enable the effective sharing or transmission of highly specialized resources to remote areas. Thus, expensive health-care resources will be effectively allocated and shared.

- **Better accuracy and efficiency of the services:** Employing all the technologies may also help in better maintenance of resources and on-time servicing of the resources. This will increase the predictability and efficiency of the whole system.
- **Efficiently analyzing patients' data (medical and nonmedical):** Getting a detailed view of patients' data that can check other factors responsible for the disease and can help the professionals in better prediction and creating more personalized treatments.
- **Efficient data analysis:** Healthcare 4.0 can help efficient data collection and transmission on a large scale, these data when analyzed for longer duration could help in better generalizations as well as results like data of infectious disease will tell the hotspots of that diseases, age groups affected, moreover it will help in controlling the rate of infection at large scale.
- **Smart decision-making supported by MCPS:** Using MCPS in Healthcare 4.0, people can develop smart equipment and automation which can be utilized to give better prediction and enhanced decision-making. This will also require less staff and error could be minimized at certain levels, furthermore providing the people with cost friendly schemes.
- **Making a cost-effective system for all:** There are many ways to achieve this in Healthcare 4.0. For example, if people allow proper sharing of advanced, costly resources and equipment across all health-care providers, the operational cost will become less and the resources will be utilized in a better way.

## 16.2.3    Health 4.0 application

This section discusses the applicability of Healthcare 4.0 for patients, for the health-care professionals, and its applications for resource management [39]. Various applications related to Healthcare 4.0 are discussed in the next subsections.

### 16.2.3.1    Application for patients

There are various applications that could be for patients in a health-care system. Few prominent are discussed in coming subsections.

- **Management of patient:** Today many applications are available for the patients for various purposes but, having similar functionality, these applications in Healthcare 4.0 can be integrated together and efficient data analysis can be done, the patients can use these applications to define their needs which will give the patient more personalized experience in the system. The huge databases having patient records can be also managed effectively using technologies like big data and the HC. These data can thus be accessible to the patients, pharmacies, laboratories, medical professionals, etc. at any time. Furthermore, the technologies can enable us to support these functionalities like integrating different systems. For example, doctors can access patients' fitness and other activity records from their personal devices maintaining the integrity and privacy of patients.
- **Boosting public healthcare:** Healthcare 4.0 enables to boost the maintenance of overall healthcare of the public in several ways, each way using the technologies

in a synchronized way. For example, employing ML and DL algorithms integrated within big data, HC, MCPS technologies over large data accumulated over a period of time can help to predict future outcomes of certain infectious diseases, health trends, etc. This will help to reduce the vulnerability and risk of loss of life during a medical pandemic. These technologies will also get us to know the hotspots of these diseases and these things will result in efficient management by health-care services.

- **Inpatient care:** This refers to how Healthcare 4.0 will facilitate the patient after he/she is admitted to a health-care facility by making the task convenient for both patient and medical professionals. This includes digital monitoring of patients, treatment devices, and other applications. These services can be integrated easily with the given technologies and will provide the patient with personalized and enhanced health-care experiences such as customized rooms and meals. Data of a patient can be fetched from other health-care facilities using network devices and can be employed for better outcomes. Applications can be used for scheduling medications and lab timings accordingly with proper alerts. This will help to reduce time loss and saved time can be utilized efficiently. Similarly, technology like blockchain will help to manage the transactions of patients efficiently and proper discharge of patients from the health-care facilities can be done.

### 16.2.3.2 Application for health-care professionals

There are various applications that could be for health-care professionals. Few prominent are discussed in coming subsections.

- **Efficient management:** Management of health-care services by all the medical professionals is a perplexing task like administration of various types of doctors, medical staffs, 24×7 work tasks, and regular scheduling. These all are the challenges to the efficiency of whole health-care systems. But, Healthcare 4.0 provides various applications and technology that can make this complex task insanely convenient. Integrating these technologies within themselves will benefit us first with better collection of data helping in managing operational procedures, scheduling, alert management, etc. Second, by easily accessible resources through fast transmission. Third, by better decision-making after deploying different algorithms. Fourthly, by efficient predictability for future needs and exploring new trends in healthcare, etc., and finally by deploying analytical models for providing personalized treatment facilities to each and every patient. Similarly, there are many more examples. These techniques will ease out the mundane task of management of the health-care services and will save a lot of time which can be later used to focus on the patient treatments more efficiently.
- **Better scheduling and resource allocation:** A health-care system requires scheduling in such a way that it can efficiently work 24×7 shifts, this is a mundane task, and many other factors related to each medical personnel are also required to be considered to create a well-optimized schedule. Similarly,

health-care professionals require a lot of resources to complete their jobs. These resources need to be well organized to become available for access at the required time. To ease out these tasks, Healthcare 4.0 applications can be designed to work on each medical professional's data related to resources, experiences, demands, history, etc. which can be used to put him/her in a proper schedule. This can help in better optimization and can also help to manage the emergency conditions. For resource allocation, people can use transmission of data, resource inventory management to utilize the resources efficiently.

- **Collaboration:** Collaboration is required among various health-care systems in several cases. These can be either within the same health-care facilities or between diverse health-care facilities and entities. For example, doctors require consulting with other doctors for some critical cases, connecting with other facilities for suppliers of pharmaceuticals, medicines, etc. This collaboration requires the exchange of data over the systems maintaining security as well as privacy of data. These are basically the task of administrators in the health-care system. Healthcare 4.0 provides various applications by combining different technologies and facilitating easy communications between different organizations.

### 16.2.3.3　Application for resource management

Any health-care system largely depends on its resources for its efficient functioning. Resources include medical components like medical devices, laboratory tools, surgical equipment, diagnostic tools, medications, protection gears and instruments, etc. It also includes physical infrastructural tools like a fire alarm, beds, systems, furniture, water, and power supply. Moreover, all staff, professionals in healthcare using the abovementioned resources are also resources for the system. These all resources need to be efficiently utilized and managed in the system. Users need to consider different aspects for the maintenance of the resources. First, the availability of resources is an important aspect, which means the resources need to be available when required. These resources should be equipped with connectivity like Bluetooth, wired, and wireless. This will help Healthcare 4.0 applications to link all the resources in order to collect, exchange, and transfer the data from these resources to the analysis modules. Second, users need proper allocation of resources to the respective professionals according to the procedures and operations. These include X-ray machines, magnetic resonance imaging (MRI) scans, ICU equipment, etc. Thus, there is a need to optimize the allocation of all these resources using the Healthcare 4.0 applications for scheduling of resources using data and this can benefit in reducing waiting time and enhanced utilization. Lastly, the resources must be checked for faults from time to time, and the management of this fault checking should be properly synchronized with other schedules.

### 16.2.3.4　Applications and enabling technologies mapping

The chapter has researched till now that Healthcare 4.0 is the integration of various technologies to serve great objectives for the overall systems. HF is known to provide local storage and accessibility of data enabling smooth communication, while IoS is essential to all the services used by the people or users. Thus, proper mapping of these technologies is a must. Some technologies like HF and IoS are almost required in every health-care application. IoT is required for most of the monitoring devices, blockchain, cloud, and big data for scheduling and collaboration. So, there is a need to properly integrate these technologies so that they can be utilized to their full potential.

## 16.3    Machine learning algorithms

ML is based on the concept of learning, training, and then decision-making by machine based on dataset [45]. This learning can be broadly classified into three types that are supervised learning (SL), unsupervised learning (UL), and reinforcement learning (RL). SL means it provides the model with labeled data, i.e., the user supervises the model to learn, while in UL there is no labeled data, the model learns all by itself. RL is different from these two as it uses reward or punishment-based approach to making the model learn and predict. Some popular and widely used algorithms of SL are logistic regression, linear regression (LR), support vector machine (SVM), decision tree (DT), artificial neural network (ANN), etc., whereas principal component analysis (PCA) is one of the most popular algorithms of UL.

### 16.3.1    Linear regression

In LR, the machine models the relationship between independent variables and a dependent variable (labels and features) and finds a line that best fits the data. To check closeness of data, the regression line fits the data and users use statistical measures such as R squared, mean squared error (MSE). A higher R squared value and lower MSE mean the model fits the data better. The LR technique can be used for three purposes, determining the strength of predictors, forecasting an effect, and trend forecasting. Further, it uses cost function and gradient descent techniques to minimize the error.

### 16.3.2    Logistic regression

This algorithm is used in classification problems that models conditional probability (0 or 1). In other words, it is similar to the LR model that tries to predict an outcome for a dependent variable from one or more independent variables but, in logistic regression, the independent variable can be categorical or continuous. It uses a logistic function also known as the sigmoid function to classify the data. Logistic regression is mostly used in binary classification problems. It uses a decision boundary approach to classify the data into two categories. It also uses optimization techniques like cost function and gradient descent.

### 16.3.3    Support vector machines

SVM is another SL algorithm that can be used for both regression and classification problems. However, it is mostly preferred for classification problems. It can classify both linear and nonlinear data. It works by plotting each data item as a point in $n$-dimensional space (where $n$ is the number of features) with the value of each feature being the value of a particular coordinate. Then, it performs classification by finding the hyperplane that differentiates the two classes very well. Data points are decided on the basis of boundaries which are overlaid by hyperplanes. Data points that fall on any side of the given plane are attributed to various classes. Moreover, the dimension highly depends upon the total number of features. For example, the output would be only one line if in case there are two inputs to machine. Support vectors are set of data that directs toward the hyperplane and these will help users to maximize the margin of the classifier. For nonlinear data, SVM uses kernel functions that take input as low dimension feature space and outputs high-dimension feature space due to which classification becomes easy. SVM classifiers like one versus all and one versus one are used for multiclass classification.

### 16.3.4   Artificial neural network

These are the algorithms that model similar functioning to the human brain. As the human brain consists of a network of neurons that are interconnected, ANN also consists of neurons that are arranged in several layers. There are different types of ANN such as feedforward neural network (FFNN), recurrent neural network, and convoluted neural network (CNN). It contains a network of interconnected nodes. Each node is a perceptron showing similarity to multiple LRs which produces signals that are fed into an activation function by the perceptron. FFNN consists of an input and output layer with a hidden layer within itself. It feeds the signal in the forwarding direction only. A training algorithm is used by ANN to minimize the error among targeted and predicted output by adjusting the weight of each neuron. This training algorithm is known as backpropagation. Similarly, recurrent neural network (RNN) uses loops in hidden layers due to which it has internal memory. This memory feature of RNN, in combination to long short term memory (LSTM) technique (that enhances the memory time), is used in major technologies today.

### 16.3.5   Decision tree

DT is a nonparametric supervised algorithm that can be used for both classification and regression problems. It is basically a flowchart drawn upside down, consisting of internal nodes, leaf nodes, and a root node. Each internal node represents a test on a feature, whereas each leaf node represents the class labels and branches represent conjunctions of features that lead to those class labels. The paths from the root to leaf represent classification rules. By drawing this flowchart, users can easily understand the relations. It is also known as classification and regression trees labels. The paths from the root to leaf represent classification rules. DT is very useful where concepts for statistics of data are used such as in the case of ML and data mining. DT falls under domain of SL and it differentiates the data according to the conditions involved in decision-making process.

## 16.3.6 Random forests

Random-forest-SL is a network of DTs. The group of DTs is trained with the bagging method. In other words, it is a multiple DT that is merged together to give better predictive results with more accuracy and reliability. It also provides versatility as it can be used for both classifications and falls under regression problems. It gives better prediction than DT as it adds more randomness to the trees and during the splitting of a node, it uses the best feature among a random subset of features. There is less chance of overfitting in this algorithm, which is a big advantage.

## 16.3.7 K means

It is an unsupervised algorithm that comes under type of clustering technique. Clustering in UL is an important approach as it uses patterns in a collection of uncategorized data and finds natural clusters or groups within the data. $K$ Means is a subtype of types of clustering and comes under partitioned clustering. It is basically a centroid-based clustering. $K$ Here represents a number of groups and the algorithm starts from identifying the $k$ centroids and then iterates between two steps of assigning the data points and updating these centroids. Euclidean distance measures the next step for updating centroids by taking the mean of all data points assigned to a particular cluster.

## 16.3.8 Naïve Bayes

It is a classification algorithm that uses the Bayes theorem assuming that the presence of a particular feature in a class is unrelated to the presence of any other feature. It is easy to build and even works efficiently on large datasets. In spite of its simplicity, naïve Bayes outperforms many complex sophisticated algorithms.

## 16.3.9 Dimensionality reduction algorithm

These algorithms are applied to datasets with $p$ dimension of data into subsets of $k$ dimensions $(k<<<n)$. They serve many benefits in handling and processing large datasets in ML models such as the space required is reduced, less computational or training time is required, reduced dimension, which is beneficial to some algorithms, dimension reduction techniques that take care of multicollinearity, reduced dimensions of datasets, which helps to visualize better, and many more. The common dimensionality reduction techniques used are feature selection in which the user only keeps the most relevant variables from the original datasets, while another technique includes finding a smaller set of new variables, each being a combination of the input variables, containing basically the same information as the input variables.

## 16.3.10 Gradient boosting algorithm and AdaBoosting algorithm

Boosting algorithms come under ensemble learning techniques. Ensemble learning increases the accuracy of prediction by combining the decisions by multiple models. This diversification increases the overall performance. Boosting algorithms are very useful for conversion from weak learner to stronger one. It fits a sequence of weak learner models, which are approximately little stronger to random one. Due to their ability to enhance the accuracy of predictions, it is the most preferred ML algorithm.

## 16.4    Machine learning for Healthcare 4.0

In the previous section, the chapter has discussed different ML algorithms and the type of learning it follows; in context to this user will now see how these algorithms can be utilized to build health-care applications. UL algorithms (learning from unlabeled data) like clustering can be used for anomaly detection [45]. Some other examples can be predicting hepatitis using PCA [46], heart diseases can be predicted using clustering [47], etc. SL includes classification and regression problems. Moreover, classification techniques are widely used in healthcare for purposes such as recognizing different body organs for medical images [48], classifying different lung diseases [49], etc., whereas semi-SL (where the data is both labeled and unlabeled) techniques are particularly useful for health-care applications as it is generally difficult to collect sufficient amounts of labeled data. In [50], clustering based on semi-SL facilitating health-care applications is discussed. Data sensors used in activity recognition using semi-supervised algorithms are presented in [51]. In [48,52], medical image segmentation using a semi-supervised approach is applied by the authors. Apart from these, RL is another learning paradigm in which the model learns to make a sequence of decisions and the model gets either rewards or penalties for the actions it performs [6]. RL is known to have great potential to transform health-care applications. Some uses of RL such as checking context-free symptom in disease diagnosis are presented in [51].

Further, the healthcare on the basis of using ML can be divided into four applications: prognosis, diagnosis, treatment, and clinical workflow. Prognosis is the stage of prediction of the development of disease in patients. In this phase, symptoms and signs for the disease are identified by predicting if these symptoms will deteriorate, enhance, or remain steady over a period of time, chances of survival, etc. ML is used for cancer detecting in brain tumor [53] and lung nodules [54] are designed to facilitate disease prognosis [55]. These models are tested and trained on the data collected from patients during this stage. This data comprises medical images, phenotypic, genotypic, pathology results, etc. ML is useful for disease prognosis and has been efficiently utilized to achieve the aim of "personalized medicine" but this field is still budding and many new techniques are yet to be explored in this. The next application of ML is in diagnosis. Medical image analysis is one of the methods used for diagnosis. In this ML algorithms are used to efficiently analyze the medical images for diverse information to be used later in the treatment phase. There are various imaging appliances like MRI and computed tomography that provide the medical images of various organs of bodies, which helps in diagnosing the body for a particular disease, its sign, and symptom.

Medical image analysis includes detection (identifying specific disease patterns), classification (identifying different organs and abnormalities), segmentation (segmenting different tissues and organs for quantitative analysis), retrieval (to manage and query huge databases of the present as well as past diagnosis), reconstruction (raw data from image sensors are used to generate new images), and image registration (mapping input image to a reference image) tasks. These tasks are efficiently performed by deploying ML models in designing fully automated intelligent systems. Today, hospitals and other health-care facilities are producing EHRs in huge amounts. It comprises structured and unstructured data. ML models have been designed to extract the clinical features out of these dates which help in improved diagnosis [56]. In [57], semi-supervised models are designed to extract the data from unstructured data and they are presented using ML models used for diabetes diagnosis [58]. The third application is treatment, in which people can use techniques like real-time health monitoring using ML, which helps in efficient monitoring of critical patients, IoT sensors, health tracker smart devices, etc. All the techniques collect health data of patients, which is communicated over cloud and later analyzed via ML models, later the predictions are transferred back to originating devices via the cloud and necessary actions are taken accordingly [59]. Image interpretation of the medical images by experts is also used in the treatment phase. These interpretations are vital to prepare clinical reports. Not all health-care service providers are equipped with expertise like experienced radiologists, technicians. Therefore, making clinical reports in these cases is challenging. On the other hand, even if hospitals are having experts with them, making high-quality reports is very time-consuming and troublesome. Natural language processing (NLP) with ML technique can be solutions to these problems, for example, annotating clinical reports using NLP-based method is used for such precise analysis [60], an automatic report can be generated by deploying models that use CNN along with LSTM network [61]. Thorax disease classification as well as reporting of chest X-rays model can be developed by integrating CNN and RNN [62] and many more. Ahmad *et al.* [63] have presented interpretable ML models that are needed in healthcare and discussed, including their deployed. Figure 16.1 illustrates the different phases of ML in health-care systems.

Deploying different ML models for early prediction and diagnosis of diseases enables efficient and enhanced treatment for the disease. This is so far one of the best applications of ML. In a similar study [64], it was concluded that ML techniques improve efficient predictions by studying ML algorithms that are tested and trained on clinical data for predicting the risk of cardiovascular disease. Fatima *et al.* [64] surveyed various ML concepts in order to detect various diseases like liver disease, dengue, diabetes. ML model can diagnose as well as predict worsening of cancer [65]. Apart from this, computer-aided detection (CADe) and computer-aided diagnosis (CADx) systems are developed, which use integrated technologies like image processing techniques. One such system is IBM's Watson. As discussed earlier, RL-based models are also used for diagnosis and treatment [66]. ML models are used in modeling the clinical time-series data, which help in applications such as prediction of clinical intervention in ICUs using models with CNN and LSTM [67], managing ICU's predictions using attention model [68], and so on. To improve clinical research and

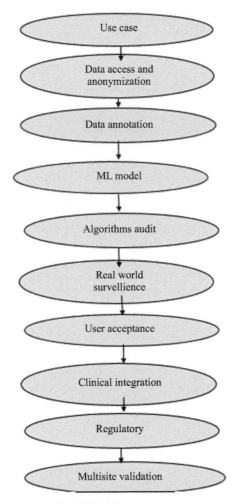

*Figure 16.1    Phases of deploying ML in healthcare*

practice, NLP techniques are used with other medical related software for analyzing information from unstructured medical data [69]. ML model is also facilitating the clinicians with applications for the processing of clinical speech as well as audio data, which helps in saving their time and reducing workload. It also helps in the diagnosis of disease related to speech such as dementia [70] and Alzheimer's disease [71].

## 16.5    Vulnerabilities for ML in Healthcare 4.0

Deploying ML in health-care provides many benefits to the system but creates many sources of vulnerabilities due to its security and privacy risks. Figure 16.2 depicts various vulnerability sources in deploying ML for healthcare.

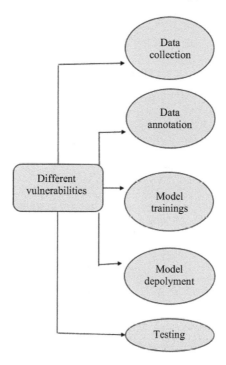

*Figure 16.2    Different sources of vulnerability and security threats for ML in healthcare*

## 16.5.1    Vulnerabilities in data collection

ML models require training and testing of models by using large amounts of data. The healthcare can use these data in the form of medical image, radiology report, EHR, etc. that require human efforts in collecting it and it is a time-consuming task. These data can have various sources for vulnerabilities that might affect ML implementations. Many times these data collected can have noise (instrumental and environmental disturbances) in them, which can cause the model to over fit the data. For example, multi-shot MRI is highly sensitive to motion, thus a small change in the subject's head or respiration can cause undesirable noises in images, which will increase the chances of misdiagnosis. ML/DL system in healthcare requires qualified technical staff like engineers and data scientists for their efficient functioning. Since a health-care system is an ecosystem of interdisciplinary technical and nontechnical staff, it often lacks qualified personnel required for developing and maintaining the ML/DL systems. This results in inefficient functioning and the benefits of ML systems cannot be fully utilized. Many times, the hospitals depend only on their physician or researchers to operate these ML/DL-based systems considering the clinical usability of these systems as important. But these people lack the computational experience to develop or operate this system resulting in adverse effects in the health-care system.

## 16.5.2    Vulnerabilities due to data annotation

Since most of the models used in ML-based systems are supervised ones and these models require huge labeled data to be trained upon, thus, these labels are assigned to each sample of data (such as medical images). This process of assigning labels is known as data annotation and it is an important part of designing an ML model, which requires trained and expert personnel. But often due to the lack of such expertise problems such as label leakage, class imbalance, etc. arises leading to several vulnerabilities. One such vulnerability can be the ambiguity in medical datasets such as medical images [72] and even the expert physicians can disagree on precise diagnostic tasks [73]. Some spiteful users can make the situation much more difficult by disturbing the data which will make the diagnosis more difficult and complicated. Vulnerability can arise due to improper annotation. Proper guidelines are given with privacy and legal considerations, which are to be followed by annotating the dataset for life-critical health-care situations [74]. Datasets that are frequently used in healthcare are generally annotated for coarse-grained labels but, in practical the ML as well as DL model uses fine-grained labels within the clinical environment. If the label annotation is not done properly, it can lead to problems such as improper distribution of samples in classes, which can lead to biasing in models, availability of datasets required, augmentation of datasets, data missing, etc.

## 16.5.3    Vulnerabilities in model training

A model training (MT) can give targeted outputs efficiently only when it has been trained properly. Training of an ML model depends on many parameters (such as learning rates, epochs, and batch size) all of these are needed to be fulfilled. Incomplete training, privacy breaching, stealing, or model poisoning are some of the vulnerabilities in the model. MT is at high risk of security threats such as adversarial attacks [75], model-based attacks [76], data poisoning attacks. In poisoning attack, originality and availability of data are deteriorated by poising the data with the payload. The poisoning modifies the original dataset and produces anomaly for the boundaries of victimized ML-based model. The attack is carried out during training phase to illegally gather sensitive information rather than seizing the whole system. The main objective of this attack is to get those preserved dataset in order to carry out further more devastating attacks. These vulnerabilities are required to be checked as it affects the functioning of ML models, thus reducing their advantages in the health-care system. These models can be deployed in security-critical applications like biometrics, fingerprint sensors, and in life-critical applications. Health-care sector tries their best to keep security hygiene that defends them against adversary in all possible ways. Therefore, the ML-based healthcare should also overlay themselves on the concept of cyber defense against hacker.

## 16.5.4    Vulnerabilities in deployment phase

The deployment phase is crucial as it involves the deployment of ML models in various functions and operations in the health-care system. This requires huge human resources and decisions made by health-care personnel. This deployment phase also suffers from various vulnerabilities, which is needed to be checked. The distribution shifts, and incomplete values or data, hold a major problem in deployment as the data collected has incomplete values which are simply ignored during analysis. This kind of model leads to the problem of a healthy person diagnosed with a disease called false positive and a patient having a disease identified as healthy known as a false negative. Both of these problems are severe and affect the integrity of the system.

### 16.5.5   Vulnerabilities in testing phase

The testing phase of an ML model comes after the training phase. If the training of the model is not done properly, there can be vulnerabilities in the testing phase. Such as the outcomes of false positive and false negative come from inadequate data fed to the model in the training phase. Misinterpretation during the testing phase is also a common issue. The testing phase is the last phase; hence, these issues can be checked by considering the vulnerabilities of the sections discussed earlier. At last, the true meaning of ML-powered health-care system is to deploy ML in critical health-care applications using analytical methods [77].

## 16.6   ML-based solutions for Healthcare 4.0

This section will discuss the various solutions and applicability of ML to ensure secure, private, and robust processing.

### 16.6.1   Privacy preservation

Ensuring the safety of the privacy of the users is necessary for the health-care system. As discussed, health-care application built on various technologies such as ML and DL requires huge datasets, these data can be personal to the users, therefore, any breach in such data can affect the system with unavoidable consequences. Preservation of privacy while deploying ML models essentially means that training the model should not include any additional information regarding the users. The information/data are basically available as cloud storage; thus, they can be breached. Data anonymization techniques are used to check data breaches. However, it is said that even if the data is anonymized, meaningful information can be inferred from an individual's private data [78]. There are many efforts addressing this problem of privacy in ML-powered healthcare, such as the two server model with three different protocols. There are various methods that are adopted for executing secured arithmetic processes over a secure multiparty computation-based environment [79]. Moreover, softmax and sigmoid functions have been proposed as alternatives for the nonlinear activation functions used in ML models.

Other techniques are also used to preserve privacy such as cryptographic approaches. It is used for the training and testing of models where encrypted data are accessed from multiple parties. Cryptographic approaches use methods like homomorphic encryption where, addition, multiplication operations can be done on the encrypted data which serves as the basis for computing complex functions. The second method is garbled circuits, which is used in the case where, the private data of two parties are used to get the results. Using the homophobic encryption and garbled circuits, some classification techniques such as naïve Bayes, DT, and hyperplane decision can be used to build cryptographic blocks [80]. Third method is secret sharing in which assets can be shared among different parties, including shareholder, having secret data. Lastly, secure processors are also used which account for the security of sensitive code from the unauthorized elements at higher levels.

### 16.6.2    Differential privacy

It refers to the process of adding disturbances to the dataset in order to protect that data. This idea was first proposed in 2006 [81], it guarantees the privacy of the algorithm, which analyses aggregate datasets [82]. The group privacy and sturdiness additional data, which serves many benefits to the health-care applications, uses the differential privacy (DP) concept. Group privacy is useful when the dataset contains correlated samples and composability is used for modularity of algorithm designed. Moreover, this archives robustness without hindering the system's privacy while using additional information/data. The model for healthcare could also be developed by working upon the available encrypted datasets that usually have noise involved in them [83]. Private ML designed by using Private Aggregation of Teacher Ensembles is also very useful for such system [84]. Other privacy mechanisms are differentially private stochastic gradient descent [85], hyper parameter selection [86], Laplace [87], and Exponential Noise Differential Privacy Mechanisms [88,89], which are beneficial for health-care system.

### 16.6.3    Federated learning

Google Inc. recently proposed the ideas of federated learning (FL), also known as collaborative learning, which is a learning technique that the model has trained an algorithm using local data or data from multiple decentralized servers but, without any exchange of data [90]. Ye *et al.* [91] proposed edge-FL, which separates the process of updating the local model that is supposed to be completed independently by mobile devices.

## 16.7    Conclusion

This chapter worked on a way to demonstrate the role of different technologies, keeping the main focus on ML for Healthcare 4.0. Initially, the chapter defines Healthcare 4.0 and its applications. Then, various types of ML algorithms are highlighted. Further, it explores ML applications in healthcare, and their way of implementation. The chapter also discussed the challenges faced while deploying ML models in the health-care system. The chapter provides some solutions to ensure the security, privacy, and robustness of ML models when implemented over health-care system. ML is a vast field within itself and when this field is integrated with other technologies, it produces great results. When used in the health-care system, this field will boost efficiency and enhance its service to many subfields of healthcare which consequently benefits the human beings.

# References

[1] C. Kanchanachitra, M. Lindelow, T. Johnston *et al.*, "Human resources for health in southeast Asia: Shortages, distributional challenges, and international trade in health services," *Lancet*, vol. 377, no. 9767, pp. 769–781, 2011.

[2] M. Akay and T. Tamura, "Global healthcare: Advances and challenge [Scanning the Issue]," *Proc. IEEE*, vol. 103, no. 2, pp. 147–149, 2015.

[3] G. Alfian, M. Syafrudin, M. Ijaz, M. Syaekhoni, N. Fitriyani, and J. Rhee, "A personalized HEALTHCARE monitoring system for diabetic patients by UTILIZING BLE-based sensors and real-time data processing," *Sensors*, vol. 18, no. 7, p. 2183, 2018. doi:10.3390/s18072183.

[4] M. B. Sampa, M. R. Hoque, R. Islam *et al.*, "Redesigning portable health clinic platform as a remote healthcare system to tackle COVID-19 pandemic situation in unreached communities," *Int. J. Environ. Res. Public Health*, vol. 17, no. 13, p. 4709, 2020.

[5] M. Jindal, J. Gupta, and B. Bhushan, "Machine learning methods for IoT and their future applications," in *2019 International Conference on Computing, Communication, and Intelligent Systems (ICCCIS)*, 2019. doi:10.1109/icccis48478.2019.8974551.

[6] R. Tayal and A. Shankar, "Learning and predicting diabetes data sets using semi-supervised learning," in *2020 10th International Conference on Cloud Computing, Data Science & Engineering (Confluence)*, Noida, India, 2020, pp. 385–389. doi:10.1109/Confluence47617.2020.9058276.

[7] L. Xing, E. A. Krupinski, and J. Cai, "Artificial intelligence will soon change the landscape of medical physics research and practice," *Med. Phys.*, vol. 45, no. 5, pp. 1791–1793, 2018.

[8] A. Kumari, S. Tanwar, S. Tyagi, and N. Kumar, "Fog computing for Healthcare 4.0 environment: Opportunities and challenges," *Comput. Electr. Eng.*, vol. 72, pp. 1–13, 2018.

[9] A. A. Mutlag, M. K. A. Ghani, N. Arunkumar, M. A. Mohammed, and O. Mohd, "Enabling technologies for fog computing in healthcare IoT systems," *Future Gener. Comput. Syst.*, vol. 90, pp. 62–78, 2019, [online] Available: http://www.sciencedirect.com/science/article/pii/S0167739X18314006.

[10] B. Mohanta, P. Das, and S. Patnaik, "Healthcare 5.0: A paradigm shift in digital healthcare system using artificial intelligence, IOT and 5G communication," in *2019 International Conference on Applied Machine Learning (ICAML)*, 2019, pp. 191–196. doi:10.1109/ICAML48257.2019.00044.

[11]    G. Rong, A. Mendez, E. B. Assi, B. Zhao, and M. Sawan, "Artificial intel-
       ligence in healthcare: Review and prediction case studies," *Engineering*,
       vol. 6, no. 3, pp. 291–301, 2020, [online] Available: http://www.science-
       direct.com/science/article/pii/S2095809919301535.

[12]    J. Gaur, A. K. Goel, A. Rose, and B. Bhushan, "Emerging trends in machine
       learning," in *2019 2nd International Conference on Intelligent Computing,
       Instrumentation and Control Technologies (ICICICT)*, 2019. doi:10.1109/
       icicict46008.2019.8993192.

[13]    S. Kumar, B. Bhusan, D. Singh, and D. K. Choubey, "Classification of
       diabetes using deep learning," in *2020 International Conference on
       Communication and Signal Processing (ICCSP)*, 2020. doi:10.1109/
       iccsp48568.2020.9182293.

[14]    S. Goyal, N. Sharma, B. Bhushan, A. Shankar, and M. Sagayam, "IoT
       enabled technology in secured healthcare: Applications, challenges and
       future directions," in A. E. Hassanien, A. Khamparia, D. Gupta, K. Shankar,
       and A. Slowik (Eds.), *Cognitive Internet of Medical Things for Smart
       Healthcare Studies in Systems, Decision and Control* (Vol. 311), 2021.
       Cham: Springer. doi:10.1007/978-3-030-55833-8_2.

[15]    N. Sharma, I. Kaushik, B. Bhushan, S. Gautam, and A. Khamparia,
       "Applicability of WSN and biometric models in the field of healthcare," in
       *Deep Learning Strategies for Security Enhancement in Wireless Sensor
       Networks Advances in Information Security, Privacy, and Ethics*, 2020,
       pp. 304–329. USA: IGI Global. doi:10.4018/978-1-7998-5068-7.ch016.

[16]    C. Thuemmler and C. Bai, Health 4.0: How Virtualization and Big Data are
       Revolutionizing Healthcare. New York, NY, USA: Springer, 2017.

[17]    N. Mohamed and J. Al-Jaroodi, "The impact of Industry 4.0 on healthcare sys-
       tem engineering," in *Proc. IEEE Int. Syst. Conf. (SysCon)*, Apr. 2019, pp. 1–7.

[18]    E. AbuKhousa, N. Mohamed, and J. Al-Jaroodi, "Health 4.0: Can healthcare
       industry get smarter?" in *Proc. 13th Int. Symp. Tools Methods Competitive
       Eng. (TMCE)*, 2020.

[19]    A. Khelassi, V. V. Estrela, A. C. B. Monteiro, R. P. França, Y. Iano, and
       N. Razmjooy, "Health 4.0: Applications management technologies and
       review," *Med. Technol. J.*, vol. 2, no. 4, pp. 262–276, 2019.

[20]    J. Chanchaichujit, A. Tan, F. Meng, and S. Eaimkhong, "An introduction to
       Healthcare 4.0," in *Healthcare 4*, Singapore: Palgrave Pivot, pp. 1–15, 2019.

[21]    J. Al-Jaroodi, N. Mohamed, and E. Abukhousa, "Health 4.0: On the way to
       realizing the healthcare of the future," *IEEE Access*, vol. 8, pp. 211189–
       211210, 2020. doi:10.1109/ACCESS.2020.3038858.

[22]    S. M. R. Islam, D. Kwak, M. H. Kabir, M. Hossain, and K.-S. Kwak, "The
       Internet of Things for health care: A comprehensive survey," *IEEE Access*,
       vol. 3, pp. 678–708, 2015.

[23]    M. D'Aloia, A. Longo, G. Guadagno, *et al.*, "Low cost IoT sensor system for
       real-time remote monitoring," in *2020 IEEE International Workshop on
       Metrology for Industry 4.0 & IoT*, 2020, pp. 576–580. doi:10.1109/
       MetroInd4.0IoT48571.2020.9138251.

[24] Y. A. Qadri, A. Nauman, Y. B. Zikria, A. V. Vasilakos, and S. W. Kim, "The future of healthcare Internet of Things: A survey of emerging technologies," *IEEE Commun. Surveys Tutorials*, vol. 22, no. 2, pp. 1121–1167, Second Quarter 2020. doi:10.1109/COMST.2020.2973314.

[25] J. Cardoso, K. Voigt, and M. Winkler, "Service engineering for the Internet of services," in *Proc. Int. Conf. Enterprise Inf. Syst.* Berlin, Germany: Springer, 2008, pp. 15–27.

[26] E. AbuKhousa, N. Mohamed, and J. Al-Jaroodi, "E-health cloud: Opportunities and challenges," *Future Internet*, vol. 4, no. 3, pp. 621–645, 2012.

[27] H. B. Aziz, S. Sharmin, and T. Ahammad, "Cloud based remote healthcare monitoring system using IoT," in *2019 International Conference on Sustainable Technologies for Industry 4.0 (STI)*, 2019, pp. 1–5. doi:10.1109/STI47673.2019.9068029.

[28] A. Bahga and V. K. Madisetti, "A cloud-based approach for interoperable electronic health records (EHRs)," *IEEE J. Biomed. Health Inf.*, vol. 17, no. 5, pp. 894–906, 2013. doi:10.1109/JBHI.2013.2257818.

[29] P. Van Gorp and M. Comuzzi, "Lifelong personal health data and application software via virtual machines in the cloud," *IEEE J. Biomed. Health Inf.*, vol. 18, no. 1, pp. 36–45, 2014. doi:10.1109/JBHI.2013.2257821.

[30] C. Xu, N. Wang, L. Zhu, K. Sharif, and C. Zhang, "Achieving searchable and privacy-preserving data sharing for cloud-assisted E-healthcare system," *IEEE Internet Things J.*, vol. 6, no. 5, pp. 8345–8356, 2019. doi:10.1109/JIOT.2019.2917186.

[31] P. E. Idoga, M. Toycan, H. Nadiri, and E. Çelebi, "Factors affecting the successful adoption of e-health cloud based health system from healthcare consumers' perspective," *IEEE Access*, vol. 6, pp. 71216–71228, 2018. doi:10.1109/ACCESS.2018.2881489.

[32] M. Viceconti, P. Hunter, and R. Hose, "Big data, big knowledge: Big data for personalized healthcare," *IEEE J. Biomed. Health Inf.*, vol. 19, no. 4, pp. 1209–1215, 2015. doi:10.1109/JBHI.2015.2406883.

[33] C. Zhang, R. Ma, S. Sun, Y. Li, Y. Wang, and Z. Yan, "Optimizing the electronic health records through big data analytics: A knowledge-based view," *IEEE Access*, vol. 7, pp. 136223–136231, 2019. doi:10.1109/ACCESS.2019.2939158.

[34] Q. Li, L. Lan, N. Zeng, *et al.*, "A framework for big data governance to advance RHINs: A case study of China," *IEEE Access*, vol. 7, pp. 50330–50338, 2019. doi:10.1109/ACCESS.2019.2910838.

[35] R. Lin, Z. Ye, H. Wang, and B. Wu, "Chronic diseases and health monitoring big data: A survey," *IEEE Rev. Biomed. Eng.*, vol. 11, pp. 275–288, 2018. doi:10.1109/RBME.2018.2829704.

[36] I. Lee, O. Sokolsky, S. Chen *et al.*, "Challenges and research directions in medical cyber–physical systems," *Proc. IEEE*, vol. 100, no. 1, pp. 75–90, 2012.

[37] J. A. Hansen and N. M. Hansen, "A taxonomy of vulnerabilities in implantable medical devices," in *Proc. 2nd Annu. Workshop Secur. Privacy Med. Home-Care Syst.*, 2010, pp. 13–20.

[38]   H. Qiu, M. Qiu, M. Liu, and G. Memmi, "Secure health data sharing for medical cyber-physical systems for Healthcare 4.0," *IEEE J. Biomed. Health Inf.*, vol. 24, no. 9, pp. 2499–2505, 2020. doi:10.1109/JBHI.2020.2973467.

[39]   J. Al-Jaroodi and N. Mohamed, "Blockchain in industries: A survey," *IEEE Access*, vol. 7, pp. 36500–36515, 2019.

[40]   P. Verma and S. K. Sood, "Fog assisted-IoT enabled patient health monitoring in smart homes," *IEEE Internet Things J.*, vol. 5, no. 3, pp. 1789–1796, 2018. doi:10.1109/JIOT.2018.2803201.

[41]   D. M. West, *How 5G Technology Enables the Health Internet of Things*, Brookings Center for Technol. Innovation, vol. 3, pp. 1–20, 2016.

[42]   N. Mohamed and J. Al-Jaroodi, "Applying blockchain in industry 4.0 applications," in *Proc. IEEE 9th Annu. Comput. Commun. Workshop Conf. (CCWC)*, 2019, pp. 0852–0858.

[43]   S. Wang, J. Wang, X. Wang, *et al.*, "Blockchain-powered parallel healthcare systems based on the ACP approach," *IEEE Trans. Comput. Soc. Syst.*, vol. 5, no. 4, pp. 942–950, 2018. doi:10.1109/TCSS.2018.2865526.

[44]   M. Zarour, M. T. Ansari, M. Alenezi, *et al.*, "Evaluating the impact of Blockchain Models for secure and trustworthy electronic healthcare records," *IEEE Access*, vol. 8, pp. 157959–157973, 2020. doi:10.1109/ACCESS.2020.3019829.

[45]   V. Chandola, A. Banerjee, and V. Kumar, "Anomaly detection: A survey," *ACM Comput. Surv. (CSUR)*, vol. 41, no. 3, p. 15, 2009.

[46]   K. Polat and S. Gunes, "Prediction of hepatitis disease based on principal component analysis and artificial immune recognition system," *Appl. Math. Comput.*, vol. 189, no. 2, pp. 1282–1291, 2007.

[47]   A. K. Pandey, P. Pandey, K. Jaiswal, and A. K. Sen, "Data Mining clustering techniques in the prediction of heart disease using attribute selection method," *Heart Disease*, vol. 14, pp. 16–17, 2013.

[48]   D. Mahapatra, "Semi-supervised learning and graph cuts for consensus based medical image segmentation," *Pattern Recognit.*, vol. 63, pp. 700–709, 2017.

[49]   W. Shen, M. Zhou, F. Yang, C. Yang, and J. Tian, "Multi-scale convolutional neural networks for lung nodule classification," in *International Conference on Information Processing in Medical Imaging*. Springer, 2015, pp. 588–599.

[50]   M. N. Sohail, J. Ren, and M. Uba Muhammad, "A Euclidean group assessment on semi-supervised clustering for healthcare clinical implications based on real-life data," *Int. J. Environ. Public Health*, vol. 16, no. 9, p. 1581, 2019.

[51]   H.-C. Kao, K.-F. Tang, and E. Y. Chang, "Context-aware symptom checking for disease diagnosis using hierarchical reinforcement learning," in *Thirty-Second AAAI Conference on Artificial Intelligence*, 2018.

[52]   W. Bai, O. Oktay, M. Sinclair *et al.*, "Semi- supervised learning for network-based cardiac MR image segmentation," in *International Conference on Medical Image Computing and Computer-Assisted Intervention*. Springer, 2017, pp. 253–260.

[53]  P. Afshar, A. Mohammadi, and K. N. Plataniotis, "Brain tumor type classi-
      fication via capsule networks," in *2018 25th IEEE International Conference
      on Image Processing (ICIP)*. IEEE, 2018, pp. 3129–3133.

[54]  W. Zhu, C. Liu, W. Fan, and X. Xie, "DeepLung: Deep 3d dual path nets for
      automated pulmonary nodule detection and classification," in *2018 IEEE
      Winter Conference on Applications of Computer Vision (WACV)*. IEEE,
      2018, pp. 673–681.

[55]  A. Collins and Y. Yao, "Machine learning approaches: Data integration for
      disease prediction and prognosis," in *Applied Computational Genomics*.
      Springer, 2018, pp. 137–141.

[56]  P. B. Jensen, L. J. Jensen, and S. Brunak, "Mining electronic health records:
      Towards better research applications and clinical care," *Nat. Rev. Genet.*,
      vol. 13, no. 6, p. 395, 2012.

[57]  Z. Wang, A. D. Shah, A. R. Tate, S. Denaxas, J. Shawe-Taylor, and H.
      Hemingway, "Extracting diagnoses and investigation results from unstruc-
      tured text in electronic health records by semi-supervised machine learning,"
      *PLoS One*, vol. 7, no. 1, p. e30412, 2012.

[58]  T. Zheng, W. Xie, L. Xu *et al.*, "A machine learning-based framework to
      identify type 2 diabetes through electronic health records," *Int. J. Med. Inf.*,
      vol. 97, pp. 120–127, 2017.

[59]  V. Jindal, "Integrating mobile and cloud for PPG signal selection to monitor
      heart rate during intensive physical exercise," in *Proceedings of the
      International Conference on Mobile Software Engineering and Systems*.
      ACM, 2016, pp. 36–37. Selection method, heart disease, vol. 14, pp. 16–17,
      2013.

[60]  J. Zech, M. Pain, J. Titano *et al.*, "Natural language-based machine learning
      models for the annotation of clinical radiology reports," *Radiology*, vol. 287,
      no. 2, pp. 570–580, 2018.

[61]  Y. Xue, T. Xu, L. R. Long *et al.*, "Multimodal recurrent model with attention
      for automated radiology report generation," in *International Conference on
      Medical Image Computing and Computer-Assisted Intervention*. Springer,
      2018, pp. 457–466.

[62]  X. Wang, Y. Peng, L. Lu, Z. Lu, and R. M. Summers, "TieNet: Text-image
      embedding network for common thorax disease classification and reporting
      in chest x-rays," in *Proceedings of the IEEE Conference on Computer Vision
      and Pattern Recognition*, 2018, pp. 9049–9058.

[63]  M. A. Ahmad, A. Teredesai, and C. Eckert, "Interpretable Machine
      Learning in Healthcare," in *2018 IEEE International Conference on
      Healthcare Informatics (ICHI)*, 2018, pp. 447–447. doi:10.1109/ICHI.
      2018.00095.

[64]  M. Fatima and M. Pasha, "Survey of machine learning algorithms for disease
      diagnostic," *J. Intell. Learn. Syst. Appl.*, vol. 9, no. 01, p. 1, 2017.

[65]  J. A. Cruz and D. S. Wishart, "Applications of machine learning in cancer
      prediction and prognosis," *Cancer Inf.*, vol. 2, p. 117693510600200030,
      2006.

[66]    Z. Zhang, "Reinforcement learning in clinical medicine: A method to optimize dynamic treatment regime over time," *Ann. Transl. Med.*, vol. 7, no. 14, p. 345, 2019. doi:10.21037/atm.2019.06.75.

[67]    H. Suresh, "Clinical event prediction and understanding with deep neural networks," Ph.D. dissertation, Massachusetts Institute of Technology, 2017.

[68]    H. Song, D. Rajan, J. J. Thiagarajan, and A. Spanias, "Attend and diagnose: Clinical time series analysis using attention models," in *Thirty-Second AAAI Conference on Artificial Intelligence*, 2018.

[69]    A. Névéol, H. Dalianis, S. Velupillai, G. Savova, and P. Zweigenbaum´, "Clinical natural language processing in languages other than English: Opportunities and challenges," *J. Biomed. Semant.*, vol. 9, no. 1, p. 12, 2018.

[70]    C. Pou-Prom and F. Rudzicz, "Learning multiview embeddings for assessing dementia," in *Proceedings of the 2018 Conference on Empirical Methods in Natural Language Processing*, 2018, pp. 2812–2817.

[71]    K. C. Fraser, J. A. Meltzer, and F. Rudzicz, "Linguistic features identify Alzheimer's disease in narrative speech," *J. Alzheimer's Dis.*, vol. 49, no. 2, pp. 407–422, 2016.

[72]    A. Zahin, L. T. Tan, and R. Q. Hu, "Sensor-based human activity recognition for smart healthcare: A semi-supervised machine learning," in *The International Conference on Artificial Intelligence for Communications and Networks*. Springer, 2019, pp. 450–472. https://doi.org/10.1007/978-3-030-22971-9_39.

[73]    X. A. Li, A. Tai, D. W. Arthur *et al.*, "Variability of target and normal structure delineation for breast cancer radiotherapy: An RTOG multi-institutional and multi observer study," *Int. J. Radiat. Oncol. Biol. Phys.*, vol. 73, no. 3, pp. 944–951, 2009.

[74]    F. Xia and M. Yetisgen-Yildiz, "Clinical corpus annotation: Challenges and strategies," in *Proceedings of the Third Workshop on Building and Evaluating Resources for Biomedical Text Mining (BioTxtM 2012) in conjunction with the International Conference on Language Resources and Evaluation (LREC)*, Istanbul, Turkey, 2012.

[75]    C. Szegedy, W. Zaremba, I. Sutskever, J. Bruna, D. Erhan, I. Goodfel-low, and R. Fergus, "Intriguing properties of neural networks," arXiv preprint arXiv:1312.6199, 2013.

[76]    B. Biggio, B. Nelson, and P. Laskov, "Poisoning attacks against support vector machines," in *29th International Conference on Machine Learning*, 2012, pp. 1807–1814.

[77]    T. J. Pollard, I. Chen, J. Wiens *et al.*, "Turning the crank for machine learning: Ease, at what expense?," *Lancet Digital Health*, vol. 1, no. 5, pp. e198–e199, 2019.

[78]    A. Narayanan and V. Shmatikov, *Robust De-Anonymization of Large Datasets (How to Break Anonymity of the Netflix Prize Dataset)*, University of Texas at Austin, 2008.

[79]    P. Mohassel and Y. Zhang, "SecureML: A system for scalable privacy-preserving machine learning," in *2017 IEEE Symposium on Security and Privacy (SP)*. IEEE, 2017, pp. 19–38.

[80]   R. Bost, R. A. Popa, S. Tu, and S. Goldwasser, "Machine learning classifi- cation over encrypted data," in *NDSS*, vol. 4324, 2015, p. 4325.

[81]   C. Dwork, Differential privacy. In H. C. A van Tilborg and S. Jajodia (Eds.), *Encyclopedia of Cryptography and Security*. Boston, MA: Springer. https:// doi.org/10.1007/978-1-4419-5906-5_752.

[82]   M. Abadi, A. Chu, I. Goodfellow *et al.*, "Deep learning with differential privacy," in *Proceedings of the 2016 ACM SIGSAC Conference on Computer and Communications Security*. ACM, 2016, pp. 308–318.

[83]   M. McDermott, S. Wang, N. Marinsek, R. Ranganath, M. Ghassemi, and L. Foschini, "Reproducibility in machine learning for health," in *Presented at the International Conference on Learning Representative (ICLR) 2019, Reproducibility in Machine Learning Workshop*, 2019.

[84]   N. Papernot, S. Song, I. Mironov, A. Raghunathan, K. Talwar, and U. Erlingsson, "Scalable private learning with pate," in *International Conference on Learning Representations (ICLR)*, 2018.

[85]   Y.-X. Wang, B. Balle, and S. Kasiviswanathan, "Subsampled Rényi differ- ential privacy and analytical moments accountant," arXiv preprint arXiv:1808.00087, 2018.

[86]   H. B. McMahan, G. Andrew, U. Erlingsson *et al.*, "A general approach to adding differential privacy to iterative training procedures," in *NeurIPS 2018 Workshop on Privacy Preserving Machine Learning*, 2018.

[87]   N. Phan, X. Wu, H. Hu, and D. Dou, "Adaptive Laplace mechanism: Differential privacy preservation in deep learning," in *2017 IEEE International Conference on Data Mining (ICDM)*. IEEE, 2017, pp. 385–394.

[88]   F. McSherry and K. Talwar, "Mechanism design via differential privacy." in *FOCS*, vol. 7, 2007, pp. 94–103.

[89]   C. Dwork and F. D. McSherry, "Exponential noise distribution to optimize database privacy and output utility," Jul. 14 2009, US Patent 7,562,071.

[90]   H. B. McMahan, E. Moore, D. Ramage *et al.*, "Communication-efficient learning of deep networks from decentralized data," in *Proceedings of the 20th International Conference on Artificial Intelligence and Statistics (AISTATS) JMLR*. WCP, vol. 54, 2017.

[91]   Y. Ye, S. Li, F. Liu, Y. Tang, and W. Hu, "EdgeFed: Optimized federated learning based on edge computing," *IEEE Access*, vol. 8, pp. 209191– 209198, 2020. doi:10.1109/ACCESS.2020.3038287.

*Chapter 17*

# Big data analytics and data mining for healthcare and smart city applications

*Sohit Kummar[1] and Bharat Bhushan[1]*

The unprecedented growth of population in urban areas has been causing a challenge for the citizens in their day-to-day lives such as road congestion, public security, environmental pollution, electricity shortage and water shortage. To control and resolve all these issues, new technologies have been developed for smart cities. Intelligent services and better applications are deployed in smart cities, by combining the Internet of Things (IoT) with the technologies like data mining (DM) and deep learning (DL). Many sectors like healthcare, governance, agriculture and public safety can increase their efficiency with the help of these new technologies and can convert these into smart applications for smart cities. Different kinds of computing like edge computing, fog computing and cloud computing support to provide better insights into analytics with the help of big data in smart cities. All these technologies are transforming or raising healthcare ecosystems, leading them in the direction of smart healthcare. This permits surgeons to get real-time data of their patients distantly with the help of wireless communication. Smart healthcare is established on new technologies to convey enriched and valued healthcare facilities for patients. This chapter explores the current challenges that are faced during the indigenous development of the smart cities. Furthermore, the chapter discusses the theoretical background of smart cities with the explanation of their components. Moreover, the chapter describes the necessity of computational infrastructure for smart cities in a framework of big data and DM. The chapter highlights some mining methods for extracting important information from huge and mixed data. Additionally, the chapter examines the advancement of healthcare sector in smart cities in context of big data and DM.

## 17.1 Introduction

Today almost 55% of the population are living in the urban cities, and it is calculated that in the coming 30 years about 68% of the population will be living in

[1]School of Engineering and Technology (SET), Sharda University, Greater Noida, India

smart cities [1]. According to an estimation by the United Nations, it is said that the population will increase by 2.5 billion by the year 2050. This huge amount of population will pose a great challenge, as it is highly difficult for the development and sustainable management of the urban cities areas [2]. It will also be a great challenge for the people to provide a very good quality of life (QoL) for the citizens of smart cities [3]. Therefore, it is very important to understand the need for urgent and effective solutions to support various demands of the population that grow at a very fast speed [4]. On the other side, the evolutions of the big data analytics (BDA) and the IoT [5] are the major factors that are responsible for the highly efficient implementation of the smart cities' services [6]. The BDA and IoT have gained immense popularity and attention as shown in Figure 17.1.

Across various domains, various intelligent systems have been developed with the emerging technologies [7], which help us to make different domains that are highly efficient. The benefit of smart cities is the processing and collection of data by a different technology of computing, to provide better interconnection and communication [8]. This leads to a better service in the smart services by uplifting the security, privacy, availability, sink and transportation. After looking at these issues, to support the development of the smart cities, authorities have shown a great interest toward the smart cities and invested billions of dollars [9]. IoT can be referred to as making the interconnection between the infinite numbers of the smart devices [10]. This technology helps the physical objects to enact as human and does their behaviors such as decision-making, thinking, hearing, sensing and seeing in order to coordinate actions, share information and communicate with other [11]. By these abilities, one can transform these normally simple objects or physical devices into intelligent devices that can operate on their own and adjust to the real-time circumstances and work peacefully without any disturbance of a third member like humans [12].

BDA and DM concepts are specific to smart cities as a whole and especially to smart healthcare systems in many ways [13]. Social media is reconstructing the health-related communications and share medical information, by varying the way of keeping the health records that evaluate by specialists. The availability of web resources on social media feeds and online forums delivers very important facts [14]. Indeed, BDA

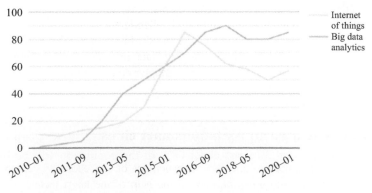

*Figure 17.1    Google search trends for BDA and IoT*

and DM techniques, broadcast management schemes look at people's real-life situations, producing large amounts of formal and informal information due to the rapid and massive market of human devices and the development of wireless sensors and mobile communication technologies [15]. In addition, clinical trials, photographs and descriptions from clinics lead to patients' medical supplies, compiled by records that can take several forms and programs. The most common are electronic health records (EHR), electrical medical records (EMR) and personal health records (PHR). While the EHR is expected to report care incidents in most management delivery management, EMRs of real-time patient health records are validated in decision-making tools, which can be used to assist physicians in decision-making [16]. PHR is a complete tool; a lifelong tool for dealing with health-related data, promoting healthcare and supporting the management of chronic diseases unlike EHR and EMR and is often managed by patients. Moreover, the methodical static texts reveal an important cause of environmental familiarity [17]. It needs web tools in dedicated mines to hold and refine recovery. Finally, a large number of biological data (genomics, macrobiotic, proteomics, metabolomics, epigenetics and transcriptomics) are produced and invented at an unparalleled rate, as the cost of obtaining and testing data decreases with these technologies [18]. A summary contribution of this work is enumerated as follows:

- This chapter highlights various requirements and explores the characteristic features of a smart city.
- This chapter describes different kinds of requirements for cloud, fog and edge computing.
- This chapter presents a brief description of the use of new technology like DM and DL for smart cities.
- This chapter discusses the environmental sustainability, public safety, health and urban land planning for smart cities.
- This chapter explores the role of BDA and DM in the healthcare sector.

The remainder of the chapter is organized as follows. Section 17.2 presents the theoretical background knowledge of the smart cities, in which all the smart functions of the smart cities highlights. Section 17.3 describes the function of computational infrastructure to provide the analytics in smart cities along with overall functioning of cloud computing, fog computing, edge computing and big data concepts based on machine learning (ML). Section 17.4 provides the insightful knowledge of mining methods that are available for big data to mine heterogeneous data. Section 17.5 highlights the role of big data in designing and planning of healthcare sector of smart cities. Finally, the chapter concludes in Section 17.6 with some important future research directions.

## 17.2 Theoretical background of smart cities

Smart cities can be termed as efficient management of the economy, environment, mobility, living, people and government with the help of the latest technologies. It is deeply studied and surveyed different aspects of smart city themes and concepts [19].

Lazaroiu *et al.* [20] investigated the different aspects of energy consumption and energy efficacy problems and were aware of the fact that cities are consuming 75% of the world's energy production capacities, and these cities are also responsible for generating 80% of carbon dioxide emissions. For a balanced use of the world's precious energy resources, a model is developed that helped us to resolve the issues with energy efficiency. Some components of smart cities are discussed in the succeeding subsection [21].

### 17.2.1　Smart people

The two main aims for the smart cities are to improve the QoL and a better living environment, as services and smart devices are mainly used by the users, which makes it crucial to be well designed and properly implemented for the people [22]. Yeh [23] suggested that the people of the smart cities should be aware of the social networking platforms, which work as a bridge for learning the purpose of the efficient use of the services and systems of smart cities. Belanche-Gracia *et al.* [24] proposed the security and privacy concerns for the use of transportation and public facilities with the use of the advanced smart card with the help of radio-frequency identification technology. Chatterjee and Kar [25] discussed the factors that affect the use of information systems based on the class of systems and information. For a mutual living experience, people should exchange their thoughts and opinions on social media platforms. It also gives an immense opportunity for people to earn money by resolving resident's issues by using these social media platforms. All these data are to be collected and processed; for example, Niforatos *et al.* [26] described a crowdsourcing weather application that takes a mixture of data from manual input of people and sensors. Mone [27] suggested that it is very crucial to design the smart cities keeping in mind the analyses of traffic issues.

### 17.2.2　Smart economy

A smart economy can be defined as cities, which uses smart payment tools and smart money to uplift its economy [28]. Smart economy depends on two terms that are mobile commerce and smart business, and these two main terms are mainly responsible for providing smart economy in the smart cities. Johnson *et al.* [29] proposed a probabilistic and predictive architecture that depends on management and risk-based approach to shift the current situations of market within business. Moreover, commercial and potential benefits of smart economy are based on the interaction of smart citizens, and most of the smart cities do not have a smart and good economy due to lack of proper designing and planning. Keegan *et al.* [30] described the need for E-commerce in digital cities without creating any problem for the retailers without hampered their business. To uplift the smart economy of both, the E-commerce and the retailers should work in collaboration with each other by providing a platform to ease the business of the smart cities [31]. Mobile shopping system helps a retailer in the smart cities to know what a customer wants, which type of smartphone, which in turn helps the retailer to raise the graph of their sale. However, an equal balance should be maintained between the experience and innovation of users in terms of the smart economy, while the user's account privacy remains a challenge [32].

## 17.2.3    Smart governance

For smart governance, the government should use social media to encourage the residents to collaborate and participate in the smart cities more efficiently. Government should also take stand and be actively involved in the issues that are related to the privacy and security to provide a clear and secure communication [33]. Rana *et al.* [34] highlighted the need for transparency among citizens. For a successful smart government, there are many key factors to be kept in mind such as network integration, channel, smartphone services and smart city services [35]. We must understand that government is very efficiently managing all the governmental work and policies of residents, and this process helps the residents to be involved in the evaluation of smart cities. There were various methods proposed, which calculate the smartness of the smart cities by calculating the effectiveness, collaboration, security, transparency and easiness [36]. For all the E-governance, an infrastructure should be developed for better support over the cloud-based technology that will enhance the data-processing time, decision-making based on evidence, sustainability, resident's centricities, creativity, equality, efficiency, openness, entrepreneurialism, technology savviness, resiliency and innovation, which results in better and safe smart governance [37].

## 17.2.4    Smart mobility

The potency of transport capacities based on the congestion in the smart cities is one of the biggest tasks of the smart governance. Intelligent transportation management system is majorly discussed in the scientific articles given out by many experts in the world [38]. Internet of vehicle (IoV) is the major solution that can be considered at the solution of current problem and it also solves the issues like efficiency and traffic safety. Zhu *et al.* [39] proposed a compatible network management system that the people of smart cities can easily adapt to the newly emerging technology of IoV. It would be difficult to adapt to the IoV in the starting, but this process grows much more efficient with time and by adaptation of people.

It was mentioned that urban traffic management solutions should be introduced with a solution that drivers can reach to their destination without experiencing the traffic problems [40]. Calderoni *et al.* [41] designed a model that will take the data from different networks of the sensors by recognizing two different services, namely smartphone-based traffic control system and the wise traffic controller. These two systems do the wonderful job in smart cities with urban infrastructure, a solution with the most efficient vehicle tracking management system in which data can be collected on the basis of real-time movement of the vehicles in the smart cities. However, improvisation in the model over time resulted in tracking of multiple vehicles at a single time at much better accuracy [42].

## 17.2.5    Smart environment

Water supply, green spaces, waste management, air quality, monitoring, energy efficiency, etc. all are elements of smart environment that need to be accomplished in a way toward a better deployment of smart cities [43]. The major issue is the constant monitoring of the trees in the smart cities that will help one to build a better smart environment. It is further noticed that trees in the smart cities could also damage the network cables, and it also occurs disruption in power connections, and some researchers suggested an efficient way, which is by developing a dynamic laser-based scanning system, results in locating well-organized trees in the smart cities [44]. Castelli *et al.* [45] discussed that the pollution in the air can cause severe damage to the environment, which many urban cities are already facing. A report published by World Health Organization says many people are dying because of air pollution every year. However, making it very necessary to keep an eye on the air quality index management, this could be done through the various traffic monitoring sensors installed at the certain location in the smart cities [46]. The water management is a challenging issue if not managed properly, as it has been seen in the smart cities and few factors remain as a challenge such as maintenance cost, new contaminants, and aging water infrastructure. Some experts suggest that ICT systems improved the quality of drinking water across the smart cities. Water management is directly responsible for the QoL that people are spending, as it is also important for the governance to keep the contaminants as low as possible [47].

### 17.2.6 Smart living

Smart building for tourism, healthcare, public safety and education comes up together as smart living. When we focus on these topics and work with better governance, these sectors will automatically improve the QoL of the residents. The other factor is the public safety of the people as it directly affects the development of the smart cities. Interactive voice responses is a model that is used with the help of citizens who can efficiently report the problem with the public safety, and it is also very easy to learn [48]. Healthcare issues are very important to be assessed as healthcare impacts the QoL of smart cities. Hussain *et al.* [49] proposed a framework of hospital management that uses real-time monitoring for the disabled and elderly people of the smart cities. Pramanik *et al.* [50] defined a demonstration for the healthcare-connected business model that uses the trending technology like big data for smart-healthcare system. This healthcare system helps the governance of the smart cities to decrease the health costs, achieve better service and improve contact management. Vincent [51] commented that the important factor, which is education services, has a deep impact on the QoL of citizens of the smart cities at the local development level. Another main factor is the smart buildings that are very popular for their unique features and special design [52]. Table 17.1 presents the components of smart cities that need to be achieved.

### 17.3 Computational infrastructures for smart cities big data analytics

In few years, a great advancement is being noticed in especially DL techniques and their accuracies. However, utmost memory and high computational power are required; these things are majorly solved by some specific and advanced computational

*Table 17.1 Components of smart cities*

| Smart people [22] | Smart economy [28] | Smart governance [33] | Smart mobility [38] | Smart environment [43] | Smart living [48] |
|---|---|---|---|---|---|
| • Healthcare study<br>• Telecommunication<br>• Entertainment<br>• Cultural activities | • Employment opportunities<br>• Smart manufacturing | • IT connectivity<br>• Online citizen services<br>• Digital media<br>• Smart data protection<br>• Smart and advanced security<br>• Smart agriculture sustainability | • Transport<br>• Walkability<br>• Traffic<br>• Wireless networks | • Pollution<br>• Green building<br>• Renewable energy<br>• Smart grids<br>• Air quality<br>• Trees | • Sewerage and sanitation<br>• Water supply<br>• Electricities<br>• Building and home<br>• Public open space |

platforms. Moreover, platforms like fog, edge and cloud computing are used. Edge computing and fog computing are specially designed as extensions for the enabled data analytics and cloud network for the source of the new data creation [52]. These three computing techniques are explained in detail in the subsections.

## 17.3.1    Cloud computing

Cloud computing technology helps us to access the data from anywhere in the world at any time; we can say the data and function at our fingertips. It contains several data centers and servers that are available on the Internet for all the users in the world [53]. There are many special features of IoT as discussed in the following:

- Storage on the Internet: Cloud is a technology that connects the server to different devices through Transmission Control Protocol/Internet Protocol networks. Its major task is to help the movement of the data and to provide storage deployment.
- Service over Internet: There are many services available on cloud technology, majorly artificial intelligence (AI) and networking to support the different needs of the users.
- Applications over Internet: Cloud applications help the user to perform tasks through an Internet connection from anywhere instead of writing code, which is not at all convenient.

The data created and generated by the devices are sent to cloud infrastructure, where these data are stored and processed in real time by using various DL algorithms [54]. Despite having many advantages such as sustainability, flexibility and interoperability, cloud computing technology has few disadvantages as listed in the following:

- Computation cost: The major two phases of DL models are inference and training in which the data first is transferred to the cloud for these phases to come into the effect. Both these processes use a high amount of bandwidth that increases its cost significantly.
- Latency: To know the strength of the network, this can be said as the time taken for the server to reply. Sometimes a cloud fails when it cannot respond in a very short time. It causes a major problem with time-critical applications.
- Reliability: These services are provided wirelessly, which means any problem at the network will affect the reliability of the services provided.

## 17.3.2    Fog computing

Fog computing is developed for different kinds of IoT applications and responsible for data analytics and computing nodes formations. Vaquero *et al.* [55] discussed that a large amount of heterogeneous decentralized devices are cooperated and communicated with others universally that work with the network to perform processing and storage tasks without any interruption from a third party. Fog computing and cloud computing share the mutually similar service such as deployment, networking and storage. Furthermore, fog computing technology is only available in few geographical locations in the world, whereas cloud computing is available everywhere without any complication of the geographical location. Moreover, fog computing is specially designed for the use of real-time IoT applications. These types of computing help us with low latency, minimal issues with privacy and security, and limited network bandwidth.

## 17.3.3   Edge computing

Edge computing is a new model that is developed to decrease and remove the cons of cloud computing [56] as it is the extended version of the cloud computing. Edge computing has a high computation space so that a huge amount of data are taken and then processed at the edge before sending to the central server cloud. A difficulty in the market is a huge increment in data creation that makes it a bit difficult to transport the data to the cloud. To improve the data process, we perform analytics at the edge rather than sending it to the cloud. This series of steps is beneficial in many ways such as it decreases the response time, improves bandwidth efficiency, reduces energy utilization and also reduces network pressure [57]. Edge computing is very important for a better development of the upcoming smart cities. By using this technology, smart cities can improvise in the various sectors and people can use edge gateway by which all the smart device stands connected to the network. All the data are meant to be processed at local level, which will increase the security, privacy and overall performances.

## 17.3.4   Big data based on machine learning

Big data is available in all places and sectors around the world. Conversely, its difficulty exceeds the processing power of outdated tools. For this reason, high-performance computing platforms are mandatory to use the full capacities of big data. These needs have unquestionably converted into a real challenge. Numerous revisions focus on searching a method that permits reducing of computational costs by increasing the compliance of the extracted data [58]. The necessity to excerpt useful information has required using of different methods of ML, to compare the results obtained and to analyze them according to the features of huge data volumes. ML can perform any task that a human is capable of doing with his human intelligence. Major of this intelligence revolves around few important factors such as engrossing speech to text, translating any language and image recognition. The power of AI has grown significantly in the last few years [59]. AI provides the capability to the computer to enact and take the decision through computer programs by improving the learning behavioral changes after trained unlabeled datasets from the mixed programs. At a later stage, the finally trained program computer now has the ability to take new decisions. ML models can learn nonlinear functions and features from a huge amount of complex, raw data with much better performance than over traditional ML methods. ML can be broadly classified into four major categories, discussed as follows:

*Table 17.2   Categories of ML*

| Supervised learning [60] | Unsupervised learning [60] | Semi-supervised learning [61] | Reinforcement learning [61] |
|---|---|---|---|
| • Known labels or output | • Unknown labels or output<br>• Focus on finding patterns and gaining insight from the data | • Known labels or output for a subset of data<br>• A blend of supervised and unsupervised learning | • Focus on making decision, based on previous experience<br>• Policy-making with feedback |
| Uses: | Uses: | Uses: | Uses: |
| • Insurance underwriting<br>• Fraud detection | • Customer clustering<br>• Association rule mining | • Medical prediction | • Gaming<br>• Complex decision making<br>• Reward system |

- Supervised learning: It refers to the capability of learning from labeled training data and helps in the way of predicting the outcomes majorly for unforeseen data.
- Unsupervised learning: It refers to the capability of examining the relationship and the naturally descriptive statistic of the data. The unsupervised learning is utilized to find out the interesting, hidden structure of the data [60].
- Semi-supervised learning: It refers to the training of a huge amount of data, which mainly contain less labeled data as compared to fully unlabeled data.
- Reinforcement learning: It occurs in between unsupervised and supervised learning and gives the ability to an "agent" to extract the learning from its nearby surrounding and the environment, which in turn makes the agent highly capable of behaving and acting smartly, then the "agent" can provide direct interaction with environment by its "actions" and accepts "reward" from nearby surrounding as well as "penalty" for unwanted results to create and inspire from a very perfect behavior policy [61]. Table 17.2 presents the summarized view of above discussed ML categories.

## 17.4   Mining methods for big data

There are different kinds of heterogeneous data available in our surroundings and we need to apply the DM techniques to utilize all these heterogeneous available data, with the help of automation [62]. Some mining techniques that come under the supervised, unsupervised and reinforcement learning are discussed next.

### 17.4.1   Classification

In classification, a process is followed through which an object is assigned to the predefined category, classification techniques can predict the destination class of each object of the data. For supervised learning, the targeted labels are assumed before processing. Before the classification of unknown data/objects or unlabeled data, a classifier (prediction function) classifies the required training as most algorithms are classified into two types. The first one is computing the probability of an item whether it belongs to a particular class or not and the second is comparing it with the cut-off value [63]. The evaluation of the performance of classification model can be done as follows:

$$\text{Accuracy} = \frac{\text{number of correct prediction } (T_p + F_p)}{\text{total number of predictions } (T_p + F_p + T_n + F_n)} \quad (17.1)$$

$$\text{Error rate} = \frac{\text{number of wrong prediction } (T_n + F_n)}{\text{total number of predictions } (T_p + F_p + T_n + F_n)} \quad (17.2)$$

Precision is an alternative method through which we can find out the classification algorithm results. Precision can be defined as the probability that selection taken on a random basis always results in relevance and recall can be defined as if the probability of a randomly selected object is reclaimed [64]. The mathematical expression for both is as follows:

$$\text{Precision } (pr) = \frac{T_p}{T_p + F_p} \quad (17.3)$$

$$\text{Recall } (R) = \frac{T_p}{T_p + F_n} \quad (17.4)$$

Here, $T_n$, $T_p$, $F_n$ and $F_p$ can be truly said as a confusion matrix as shown in Table 17.3.

Based on both recall and precision, these classification results can be given an $F$-score by the following formula:

$$F - \text{score} = \frac{2 \times pr \times R}{pr + R} \quad (17.5)$$

## 17.4.2 Clustering

A cluster can be defined as the objects present in a special identical group. With the help of clustering algorithm, the clusters are segregated into a certain fixed number of subclusters on the basis of their features. Clustering follows unsupervised

*Table 17.3 Confusion matrix*

|  | Prediction class = 0 | Prediction class = 0 |
| --- | --- | --- |
| Actual class = 1 | False negative ($T_n$) | True positive ($T_p$) |
| Actual class = 0 | True negative ($T_n$) | False positive ($F_p$) |

learning technique, for example, in few medical centers, certain patients have an unknown disease but researchers of the medical field are able to uncover and provide cure of those diseases as they are having little data related to the symptom of disease and improvement made by the patients based on some treatments that are provided by the doctors [65]. This clustering will help in a way to segregate the patients on the basis of their recognized symptoms and progress, which will help the doctors to perform a better and improved treatment.

### 17.4.3    Frequent pattern mining

Frequent pattern mining can be defined as a sequence of events or a set of data objects or data object that appears frequently on the system is known as a frequent pattern. When mining is done on frequent patterns, it gives a good overview of the analytical section and understanding of the data insights of the citizen's activity in a much suitable environment. Analyzing the pattern always plays an important role by which we can correlate and find the relationship between the data [66]. With the broad application of the association rule, one can easily predict that how the customer purchases a new item. This can yield out a complete prediction of the customer's pattern of purchase, which will help one to ramp up the customer experience and boost the business sales. The patterns with some specific orders can be called sequential patterns and when we perform mining on these patterns then it is called sequential pattern mining and can be applied to transaction patterns of any type of customer [67].

### 17.4.4    Another mining method

As outliers present in the data, during DM, lots of exceptions have to be faced. Sometimes these outliers can also be called anomalous objects. Outliers always have a different identity while comparing it with the regular data, and due to this unique identity, it is called an outlier [68]. By looking at the properties, especially the inherent properties, it can find out the good insights over the data. For outlier detection, data can take from IoT applications like smart traffic, parking system, smart agriculture, healthcare and smart home. Broadly outlier detection can be seen through four methods: distance-based, statistical-based, distribution, deviation and density local outlier detection. Outlier mining method is used in E-health monitoring system, in which health parameter is calculated via metric sensors and analyzed. All these data are collected in one place and then mining is done for outlier detection. It helps one to extract all the anomalous information present in the data, which will help the healthcare management system to predict all emergencies [69].

## 17.5    Advances in healthcare sector

Data in the healthcare sector is unstructured as these come from various healthcare applications such as health information exchange, public records, genetic databases, EHR and sensor data. Owing to the huge volume, heterogeneous data formats, and other associated uncertainties, it becomes difficult to transform the raw data into proper information. Selection of class attributes and health feature identification in healthcare data requires highly architecturally specific and sophisticated tools and techniques. The applicability of BDA and DM in healthcare sector is explored in the following subsections.

### 17.5.1 Big data for healthcare

Owing to the growing global population and the consequent generation of voluminous data in a healthcare sector, big data has emerged as a new promising solution. Pharmaceutical-industry stakeholders and experts have actively started analyzing big data to improve healthcare quality. Big data-enabled healthcare systems have been established across numerous disciplines such as treatment cost determination and patient characteristic investigation. Health informatics involves the storage, retrieval and acquisition of data in order to yield efficient results to service providers. Healthcare data are heterogeneous and link to numerous biomedical sources, including demographics, laboratory tests, gene arrays, imagery and sensors. Mostly these data are unstructured and unfit for storing electronically. This leads to the concept of data digitization that is supported by the four Vs, namely veracities, velocities, volume and variety [70,71].

Viceconti *et al.* [71] combined BDA and virtual psychological human technologies to produce effective and robust medical solutions that are capable of working with heterogeneous data spaces, non-textual information and sensitive data. In another work, Zhang *et al.* [72] proposed a cyber-physical system–based healthcare application built on BDA and cloud computing. Similarly, Hossain and Muhammad [73] proposed a powerful emotion detection module for connected healthcare system that can capture image and speech signals of patients within smart homes. Sahoo *et al.* [74] proposed an improved naïve Bayes algorithm that uses cloud big data for the prediction of future health conditions. The work also proposes an optimal data distribution scheme for positioning both streaming and batch patient data toward spark nodes. In another work, Hussain *et al.* [75] proposed a novel scheme to avoid semantic loss during healthcare document partitioning in big data. The proposed model set up uniquely configured systems using clinical document architecture on HDFS. Similarly, Syed *et al.* [76] proposed a novel healthcare framework to help elderly people in ambient-assisted living scenarios. The proposed framework achieved effective decision-making, analysis, treatment recommendations. In another work, Zhou *et al.* [77] proposed a frequent pattern mining-based medical cluster behavior model by combining the association rule mining with MapReduce computing model. Nazir *et al.* [78] summarized the existing research work and discussed the issues related to large-scale data management, complex system modeling, processing voluminous data and derivations from healthcare simulations and data. Kim and Chung [79] proposed to apply a multimodal autoencoder in healthcare big data for missing data estimation. The work used denoising an autoencoder to find missing values in PHR.

*Table 17.4  Big data analytics and data mining for healthcare sector*

| Technologies | Reference | Year | Contribution |
|---|---|---|---|
| Big data for healthcare | Viceconti *et al.* [71] | 2015 | Robust medical solutions that are capable of working with heterogeneous data spaces, non-textual information and sensitive data |
| | Zhang *et al.* [72] | 2017 | Healthcare applications built on big data analytics and cloud computing |
| | Hossain and Muhammad [73] | 2018 | Emotion detection module for connected healthcare system |
| | Sahoo *et al.* [74] | 2018 | Cloud big data for prediction of future health conditions |
| | Hussain *et al.* [75] | 2019 | Avoid semantic loss during healthcare document partitioning in big data |
| | Syed *et al.* [76] | 2019 | Healthcare framework to help elderly people in ambient-assisted living scenarios |
| | Zhou *et al.* [77] | 2020 | Medical cluster behavior model |
| | Nazir *et al.* [78] | 2020 | Discussed the issues related to large-scale data management |
| | Kim and Chung [79] | 2020 | Multimodal autoencoder in healthcare big data for missing data estimation |
| Data mining for healthcare | Akay *et al.* [81] | 2015 | Framework for cancer treatment using network partitioning scheme |
| | Yassine *et al.* [82] | 2017 | Big data–based smart home model for measuring and analyzing energy used in occupants behavior |
| | Kovalchuk *et al.* [83] | 2018 | Hybrid simulation–based framework for the discovery and classification of clinical pathways for patients |
| | Amin *et al.* [84] | 2019 | Hybrid data mining–based prediction model for predicting heart disease |
| | Sun *et al.* [85] | 2019 | Network-based progressing mining method for chronic diseases |
| | Gonçalves *et al.* [86] | 2020 | Predict mental illness considering unemployment factor |
| | Kaur *et al.* [87] | 2020 | Prostate cancer prediction model |
| | Zhang *et al.* [88] | 2020 | Enhanced privacy data fusion scheme that employs mining solutions |

## 17.5.2 Data mining for healthcare

The DM methods can be helpful for pattern discovery in order to generate computational tools and theories that assist humans in useful knowledge extraction from the ever-growing voluminous data. The most common DM methods that are used in healthcare sector are data visualization, pattern matching, evolution, association, clustering, generalization, classification, meta-rule-guided mining and characterization. Considering the underutilization of healthcare data, the concepts of DM can be used to extract valuable information and thereby effectively predict and diagnose disease [80].

Akay *et al.* [81] proposed a dual-analysis framework for cancer treatment that focuses on treatment's side effects and forum posts. Word frequency data in forum posts are analyzed using the self-organizing maps, and stability measurement is achieved using network partitioning scheme. In another work, Yassine *et al.* [82] proposed a big data–based smart home model that facilitates easy discovering and learning of human activity patterns. The proposed scheme utilized prediction, cluster analysis and frequent pattern mining for measuring and analyzing energy used in occupants behavior. Kovalchuk *et al.* [83] proposed a hybrid simulation-based framework for the discovery and classification of clinical pathways for patients. Amin *et al.* [84] proposed a hybrid DM-based prediction model for predicting heart disease using seven classification algorithms and DM techniques. In another work, Sun *et al.* [85] proposed a network-based progressing mining method to improve the clarity on chronic diseases and the associated medication stages. Gonçalves *et al.* [86] aimed to predict mental illness and associate it with factors like unemployment. The work integrates the concept of DM and cross-industry standard protocol to identify the factors associated with mental illness prediction. Similarly, Kaur *et al.* [87] used Indian datasets to develop a prostate cancer prediction model and highlight various predictors related to cancer survivability. Zhang *et al.* [88] proposed an enhanced privacy data fusion scheme that employs mining solutions and multisource data integration to provide better and timely health services to patients. Table 17.4 summarizes various contributions that highlight the role of big data and DM in the healthcare sector.

## 17.6 Conclusion

Technologies like big data, ML, AI, DL and DM create a deep impact on people's lifestyle. The development of the smart cities is highly proportional to such technologies. All these technologies can be clubbed together with the IoT devices to provide more efficiency. Many issues present in the real-world cities can be solved with these technologies in the new upcoming smart cities. For example, the issues like traffic management can be resolved with the fully automated robot system and by designing it with a better infrastructure, which will increase the efficiency in traffic management. Moreover, sustainable concepts of smart cities should carry keywords like environment, land use, transportation and relations with each other. The designer of the smart cities should have few aspects in his mind before designing the smart cities' layout such as the population of the smart cities, size of the smart cities, how much it is accessible to the service center of the prominent company and how much accessible it is to the other cities that exist nearby. The main aim of our study through this chapter was to spread the awareness among the people that what are the key future trends of the smart cities and how we can build a smart healthcare to provide better treatment with ease. The chapter has described a theoretical background of smart cities in which some important components are discussed. Furthermore, the chapter highlights the need of computational infrastructure for smart cities in a correlation with BDA. Moreover, the chapter highlights some mining methods for mining of big as well as heterogeneous data. Additionally, the chapter has described the advancement of healthcare sector in smart cities in context of BD and DM techniques. In future, we enhance this study in a way of providing more security and ease.

# References

[1]    Agbali M., Trillo C., Fernando T., Oyedele L., Ibrahim I. A., and Olatunji V. O. (2019). Towards a refined conceptual framework model for a smart and sustainable cities assessment. *IEEE International Smart Cities Conference (ISC2)*, pp. 658–664, doi:10.1109/ISC246665.2019.9071697.

[2]    Suryanegara M., Prasetyo D. A., Andriyanto F., and Hayati N. (2019). A 5-step framework for measuring the quality of experience (QoE) of Internet of Things (IoT) services. *IEEE Access*, 7, 175779–175792, doi:10.1109/ACCESS.2019.2957341.

[3]    Mishra K. N. and Chakraborty C. (2020). A novel approach towards using big data and IoT for improving the efficiency of m-health systems. In: Gupta D., Hassanien A., Khanna A. (eds), *Advanced Computational Intelligence Techniques for Virtual Reality in Healthcare. Studies in Computational Intelligence*, vol. 875. Cham: Springer. https://doi.org/10.1007/978-3-030-35252-3_7.

[4]    Gupta A., Chakraborty C., and Gupta B. (2019). Medical information processing using smartphone under IoT framework. In: Mittal M., Tanwar S., Agarwal B., Goyal L. (eds), *Energy Conservation for IoT Devices. Studies in Systems, Decision and Control*, vol. 206. Singapore: Springer. https://doi.org/10.1007/978-981-13-7399-2_12.

[5]    Mishra K. N. and Chakraborty C. (2020). A novel approach toward enhancing the quality of life in smart cities using clouds and IoT-based technologies. In: Farsi M., Daneshkhah A., Hosseinian-Far A., Jahankhani H. (eds), *Digital Twin Technologies and Smart Cities. Internet of Things (Technology, Communications and Computing)*. Cham: Springer. https://doi.org/10.1007/978-3-030-18732-3_2.

[6]    Gupta A., Chakraborty C., and Gupta B. (2019). Monitoring of epileptical patients using cloud-enabled health-IoT system. *Traitement Du Signal*, 36(5), 425–431. doi:10.18280/ts.360507.

[7] Chakraborty C. and Gupta B. (2016). Adaptive filtering technique for chronic Wound analysis UNDER Tele-Wound Network. *Journal of Communication, Navigation, Sensing and Services (CONASENSE)*, (1), 57–76. doi:10.13052/jconasense2246-2120.2016.005.

[8] Haque A. K., Bhushan B., and Dhiman G. (2021). Conceptualizing smart city applications: Requirements, architecture, security issues, and emerging trends. *Expert Systems*. https://doi.org/10.1111/exsy.12753.

[9] Huynh-The T., Hua C., Doan V., Pham Q., Nguyen T., and Kim D. (2020). Deep learning for Constellation-based modulation classification under multipath fading channels. *2020 International Conference on Information and Communication Technology Convergence (ICTC)*. doi:10.1109/ictc49870.2020.9289413.

[10] Vinayakumar R., Alazab M., Srinivasan S., Pham Q., Padannayil S. K., and Simran K. (2020). A visualized botnet detection system based deep learning for the internet of things networks of smart cities. *IEEE Transactions on Industry Applications*, 56(4), 4436–4456. doi:10.1109/tia.2020.2971952.

[11] Alazab M., Khan S., Krishnan S. S., Pham Q., Reddy M. P., and Gadekallu T. R. (2020). A multidirectional LSTM model for predicting the stability of a smart grid. *IEEE Access*, 8, 85454–85463. doi:10.1109/access.2020.2991067.

[12] Nduwayezu M., Pham Q., and Hwang W. (2020). Online computation offloading in NOMA-based multi-access edge computing: A deep reinforcement learning approach. *IEEE Access*, 8, 99098–99109. doi:10.1109/access.2020.2997925.

[13] Goyal S., Sharma N., Bhushan B., Shankar A., and Sagayam M. (2021). IoT enabled technology in secured healthcare: Applications, challenges and future directions. In: Hassanien A.E., Khamparia A., Gupta D., Shankar K., Slowik A. (eds), *Cognitive Internet of Medical Things for Smart Healthcare. Studies in Systems, Decision and Control*, vol. 311. Cham: Springer. https://doi.org/10.1007/978-3-030-55833-8_2.

[14] Goyal S., Sharma N., Kaushik I., Bhushan B., and Kumar A. (2020). Precedence & Issues of IoT based on Edge Computing. *2020 IEEE 9th International Conference on Communication Systems and Network Technologies (CSNT)*. doi:10.1109/csnt48778.2020.9115789.

[15] Sharma N., Kaushik I., Bhushan B., Gautam S., and Khamparia A. (2020). Applicability of WSN and biometric models in the field of healthcare. *Deep Learning Strategies for Security Enhancement in Wireless Sensor Networks Advances in Information Security, Privacy, and Ethics*, IGI Global, USA, 304–329. doi:10.4018/ 978-1-7998-5068-7.ch016.

[16] Bhushan B., Sahoo C., Sinha P., and Khamparia A. (2020). Unification of Blockchain and Internet of Things (BIoT): Requirements, working model, challenges and future directions. *Wireless Networks*. doi:10.1007/s11276-020-02445-6.

[17] Saxena S., Bhushan B., and Ahad M. A. (2021). Blockchain based solutions to Secure IoT: Background, integration trends and a way forward. *Journal of Network and Computer Applications*, 103050. doi:10.1016/j.jnca.2021.103050.

[18]    Bhushan B., Khamparia A., Sagayam K. M., Sharma S. K., Ahad M. A., and Debnath N. C. (2020). Blockchain for smart cities: A review of architectures, integration trends and future research directions. *Sustainable Cities and Society*, 61, 102360. doi:10.1016/j.scs.2020.102360.

[19]    Khamparia A., Singh P. K., Rani P., Samanta D., Khanna A., and Bhushan B. (2020). An internet of health things-driven deep learning framework for detection and classification of skin cancer using transfer learning. *Transactions on Emerging Telecommunications Technologies.* doi:10.1002/ ett.3963.

[20]    Lazaroiu G. C. and Roscia M. (2012). Definition methodology for the smart cities model. *Energy*, 47(1), 326–332. doi:10.1016/j.energy.2012.09.028.

[21]    Sethi R., Bhushan B., Sharma N., Kumar R., and Kaushik I. (2021). Applicability of industrial IoT in diversified sectors: Evolution, applications and challenges. In: Kumar R., Sharma R., Pattnaik P.K. (eds), *Multimedia Technologies in the Internet of Things Environment, Studies in Big Data*, vol. 79. SIngapore: Springer. https://doi.org/10.1007/978-981-15-7965-3_4.

[22]    Malik A., Gautam S., Abidin S., and Bhushan B. (2019). Blockchain technology-future of IoT: Including structure, limitations and various possible attacks. *2nd International Conference on Intelligent Computing, Instrumentation and Control Technologies (ICICICT)*, Kannur, India, 2019, pp. 1100–1104, doi:10.1109/ICICICT46008.2019.8993144.

[23]    Yeh H. (2017). The effects of successful ICT-based smart cities services: From citizens' perspectives. *Government Information Quarterly*, 34(3), 556–565. https://doi.org/10.1016/j.giq.2017.05.001.

[24]    Belanche-Gracia D., Casaló-Ariño L. V., and Pérez-Rueda A. (2015). Determinants of multi-service smartcard success for smart cities development: A study based on citizens' privacy and security perceptions. *Government Information Quarterly*, 32(2), 154–163. https://doi.org/10.1016/ j.giq.2014.12.004.

[25]    Chatterjee S. and Kar A. K. (2017). Effects of successful adoption of information technology enabled services in proposed smart cities of India. *Journal of Science and Technology Policy Management*, 9(2), 189–209. https://doi.org/10.1108/jstpm-03-2017-0008.

[26]    Niforatos E., Vourvopoulos A., and Langheinrich M. (2017). Understanding the potential of human–machine crowdsourcing for weather data. *International Journal of Human-Computer Studies*, 102, 54–68. https://doi. org/10.1016/j.ijhcs.2016.10.002.

[27]    Mone G. (2015). The new smart cities. *Communications of the ACM*, 58(7), 20–21. https://doi.org/10.1145/2771297.

[28]    Gautam S., Malik A., Singh N., and Kumar S. (2019). Recent advances and countermeasures against various attacks in IoT environment. *2019 2nd International Conference on Signal Processing and Communication (ICSPC)*. https://doi.org/10.1109/icspc46172.2019.8976527.

[29]    Johnson P., Iacob M. E., Välja M., van Sinderen M., Magnusson C., and Ladhe T. (2014). A method for predicting the probability of business

network profitability. *Information Systems and e-Business Management*, 12 (4), 567–593. https://doi.org/10.1007/s10257-014-0237-4.

[30] Keegan S., O'Hare G. M. P., and O'Grady M. J. (2012). Retail in the digital cities. *International Journal of E-Business Research*, 8(3), 18–32. https://doi.org/10.4018/jebr.2012070102.

[31] An J., Le Gall F., Kim J., Yun J., Hwang J., Bauer M., and Song J. (2019). Toward global IoT-enabled smart cities interworking using adaptive semantic adapter. *IEEE Internet of Things Journal*, 6(3), 5753–5765. https://doi.org/10.1109/jiot.2019.2905275.

[32] Díaz-Díaz R. and Pérez-González D. (2019). Implementation of social media concepts for E-government: Case study of a social media tool for value co creation and citizen participation. In I. Management Association (Ed.), *Smart Cities and Smart Spaces: Concepts, Methodologies, Tools, and Applications* (pp. 1071–1091). IGI Global. http://doi:10.4018/978-1-5225-7030-1.ch049.

[33] Gascó-Hernandez M. (2018). Building a smart cities. *Communications of the ACM*, 61(4), 50–57. https://doi.org/10.1145/3117800.

[34] Rana N. P., Luthra S., Mangla S. K., Islam R., Roderick S., and Dwivedi Y. K. (2018). Barriers to the development of smart cities in Indian context. *Information Systems Frontiers*, 21(3), 503–525. https://doi.org/10.1007/s10796-018-9873-4.

[35] Cledou G., Estevez E., and Soares Barbosa L. (2018). A taxonomy for planning and designing smart mobility services. *Government Information Quarterly*, 35(1), 61–76. https://doi.org/10.1016/j.giq.2017.11.008.

[36] Fietkiewicz K. J., Mainka A., and Stock W. G. (2017). eGovernment in cities of the knowledge society. An empirical investigation of Smart Cities' governmental websites. *Government Information Quarterly*, 34(1), 75–83. https://doi.org/10.1016/j.giq.2016.08.003.

[37] Guetat S. B. and Dakhli S. B. (2016). Services-based integration of urbanized information systems. *Information Resources Management Journal*, 29(4), 17–34. https://doi.org/10.4018/irmj.2016100102.

[38] Sussman F. S. (2001). Telecommunications and transnationalism: The polarization of social space. *The Information Society*, 17(1), 49–62. https://doi.org/10.1080/019722401750067423.

[39] Zhu W., Gao D., Zhao W., Zhang H., and Chiang H.-P. (2017). SDN-enabled hybrid emergency message transmission architecture in internet-of-vehicles. *Enterprise Information Systems*, 12(4), 471–491. https://doi.org/10.1080/17517575.2017.1304578.

[40] Walravens N. (2012). Mobile business and the smart cities: Developing a business model framework to include public design parameters for mobile cities services. *Journal of Theoretical and Applied Electronic Commerce Research*, 7(3), 23–24. https://doi.org/10.4067/s0718-18762012000300012.

[41] Calderoni L., Maio D., and Rovis S. (2014). Deploying a network of smart cameras for traffic monitoring on a "cities kernel". *Expert Systems with Applications*, 41(2), 502–507. https://doi.org/10.1016/j.eswa.2013.07.076.

[42]    Lee G., Mallipeddi R., and Lee M. (2017). Trajectory-based vehicle tracking at low frame rates. *Expert Systems with Applications*, 80, 46–57. https://doi.org/10.1016/j.eswa.2017.03.023.

[43]    Anagnostopoulos T., Kolomvatsos K., Anagnostopoulos C., Zaslavsky A., and Hadjiefthymiades S. (2015). Assessing dynamic models for high priority waste collection in smart cities. *Journal of Systems and Software*, 110, 178–192. https://doi.org/10.1016/j.jss.2015.08.049.

[44]    Corbett J. and Mellouli S. (2017). Winning the SDG battle in cities: How an integrated information ecosystem can contribute to the achievement of the 2030 sustainable development goals. *Information Systems Journal*, 27(4), 427–461. https://doi.org/10.1111/isj.12138.

[45]    Castelli M., Gonçalves I., Trujillo L., and Popovic A. (2016). An evolutionary system for ozone concentration forecasting. *Information Systems Frontiers*, 19(5), 1123–1132. https://doi.org/10.1007/s10796-016-9706-2.

[46]    Polenghi-Gross I., Sabol S. A., Ritchie S. R., and Norton M. R. (2014). Water storage and gravity for urban sustainability and climate readiness. *Journal – American Water Works Association*, 106(12). https://doi.org/10.5942/jawwa.2014.106.0151.

[47]    Breetzke T. and Flowerday S. V. (2016). The usability of IVRs for smart cities crowdsourcing in developing cities. *The Electronic Journal of Information Systems in Developing Countries*, 73(1), 1–14. https://doi.org/10.1002/j.1681-4835.2016.tb00527.x.

[48]    Cilliers L. and Flowerday S. (2017). Factors that influence the usability of a participatory IVR crowdsourcing system in a smart cities. *South African Computer Journal*, 29(3). https://doi.org/10.18489/sacj.v29i3.422.

[49]    Hussain A., Wenbi R., da Silva A. L., Nadher M., and Mudhish M. (2015). Health and emergency-care platform for the elderly and disabled people in the smart cities. *Journal of Systems and Software*, 110, 253–263. https://doi.org/10.1016/j.jss.2015.08.041.

[50]    Pramanik M. I., Lau, R. Y. K., Demirkan H., and Azad M. A. (2017). Smart health: Big data enabled health paradigm within smart cities. *Expert Systems with Applications*, 87, 370–383. https://doi.org/10.1016/j.eswa.2017.06.027.

[51]    Vincent J. M. (2006). Public schools as public infrastructure. *Journal of Planning Education and Research*, 25(4), 433–437. https://doi.org/10.1177/0739456x06288092.

[52]    Mukherjee M., Shu L., and Wang D. (2018). Survey of fog computing: Fundamental, network applications, and research challenges. *IEEE Communications Surveys & Tutorials*, 20(3), 1826–1857. https://doi.org/10.1109/comst.2018.2814571.

[53]    Bonomi F., Milito R., Zhu J., and Addepalli, S. (2012). Fog computing and its role in the internet of things. *Proceedings of the First Edition of the MCC Workshop on Mobile Cloud Computing – MCC '12*. https://doi.org/10.1145/2342509.2342513.

[54]    Rashid M. and Wani U. I. (2020). Role of fog computing platform in analytics of internet of things- issues, challenges and opportunities. *Fog, Edge,*

*and Pervasive Computing in Intelligent IoT Driven Applications*, pp. 209–220. Wiley. https://doi.org/10.1002/9781119670087.ch12.

[55] Vaquero L. M. and Rodero-Merino L. (2014). Finding your way in the fog. *ACM SIGCOMM Computer Communication Review*, 44(5), 27–32. https://doi.org/10.1145/2677046.2677052.

[56] Yu W., Liang F., He X., Hatcher W. G., Lu C., Lin J., and Yang X. (2018). A survey on the edge computing for the internet of things. *IEEE Access*, 6, 6900–6919. https://doi.org/10.1109/access.2017.2778504.

[57] Wang X., Han Y., Leung V. C., Niyato D., Yan X., and Chen X. (2020). Convergence of edge computing and deep learning: A comprehensive survey. *IEEE Communications Surveys & Tutorials*, 22(2), 869–904. https://doi.org/10.1109/comst.2020.2970550.

[58] Qiu J., Wu Q., Ding G., Xu Y., and Feng S. (2016). Erratum to: A survey of machine learning for big data processing. *EURASIP Journal on Advances in Signal Processing*, 2016(1). https://doi.org/10.1186/s13634-016-0382-7.

[59] Garcia-Almanza A. L., Alexandrova-Kabadjova B., and Martinez-Jaramillo S. (2013). *Bankruptcy Prediction for Banks: An Artificial Intelligence Approach to Improve Understandability*. Studies in Computational Intelligence, 633–656. https://doi.org/10.1007/978-3-642-29694-9_24.

[60] Wen Chen X. and Lin X. (2014). Big data deep learning: Challenges and perspectives. *IEEE Access*, 2, 514–525. https://doi.org/10.1109/access.2014.2325029.

[61] Shokri R. and Shmatikov V. (2015). Privacy-preserving deep learning. *2015 53rd Annual Allerton Conference on Communication, Control, and Computing (Allerton)*. https://doi.org/10.1109/allerton.2015.7447103.

[62] Brynjolfsson E. and Mcafee A. (2017). The business of artificial intelligence, *Harvard Bus. Rev. 2017 Artificial Intelligence and Robotics (IRANOPEN)*. https://doi.org/10.1109/rios.2017.7956467.

[63] James G., Witten D. Hastie T., and Tibshirani R. (2013). *Unsupervised Learning*. Springer Texts in Statistics, 373–418. https://doi.org/10.1007/978-1-4614-7138-7_10.

[64] Hastie T., Tibshirani R., and Friedman J. (2008). *Unsupervised Learning*. The Elements of Statistical Learning, 485–585. https://doi.org/10.1007/978-0-387-84858-7_14.

[65] Kingma P., Rezende D. J., Mohamed D. S., and Welling M. (n.d.). Semi-Supervised Learning with Deep Generative Models. https://doi.org/arXiv:1406.5298.

[66] Van Hasselt H., Guez A., and Silver D. (2016). Deep reinforcement learning with double Q-learning. *Proceedings of the AAAI Conference on Artificial Intelligence*, 30(1). Retrieved from https://ojs.aaai.org/index.php/AAAI/article/view/10295.

[67] Bassolas A., Barbosa-Filho H., Dickinson B., *et al.* (2019). Hierarchical organization of urban mobility and its connection with cities livability. *Nature Communications*, 10(1). https://doi.org/10.1038/s41467-019-12809-y.

[68]    Li R., Zhao Z., Yang C., Wu C., and Zhang H. (2018). Wireless big data in cellular networks: The cornerstone of smart cities. *IET Communications*, 12 (13), 1517–1523. https://doi.org/10.1049/iet-com.2017.1278.

[69]    Luo F., Cao G., Mulligan K., and Li X. (2016). Explore spatiotemporal and demographic characteristics of human mobility via Twitter: A case study of Chicago. *Applied Geography*, 70, 11–25. https://doi.org/10.1016/j.apgeog. 2016.03.001.

[70]    O'Sullivan F. and Holzinger S. A. (2021). AI and big data in healthcare: Towards a more comprehensive research framework for multi-morbidity. *Journal of Clinical Medicine*, 10(4), 766. doi:10.3390/jcm10040766.

[71]    Viceconti M., Hunter P., and Hose R. (2015). Big data, big knowledge: Big data for personalized healthcare. *IEEE Journal of Biomedical and Health Informatics*, 19(4), 1209–1215. doi:10.1109/JBHI.2015.2406883.

[72]    Zhang Y., Qiu M., Tsai C. W., Hassan M. M., and Alamri A. (2017). Health-CPS: Healthcare cyber-physical system assisted by cloud and big data. *IEEE Systems Journal*, 11(1), 88–95. doi:10.1109/JSYST.2015. 2460747.

[73]    Hossain M. S. and Muhammad G. (2018). Emotion-aware connected healthcare big data towards 5G. *IEEE Internet of Things Journal*, 5(4), 2399–2406. doi:10.1109/JIOT.2017.2772959.

[74]    Sahoo P. K., Mohapatra S. K., and Wu S. (2018). SLA based HEALTHCARE big data analysis and computing in cloud network. *Journal of Parallel and Distributed Computing*, 119, 121–135. doi:10.1016/j. jpdc.2018.04.006.

[75]    Hussain S., Hussain M., Afzal M., Hussain J., Bang J., Seung H., and Lee S. (2019). Semantic preservation of standardized healthcare documents in big data. *International Journal of Medical Informatics*, 129, 133–145. doi:10.1016/j.ijmedinf.2019.05.024.

[76]    Syed L., Jabeen S. S. M., and Alsaeedi A. (2019). Smart healthcare framework for AMBIENT assisted living using IoMT and big data analytics techniques. *Future Generation Computer Systems*, 101, 136–151. doi:10.1016/j.future.2019.06.004.

[77]    Zhou S., He J., Yang H., Chen D., and Zhang R. (2020). Big data-driven abnormal behavior detection in healthcare based on association rules. *IEEE Access*, 8, 129002–129011. doi: 10.1109/ACCESS.2020.3009006.

[78]    Nazir S., Khan S., Khan H. U., *et al.* (2020). A comprehensive analysis of healthcare big data management, analytics and scientific programming. *IEEE Access*, 8, 95714–95733. doi:10.1109/access.2020.2995572.

[79]    Kim J. and Chung K. (2020). Multi-modal stacked denoising autoencoder for handling missing data in healthcare big data. *IEEE Access*, 8, 104933–104943. doi: 10.1109/ACCESS.2020.2997255.

[80]    Jothi N., Rashid N. A., and Husain W. (2015). Data mining in healthcare – A review. *Procedia Computer Science*, 72, 306–313. doi:10.1016/j.procs. 2015.12.145.

[81] Akay A., Dragomir A., and Erlandsson B. (2015). Network-based modeling and intelligent data mining of social media for improving care. *IEEE Journal of Biomedical and Health Informatics*, 19(1), 210–218. doi:10.1109/JBHI.2014.2336251.

[82] Yassine A., Singh S., and Alamri A. (2017). Mining human activity patterns from smart home big data for health care applications. *IEEE Access*, 5, 13131–13141. doi: 10.1109/ACCESS.2017.2719921.

[83] Kovalchuk S. V., Funkner A. A., Metsker O. G., and Yakovlev A. N. (2018). Simulation of patient flow in multiple healthcare units using process and data mining techniques for model identification. *Journal of Biomedical Informatics*, 82, 128–142. doi:10.1016/j.jbi.2018.05.004.

[84] Amin M. S., Chiam Y. K., and Varathan K. D. (2019). Identification of significant features and data mining techniques in predicting heart disease. *Telematics and Informatics*, 36, 82–93. doi:10.1016/j.tele.2018.11.007.

[85] Sun C., Li Q., Cui L., Li H., and Shi Y. (2019). Heterogeneous network-based chronic disease progression mining. *Big Data Mining and Analytics*, 2(1), 25–34. doi:10.26599/BDMA.2018.9020009.

[86] Gonçalves C., Ferreira D., Neto C., Abelha A., and Machado J. (2020). Prediction of mental illness associated with unemployment using data mining. *Procedia Computer Science*, 177, 556–561. doi:10.1016/j.procs.2020.10.078.

[87] Kaur I., Doja M., and Ahmad T. (2020). Time-range based sequential mining for survival prediction in prostate cancer. *Journal of Biomedical Informatics*, 110, 103550. doi:10.1016/j.jbi.2020.103550.

[88] Zhang Q., Lian B., Cao P., Sang Y., Huang W., and Qi L. (2020). Multi-source medical data integration and mining for healthcare services. *IEEE Access*, 8, 165010–165017. doi: 10.1109/ACCESS.2020.3023332.

# Index